The Complete Merlin Tarot

By the same author

THE MERLIN TAROT
THE WAY OF MERLIN

THE COMPLETE MERLIN TAROT

Images, Insight and Wisdom from the Age of Merlin

R. J. Stewart

Illustrated by Miranda Gray

Aquarian/Thorsons
An Imprint of HarperCollins*Publishers*

The Aquarian Press
An Imprint of HarperCollins*Publishers*
77–85 Fulham Palace Road,
Hammersmith, London W6 8JB
1160 Battery Street,
San Francisco, California 94111–1213

Published by The Aquarian Press 1992
3 5 7 9 10 8 6 4 2

A catalogue record for this book
is available from the British Library

ISBN 1 85538 091 9

Printed in Great Britain by
Woolnough Bookbinding Ltd,
Irthlingborough, Northants

CONTENTS

ILLUSTRATIONS

ACKNOWLEDGEMENTS

Before crediting sources, I must acknowledge the patience, skill and vision of Miranda Gray, who painted the Merlin Tarot from my crude sketches and written descriptions. That she finished such a monumental task within one year with such profound intuition and powerful results will always astonish me.

Tarot is essentially an anonymous organic tradition; no tarot designer or artist should fail to acknowledge the collective work of all previous tarot exponents. Specific acknowledgement must be made of the work of A. E. Waite and Pamela Coleman-Smith, in collaboration with W. B. Yeats. Their tarot pack, which formed the basis of my own initial tarot instruction, contains many sub-elements from Celtic tradition for those who are able to detect them.

The relationship of major images (Trumps) to the Tree of Life, similar to our Figure 2, was first published by W. G. Gray in *Magical Ritual Methods* (Helios, Toddington, 1969). Mr Gray's system is not derived from the *Vita Merlini* (Life of Merlin), is lettered and numbered quite differently from our Merlin Tarot, and is given a very different interpretation and subsequent development. Nevertheless, it acts as a bridge between the cosmology/psychology found within the Merlin texts and related Western esoteric traditions, and modern restatements of Kabbalah.

Substantial acknowledgement must be given to the chronicler and poet Geoffrey of Monmouth, writing in the twelfth century. He drew material from bardic, poetic, historical and magical traditions, and so assembled the Merlin texts, which contain a coherent body of symbolism virtually ignored by modern occultists, esoteric scholars and psychologists alike. Without his remarkable work, which had a most profound effect upon Western literature (perhaps because of, rather than in spite of, its magical content), the Merlin Tarot would never have been conceived or developed in its present form.

Ultimate acknowledgement in such matters must be made to Merlin, the prophet of Western consciousness. In literature, legend and imaginative vision he provides unfailing instruction and insight to those who reach his retreat and place of observation and contemplation between the worlds.

R. J. Stewart,
1987

PREFACE AND READER'S GUIDE

Many of the symbols, images and concepts found in the Merlin Tarot are also found in the *Vita Merlini*, *Prophecies of Merlin*, and in those parts of *The History of the Kings of Britain* that relate to Merlin. These sources (referred to as 'the Merlin texts') prove an early historical dating for tarot or proto-tarot images and systems, relating to mythical or magical poetry and story-telling. But the Merlin texts are not proposed as a sole source for the images and traditions described in this book; both the medieval texts and this modern restatement of tarot derive from a specific and individual tradition which underpins both.

In the Merlin texts, we can detect both Celtic and classical material, but this does not fully answer the question of the origin of inner symbolic or magical tradition that runs through the Merlin tales and prophecies. Citing parallels and sources helps to give historical thresholds for material, but seldom truly provides proof of origin. When such sources are referred to in this book, it is merely to remind the reader that early traditions involving both Merlin and tarot imagery existed in proven literature several centuries before the earliest known tarot cards. In other words, we are dealing with a living tradition, and not simply a piece of literary dissection.

The concepts discussed in the following chapters, and shown in the cards themselves, are imaginative reconstructions of that living tradition. Sources include the Merlin texts, folklore, mythology, Celtic tradition, and certain Northern and Western and Hermetic sources of esoteric instruction which have long been ignored or forgotten in modern psychological and magical texts.

When we study and use the Merlin Tarot, we are employing a symbolic alphabet from an enduring and living magical/psychological and, ultimately, spiritual tradition. This tradition, embodied by the figure of Merlin, persisted underground for many centuries after its last literary remnants appeared. Indeed, the Merlin texts represent the fragments of an ancient oral tradition reworked in the twelfth century by a writer of genius, Geoffrey of Monmouth. They are not formal magical texts, but sources of mystery, amusement, education and allegory.

When a revival of magical traditions came to the fore in the nineteenth and early twentieth centuries, the Merlin tradition was ignored. Imagery was drawn from Eastern sources, with a strong intellectual tendency to unify and universalize all traditions into a vast and often confusing 'complete' system. That much of this material worked (mainly refined by the powerful intellects and scholars of the Golden Dawn and later derivative groups) cannot be denied. But it represents only one relatively modern tradition of inner transformation, and there are many others equally effective. Most important, perhaps, is the fact that occult literary traditions from the nineteenth century are not core traditions inherent in the Western psyche, although they employ some of the units of such core traditions.

The tradition that underpins the Merlin Tarot is Western and, to a certain extent, Celtic; but it is a living tradition, and as such slowly changes and develops with each century. Although we employ reference sources that date from the twelfth century in literature, and from much earlier periods in symbolism, we are emphatically not reviving a dead ancient art when we use the Merlin Tarot; such transformative traditions reach both back and forward in time. A restatement of primal tarot and related instruction would not have been possible a generation ago, even though the Merlin texts have been known for almost 800 years. More simply, the time is now right for the Merlin Tarot; the core tradition from which it derives has emerged.

To use the Merlin Tarot, the reader should become familiar with each image, both through picturing the cards in meditation and by reading the associated chapters. Such a direct practical approach will attune consciousness to the inner or deeper levels of the tradition which underpin the visual and instructional material.

This book travels through the Trumps in their cosmological and psychological order; after the detailed examination of Trumps and their relationships to one another, there are chapters on the Court and Number or Element cards and on subsidiary uses of tarot.

There are many differences between the Merlin Tarot images and system of cosmology and psychology, and those previously published in Western esoteric literature. There are also many deep similarities and close relationships, for all tarot derives from a fundamental pattern of images, an alphabet of the imagination. If the Merlin Tarot is met openly and worked with and through in a simple manner, the power of the images and patterns will speak clearly for itself.

Working with the Deck

The Trumps, Wheels and Worlds

The Merlin Tarot comprises 22 Trumps, 40 Numbers and 16 Court cards or People, giving a deck of 78 cards. There are also 2 further cards with key figures for rapid reference while using the deck.

The system is based upon Three Worlds and Three Wheels. The Three Wheels are really three rotations of a theoretical spiral or path of ascent and descent between Earth and heaven or, in modern terms, between modes or levels of consciousness, but for practical purposes they are regarded as separate Trumps. The Three Worlds are defined by the Three Wheels and correspond to the trumps Moon, Sun and Star. Thus there are Lunar, Solar and Stellar Worlds and their inhabitants (described by the bard Taliesin) and three thresholds or Wheels: Fortune, Justice and Judgement. This system is shown in Figure 1 and forms the centre of a simple Tree of Life (Figure 2) reaching, as did all ancient cosmologies, from the Earth to the stars.

Whether you are already using tarot or are a complete beginner, the following sequence will be helpful in gaining deeper understanding of the Merlin Tarot. If you want to get the best from this deck, please do not rush into divination by looking up 'meanings' – the meanings must come from within ourselves, and not be derived mechanically from reference sources. The following method is the best way towards using the deck – it does not take much time, is designed to give you insights long before you use the cards for divination, and will empower any divinatory work that you undertake. Divination is a lesser art of tarot, the greater arts being meditation and visualization, particularly with the powerful Trumps.

The first helpful way of working with the deck is simply to lay the Trumps out in the order shown in the two reference cards. The first of these, The Creation Vision, shows the sequence of Trumps from the Earth to the stars and back again, as follows:

1 The Moon	2 The Sun	3 The Star	(The Three Worlds)
4 Fortune	5 Justice	6 Judgement	(The Three Wheels)
7 The Fool	8 The Magician	9 The Chariot	(The Three Enlighteners)
10 The Guardian	11 The Blasted Tower	12 Death	(The Three Liberators)
13 The Hanged Man	14 The Hermit	15 The Innocent	(The Three Redeemers)
16 Temperance	17 The Emperor	18 Strength	(The Three Givers)

| 19 The Empress | 20 The Lovers | 21 The Priestess | (The Three Sharers) |
| 22 The Universe | | | (One Manifest Reality) |

The card also shows the basic Tree of Life and the simple planetary attributes of each Sphere of the Tree. Our Trump 21,* for example, The Priestess, reveals the consciousness/energy of the Moon and Venus, of the emotions and the generative lunar powers.

The second reference card is The Two Dragons, an image drawn from the prophetic vision of the young Merlin, whose powers were awakened by the arousal of two dragons in the Underworld.[1] This card shows the Trump relationships in a simpler form, as they relate to one another through the Three Worlds.

If you lay the Trumps out in the order shown in these two reference cards, you will find a harmony, a living pattern, revealing the *energies* from the Earth to the stars, their collective or ancestral pattern, and how they resonate within each of us.

The next stage is to meditate upon each Trump separately, in the order shown. You will see that they fit in pairs, triads and groups of relationships of various kinds. Try to feel these patterns within yourself, try to see them in the environment from land to sky, Earth to stars. They are part of our consciousness and energy, the Microcosm, and part of the greater worlds of the planet, solar system and universe, the Macrocosm. The two mirror one another.

At all stages, refer to the various illustrations, and try always to lay out cards in the patterns shown. Our own energies and relative position as humans upon the planet are represented by the Seven Directions (see Figure 5): if you work with this concept, it comes alive, and the tarot cards achieve new depths of resonance and meaning when they are returned to their primal order based upon Moon, Sun and Star.

---

*The numbering of the Merlin Tarot is purely for reference, and is not connected to the so-called 'traditional' numbering or order of tarot Trumps that has appeared from the nineteenth century onwards. The difference between contrived literary systems of tarot correspondences and the perennial natural or holistic traditions is discussed in later chapters.

Figure 1: THE THREE WORLDS AND THREE WHEELS

1	Fortune	Lunar World
2	Justice	Solar World
3	Judgement	Stellar World

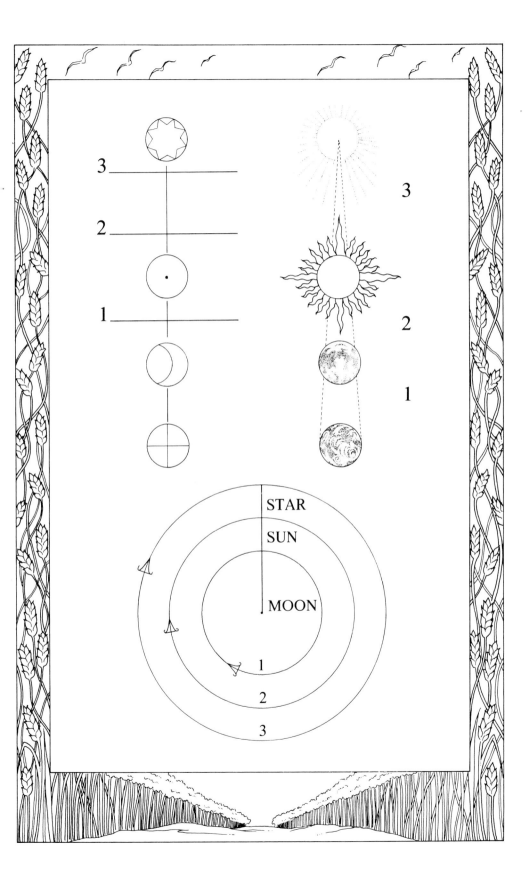

The Numbers

Once you have become familiar with the Trump patterns, begin to work through the Number cards. There are four suits, one for each Element (Air, Fire, Water and Earth), from Ace to Ten. (The numbers are discussed in detail in Chapters 25, 26 and 27.)

If you lay the Number cards out around the Wheel of Life (Figure 6), you will discover how they relate to one another. You will also see that certain numbers relate to certain Trumps, as shown upon the Tree of Life (Figure 2). Trump 3, The Star, for example, has affinity with the Four Aces and the Four Sixes, for it reveals the powers of the 1st and 6th Spheres, the Crown of Stars and the Sun of Beauty. Trump 7, The Fool, has affinity with the Four Eights and the Four Tens, and so forth.

You can also lay the numbers out according to the Tree of Life, from the Four Aces at the Crown to the Four Tens in the Kingdom. When setting the Number cards out in this pattern, lay the relevant Trumps between them as shown in our key cards and various figures. This will show how the entire deck begins to relate throughout.

Figure 2: (opposite) THE TREE OF LIFE

Spheres

1st:	*Primum Mobile*/Crown	
2nd:	The Zodiac/Wisdom	
3rd:	Understanding	♄
4th:	Mercy	♃
5th:	Severity	♂
6th:	Beauty	☉
7th:	Victory	♀
8th:	Honour	☿
9th:	Foundation	☽
10th:	Kingdom	⊕

Trumps or Paths

1: The Moon; 2: The Sun; 3: Star (The Three Worlds); 4: The Wheel of Fortune; 5: Justice; 6: Judgement (The Three Wheels); 7: The Fool; 8: The Magician; 9: The Chariot; 10: The Guardian; 11: The Blasted Tower; 12: Death; 13: The Hanged Man; 14: The Hermit (The Eight Ascending Images); 15: The Innocent; 16: Temperance; 17: The Emperor; 18: Strength; 19: The Empress; 20: The Lovers; 21: The Priestess; 22: The Universe (The Eight Descending Images).

NOTE: The Trump or Path numbers relate to the cycle of ascent and descent (see p.33). They are not related to mystical numerology or alphabetic correspondences.

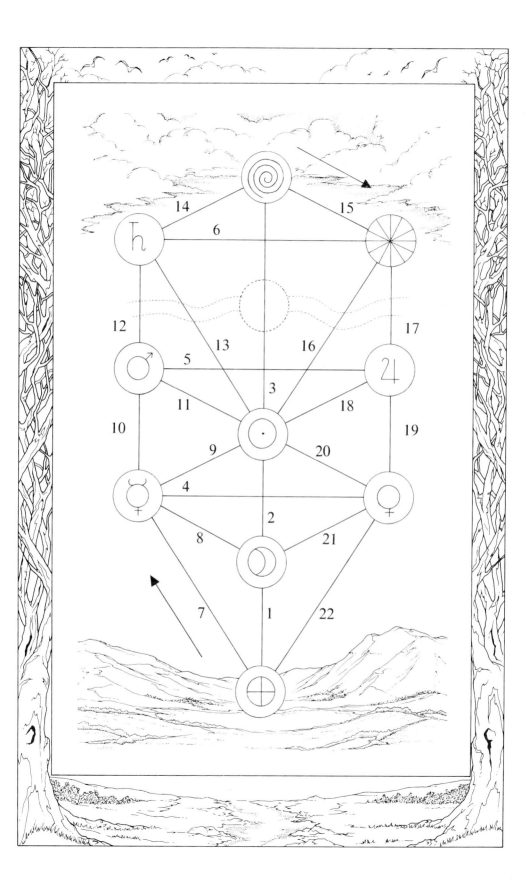

The Court Cards or People

The 16 Court cards can now be approached. (The Courts are discussed further in Chapter 28.)

Lay them out according to the Court Circle (Figure 18, p.287) and meditate upon their relationship to one another and to the Four Elements, Seasons and Directions around the Wheel of Life.

The Wheel or Circle of Court cards can also be laid out around any of the Three Wheels and Worlds, with the Court of Birds or Air at the crown, Serpents or Fire at the right, Fishes or Water below, and Beasts or Earth at the left. Try laying them around each of the Three Wheels and Worlds in turn. Finally, assemble the entire universe of Trumps and Number cards according to the Dragons (the Tree of Life) and then add the Courts: Air at the top of the Tree, Fire to the right, Water beneath, Earth to the left. Meditate upon this pattern and its holism of relationships.

You may also work with the Court cards by relating them to the central Spheres of the *Axis Mundi* or Tree of Life: Earth, Moon, Sun and Crown. Planet Earth has the Court of Earth/Beasts rotating around it, the planetary Moon has the Court of Water/Fishes, the Sun has the Court of Fire/Serpents and the Crown has the Court of Air/Birds. This pattern is shown in Figure 23, p.326.

Divination, Farsight and Insight

When you have worked through the patterns of layout, meditation and vision briefly described above, you will find that divinatory work comes alive most powerfully, and you can work with the specific new layouts described in Chapter 30. At first, it will be necessary to refer to the summaries and attributes given, but you will need these less and less as you become more familiar with the Merlin Tarot.

The relationship between divination, farsight and insight is inherent in tarot, and a good tarot worker uses all three, but most of all he or she uses insight, working with the images to reveal truth. This may be truth about yourself, about a question, about other people or about a situation.

In its true function and power, tarot tells the story of the Creation of the Worlds, so it reveals truths about powers, energies, consciousness and the countless patterns that combine and recombine to form our manifest world.

INTRODUCTION

I began work on the Merlin Tarot in 1985, and had published many of the ideas developed in the deck in earlier books and articles. *The Merlin Tarot* book and cards appeared in 1988; the book covering the entire deck, but dealing only briefly with the Court and Number cards. *The Complete Merlin Tarot* contains material that was left out of the main chapters of that first book for various reasons (mainly limitations of space), plus a full development of all the Number and Court cards.

When I began the Merlin Tarot the revival of interest in tarot was well under way, and this deck was the first of the so-called 'alternative' decks that have appeared in the 1980s and 1990s. Such modern decks range from the whimsical to the absurdly intellectual; some are true visionary works, others are pot-boilers catering to an enthusiastic new market. But the custom of varying tarot packs is not a new one, as variations have been used since the cards first appeared during the Renaissance. The *images* of tarot (Trumps, Courts and Numbers) are far older than any historical *cards*, and it is upon such a primal set of images, with a known and dated set of threshold texts, that the Merlin Tarot is based.

The truth is that there is no definitive tarot, no authoritative source or original deck. There is, however, a tradition containing images and patterns. Early tarot card images were taken from oral poetic and prophetic traditions, setting out as pictures certain themes and visions found in the wisdom teachings and story-telling repertoire of the Northern and Western world. These were made available to the Renaissance princes as the first hand-painted tarot packs, later to be spread by the advent of printing.

Even earlier images, such as those used in the Merlin Tarot, remained unnoticed by modern tarot enthusiasts and scholars alike, until I began to publish the connections in *The Prophetic Vision of Merlin* and *The Mystic Life of Merlin* (Penguin Arkana, 1986). The Merlin Tarot, as already mentioned, is founded upon images and expositions or teachings in the medieval Merlin texts known as the *Prophecies* and *Life of Merlin*, set out into Latin by Geoffrey of Monmouth in the middle of the twelfth century. But these sources are themselves taken from much older oral bardic material, using a storehouse of images and tales rooted into the ancient wisdom traditions of the Western and Northern world. The sources used by Geoffrey were, broadly speaking, Celtic, but with many connections to other cultures.

The Merlin Tarot does not, therefore, claim any false 'authority', merely to be rooted in a powerful enduring visionary tradition, that same ancient tradition embodied by seers and seeresses, bards and poets and, of course, the figure of Merlin. The value of such a tradition is not its age or authenticity, but its inherent power. It either has that power or it does not. You will discover for yourself, after working with the Merlin Tarot, how powerful it can be.

Before developing the Merlin Tarot, I had been working with tarot since 1969, so 15 years or more had passed between the time of my first introduction to tarot and my discovery of the source images in the Merlin texts, leading to the Merlin Tarot. A total of 22 years leads to the production of *The Complete Merlin Tarot*, written in 1991.

When I bought my first tarot deck, it came by post in a plain brown-paper wrapper. There were no shops selling tarot in the high street as there are today, but there were still several decks to choose from, all more or less related to one other. The decks in print in the 1960s were generally derived from a simple tarot deck found throughout Europe (excepting Britain), with national variations, from approximately the eighteenth century onwards. This deck, still available today, is often wrongly described as the 'original' tarot in modern books, for, although it has the weight of popular use for divination, it is a relatively late printed version, and one of a number in and out of print in Europe during the course of the eighteenth to the twentieth centuries.

The major exception within the modern variant decks was, of course, the astonishing set produced by Aleister Crowley and Lady Freda Harris, which remains to this day a unique and remarkable visionary work. Another tarot was developed by A. E. Waite and Pamela Coleman-Smith, with some level of contribution from W. B. Yeats (first published by Rider in 1910). It was this Rider–Waite deck that I drew from its concealing postal wrapper in 1969, thus beginning my practical experience of tarot at the age of 20.

Several years were to pass before I realized the deeper Celtic ambience of the Waite deck, which has a superficially Renaissance style, with images of people in late medieval costume. At first I attributed this inner level to the influence of Yeats,[2] which may indeed be the case, but I have gradually realized that in certain decks the inner tradition simply resonates, almost regardless of the details on the cards themselves.

The Waite tarot had an interesting effect upon me, not due to the deck itself, but to the deeper levels of vision and energy inherent in tarot. For many nights I dreamed my way through the deck, being carried from card to card by the flowing water, roads, gateways, paths and so forth that appear within them. Much of what I learned in these powerful dreams was not directly related to the Waite deck, and I had many difficulties relating this dream-lore to the actual cards that I was studying. In retrospect I can see the dream learning as part of a living tradition, and the printed cards merely as variant examples of that tradition. Some of those early dreams have been woven into the Merlin Tarot, not by consulting notes or intellectual contrivance, but simply because they are still living in the visionary storehouse of tarot, and so they regenerated when I began work on the deck.

Tarot and Sacred Space

Most books on tarot give a quite artificial and absurd set of relationships between the Trumps. These contrived relationships are mainly the work of Victorian occultists who were struggling to recover the old traditions, yet were driven by the pedantic and obscure style and mentality of the day. They were also bedevilled with secrecy – often for good reasons in a bigoted orthodox society – and sometimes childishly delighted in publishing and teaching correspondences which were plainly nonsense.

The Merlin Tarot and tradition is based upon the idea of Sacred Space, with all energies and consciousness turning about the Three Worlds of Moon, Sun and Star. It uses a simple pattern based upon Sacred Space and the Seven Directions: Above, Below, Within, Before or East, Right or South, Behind or West and Left or North (see Figure 5, p.77). This is not a contrivance or a false antiquarian pattern, but drawn from venerable traditions concerning the relationship between humanity and the environment. The Seven Directions are the basis of all human relative orientation, and the Cardinal Directions of East, South, West and North play a major role in all wisdom traditions world-wide. Any tarot book that does not take account of the Directions, and the central axis of Moon, Sun and Star, leading from the Earth to the stars, is divorced from such traditions.

Furthermore, tarot correspondences that ignore, or are ignorant of, the *holism* of Trumps, based upon the Seven Directions, are cut off from the collective wisdom of our ancestors. We have been standing upon the surface of the planet, passing through the Seasons, feeling the affects of the moon, sun and stars for millennia; their patterns and rhythms flow deeply within us. Throw away any tarot book that does not take this into account!

Likewise I would urge you to forget the nonsense about tarot on Egyptian temple walls or the secret preservation of tarot from lost civilizations – this is all the obscurantist fantasy of the Victorians or of later writers who simply copied them without doing any actual work upon the deeper levels of tarot itself.

The true mystery and wonder of tarot is far greater than any romantic notion concerning adepts and ancient temples, for tarot comes from the rotation of energy and consciousness within the Three Worlds of Moon, Sun and Star. It works in so many ways because its flow and rhythm is inherent within ourselves. This is the power of tarot, and to bring it alive we must be aware of its roots in Sacred Space and the images that arise within that Space and which are found in mythic forms world-wide.

Most of all I would urge you to work directly with the tarot, and learn to rely upon your own meditations, intuitions and insights. The Merlin Tarot is particularly powerful for meditative and intuitive work, for it uses clear images and patterns uncorrupted by religious propaganda or the maundering of intellectual occultists. Like all living holisms, there are levels within or behind the Merlin Tarot which cannot be put into words, but which you will contact if you work with the deck regularly.

Merlin's original adventure was to come into contact with all living beings upon the Wheel of Life, to experience the Seasons, the Elements and the Powers directly within himself. At the close of his adventure, he retired into spiritual contemplation, or, some say, merged with the land. The two are the same.[3] This cycle of Merlin's life is epitomized by the Trumps, from The Fool to The Hermit, which form the Ascending images of the Merlin Tarot (see Figure 4, p.33).

The original Merlin tradition was prophetic, with human consciousness fired by the living energy of the Sacred Land and the dragons of the Goddess. This tradition also runs through the Merlin Tarot: working with the deck will bring about such an adventure within yourself. It will vary according to your sex, for the visionary and prophetic powers work in slightly different ways in men and women; the deeper experiences, however, transcend and underpin such polarized differences.

When I began work on the Merlin Tarot it was my intention to create a deck primarily for insight, visualization and deep inner work within the Northern and Western tradition. It was also important to restore several Trumps (Death, The Guardian, The Hierophant and Judgement) in modern publication, disposing of propaganda and corrupt repressive versions (see the relevant chapters on the Trumps). I was, and still am, less concerned with divination and farsight or prediction. The impetus of the Merlin tradition, however, overtook my own small intentions, and the deck has very powerful divinatory potential, a potential which works just as well for the complete beginner as for the more expert tarot reader.

The true value of the Merlin Tarot is in a combination of all inner arts and disciplines, for tarot mirrors the universe within ourselves as well as the universe that is, seemingly, outside. Throughout this book I encourage you to do away with texts, tables, lists, correspondences and keywords as soon as possible. At a later stage, when the universes within and without come together and are realized to be one, we can even throw away the deck of cards.

Does that seem such an absurd statement? If you work with the deck for long enough the images will come alive within you, and you will have no need of prompts or clues as to their meaning even in widely varying contexts and patterns of cards. Eventually you will be able work directly with the images themselves, as they appear in visualization or intuitive perception. That is how I designed *The Complete Merlin Tarot*, for though I began with some ancient poems that held the key visions, it was the living visions themselves that I used to create the deck.

There are other connected visions, of cosmology and prophecy, that arise from the Merlin Tarot. Those cannot be described in words, but are available to you when you use the images of the deck. Conversely, you need not bother about such visions, for like all tarot, the Merlin Tarot can be used in the simplest of ways, for imagery and story-telling. The choice is yours, for universal vision and the simplest of stories are not so far apart from one another.

R. J. Stewart,
1991

THE HISTORY, COSMOLOGY AND PSYCHOLOGY OF THE MERLIN TAROT

Historical Background

The Merlin Tarot is a modern restatement of the earliest known set of tarot images and tarot cosmology and psychology in Western literature. It is drawn from the *Vita Merlini* and *The Prophecies of Merlin* written out (but not created) by Geoffrey of Monmouth in the middle of the twelfth century. Some further material is drawn from Geoffrey's major work, *The History of the Kings of Britain*, which gives the background to Merlin's early life.

Modern research into tarot has proposed that the Trumps derive from the *Triumphs* of Petrarch, written around 1340.[4] The earliest actual cards date from the middle of the fifteenth century, but these were drawn from existing images and traditions, and not created out of a vacuum. The undeniable tarot Trump images and elemental system described in the Merlin texts, however, set a historical dating at least two centuries earlier than the presumed sources in Petrarch.

When the more fanciful theories regarding tarot were formulated in the nineteenth century, and when the literary watershed of Petrarch's *Triumphs* was proposed, no one had examined the Merlin texts. Yet these texts contain a clear cosmology and elemental psychology, plus a number of images and characters which are identical to those later found in picture form as tarot cards. They pre-date both the earliest hand-painted cards and the works of Petrarch, and we may presume that all such variants – literary, poetical and visual – derive from a general tradition. In the case of the Merlin texts, much of this tradition is from Celtic bardic poetry and oral lore, reworked extensively and combined with classical Greek motifs by Geoffrey of Monmouth.

Story-Telling and the Merlin Tarot

In the Merlin texts, as in the later *Triumphs* of Petrarch, the Grail texts and many other poetical and mystical works, the central character takes part in a series or cycle of adventures. As prophet of the land of Britain, Merlin represents not only Otherworld powers from his daemon father, but humanity in general, from his Welsh mother. In this context we must remember that *daemon* is a quite different term from the later *demon*, for the first is a type of advisory spirit, such as inspired Socrates, or one that may become wise through carrying prayers to Divinity (in the *Vita*), while the second is a development of religious propaganda and psychological conditioning.

Many motifs and themes within Merlin's adventures are also found in other Celtic legends, such as *The Mabinogion*.[5] We may reasonably presume that the Merlin texts, the earliest collection of tarot images in literature, are intimately connected to an oral story-telling tradition. This bardic tradition was eventually set down as various collections of tales, including *The Mabinogion*, or was incorporated in Ireland into various monastic books. Thus there are many clear and direct parallels between sources from early tradition and story-telling, legendary and heroic themes.

Such traditions always contain the collective wisdom and magical symbolism of the culture in which they developed; they often preserve this wisdom long after its deeper aspects have been removed from formal religion by the arrival of new cults or political restrictions. There is nothing remarkable, therefore, in the fact that tarot, as picture cards preserving an ancient system of symbols and images, should contain mystical and magical material. Tarot cards derived from poems and tales, in which the primal images were reiterated in endless cycles and combinations. This is the basis for the Merlin Tarot, taken from the adventures and wonders experienced by Merlin on his journey around the Wheel of Life towards spiritual maturity.

The Creation Vision

We can now proceed directly to the heart of the Merlin Tarot, which is a cosmology and magical psychology. This system, which we may call the Creation Vision, is expounded in the *Vita* to Merlin by the bard Taliesin. The Creation Vision forms a framework upon which key images (Trumps) fit in a lucid and coherent fashion. The adventures and visions of Merlin himself provide the basis for many of the Trumps, and the Creation is balanced by an apocalyptic vision of the ending of the solar system, found as the dramatic conclusion to the *Prophecies*.

Although the system described in the Merlin texts pre-dates the introduction of Kabbalah into western Europe, it clearly has many parallels with the Tree of Life. For the benefit of modern readers and students, I have employed a very simple Tree of Life as a working model for the Merlin Tarot, but the allocation of Trumps is totally different from the nineteenth- and twentieth-century systems deriving from magical orders such as the Golden Dawn. The Merlin Tarot follows the creation and reflection of the worlds and orders of life found in the *Vita* and *Prophecies*, which, it need hardly be stated, long pre-date modern occult literature. [1]

The resulting tarot system is powerful and simple, and includes original forms of Trumps which were later influenced, or even corrupted, by political religion. The primal quality that results, in both the system and the individual cards, makes it possible to work with the Merlin Tarot directly and effectively. Both the individual or group already experienced with tarot and Kabbalah, and the new student, will find this previously ignored or little known system to be very effective and absorbing.

In some ways the Creation Vision of the Merlin Tarot returns to the original spirit of Kabbalah or esoteric tuition in general, for it is an oral and visionary system. It does not work through complex multi-lingual and mathematical intellectual correspondences, but through a story that gives imaginative insight into higher orders of reality or truth. These orders may be properties of consciousness, or actual beings, creatures and natural events in the 'Worlds'.

The Three Worlds and the Three Wheels

As already mentioned, the Merlin Tarot is based upon Three Worlds and Three Wheels (see Figures 1–3). The Three Worlds are defined by the Three Wheels, and correspond to the Trumps Moon, Sun and Star. Thus there are Lunar, Solar and Stellar Worlds, and three thresholds or Wheels: Fortune, Justice and Judgement. The Earth is included in the Lunar World, though it also partakes of all Three Worlds.

The other Trumps are related harmonically to this *Axis Mundi* of Worlds, taking positions that correspond to their roles within the Merlin texts. This gives rise to a harmonic or organic set of relationships and Trump positions which probably derives from an ancient story-telling symbolic 'alphabet', an alphabet not of letters, but of images.

The Illustrations

There are a number of sets of relationships inherent in the Merlin Tarot, mainly defined and described within the Merlin texts already mentioned.

The Merlin Tarot is particularly concerned with *polarity* and *reflection* of images, a subject which is hardly touched upon in other tarot systems. The various illustrations given throughout this book show in diagrammatic form the partnerships, triads and harmonic relationships between Trumps. An obvious example is the *Axis Mundi*, Tree of Life, or Spiral of Worlds (see Figure 2): the levels of Moon, Sun and Star are *harmonics* of one another, as are the thresholds or Wheels of Fortune, Justice and Judgement.

Before studying the individual chapters on the Trumps, the reader should examine the illustrations, and will find it helpful to refer to them frequently until their patterns are familiar. They are simple maps and patterns of relationship, and effectively replace many thousands of words of theory and description. In all cases, the actual cards should be laid out in the configurations shown in the illustrations.

The illustrations show that each Trump has a polar partner (similar to, but not necessarily, a sexual or marriage partner) and has higher and lower harmonics. Some Trumps reflect one another at ultimate extremes, in the upper and lower regions of the Tree of Life or Spiral of Worlds. Each of the chapters on the Trumps begins with a short summary of a particular Trump's attributes, and its symbolism and relationships are described in the main text, with reference to the illustrations. (See Figures 1, 2 and 8.)

Figure 3: (opposite) THE CREATION VISION (based on the *Vita Merlini* and *Prophecies*)

The First Wheel: The Lunar World – centred upon the Moon.
☉   Energy/spirit/transpersonal consciousness.
☽   Psyche/sexual energies/subconscious and collective or ancestral consciousness.
♀   Emotions.
☿   Intellect.
⊕   Body and outer events.

The Second Wheel: The Solar World – centred upon the Sun.
♀   The Abyss (crossed by Trumps 3, 13, 16).
☉   Transpersonal consciousness.
☽   Psyche, subconscious (supporting emotions and intellect).
♂   Catabolic energies/consciousness.
♃   Anabolic energies/consciousness.

The Third Wheel: The Stellar World – centred upon the unknown or void.
♅   *Primum Mobile*/seed of being.
♀   The Abyss or void.
☉   Transpersonal consciousness (source of lower consciousness).
♄   Universal Understanding.
♆   Universal Wisdom.

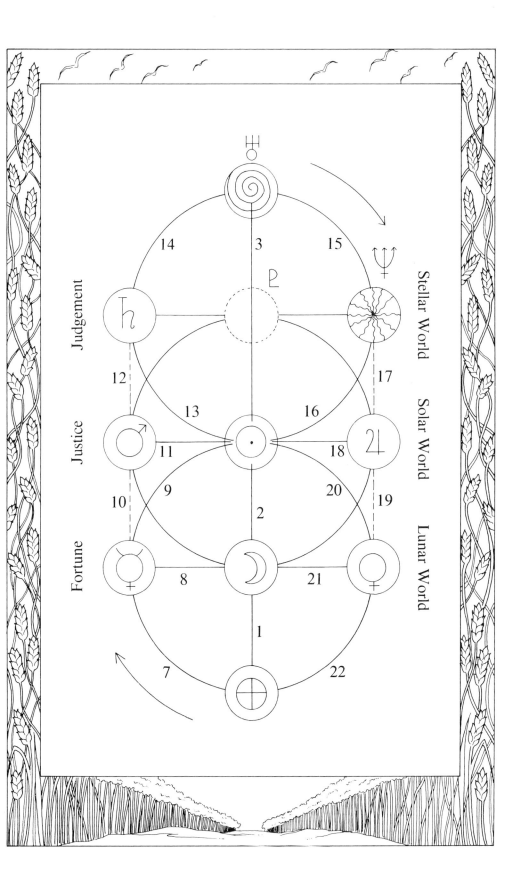

Using the Merlin Tarot

As with any tarot pack, The Merlin Tarot may be used in a number of different ways. Ultimately, tarot provides many truths and transformations through meditation, visualization and pattern making. It may also be used for insight, farsight and prevision, though these are lesser arts.

Tarot has always been used, from the earliest times (before picture cards and the words 'Trump' or 'tarot'), for story-telling. This gives us an insight into the predictive power of tarot images, for they show the implied story behind any query, and often project the energies inherent in such a story into the future. The Merlin Tarot is particularly powerful as a story-telling or myth-defining system, as it is free of many corruptions and superstitions that have become attached to tarot from the fifteenth century to the present day. Because of this, modern students will find the Merlin Tarot a readily accessible method of exploring inner space, the modes and dimensions of consciousness.

The Holism of the Merlin Tarot

In popular use of tarot, the Trumps and minor cards are ascribed a basic meaning, either for prediction or meditation; many methods of use take the subject no further. But there are a number of systems of relationship within published tarot studies and packs, and such systems are essential to development through meditation and visualization. Tarot is a *holism* and not a collection of loosely related units.

The system connected to the Merlin Tarot is very different from those in general publication. It is likely to derive from a coherent oral wisdom tradition that once permeated the Western world and was inherent in the material set from Welsh or Breton into Latin by Geoffrey of Monmouth.

The Threefold Pattern found in Geoffrey's *Vita Merlini*, as well as in many other cosmologies, is developed from the concept of reflections or harmonics deriving from an original unity or source. The three reflections are the Stellar, Solar and Lunar Worlds, which are shown upon the Middle Pillar of the Tree of Life with connecting Paths between their associated Spheres of energy. The Paths are related in Western esoteric tradition to tarot Trumps, not because the cards were devised through direct contact with such tradition, but because they formalized diffuse variants of it at a very late date. They were painted, and later printed, as educational and exemplary or story-telling sets of images, but preserved organically the original cosmological and mythical story, which is finely defined through conceptual models such as the Tree of Life.

By setting the patterns found in the *Vita* and the *Prophecies* upon the Tree of Life and, conversely, by adjusting the attributes of the paths

(Trumps) on the Tree of Life to match the visions of the Merlin texts, we arrive at a simple primal system of relationship. This system is founded upon the concept of the Three Wheels and a cycle of ascent and descent which moves across the illusory or relative limits set by our consciousness within each Wheel.

The Cycle of Ascent and Descent

The tradition of ascending and descending is found in magical arts, religious and mystical contemplation, and some important but little understood physical disciplines in both the West and the East. It has expression in yoga, tantric practices, rituals such as the Mass, Hermetic alchemy and a number of other physical forms. These are all refined specialized variants of natural patterns and laws, and are not in any way strange, unnatural or superior.

The cycle of ascent and descent, or circulation, is essential to our physical well-being, through our breathing and our bloodstream. In certain mystical or metaphysical arts, this analogy is carried to deeper or inner levels through conceptual models and sets of images which act upon our entire complex of body/consciousness; tarot is the major set of images of this type within Western traditions. When we combine enduring traditional symbols, such as the Spindle or Tree of Life, with the cosmology and psychology of the Merlin texts (which, as mentioned earlier, are merely early sources and examples of the same tradition overlooked or ignored in literary and revival 'occultism'), an order of relationship for the Trumps appears. This order may be *ascended* and *descended*.

The Technique and Practice
In practical work, we ascend one side of the Tree or Spindle or Spiral of Worlds, and descend the other. This is not the only way of encountering the symbols, but is a proven method taught in many systems of inner development. The order relates to the *Great Story* or adventures of The Fool, or first and last human; furthermore, it is found within the Merlin texts as the pattern for Merlin's adventures, visions and transformations. We may assume, therefore, that this technique formed part of the bardic tradition of magical psychology and cosmology, much of which is now lost.

First, we examine the Three Worlds through which all such transformative journeys and changes of consciousness occur (Moon, Sun and Star). After this central cosmology/psychology, we encounter the Three Wheels (Fortune, Justice and Judgement) which act as thresholds of energy and consciousness.

We then return to Earth and begin the *ascent*, the dramatic series of transformations undertaken by The Fool. The ascent works harmonically through the catalytic Trumps (on the left-hand side of the Tree of Life, Figure 2): Fool/Magician/Chariot/Guardian/Blasted Tower/Death/Hanged Man/Hermit. The peak of our ascent is The Hermit, who withdraws consciousness into universal being or the void. This Trump is represented by in the Merlin tradition by the aged Merlin, who withdraws into a stellar observatory leaving the outer world behind.[1]

The path of *descent* travels down the right-hand side of the Tree of Life, following harmonically the anabolic or building Trumps. The order is: Innocent/Temperance/Emperor/Strength/Empress/Lovers/Priestess/Universe. The image of The Universe is represented in the Merlin tradition by a figure who purifies and transforms the outer world, a type of Goddess of Sovereignty,[6] and by the fourfold pattern of The Creation Vision.

The overall movement describes a Great Circle encompassing the entire Tree of Life, but within this are the cycles of the Three Wheels or Three Worlds. The legend of the red and white dragons, associated with the youthful Merlin and his visions of the future, is based upon an energetic or circulatory system of this sort. The concept has harmonics within the human body, consciousness, regional and planetary locations. It resonates through the Three Worlds of Moon, Sun and Star, as shown in the Trumps of the same name, and the Wheels of Fortune, Justice and Judgement. (Figure 7, p.89, is a key illustration of this concept.)

Stellar Patterns

Another major concept is that the Worlds are initially defined by a series of harmonics reaching from the Earth to the moon, the sun and on to the stars or a selected star. In ancient tradition the Pleiades often acted as an observed stellar focus, for this group of stars in the constellation of Taurus can be seen from both hemispheres of our planet, and was used to mark to turning of the year. There is a poetic or mystical correlation between the Seven Pleiades and the Seven Planets, though, curiously, there are only six stars to be seen in the physical grouping itself.

Another stellar focus found in magical tradition is the Pole Star, used to define spherical orientations of Above, Below, East, South, West and North. This simple pattern hides a profound operational system for directing and enhancing consciousness. When we examine *The Prophecies of Merlin* we find that stellar patterns, including the Pleiades, are a central theme of certain visions, particularly the Apocalypse or mystical vision of the goddess Ariadne unravelling the universe.

Overall, it is the concept of a *threefold relativity* that is important, rather than precise correlation and measurement. In early magical astronomy, the forerunner of astrology, direct observations were made of patterns in the night sky, and poetical conclusions or mystical affirmations drawn from

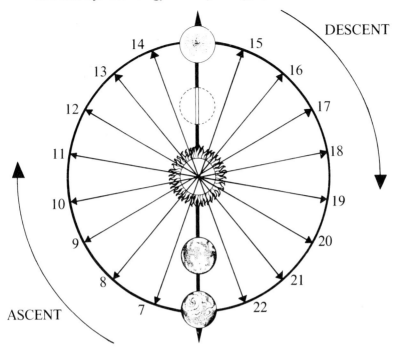

Figure 4: TRUMP RELATIONSHIPS: The Cycle of Ascent and Descent

Partners or polar pairs of Trumps

A	14	Hermit–Innocent	15	D
S	13	Hanged Man–Temperance	16	E
C	12	Death–Emperor	17	S
E	11	Blasted Tower–Strength	18	C
N	10	Guardian–Empress	19	E
D	9	Chariot–Lovers	20	N
I	8	Magician–Priestess	21	D
N	7	Fool–Universe	22	I
G				N
				G

Ultimate or Extreme Pairs of Trumps

7	The Fool–The Innocent	15
8	The Magician–Temperance	16
9	The Chariot–The Emperor	17
10	The Guardian–Strength	18
11	The Blasted Tower–The Empress	19
12	Death–The Lovers	20
13	The Hanged Man–The Priestess	21
14	The Hermit–The Universe	22

them. The connections made between the physical environment and stellar patterns were intuitive as well as mathematical – temple sites were aligned to certain stars or planets very accurately by measurement, but the reasons for such relationships lived in the deeper consciousness before the measurements were made for physical alignment. Detailed measurements and proportions are not essential to structures such as the Tree of Life or tarot cosmology; indeed, for many students they can become a positive snare and maze of distraction. But in certain advanced astrological and philosophical or metaphysical sciences, an element of precision and calculation is essential, though it is difficult to judge what relationship these artistic sciences bear to popular modern astrology – if indeed there is any relationship at all.

Method of Working

We may approach the triple pattern initially through an examination of words, images, symbols and maps. This preliminary but vitally important stage tends to occupy the sole attention of modern esoteric literature, but its true function is to provide a set of guidelines for actual experience, rather than a rigid or so-called 'authoritative' definition of apparent reality. Once we have learned the initial units and maps of arrangement, we can employ the symbols and images to meditate upon each World or mode of being. This practice is aimed at an understanding of the relationship between relative states or spheres of activity in the universe (planetary, solar and stellar) and modes or levels of human awareness. They are harmonics of one another, and this concept is so important, so central to tarot, that we shall return to it repeatedly, for it is both the foundation and the crown of mystical cosmology.

More significant in our present context, however, is the affirmation that this idea works as a practical model by which our consciousness may be transformed and expanded. But the Merlin Tarot is not designed with the intention of making any grandiose or sweeping pseudo-religious statement, simply for one purpose only: spiritual or inner work.

When working with tarot, as we approach the patterns, examples, illustrations, or each single Trump, the associated cards should be laid out as illustrated. Visual and imaginative work with tarot will reveal the relationships very directly, and is more effective than any verbal description.

Basic Table of Trumps
(See also Figures 1–3, 6, 7)

1	Moon	⎫
2	Sun	⎬ The Three Worlds
3	Star	⎭
4	Fortune	⎫
5	Justice	⎬ The Three Wheels
6	Judgement	⎭
7	Fool	⎫
8	Magician	⎪
9	Chariot	⎪
10	Guardian	⎬ Ascending
11	Blasted Tower	⎪ or Internalizing Trumps
12	Death	⎪
13	Hanged Man	⎪
14	Hermit	⎭
15	Innocent	⎫
16	Temperance	⎪
17	Emperor	⎪
18	Strength	⎬ Descending
19	Empress	⎪ or Externalizing Trumps
20	Lovers	⎪
21	Priestess	⎪
22	Universe	⎭

The Pattern of Ascent and Descent

By ascending the left-hand of the Spiral or Tree, via the connecting paths, we immediately encounter images which liberate us from conditioning, preconception, self-inflation, imbalance and the rigid habitual abuses of our essential energies. By descending the right-hand side of the Spiral or Tree, we encounter the balancing polar images which restore and regenerate energies right through into the outer physical world. This is the basic death/life cycle of taking and giving, catabolism and anabolism. In tarot Trumps specific images are set into patterns of relationship; these patterns act to transform our entity or consciousness/body relationship.

So, working in the manner outlined, we follow a natural pattern, but apply it in a very specific and powerful manner through our imagination. All existence circulates, moves in cycles, rotates, breathes in and out of being, moves from life to death to life. This concept of relativity or circular motion is apparent in all forms and energies, from crystals to stones, to animals and planets, to humans, to the solar system, to the stars. Nothing that exists may do so without rotation, polarity and interaction. Modern physics approaches this truth through relativity and energy, space and time, restating, in a profound scientific and mathematical way, a theory taught for millennia in the Mysteries or esoteric schools of magical and metaphysical development.

Ascending and descending may be combined, in advanced stages of work, with groups or related Trumps in pairs, triplicates and other sets; but to prove the circulation of images within ourselves is a major work of meditation and visualization in its own right. When we practise the major circulation we travel around the Great Circle of the Tree of Life; when we ascend and descend using sets of Trumps, we travel up and down the Middle Pillar or pivot, just as is initially undertaken with the Trumps of Moon, Sun, Star and the Three Wheels. Ultimately, we may be able to work the entirety of the Tree of Life and the tarot images by using only the Middle Pillar or the Three Wheels, thus the most advanced stage is a higher harmonic of the early development.

Alphabetic and Numerological Systems
The method of approaching tarot most frequently found in publication, in which numbers are given to Trumps, and these in turn are juggled or forced into alphabetic and astrological correspondences, is most unfortunate, and has had a prolonged debilitating effect upon the Western esoteric traditions, although in their original form, that is, derived from genuine Jewish mysticism, the alphabet and numbers of the Kabbalah provide a profound insight into mystical truth, embodied within the religion and culture in which such a system was developed over thousands of years. A similar system was supported by the druidic or bardic traditions, most of which is now lost, in which natural phenomena, such as trees, seasons, flights of birds and locations upon the landscape, all provided an alphabet of inner reality. Some of this system appears within the *Vita Merlini* in a rather literary and confused form. Neither of these ancient systems, however, are those proposed by standard occultism, which is mainly a contrivance devised by nineteenth-century thinkers and researchers who were totally divorced, by culture, education and inclination, from both Jewish mysticism and Celtic tradition.

The common tendency to aim for 'completeness' or pan-cultural cross-reference simply cannot be fulfilled in esoteric work; what is required is repeated effort with a simple organic symbol structure. Work of this sort will lead to insights into similar systems world-wide, but intellectual correspondences will not lead to such insight any more than computers will truly develop consciousness. There is a great and vital difference between ordering and reordering fragments of information and moving symbols into higher modes of awareness. The first may be done forever without ever reaching a new level of consciousness, but the second may be gained from relatively simple sets of images or symbols; and this is precisely the aim of tarot and related wisdom traditions.

The Pattern of Ascent

The cycle of ascent begins in the human consensual world, but solely from the initiation or starting-point of an individual seeking altered consciousness, new thresholds of reality. To gain such altered states of consciousness, we ascend the left-hand side of the Tree of Life or Spindle and descend the right-hand side. These relative areas of symbols are shown as the Right and Left-Hand Pillars in Figure 2, and depend upon the conceptual model of polarity that runs through magical and mystical tuition. By ascending 'left' and descending 'right', we circulate our imagination and related energies, with the middle or pivotal Trumps as balancing and reference locations. This is essentially an inner journey, but, as in the adventures of Merlin, it has powerful outer and individual counterparts, and is by no means a mere flight of frivolous fantasy. In tarot the imagination is used as a transformative power, not as a drifting alternative form of television or mild entertainment.

Ascent of the pattern begins with the Three Worlds or the Middle Pillar – Moon, Sun and Star – crossed by the three thresholds, the Three Wheels of Fortune, Justice and Judgement. The triplicity may be ascended and descended in meditation (see the appropriate sections on each Trump). Once these six Trumps have been encountered as pivotal and defining areas of symbolism and consciousness, we can return to the outer world for the circulation or cycle of ascent and descent.

The pattern of ascent, as mentioned earlier, uses the following sequence of Trumps: Fool / Magician / Chariot / Guardian / Blasted Tower / Death / Hanged Man / Hermit.

The Pattern of Descent

Having reached the top of the Spindle, or the Crown of the Tree of Life, the originative state from which all other states are reflected, we begin our descent. We thus encounter the polar partners to those Trumps which we met during our ascent. The pattern of descent uses the following sequence of Trumps: Innocent / Temperance / Emperor / Strength / Empress / Lovers / Priestess / World or Universe. This is shown upon Figure 4.

Only after experiencing the powers of taking or breaking down may we truly accept those of giving or building up. This is a law found in nature, perhaps most obviously expressed in the nutrition of our physical bodies. If we take in too much in the way of nutrition (or try to relate only to the positive and anabolic Trump images) we run the risk of becoming poisoned, ill, unbalanced. The corresponding elimination or catabolic process and energies are essential for balanced development. This analogy is as true in the psyche and spirit as it is in the physical body; you cannot receive without giving, you cannot build up without first breaking down.

Traditionally, we begin the cycle of inner change through purification; this is why we ascend the purifying and clarifying images (those of negative catabolic effect). Such Trumps may be disturbing or even terrifying if we seek to retain our inflated self-polluted delusions, but they are agents of health if we seek true liberation through inner transformation.

This is why the corruption of the Trumps of Death and The Guardian (The Devil) is so pernicious, for their orthodox propagandized forms unbalance the true action of each image. They are, of course, designed to force us into a religious system through which we might hope to escape our fears of those very same images; but imbalance in two Trumps has an ongoing effect upon all of the others, and many of our culture's deep problems today are derived from this 'domino' effect.

The Relationship of Ascent and Descent

Only experience and effort will properly reveal the effect of the cycle of ascent and descent upon the individual, but it is a well established method of working, taught for many centuries in esoteric disciplines. The purifying (ascending) Trumps enable our expanding consciousness to relate to each of the Three Worlds safely without overload; the energizing (descending) Trumps reveal to us how these Worlds are originated, created, formed and, finally, reach physical expression in time and space.

It should be emphasized that Trumps are not restricted to any direction of movement from one extreme to another; the concepts of ascent and descent are operational or working patterns for our use. The Trumps themselves may polarize in either relative 'direction' or may be perfectly balanced between their respective extremes, which are shown by the Spheres or Planets upon the Tree of Life, each Sphere symbolizing a pure mode of energy or aspect of consciousness.

Once a Trump image is polarized beyond its extremes of energy, it transforms into another image. Thus an 'upward' movement for The Empress transforms this image into The Emperor, which is the same energy within the Stellar World rather than the Solar; a downward movement for The Empress transforms the image into The Priestess or the World, modifying the image into the Lunar World. In either case the transformations are due to the energies or relative modes of consciousness in the Spheres towards which the image is polarized.

A 'sideways' or rotational movement is also possible, moving towards balance at the centre of the Tree or Spindle, and to the polar opposite image at the far extreme of right or left.

A further sequence of harmonic relationships is discovered when we place the ascending and descending orders of Trumps together as follows:

THE FOOL	THE INNOCENT
THE MAGICIAN	TEMPERANCE
THE CHARIOT	THE EMPEROR
THE GUARDIAN	STRENGTH
THE BLASTED TOWER	THE EMPRESS
DEATH	THE LOVERS
THE HANGED MAN	THE PRIESTESS
THE HERMIT	THE UNIVERSE

This is a meditational and visualizing aid of considerable value, and is shown in full in Figure 7, p.89. In the illustration we can see the relationship of 'opposites' given by reading the lists above from right to left, but also the relationship of 'partners' as shown upon the Tree of Life. Laying the Trump cards out in these patterns gives many meditational insights; furthermore, these relationships are employed in legend and myth world-wide, and form the basis for creative story-telling generated out of a symbolic or floating repertoire. When paired in the manner shown above, the images are not so much 'opposites' but ultimate *extremes* of one another – partners that are not subject to rotation or temporal polarization, but are always inherent in one another.

Tarot and Energy

The pattern of ascent and descent is the magical or psychic aspect of the normal processes of a healthy body: it is a balanced circulatory system. On a more subtle level, therefore, the cycle is linked to what might be broadly termed our *vital energies*. Many mystical and magical traditions teach that such energies may be moved or amplified at will, rather than through habitual or involuntary responses and processes. The relationship between Trumps, even in standard packs and systems of relationship, has this important but frequently confused correspondence between cosmology, psychology and the vital energies. In the Merlin Tarot, it is the visualization and encountering of the Trumps in a very specific order that leads to these transformations of energy within the individual.

Most important of all is the basic rule that we must follow any pattern or system through to its ultimate end. Tarot is a spiral rather than a closed circle, but jumping from one set of attributes to another without completing any is a very subtle form of imprisonment. This is, unfortunately, why 'comprehensive' or pan-cultural esoteric systems frequently fail or even have adverse effects upon the student.

Universal Cycles

There is no suggestion whatsoever that the cycles of tarot and their simple visionary or poetic cosmology (the Three Worlds and their occupying or threshold images) should be taken literally. They work as analogies of the primal forces of creation and destruction, and are not dogmatic or religious in the usual sense of the words, even though they relate to the primal roots of religion world-wide.

Thus we do not expect to believe literally in a geocentric universe, even though this forms the initial analogy for beginning to work with tarot. It even seems likely that ancient cultures may not have taken geocentrism literally, for there is ample evidence to the contrary. Literal geocentrism was a dogma of the political Church, a dogma from which the analogical spirit had been withdrawn.

Due to our physical stance as humans upon the Earth, we have a primal map of the Seven Directions: East, South, West, North or Forward, Right, Behind, Left, Above, Below and Within. Being Within is centrism of a physical locus, the body, with a metaphysical truth inherent within it. This metaphysical truth is the ancient formula that any given point or location is surrounded by an ever-expanding sphere of time, space and energy. These concepts are fundamentals of relativity, regardless of refined mathematical proofs developed during the twentieth century.

Tarot is an imaginative (image-based) model of such a system of relativity – every time we shuffle a tarot pack and lay out cards, we are re-creating the universe. Absurd as this may seem upon a superficial intellectual level, it works dynamically upon archetypical levels of consciousness. When we see the pictures of the Trumps Moon, Sun and Star, some deep region of our awareness makes that ancient enduring human relationship (nowadays termed 'geocentric') between our position on the Earth and the lights within the wheeling patterns of the sky. No one literally believes that the Trumps are the power of the stars, sun or moon in physical space, but we respond as if they are. This is why tarot works regardless of wisdom, folly, scepticism or belief. From this inherent effect of the images we may trace the cycles of connectives and symbols running through the entire tarot pack. If we seriously employ the patterns and images, results will occur.

THE HIDDEN STORY

Within tarot, no matter what form the pack may take, is an implicit story, a cycle of interactions with many levels of change, adventure or fulfilment. On its most basic level, it tells the adventures of any individual (and this may be the real key to tarot and prediction); on its most subtle level, it tells of the transpersonal quest for spiritual maturity and realization. The images also have a macrocosmic or universal level. These three levels outlined correspond to the Three Wheels or Three Worlds which are central to the Merlin Tarot, and indeed to any tarot pattern or pack.

The basic theme revolves around the adventures of an individual. Usually the character is male, but this may only be superficial, for roles change rapidly within tarot, and the primal character is both male and female, an androgynous primal human, reflecting the unity of universal being. This motif is common to myth, legend and religion world-wide, so is not unique to tarot in any way.

On a human level, the character is known as The Fool, who is paradoxically the human beginning a quest for truth and also the highest form of spirit or pure consciousness within each of us. On other levels of symbolism, The Fool appears as other trump images: The Hanged Man, Temperance, The World or Universe, The Hermit and even The Hierophant or Innocent, the ultimate expression of spirit within individuality.

In the Merlin texts, it is the prophet himself who undertakes the journey and enacts the story, standing for all men and women upon the quest. He is also connected to the Celtic story cycle of Mabon, a divine child stolen away at birth; both are connected in turn with an earlier cycle involving the life of a sun-god or hero and the goddess of life, procreation and death. The quest for Mabon and the mystery of his disappearance are the foundation for the famous Welsh collection of tales *The Mabinogion*;[5, 6] but whereas the Mabon tales are very diffuse (though invaluable as repositories of tradition), the Merlin tales reveal a complete life cycle. We know much of Merlin, from his conception and birth right through to his retirement into spiritual contemplation, yet far more is left unrevealed, hidden within the stories, motifs and imagery. The use of tarot continually brings the Great Story to life, whoever may be cast within it, revealing hitherto unknown variations and truths.

In the context of the Merlin Tarot, we can establish the basic story of the journey around the Wheel. This can be directly applied as an open-ended system of inner development and change. In other words we are less concerned with *reading* the story than with *being* the story, and powerful images such as tarot Trumps can act directly upon the imagination to effect changes within the entire being.

Merlin's adventures and visions in the Merlin texts cover a very wide range of events and transformations, from mysterious birth to sacrificial death, from cosmic vision to spiritual withdrawal, from grief and suffering to the embodiment of the power of nature. All of these experiences, and more, are within the *Vita* and the *Prophecies* and in the parts of *The History of the British Kings* which tell of Merlin. They may be regarded as allegories of human experience, or they may be applied as dynamic archetypes of changing consciousness. The choice is ours to make and to put into effect.

Three levels of experience and understanding are clearly defined in the Merlin texts:

1. Human psychology.
2. Spiritual and magical transformative arts and disciplines.
3. Higher consciousness or universal awareness.

In any genuine oral tradition, these three levels of exposition or reality are often fused inseparably. They correspond to the Lunar, Solar and Stellar Worlds, or the Three Wheels of tarot. The three levels are all expressed through Elemental symbolism, the great philosophical system that underpinned ancient world views. In this, a fourfold rotation of relative states of energy is defined through the Elements of Air, Fire, Water and Earth. This pattern, shown in Figure 3, gives relative phases to all manifest cycles, from the Seasons of the Year to human life, to the rotation of the great galaxies. Merlin experiences each of the three levels, Wheels or Worlds in turn, spiralling ceaselessly towards truth. With each turn or flowing of the seasons he undergoes changes, and the patterns of such changes may be applied by any of us in our use of tarot symbols or other aids to inner development and transformation.

Detailed Symbolism of the Three Wheels

The Three Wheels, as defined above, consist of:

1. The Lunar World, encompassed by the Wheel of Fortune.

2. The Solar World, encompassed by the Wheel of Justice.

3. The Stellar World, encompassed by the Wheel of Judgement.

The combination of traditional and modern attributes to the Wheels are shown in Figures 4–6. This simple system makes a very effective pattern, and its profound psychological insight pre-dates modern psychology by seven centuries at least. Much of the *Vita* is concerned with Merlin's journey around the First Wheel, which is the area covered by both ancient and modern psychology. But whereas modern psychology remains upon the First Wheel, the enduring traditions of insight spiral through two further modes of consciousness in which the persona and the conditioned psyche are transformed.

The images of Fortune, Justice and Judgement are usually female in tarot Trumps (though Fortune often takes the form of a Wheel with various supporting symbols or characters). This feminine presentation of three major Trumps derives from the ancient Mystery of the Weaver, and her effect upon the Three Worlds of Moon, Sun and Stars.

The First Wheel: Fortune
This Wheel encompasses the Earth, which is within the Lunar World, and touches upon the Solar World. It rings the Spheres of Kingdom, Honour and Victory upon the basic Tree of Life (see Figure 2) symbolized by the planets Earth, Mercury and Venus. These in turn correspond to modes of consciousness, as shown in Figures 1 and 8. This Wheel is centred upon The Moon.

The Second Wheel: Justice
This rotation of energy or limit of consciousness encompasses the Solar World and touches upon the Stellar World. It encompasses the Spheres of Severity and Mercy upon the Tree of Life, and also encompasses those Spheres directly within the First Wheel, that of Fortune. This Wheel is centred upon The Sun, and is further defined by the qualities or modes of consciousness shown in Figure 5.

The Third Wheel: Judgement
This rotation or limit of consciousness or energy encompasses all Worlds, thus it corresponds to the Stellar World, which by its nature enfolds harmonically the First and Second Wheels.

The Wheels' correspondence with Merlin is as follows:

1. While Merlin lives close to nature and suffers from human grief and torment, he is circling the Wheel of Fortune, under the consciousness of The Moon.

2. While Merlin observes the motion of the planets and grows beyond

personal considerations into transpersonal or deeper levels of understanding, he is circling the Wheel of Justice, under the consciousness of The Sun.

3. While Merlin comprehends the patterns of the stellar universe, and sees beyond the patterns to the truth of creation destruction and origination, he circles the Wheel of Judgement, under the consciousness of The Star.

These three levels of awareness are inherent in us all; this is the core of the traditional teaching embodied in the Merlin Tarot.

The Analogy of Mirrors

In a set of mirrors the first reflection of an image reverses right and left, which is to say, it reverses the polarity of the original image. The second reflection reverses again, but this re-reversed third image is not identical to the original first image. A correctly aligned arrangement of mirrors seems to reflect to infinity, as can be easily demonstrated. Models and structures of this sort played an important role in the education of the Mysteries or in some schools of magical art, but they were never regarded as physical experiments, merely demonstrations that physical laws were analogues of modes of consciousness.

An infinity of reflections, of polarized relationships, is inherent in the cosmology of the Merlin Tarot, as in its traditional sources and parallels. Just as an 'infinity' of actual mirror images, although instantaneous, or related to the speed of light, appears to us in a serial or linear form and perspective, so tarot images form a holism with many related parts that need to be approached separately or in sets before we can grasp the original unity.

The examination must be undertaken by separation in order to work for our conditioned consciousness. First we consider the Trumps singly for their imagery and meaning; next, we combine them in pairs, triads, quaternities and septenaries; finally, we grasp their harmonic transcendent unity. If tarot Trumps are mediated upon and worked with in this manner, they will begin to activate or transform our awareness.

The normally published arrangement of Trumps, however, and the subtly, or less than subtly, altered polarities of certain Trumps in popular packs of cards, are similar to an arrangement of mirrors in which certain units are out of alignment. The natural laws of reflection and polarity still apply, and many paths and glimpses of connection are still open to us, but the overall structure cannot reflect to infinity. It must be emphasized that infinity is an open-ended or open-question concept, not a complete system, universe or totality without variables.

Thus the balance of polarities within the Merlin Tarot, which is not that shown in regular tarot packs, is not a contrivance for the sake of intellectual completeness. It actually opens and renders the tarot less rigid through its generation of infinite reflections. This concept runs through the Merlin texts which provide the vocabulary of tarot images and relationships, and we may presume that it underpinned primal story and myth cycles. Like the 'geocentric' world of the First Wheel, repetition and completion are found in fairy tales and legends world-wide: this does not mean that they are narrow and limited, but that through their cycle of relationship the imagination may move to new levels of consciousness.

So much of this conceptual matter is difficult to render into words that tarot, music and poems or tales by oral tradition still seem to be the ideal vehicles for such imagery. Such sources will still work upon the 'heliocentric' level, the Second Wheel, where familiar themes take on a transformed meaning. By the Third Wheel, the World of stellar unity, our consciousness may draw very few analogies, for the experience has to be filtered through the Second and Third Wheels. All of this is shown in the Merlin Tarot as located upon the Spindle or Tree of Life.

Table of Reflections in the Merlin Tarot

(F = Feminine, M = Masculine, A = Androgynous, N = Neutral or Balanced. Please refer to Figure 7 and the actual Trump cards or images.)

1 Innocent–Emperor/F–M.   Hermit–Death/M–F.
2 Emperor–Empress/M–F.   Death–Guardian/F–M.
3 Empress–World/F–A.   Guardian–Fool/M–A.

1 Hanged Man–Tower/A–M.   Temperance–Strength/A–F.
2 Tower–Chariot/M–F.   Strength–Lovers/F–M.
3 Chariot–Magician/F–M.   Lovers–Priestess/M–F.

1 Star/A.   Judgement/N.
2 Sun/A.(M)   Justice/N.
3 Moon/A. (F)   Fortune/N.

The Three Pillars or Degrees of Polarity

Left-Hand	Radial	Central	Radial	Right-Hand
Hermit/M	H'man/A	Star/A	Temperance/A	Innocent/F
Death/F	Tower/M	Sun/A(M)	Strength/F	Emperor/M
Guardian/M	Chariot/F	Moon/A(F)	Priestess/F	World/A

Judgement/Justice/Wheel of Fortune connect all together in the Three Worlds of Star, Sun, and Moon (see Figure 1).

The Harmonic Relationship between Trumps

Harmonic relationship between Trumps is generally, but not exclusively, defined by sexual polarity; thus female images are often harmonics of one another, as are male images. Such rules are general rather than rigidly definitive, but they help us considerably in our attempts to grasp the tarot system. In some cases the sexual polarity of the image will reverse with a raising or lowering its harmonic (i.e. crossing from one spiral or Wheel to another). An example of such role reversal will help to demonstrate the concept.

The Emperor and Empress (see relative positions in Figures 2 and 4) are often assumed to have a marital or sexual relationship, but in the Merlin Tarot The Empress is the feminine *reflection* or *harmonic* of The Emperor. When we examine each Trump in depth, we will find that the partner for The Emperor (Lord of Life) is a feminine image of Death, while that of The Empress (Lady of Nature) is The Guardian (Lord of the Animals). These partnerships are supported and defined by the *personae* in the *Vita Merlini* by way of literary evidence and, more significantly, by the cosmology and psychology which underpins the system.

Thus The Emperor and Empress are rather like brother and sister, reflections of one another, or a reversal of role, rather than sexual partners or balanced opposites. This type of relationship between Trumps is radically redefined in the Merlin Tarot, drawing directly upon the mystical and magical patterns taught in the Mysteries of Merlin.[1, 3]

There are two properties of harmonic relationship at work in the major images (Trumps), and to a lesser extent within the Court cards: *interaction* and *archetypical resonance*. In harmonics of interaction, sexual polarity is reversed between levels or Wheels; in archetypical resonance sexual polarity tends to remain constant between levels or Wheels. The full table of relationships is shown below, and reference should be made to Figure 4, p.33. To grasp this essentially simple (although superficially complex) set of relationships, it will be helpful to lay out the actual cards in the patterns shown, and to relate to the images as well as to follow the text.

Archetypical Resonance

The following sets of relationships between Trumps broadly correspond to god and goddess forms in world religions. In a Western context they relate more specifically to Celtic, classical pagan and early Christian imagery.

Male	Female
The Hermit	The Innocent (Hierophant) (male in late tarot packs)
The Emperor	Death (male in late tarot packs)

Male	Female
The Guardian	The Empress
The Blasted Tower	Strength
The Magician	The Priestess
The Fool	The Universe or World

Androgynous or Rotating Images of Archetypical Resonance

Androgyne	Usual polarity in myth or tarot
Judgement	Female divinity (Ariadne in the Merlin texts)
The Hanged Man	Male divinity (all sacrificed gods and saviours)
Temperance	Female divinity
Justice	Female divinity
The Chariot	Female divinity (Minerva/Athena/Briggidda)
The Lovers	Male divinity (Eros)
The Wheel of Fortune	Female divinity
The Moon	Female divinity (Luna)
The Sun	Male divinity (Sol/Apollo/Belenos)
The Star	Female divinity (Astraea)

These androgynous images underlie the customary polarity shown in tarot or in other visual forms. They are androgynous because they rotate, therefore we may encounter them as either sex or as perfectly balanced. The Trumps upon the Middle Pillar of the Tree of Life, or the Spindle, are The Moon, Sun and Star. Images for these powers or modes of consciousness may be male or female, and god forms from varying cultures will take different polarities. Ultimately, these Trumps are beyond difference of polarity: they are transcendent.

Other major images, however, represent the *extremes* of polarity in the Three Worlds; thus The Empress is the extreme of feminine power in nature, while the Guardian is the extreme of masculine power in nature. The Emperor, by contrast, is the extreme of creative outgoing 'male' energy upon a higher level, while Death is the extreme of ingoing destructive 'female' power upon the same level. The extreme images are found upon the Left-Hand and Right-Hand Pillars of polarity on the Tree of Life, while the rotating or androgynous, balanced images are found towards or upon the Middle Pillar (see Figure 2).

In the archetypical resonance shown above all gods and goddesses relate harmonically, each feminine or masculine image partaking of a primal polarized archetype but varying in form and function through each of the Three Worlds. This superficially complex concept is merely a development in a cycle of images (the Trumps) of the basic concept of Three: there are positive, negative and balanced states of energy within time and space, continually changing and interacting. These energies are the mystical and biological polarities of Male, Female and Androgyne, and upon the archetypical level their relationships are less subject to the dance of change as our understanding moves into the higher or transcendent modes (the higher Worlds or Spheres).

Within the pattern of archetypical resonance is found the pattern of interaction: interactive resonance.

Interactive Resonance
With each harmonic change of consciousness or movement through the Worlds, sexual roles reverse (see Figure 1):

Left-Hand	Middle	Right-Hand
Hermit/male	Judgement	Innocent/female
Death/female	Justice	Emperor/male
Guardian/male	Wheel of Fortune	Empress/female
Fool/androgyne		World/androgyne
Hanged Man	Star	Temperance (androgyne)
Blasted Tower/male	Sun	Strength/female
Chariot/female	Moon	Lovers/male
Magician/male		Priestess/female

The Trumps from the Solar World and Lunar World show increasingly complex elements of polarity: thus The Chariot and The Lovers are actually *tri*polar, with a central figure and two polarized lesser figures in each case (see individual cards for details).

Reflection of Major Images

The polarity exchanges between the 22 Trumps may be regarded as a set of *reflections*. This concept helps us considerably in our grasp of the fusion of cosmology/psychology which underpins the Merlin texts and is demonstrated by the Merlin Tarot. Energies are reflected through the Stellar, Solar and Lunar Worlds, and this reflection causes the role reversals that are apparent in the tarot images.

The process of reflection works in either direction on the analogous map of the Wheels or Tree of Life: from Earth to stars, or from originative being to human individual. The *harmonic* theory outlined above is broadly based upon an analogy to music, but the *reflective* theory is based upon an analogy to light.

A traditional analogy, frequently employed in magical and mystical tuition, is that of vessels pouring energy into one another. Each vessel receives and modifies the energies from the one above, the last vessel being the material or outer world. This analogy tends to slightly mislead the modern mind into a serial or linear interpretation, however, when we should seek a spiralling or spherical interpretation. The tradition of vessels should be seen as one of vessels of light (rather than fluids), symbolized by mirrors or crystals. Light is received and reradiated, making a twofold process of reflection. With each reflection, it is transformed. This analogy is very helpful in grasping the relationship between the Wheels and Worlds and the Trumps that symbolize these levels of perception, consciousness and energy. Traditionally, a threefold sequence is employed to demonstrate the concept.

The Threefold Sequence of Reflection
1. An unknowable source of origination or being arises from non-being. This is the primal event that leads to all existence; it is both a mystical statement of truth and a rational but unprovable deduction employed in modern theories of stellar and quantum physics.
2. The Source emits or causes energy: in esoteric traditions this is termed the utterance of the Name, or the primary consciousness of being. In Biblical mythology, as in other creation myths world-wide, this is symbolized as Light over the waters of Darkness; we shall follow the analogy of Light from this point of the exposition.
3. Upon the utterance of Light, time and space coalesce. The reflections symbolized by the major images are both timeless and temporal simultaneously; they originate beyond time but are expressed in modified forms through time to our limited, superficially serial mode of consciousness. The description of such a sequence of reflections must be serial, due to the mode of verbal unitary communications, or the very obvious serial nature of chosen events in apparent time; but there is no suggestion that this serial pattern is immutable or anything more than a relative mode of consciousness.

In the esoteric traditions, time is merely a product of the Third Wheel within our consciousness – this is precisely why lower stages of the magical arts, tarot and transcendent traditions seem to dramatically obviate certain laws of time, space and perception: they are merely breaking out of the conditions of the Third Wheel. Significantly, such so-called 'powers' are left behind in the advanced stages of initiation or enlightenment. This is clearly found in the *Vita Merlini*, when Merlin chooses spiritual contemplation over both worldly power and prophetic or magical vision.

The Great Story, of which tarot is a visual form, runs from the beginning of time (as far as humans are concerned) to the end of the universe. The Merlin texts define this journey very clearly, through the Seasons, the planets, the stars, and ultimately into the unknown. But beyond the abyss of comprehension that separates the Third and Second Wheels from the First, or human consciousness from stellar unity, all our apparent reflections and interactions are simultaneous in a state of no-time.

We can now move on and begin our journey of ascent and descent through the Trumps of the Merlin Tarot.

I MOON

THE MOON

WORLD The Lunar World, including planet Earth.
WHEEL The First Wheel, Fortune.
BEINGS Spirits, *daemones*, ex-humans, elementals and nature spirits. Beings from other dimensions and worlds such as fairies or ancestral beings.

CONSCIOUSNESS Human, ancestral and collective, personal or masked. The entire range of thought, emotion and energies within any entity, including dream consciousness and hidden realms of awareness within the psyche.

PARTNER TRUMPS The Sun. Also polarized rotation of Trumps around the central Moon and connecting to Earth (see Figure 3).

SPHERES AND PLANETS *Spheres:* The 9th and 10th Spheres, Foundation and Kingdom. *Planets:* Luna and Earth.

ATTRIBUTES The lower third of the *Axis Mundi*, Middle Pillar or Spindle of Worlds. Life power in formation and expression. The Four Elements and their inner reflections or harmonics of consciousness.

GOD AND GODDESS FORMS Luna and the Earth Mother. All goddesses of fertility, birth, life, death and nature. Also goddesses of prevision, prophecy and magical or supernatural practices.

KEY PHRASES The Kingdom of Life/the foundation of power/passage of awareness inwards and outwards/reflection and reproduction/the Mysteries behind nature.

MERLIN TEXTS[7] *PVM* The Goddess of the Land; *VM* Description of the Lunar World and its inhabitants, description of the Earth and its regions, energies, creatures and hidden dimensions.

DIVINATORY MEANING Unconscious forces or unseen influences from within materialize into outer life. Matters relating to birth and death, dreams and desires. Collective or group modes of behaviour and awareness. May also indicate the early stages of inner transformation or initiation.

RELATED NUMBER CARDS Nines and Tens (or Aces).

Nines: Misfortune, Endurance, Fulfilment, Means.

Tens: Disaster, Responsibility, Friendship, Opportunity.

Origins of the Image

The Moon defines the first level of the Spindle of the Universe from its lowermost point in the centre of the planet Earth, to the outermost limit of the relative sphere defined by the orbit of the physical moon around the planet. In simpler terms, it is the path or connection seen (in a geocentric sense) between humankind upon the ground and the closest light in the night sky. The image reveals connections between the known and the unknown, seen and unseen.

The physical analogy, of relative positions in time and space, applies equally to our psyche; The Moon represents hidden and mysterious realms of consciousness that seem both powerful and close yet distant and inaccessible. By meditation upon this mystery, we begin to realize that our outer world is part of a greater sphere, with an inner or reflective aspect that includes yet transcends our physical body and accustomed or conditioned modes of consciousness.

In primal astrology, the Trump of The Moon fuses planetary concepts of Earth and Luna. This fusion expresses an interplay of life and death. Luna, or Foundation, is the Sphere of life in essence, pre-expression, formation; the life energies immediately before and after physical birth or death.

Meditation upon this image reveals that birth and death are inseparable: to be born into the expressed world is to die to the foundational or pre-material world; to die in the outer world is to pass into the inner world. In both transitions, birth or death, we pass a threshold or gateway beyond which energies change relationship and form.

This reflective or threshold situation is relative; it is not an immutable law, but a condition of consciousness. In other words, we may transform our awareness of the Trump, and activate a conscious fusion of qualities and energies inherent within the symbols of Earth and Moon. This is the ancient art of initiation (which simply means *beginning*), and on the path of The Moon, it involves a change of direction of attention, from outward-seeking to inward.

Sleep is a direct result of the interaction of energies connected by this Trump; it is sometimes known as the lesser death, a temporary passage through the Gate of the Moon, resulting in dreams. If we exist solely through cyclical patterns and rhythms that define outer life, sleep and dreaming are often our only access to the inner life. Meditation and visualization radically transform this customary situation.

The Moon is that area of the Spindle or Middle Pillar of the Tree of Life (see Figures 2–3) that forms the axis for the Lunar World of tarot. This World incorporates and defines our body, life energies, thoughts, feelings and spiritual potential. Its ultimate threshold or sphere of influence is defined by the Wheel of Fortune, which is the Wheel upon which all life on Earth circles endlessly; beyond this Wheel we reach into the Solar World, which has as its axis the Trump The Sun.

In basic astrology, the Moon rules the Sign of Cancer, the crab. In ancient metaphysics Cancer signified the gate of souls passing to and fro from physical to spiritual realms; many tarot cards have a crab or similar creature emerging from a pool to symbolize this enduring concept and intuition. The image of The Moon is our first key to the Mysteries of polarity and transformation: here they are seen by moonlight in their natural forms within the outer and expressed world.

The Pool of the image is the pool of life, water, the universal vehicle of life forms. But it also represents consciousness; here we encounter the ancestral rivers and seas of collective enduring consciousness which are so essential to magical traditions of transformation. If we dive into the Pool, we find another gate, the counterpoint, or reflection, of the Lunar Gate, leading downwards into the mysterious Underworld.[8] The Pool gives birth to life, it has transformative and therapeutic powers; as the manifest essence of the potent Underworld, it is a deep source of energy.

The Pool causes our irrational fear of the unknown; not because unknown mysteries are in any way evil, but because we dread change, and the unknown inevitably brings transformation and change. To dive into the Pool shown in our image may seem a drastic step, but we can at least observe and meditate upon the changing reflections shown on its surface. Such reflections must be seen only as hints, indications and intimations, and not as any type of ultimate or alternative reality.

Reflections

We all encounter reflections from the Moon Pool in dreams; some dreams arise from our individual consciousness, while others are reflections of inhabitants or energies of the greater Lunar World. It is in this realm that the much maligned and misunderstood 'astral plane' of popular occultism is found; originally the term 'astral plane' meant something more exalted and sublime, for it referred to the stars.

Tarot cosmology is defined in the *Vita Merlini* through worlds or dimensions reaching from the stars to the Earth; the dimensions between Moon and Earth (shown by the Path or Trump of The Moon) are said to be occupied by *daemones*. These are communicating entities who may, just as humans, do good or ill. Many of the dead-ends and follies of popular occultism are related to this concept, but a clarification and definition of such entities in modern practice provides genuine instruction and interaction. The *daemon*, or advising entity, of Socrates is the classical example of the proper form and function of such an entity, which is quite different from either the medieval 'demon' or the confused modern notion of the 'spirit guide'.

In Celtic tradition the Lunar World is one of the realms occupied by *faeries*, which are powerful semi-material beings seen only through Second Sight.[8] This is such a specific and enduring tradition that it seems most unfortunate that it has become polluted by absurd Victorian notions of cozy little people with gossamer wings. Faeries are in many ways identical to the *daemones* or spirits described in the *Vita*; both types of entity are further related to images of ancestral memory or *personae*. Faeries, however, have many forms quite independent of ancestral images, and it is unwise to generalize on such relationships. If we blandly reduce all such entities in the Lunar consciousness to equate to one another, we merely side-step and ignore a number of valuable and effective methods of expanding and transforming our awareness; it is the precise differences that enable us to relate and interact, not the general similarities.

Initial teachers of transformative arts and spiritual wisdom are encountered in the Lunar World; during later developments of consciousness such teachers may disappear or transform into new contacts. It is worth emphasizing that in Western tradition, and in the Mysteries of Merlin, such teachers are not necessarily human; they are innerworld images and contacts or interactions established through meditation, visualization and ritual art. Merlin himself is the primary contact for the Merlin Tarot system of expanding consciousness; but there are many others connected to each World and to each Trump, working in ways which are not possible or advisable through human teachers. In each World there are well-defined sets of contacts reached through working with the Trump images; work with The Moon will reveal a great deal of this reflective communicative art.

Contents of the Image

The Pool/The Newt/The Steps/The Dog and Wolf/The Path/The Tower and Tree/Mountains and Forest/Moon and Stars

The Pool
This has been described above, as the watery vehicle and source of living creatures, as the mysterious Gate to the Underworld or Otherworld, and as the ever-changing mirror of dream consciousness.

The Newt
In the Merlin Tarot the Newt is the equivalent symbol of the crab found in standard packs: as an amphibian partaking of both land and water, it represents *life in two worlds*. An older name for the newt is the *eft*, which also means a faery; the creature symbolizes primal or simple life taking on form, both earthy and watery, yet with clear hints of further dimensions and worlds. These worlds are not far remote or ethereal, but directly accessible from the most simple and primitive roots. The newt or eft is the simplest, earthiest form of the dragon (in poetic terms), and this theme is repeated throughout the Merlin Tarot with the appearance of serpents or dragons, which play an important role in the Merlin texts. We encounter the Newt as a transformed symbol in the higher Trump of Temperance, where it has become the legendary fiery Salamander. It is the first of a series of spiritual creatures that runs through the Merlin Tarot; the transformations of these spiritual animals are as important in esoteric traditions as the higher images of archetypes that they support within any Trump.

The Newt stands upon the rocks that surround the Pool; this represents life in the material world, upon Earth. The Newt can, by a long tedious climb around the Pool, reach the steps without ever entering the water. Such an approach takes a very long time. Some of us reach the inner worlds through long, hard life experience, perhaps through a cycle of many lifetimes during which our vitalizing and transforming energies of the imagination are hardly ever employed or developed. The amphibious Newt may therefore represent our consciousness – we are able to pass easily from earth to water (from outer conditions to inner imagination), and to move more easily through water than upon land, but our preference varies at key stages in our life experience and development.

The Pool is not merely individual imagination or consciousness, it is also a collective and potent vessel of consciousness that may be tapped by any questing individual. In this sense it purifies and energizes us; it speeds our progress towards the Steps if only we have the courage to plunge in. There is an added theme of cleansing and purification, for the action of the Moon Pool is to wash away illusions of fixed or rigid personality and open awareness to deeper levels of perception. Some of us, however, are most determined never to dive into that Pool, and take the long Path or wheel of interaction around it. But to go around the Pool may lead us dangerously close to the Dog or Wolf, two beasts described below.

The Steps

These are worn and ancient; many beings have emerged from the primal Pool over thousands of years, all seeking a path into the unknown. All living beings that are born or die cross the upper Three Steps; each Step represents one of the Three Worlds: Lunar, Solar or Stellar. Here the Worlds are hidden, so to speak, openly for all to see and cross repeatedly at the very Foundation of the Tree of Life. Triple symbolism also hides yet reveals aspects of the Goddess who rules the dimensions represented by our Trump of The Moon (the realm of both Earth and Moon or the Lunar World). The fourth or lowermost Step is the outer world, the expressed Element of Earth, and the physical body.

The Great Goddess of primal religion and fundamental consciousness has three aspects: youth, maturity and age. She is Maiden, Lover and Crone, the Triple Goddess known to ancient culture. To approach her we must take the upper Three Steps beyond the collective Pool onto the Path – and with each Step we leave behind something of our conditioned illusory or habitual lives. Thus the Steps are a paradox: if we could understand them fully we would have freedom of all Three Worlds, yet they are a great mystery that we are unable to solve.

In dreams we cross back and forward fleetingly; the little death and birth of sleep and waking may be attended by pleasures or horrors. In meditation, however, for which tarot is the symbolic alphabet of images in Western culture, the Three Steps may be regarded in new light. They become three stages of liberation from illusions which bind us to unthinking acceptance of the consensual or habitual outer world. A person who is content with such a world or limited reality regards all hints of alternative states of consciousness as 'dreams'; he or she may be only too pleased when dreams are ended and conditioned waking outer life begins its daily cycle.

Thus the Three Steps, like all threshold symbols within tarot, have a multifold function and meaning. The Steps act as three levels of liberation, or degrees of initiation, expanding awareness; they also act as a wall or dam limiting the Pool, or perhaps protecting and conserving it. Consciousness that is below a certain level or 'size' cannot cross the threshold of the Steps; thus, a further meaning to the emerging crab or Newt is that of a life-form or consciousness ready to climb the Three Steps, just able to span their height. In the sense of a containing dam or wall, the Steps are a reflection of the Three Worlds, each defined by a Wheel. Although the true vision is that of a spiral, and not three separate spheres or circles, to our limited perception our first indication of this truth is in the form of the Three Steps: they contain the Pool, just as the Three Wheels (which they are, upon levels that we cannot yet grasp) contain the universe.

The concept of the Steps and the creature that crosses them reveals our usual condition as humans: we are developed enough to cross the threshold into the inner world, but we may not see its truth in any form that is not either reduced or reflected. Many falter and slide back from the Steps. There is no guardian upon this first threshold in willed changes of consciousness; we make our own choices and act as our own guardians. Here is one of the great open secrets of magical art or meditative transformation: we are our own guardians – nothing else prevents us from development. In the higher Trumps we shall encounter certain clearly defined and powerful guardian images; these are keys to liberation rather than locks for confinement.

The change of direction, or liberation, associated with the Path of The Moon is gained by will, imagination and effort. We may regard the upper Three Steps as modes of consciousness, reaching progressively beyond the outer world of the lowermost Step.

First Step: Intuition, the call of an unknown but intuitively felt reality – the inner certainty, without tangible form, that there is more to life than the consensual or habitual world.

Second Step: Determination, the will to change and resist falling back into habitual life patterns which imbalance and destroy.

Third Step: Realization, in which we finally apprehend the inner landscape or realm of expanded consciousness, of transformed reality.

The Three Steps must be balanced by our three inherent guarding/liberating qualities;

1. Intuition should be fused with *will* to give it dynamic thrust rather than inactive hints.

2. Determination should be fused with *imagination* to enliven action with a vision of a goal.
3. Realization should be fused with *effort* to climb beyond the threshold of the last Step and actually enter into the inner worlds.

This third level is one upon which many of us fail; it is relatively easy to summon the energy to climb the Steps and peep into the Lunar World beyond, but this realization often slides into a passive observing condition. From this passive condition (similar to watching television) we slip back into the Pool, and thence to the outer habitual world. Many popular techniques of visualization and guided imagery suffer from this enervating problem; they do not reach beyond the realization of the Third Step.

The Dog and Wolf

We have now climbed the Three Steps and stand upon the beginning/ending of the Path. We are immediately confronted by two creatures symbolizing the first of many polar interactions or relative sets of energy. Traditionally these are the Wolf and the Dog or Hound; a perfectly balanced awareness passes freely to and fro between them, equidistant from each. Many of us, of course, emerge from the Pool only to be devoured by the Wolf, chased back by the Dog or, worse still, pinned down and quarrelled over by both beasts for the remainder of our lifetime.

The Dog is obedient energy/consciousness, while the Wolf is wild and instinctive energy/consciousness. We must have a balance of both to function properly. The Wolf tries to serve only himself, while the Dog tries to serve a collective family, purpose or even a tribe or culture. Both beasts are closely related: the Dog was once a Wolf. Either may change into the other through the turning of the Wheel of Fortune which contains the Lunar World around the axis of the Spindle.

We need both the wild energy of the Wolf and the devotion of the Dog; passage between these beasts will carry us on into the inner worlds of growth, transformation and maturity. They may become specific totems or companions during phases of the Great Journey, and may reappear in higher Trumps. Merlin has a Wolf as his companion (in the *Vita*) when he is driven mad through grief and lives in the wildwood. We can see a Forest within the image, and a period such as that experienced by Merlin – living as a hermit, close to nature through rejection of the world, and torn by compassion and suffering – is one of the transformative states found in spiritual traditions.

The Tower and Tree

Moving further into the image we find a transformed and reversed polar pair: the Tower is beyond the Wolf, while the Tree is beyond the Dog. There is a rhythm or mirroring of imagery in tarot, and our first examples are found within the Trump of The Moon, revealing themes and truths which run through the entire pack.

The Tower represents consciousness in its *assembled* or disciplined and structured state, while the Tree represents consciousness in its *organic* or natural state. Both reach from the Earth to the stars; both play major roles in the Mysteries of Merlin and in esoteric tradition generally. The Tower is a construct of strength, experience and science; it may also be misused as a hiding place or prison. The Tree grows out of the hidden Underworld (in the roots) towards the light, but may also become an escape into the worlds of nature or faery which should not dominate human development. Thus each pole or extreme has its powers and its dangers. We will encounter each one again in higher Trumps, and their presence upon the Path of The Moon is a prevision of inner transformation yet to be experienced.

As with the Wolf and Dog, we need to partake equally of both extremes and to pass between them freely. The interaction between Tree and Tower, Wolf and Dog is an interesting example of a symbolic psychology, exhibited openly in tarot long before modern theories regarding the psyche were developed. An effective meditational exercise is to draw, or preferably visualize, a square with these images at each corner. This is a map of the human psyche, and we may reflect upon the interactions in all directions around or across the square.

Mountains and Forest
The Path winds gently away passing between the moonlit Mountains and Forest. This is our final horizon in the image; beyond is the Solar World. Once again, this horizon reverses the quality of the polar extremes: from Tower to Forest, from Tree to Mountains. The defined and refined stones of the Tower are replaced by the primal Forest of darkness and mystery, while the single aspiring and magical Tree is replaced by the enduring stone masses of the Mountains, the body of matter through vast cycles of time.

These are the ultimate poles or extremes found within the Trump: Merlin lives as a mad hermit in the Forest, and as an observer of the stars upon the summit of the Mountains. But in the image of The Moon, the Mountains are the first range of an increasing climb; they are relatively gentle. In the *Vita* these are the mountains upon which Merlin begins to observe the stars and seek a new order within his life after emerging from the wildwood. We shall find higher mountains in tarot, culminating in the solitary peak upon which The Hermit stands.

The Path, however, leads between the two regions of extreme consciousness, just as the allegory of the legend of Merlin helps us to define and understand the extremes of our life experience and of potential transformation towards enlightenment.

Moon and Stars

The Moon in the night sky contains the face of Luna, goddess of all tides, rhythms and changes in life patterns. She carries a distaff upon which the spiralling symbol of the Three Worlds, the Thread of Truth, is shown. Both full and crescent Moon are in her image, for she rules all rotations or cycles in the Lunar World. The Trump of The Moon includes Earth, Moon and Stars in its imagery, but not the sun. The goddess rules the reflective light of night, in which the nearest and further lights, moon and stars, travel together. The illumination of this Trump is mainly from the Moon, but the Stars are present as indicators of unknown light yet to be experienced.

Astrology and prevision belong to this Trump initially, for both are arts in which the lights of night or reflection define truths which may not be seen in full daylight. But both astrology and prevision may be developed along paths shown by other Trumps, and are not limited to a lunar level of operation.

The Moon includes and prefigures many of the essentials of the entire sequence of Trumps. The Four Elements, in the form of expressed Earth world and foundational lunar realm, the laws of polarity and exchange, and the transcendent power of the stars, one of which is the sun, are all defined within The Moon. If we follow the Path, balancing the energies within us, we eventually reach the horizon; the Moon sets behind us as we pass over the threshold, and we enter the dawn of a new day. For the first time we consciously experience the sun as The Sun, the next Trump in the sequence of tarot.

II SUN

THE SUN

WORLD   The Solar World (crossing into the Lunar).
WHEEL   The Second Wheel, Justice, *and* the Third Wheel, Fortune.
BEINGS   The Solar Entity (includes the planetary entities) Angels, Innerworld Masters and Saints (both male and female), Illuminated Ones, transpersonal teachers and guides. Saviours and Redeemers

in world religion and mystical comprehension.

CONSCIOUSNESS   Solar   or   central   knowledge,   transpersonal consciousness, illuminated awareness.

PARTNER TRUMPS   The Star above, The Moon below. The rotation of polarized Trumps located upon the solar or 6th Sphere (see Figures 1, 2 and 7).

SPHERES AND PLANETS   *Spheres:* The 6th and 9th Spheres, Beauty and Foundation. *Planets:* Sol and Luna.

ATTRIBUTES   The middle third of the *Axis Mundi*, Middle Pillar or Spindle of Worlds. Balance of Power in motion; full awareness and natural harmonious relationship of polarized energies. Arousal and direction of life forces from their origin. Creative consciousness.

GOD AND GODDESS FORMS   The Son of Light and the Mother of Life/Mabon and Modron/Sol and Luna. All divine sons, children and their mothers.

KEY PHRASES   The equal light of sun and moon/perfected power/ knowledge of life/central consciousness/the foundation of harmony.

MERLIN TEXTS   *H* The young Merlin; *PVM* Vision of a rider upon a white horse who directs rivers; *VM* Description of the Solar World.

DIVINATORY MEANING   A powerful harmonizing, centralizing influence or energy upon life patterns. Emergence of new meaning, knowledge and higher levels of awareness within the inquirer. Creative adjustment of inner energies, movement towards transpersonal consciousness. General indication of positive, beneficial therapy both inwardly and outwardly.

RELATED NUMBER CARDS   Sixes and Nines.

Sixes: Transition, Balance, Joy, Benefit.

Nines: Misfortune, Endurance, Fulfilment, Means.

Origins of the Image

The Sun is an image of increasing illumination, in all possible senses. It reveals connections between lunar, foundational, generative forces of life, and the central source or seed of energy from which such forces are derived. The Sun represents a physical star, our sun, at the heart of the solar system, the source of all energy that defines our sphere of existence. This sphere is termed the Solar World, the second spiral turning of the Spindle, and has its microcosm or reflection within human consciousness.

All traditions of mystical or religious illumination lead towards this consciousness, and the esoteric art of the arousal of Inner Fire is inherent in work with the Trump of The Sun, as part of a triple pattern of Moon, Sun and Star. The primal astrological planetary concepts of sun and moon, Sol and Luna, are fused together upon this path.

All physical and metaphysical concepts and energies of light, motion, expansion, centrality, balance and harmony are found upon this path, represented by this Trump image. It commences where The Moon concludes; our journey is now undertaken in the light of full day, which in inner terms is the spiritual and creative light, the archetypical light of which the physical sun is a body or manifestation.

Contents of the Image

The Path/The Horse or Mare/The Child/The Hill and Cave/The Landscape/The Hawk/The Sun God

The Path
We now enter upon a higher level or harmonic of the Path first encountered within the image of The Moon, the first Trump to be experienced on turning attention inwards in meditation. This second level (see Figure 2, The Tree of Life) is marked in most Mystery systems or esoteric schools of training by a key symbol. In the Merlin Tarot the key symbol is the ancient 'Z' sign found carved upon standing stones (known as Pictish stones) in Scotland, but with world-wide parallels and similarities. This sign has been the subject of much debate among archaeologists and interpreters of symbols, but its meaning has long been known and taught in Western traditions of magical art and spiritual development.

The 'Z' sign may be seen as a lightning flash, the passage of power between Earth and heaven. In mystical traditions linked to the Tree of Life, such a flash is shown reaching from ultimate origination, the Crown, to extreme expression, the Kingdom or outer world. As a serpentine or undulating sign, it represents the path through all Worlds, Elements, and dimensions or spheres taken by the great saviours or sacred kings. This flashing serpentine motion cuts across all regular cycles of the Wheel of Life; we shall encounter it again in other Trumps, and in a very specific form in The Hanged Man.

The Horse or Mare
Traditionally the power and motion of solar and lunar energies is represented by a Horse or Mare. Male or female, the Horse shows living energy in motion. In the Merlin Tarot the White Mare connects to a Celtic goddess, sometimes known as Epona, from Romano-Celtic inscriptions, and to a vision of a white horse that features in *The Prophecies of Merlin*. More precisely the White Mare represents solar energy (be it of the sun or psyche), modified through a feminine lunar form or aspect. This is a typical relationship and reflection of tarot: when levels of energy change,

the imagery changes form and gender. The traditionally male solar image may become fused with a female lunar image: this is a property both of sexuality and of consciousness at one and the same time.

The White Mare is further connected to the Great Story; the divine solar child, Mabon, Apollo of the Celts, is the son of a horse goddess. This theme is found in the story of Rhiannon in *The Mabinogion*, where the myth of a child taken from his mother at birth is woven among many other tales.

The Child

The Child who rides the White Mare is a divine Child of Light, found in various religious and mystical traditions throughout the world. In Celtic legend, he is Mabon son of Modron, 'Son, son of Mother'; his image shows spiritual innocence and divine perfection carried outwards by natural power in motion. The Child on the Mare rides out to greet us at the threshold of the Trump. This motion of solar or spiritual consciousness is important in magical or mystical practices, and is enhanced by our powers of imagination.

In human terms we unite our sexual generative powers (Luna) of body/psyche with the inner Child of Light – found by meditation or, more rarely, through revelation. A perfect balance and partnership of these energies (Sol and Luna) travels the path between the worlds under a special grace or blessing. The youthful Merlin is a child born of a human mother and Otherworldly father – this legend reflects that of Mabon, and defines the operation of the Trump of The Sun. He has the power of innocent perfection of knowledge, of prophecy, of arousing dragons from within the Earth.

Imagery of this sort leads us back to a primal image of a divine Child, the first image in certain major mythical cycles; there are many connections between Merlin, Mabon and solar deities. But the theme is not confined to nature worship or paganism, for it merges perfectly with the concept of sacred kingship and a universal saviour, as expressed in the highest forms of religion and mysticism.

If we employ the Trump image for visualization, both Child and Mare come to the threshold to meet us; if we seek to go further into the Trump, and travel along the Path of The Sun, we must ride with combined lunar and solar energies, arousing them within ourselves and fusing them through visualization with the archetypical forms represented in the Trump. This is one of the open secrets of mystical and magical arts for expanding consciousness.

The Hill and Cave

The Path leads towards a Hill or Tor, with a Cave mouth visible near its summit. We may ride with the Child to this Hill, following the increasingly spiral Path upwards. The motif is one of spiritual or inner transformation; in the Merlin texts it is represented by young Merlin in a cavern within Dinas Emrys (an actual hill site in Wales), where he causes a pair of red and white dragons to appear. The theme endures as one of the great initiatory patterns: within a cave is both death and rebirth. In orthodox Christianity it is the cave of resurrection; in pagan religion it is the womb or tomb of death, rebirth, prophecy.

Within the Cave an individual may be reborn into other dimensions, other worlds; here is where we learn that the sun becomes a star, or where a mortal man or woman becomes a deity. In the depths of the Cave, saviours or sacred kings appear and take on human form to mediate light to the worlds of Moon and Earth. Conversely, within the vessel of the Cave, our individual energies are reshaped for living in higher dimensions. As with the Lunar World, so with the higher reflection or harmonic of the Solar World – birth and death are inseparable transformations. There is a parallel here to alchemy, for the Cave (a symbol often used in early alchemical texts) is a containing vessel for alchemical reaction and transmutation; in this case, the human within holds the basic Elements which are transformed through solar heat penetrating the stone sides of the chamber.

There is a further paradox here, for caves may be entrances to the Underworld, which we first encountered below the Pool of The Moon. In each of the axis Trumps (Moon, Sun, Star) there is a direct route to the Underworld: the Pool, the Cave and the Abyss. This theme symbolizes an important tradition which is virtually ignored in modern meditative or magical arts: the stars, or the ultimate reality, may be attained by passing *below* as well as by climbing above. This is due to the reflective property of metaphysics, whereby highest is inherent within lowest, or spirit inherent within matter. Each axis Trump has this truth symbolized within its own World or level: the Cave of resurrection is probably the highest level of this transformative process that we may relate to as humans; beyond this level we deal with universal consciousness or abstract concepts and stellar energies.

Not all travellers enter the Cave, or emerge from it; it is not inevitable to pass that way. There are in fact three choices in the Trump: to enter the Cave and seek out the unknown; to climb to the Hill top and meditate upon surrounding light; or to turn and retrace our steps back to the Lunar World. The first choice is that of the dedicated mystic, magician, seer, priest or priestess. The second choice is that of the religious worshipper, though it may also include meditation and ritual. The third choice is that made consciously by those of us who fear to travel further, or unconsciously by those who are not yet able to control their imaginative powers and are yet bound by the action of the Wheel of Fortune, which is the threshold crossing this particular Path.

We might add that during any of the three choices, there are points along the spiral Path where we may pause and rest. Many innerworld communicators or spiritual teachers are found at such points; they may be contacted through meditation and controlled visualization. The results from such exercises are surprisingly coherent and powerful, and tarot helps to define symbols, relationships and situations in which such visualizations are brought to life. The Court cards (People), for example, are usually interpreted as representing human types, due to their Elemental pattern; but on a higher level they may be employed in meditation and visualization for imaginative contact with innerworld entities, teachers and communicators, as they define very precisely the qualities to which we may choose to relate in any specified contact.

The Landscape
The brightly lit Summer Landscape is a higher harmonic or daylight version of that mysterious Otherworld which we first entered through The Moon. It is a variant of the Summer Land of Celtic legend, and many powerful spiritual beings live in such realms.

In the *Vita Merlini* the occupants of this dimension or world are described as angels of the solar heavens; in pagan philosophy they are solar heroes or sacred kings, who are transhuman rather than angelic in origin. In orthodox religions they are saints, holy men and women, or the convocation of enlightened ones. In magical traditions this is the realm in which teachers or guides reveal the Mysteries of Light.

In the Solar World our sun is the expressed location of a star; it may be termed a divine entity or, in some systems, an archangelic being. In Gnostic magical arts and Jewish Kabbalah, the archangelic entity of the sun is Michael, Guardian of Light. In the Merlin Tarot, however, we return to a primal image, suggested by the solar face that overlooks the divine Child and the Mare.

Although we have summarized the Solar World, symbolized by the Landscape, as the location or realm of certain highly evolved entities, there is another practical way of expressing this mystical tradition. Just as The Moon represents a mode of consciousness that is both individual and collective, so The Sun represents a higher mode that may be attained through individual meditation or collective visualization. In a collective sense, enlightened or advanced beings 'dwell' in the Solar World because they share a mode or degree of awareness.

The central sun is sometimes called the Knower, or universal mind, or unifying consciousness; if we examine the Tree of Life we find the 6th Sphere, the Sun or Harmony, at the centre of the Tree, connected directly to all other Spheres except the Kingdom or outer world, which is mediated through the Foundation of the 9th or Lunar Sphere. The Landscape, and the operations or functions of its various symbols, all indicate how we might attune to this central consciousness which has its heart within each of us.

The Hawk

As we found in our first Trump, The Moon, spiritual animals play an important role in the Merlin Tarot. Upon moving into the Solar World, flying, soaring awareness is symbolized by the Hawk reaching high into the light of the sun. The slow, earth- and water-bound Newt is replaced by the fast, keen-sighted, darting Hawk. Similarly the alternating qualities of Wolf and Hound are replaced and perfectly merged in the symbol of the White Mare.

The Hawk is seen as a mediator, travelling between sky and earth, and is traditionally associated with the month of May, when the year is reborn into Summer at the turning of the Pleiades. [6]

The Sun God

At the crown of the Trump we see the blazing sun; within it is the face of the deity Belenos, Bel or Apollo. The name simply means 'light' or 'beautiful'. Our image is taken from a first-century carving in the Temple of Sulis Minerva, at Aquae Sulis, Bath, England. According to Geoffrey of Monmouth (in the *History*) this temple was founded by King Bladud, a legendary flying king who was the founder of many arts and sciences in Britain. [10]

In this legend we meet the theme that solar kings help to develop civilization and harmony in the culture or land; this derives from a primal concept that the power of the king and land are, or should, be unified. Bladud is also mentioned as guardian of sacred springs and wells in the *Vita* and has many druidic attributes that suggest that he is a god, or vessel of a god, similar to Apollo. He is the expressed power of the sun ruling at midsummer, his face is stylized into a disc or wheel, with wings to denote power of flight. This image is a visual expression of central consciousness, the Knower; his attributes of wings, large ears and staring eyes are all very clear on the Romano-Celtic carving. A number of other themes are rooted into this image: that of the sacred hero, the magical head, the Wheel of the Seasons, the power of Light and Fire, and the important concept of guardianship and protection, which was later contained within the images of St Michael and St George.

This symbolic face is a mask before the true likeness of divine reality; it is a modified or mediating image that we may look upon safely. The mask is present not to mislead us, but to protect us from an intensity of light that we might not otherwise survive. Such images, masks and filters are central and essential to all magical, mystical and metaphysical traditions.

III STAR

THE STAR

WORLD The Stellar World (crossing into the Solar).
WHEEL The Third Wheel, Judgement, (crossing the Second Wheel, Justice).
BEINGS Stellar entities, Archangels. Originative Being.
CONSCIOUSNESS Universal, transhuman, transcendent.

PARTNER TRUMPS   Higher harmonic of The Sun and The Moon.

SPHERES AND PLANETS   *Spheres:* The 1st and 6th Spheres, Crown and Beauty. *Planets:* The Pleiades and the sun; the sun as a star.

ATTRIBUTES   The upper third of the *Axis Mundi*, Spindle or Middle Pillar of the Tree of Life; the ultimate pivot of universal consciousness; crossing the Abyss between the Stellar and Solar Worlds.

GOD AND GODDESS FORMS   The Holy Spirit or First Breath *with* The Son of Light; Astraea or the Weaver of Stars *with* Apollo, Lugh, Belenos, Christ.

KEY PHRASES   Harmony of spirit/innermost light/universal truth/ knowledge of being/transcendent illumination/grace.

MERLIN TEXTS   *PVM* The goddess Ariadne who weaves stars; *VM* Description of the Stellar World and its inhabitants.

DIVINATORY MEANING   A profound spiritual impulse or transcendent energy at work, usually within the inquirer, but sometimes also within a personal situation involving the inquirer. May also mean a collective or cosmic energy pattern involving many people, including the inquirer.

RELATED NUMBER CARDS   Aces and Sixes.

Aces: Life, Light, Love and Law.

Sixes: Transition, Balance, Joy, Benefit.

Origins of the Image

The Star is an image of transcendent universal light. It reveals the identity of our sun with all other stars as entities within the universe. As a symbol of relative existence, both physical and metaphysical, it is a universal state held harmoniously in common by all stars, for they are each uttered forth by an originative source of being.

The Inner Fire which we as humans reflect and share with both moon and sun reaches its highest rate as inner light: it begins (for us) as our biological or Earth energies in the physical body, it expands and illuminates our consciousness with the gentle watery light of the Lunar World, and rapidly rises to the fiery incandescence of the Solar World. In its highest aspect or rate, it becomes the pure 'light' of the starry universe; a constant power. The Star represents both radiation from individual suns/stars and the origin of all light or energy out of darkness or 'nothing'.

This Trump forms the distaff or uppermost part of the Middle Pillar or Axis of Worlds. Here the original utterance or seed of being defines and bridges an immeasurable Abyss of time and space by setting stars and stellar systems into motion. The image reveals both creative and destructive power (the stars) and the essence or pure, balanced, primal energy behind such power.

The simple planetary astrological attributes of the sun and a star (or in modern astrology, Uranus) are fused within this image. In geocentric astrology for the northern hemisphere the Pole Star is sometimes used as a relative location. Alternatively, the Pleiades are employed, as they are visible in both hemispheres, and act as stellar archetypes for the planets of the solar system.

All concepts of light beyond embodiment, energy in potential universal being and ultimate truth or divinity are seeded upon this path. It is the direct route across the Abyss separating universal and individual consciousness, defined physically by the vast reaches of time and space that seem to separate individual stars.

Contents of the Image

The Solar System and Abyss/The Supernal or Universal World/The Goddess Astraea/The Two Vessels and Stars

The Solar System and Abyss
If we follow the straight path along the axis of the Spindle or Middle Pillar (see Figures 1–3) it leads through a moonlit landscape as The Moon into the Hill or Tor under full sunlight in The Sun. Within the Cave of death and resurrection are found stars.

The link between the physical sun and other stars, as inhabitants of the Stellar World, may be understood through initiation into the Mysteries. In the simplest sense the stars within the Cave represent a spiritual truth known through contemplation or vision, and discovered briefly by us all at the moment of physical death.

Most of us may not pass across the Abyss between solar and universal consciousness; our cycle of lives rotates between the upper extreme of The Sun and the lower extreme of The Moon. This cycle results in birth and death between the worlds. We have the ability, however, to comprehend supernal or stellar consciousness by using symbols as interfaces, lenses, mirrors: many of the higher Trumps serve precisely this purpose. Such interfaces enable our consciousness to relate to concepts or energies which are usually beyond our conditioned states of operation in terms of thought, emotion or imagination.

Poetically, we might say that at the heart of the sun is the seed of a star: scientifically, this has been defined as the nucleus; metaphysically, it is the reality of a common status of *being* which connects all superficially separated forces and forms. All entities *are*, regardless of observed or relative states or conditions. This statement is being re-presented by modern physics, attempting to define scientifically that which has been taught for many centuries in mystical tradition.

For human consciousness the path of The Star is realized through cosmic or universal vision, by formless contemplation or moments of inspired enlightenment. The lower part of our image (lower left-hand area of the card) shows the expressed Solar System 'below' the Abyss; such is the cosmic reality of the Solar World. In the Merlin texts the powers of universal creation and destruction, either in a primal land or in the Solar System, are vested in feminine archetypes. Thus, a female figure steps across the Abyss to join Solar and Stellar Worlds.

The Abyss is that which separates; it is depth of time and space, relative distance between modes of consciousness, and the cloud or veil before our innermost energies, hidden through our temporary or temporal limitations. It is also the Veil before the face of the Goddess shown in our Trump of Judgement.

The Abyss is literally the power of *separation*; it is balanced by a power of *cohesion* within the universe. No one 'falls' into the Abyss unless they choose wilfully to do so. Within world traditions of religion, magic and mysticism, paths across the Abyss are clearly marked and described. Tarot reveals three such paths: The Star, The Hanged Man and Temperance.

The Star is a direct path along the Axis of Worlds, linking originative divinity or being with creative entities (stars generating planets and life forms). The remaining two tarot paths across the Abyss operate in a different manner, which we will discuss when we come to each relevant Trump, but all three symbolize divine potential within the human being, all three raise this potential into a higher mode and link symbolically to the great saviours or Sons of Light. Such figures are found in world religion, and represent an enduring truth rather than mere dogma. We might also say that the three paths of Star, Hanged Man and Temperance are three relative aspects of one being. This theme of polarity in unity is repeated throughout tarot.

The Supernal or Universal World

In our image the Stellar World is shown in the upper part, 'above' the Abyss. Here we see stars being uttered or born in their own realm. Traditionally the Pleiades are shown in some tarot cards, symbolizing an idealized septenary as a stellar archetype for the seven planets of the solar system in basic astrology. Curiously, there are only six Pleiades visible, and many theories have been put forward as to the missing seventh star; possibly the paradox may relate to legends of a fallen star that generated our outer world.

The cycle of the year was marked by the rising and setting of the Pleiades, and they featured in esoteric tuition and initiation. They define the cycle of the Great Year, an actual astronomical period that was originally grasped through contemplation or transcendent vision. More simply, we might say that whatever happens in the universe is reflected in a lesser form in the solar worlds – all stars are also suns or solar systems.

The Goddess Astraea

The Goddess, sometimes called Astraea (which simply means 'star'), crosses the Abyss. She gives energy to all worlds and dimensions; we see her as a transhuman form, at once beautiful and terrible. In tarot her power is modified and harmonized into a vision of a beautiful maiden; thus we see her image through the filter or interface of the Solar and Lunar Worlds.

The Two Vessels and Stars

In her right hand the Goddess holds a Vessel which pours energy downwards across the Abyss; this Vessel represents the source of creation, which develops as formation and expression, generating the solar system, the planets and life forms of all sorts until it reaches the sub-Lunar world of Earth, our consensual world and planet.

In her left hand is an upright Vessel from which originative energies radiate; this is the source of power that utters forth Light and Stars universally, the highest state or condition of existence. The Two Vessels are connected by a sweeping line, symbolizing the serpentine nature of universal energy. The originative and creative Vessels and Worlds are united by Astraea; if we could enter within her image we would find the seed or heart of all being, where original divinity emerges from incomprehensible void. Traditionally, this unattainable point or seed is geometrically at the centre of the image: if we locate this point we see that all other proportions of the Trump rotate around it.

IV FORTUNE

THE WHEEL OF FORTUNE

WORLD The Lunar World into the Solar. (Threshold between Lunar and Solar Worlds.)
WHEEL The First Wheel or threshold of consciousness.
BEINGS Angels, innerworld communicators, humans, ex-humans, lunar spirits or *daemones*. Also encompasses Elementals and other worlds such as faery realms.

CONSCIOUSNESS Individual and collective thoughts and emotions; may be limited to one *persona* or include the fortunes of a family, group, race or nation. The interaction, in consciousness, between human beings and all other life forms on the planet.

PARTNER TRUMPS Justice and Judgement (as higher harmonics).

SPHERES AND PLANETS *Spheres:* The 7th and 8th Spheres, Victory and Glory. *Planets:* Mercury and Venus.

ATTRIBUTES Fusion of thoughts and emotions: threshold of limiting consciousness between outer and inner energies of life. The wheel of a life cycle, the seasons within humankind. Also the cycle of the Four Elements within the outer, or sub-Lunar, and Lunar World. Consciousness behind or within physical expression as form and interaction.

GOD AND GODDESS FORMS Fortuna (feminine image), Mercury and Venus. Minerva/Briggidda and the Flower Maiden in Celtic tradition. Relates to deities that cause changes in situations through their effect upon humankind (i.e. Mercury/Minerva as patrons of cultural development, Venus as goddess of love).

KEY PHRASES Honour and victory/energy polarized as thoughts and feelings/change of fortune.

MERLIN TEXTS *VM* Merlin's journey around the Wheel of the Seasons.

DIVINATORY MEANING A change of fortune (may be positive or negative). Often indicates, in association with other cards, how the individual's reaction will affect a cycle of events.

RELATED NUMBER CARDS Sevens and Eights.

  Sevens: Dishonesty, Ability, Humour, Attention.

  Eights: Danger, Expediency, Excitement, Skill.

Origins of the Image

The Wheel of Fortune defines the boundary of relative energy/consciousness around the Earth. In this inclusive sense it contains all life upon our planet, the planet itself, and the sphere of energies that extends into and interacts with the field of the solar system in which the planet orbits. All wheels in esoteric symbolism are variants or harmonics of the Wheel or Sphere of the Universe (see Figure 1) and are flat maps of spherical or spiral conceptual models (see Figure 3). Thus, The Wheel of Fortune is one spiral or level of the Wheel, a pattern of relativity that is used to define all existence. This harmonic or holistic character enables such symbols to define not only relative cosmic patterns (such as the lunar, solar and stellar spheres or Worlds) but reflections of such patterns within human consciousness. The Wheel of Fortune has particular relevance to individual life rhythms.

In modern interpretations we find the Four Elements and Four Seasons, which are the basis of The Wheel of Fortune, increasingly separated from one another. Popularly, the Wheel is associated with 'fate', a concept inherited from medieval and Renaissance motifs of fortune combined with misrepresentations of Eastern theories of karma or interaction. By such means, the Wheel becomes a concept that limits, or even imprisons, the individual, and its intense development as a suppressive concept was a major aspect of late medieval popular belief, tied closely to orthodox religion.

In the Merlin Tarot a simpler and less restrictive interpretation is given, drawn directly from the *Vita Merlini*, which in turn drew upon enduring traditions. The Elements, Seasons, weather, environment, and personal and collective changes of fortune are woven together within the sphere of The Wheel of Fortune. This world view derives from a primal conceptual model that underpins all mystical and magical techniques. The interweaving of these energies seems at first to be complex and unavoidable, but, like the thread of Ariadne, forms a pattern that may be unravelled.

The theme of a thread or weaving is inherent in the Merlin Tarot, and a higher form is found in the vision of Judgement taken from the Apocalypse in the *Prophecies*; furthermore, the entire Tree of Life (Figure 2) is a variant of the symbol of the Spindle or Distaff, carried by the Goddess.

In the Merlin texts she is called Ariadne, referring to the Greek myth of Ariadne and the Minotaur, in which a thread, given by Ariadne, leads a hero through a labyrinth towards its centre. But a number of goddesses take the form of Weavers, and we should read Geoffrey of Monmouth's 'Ariadne' as a descriptive term rather than a proper name that pin-points a specific legend. In Welsh legend, a woman called Arianrhod ('Silver Wheel') exhibits many of the powers or attributes of a goddess, and wheel deities play a major role in Celtic mythology.

The overall concept is that of the circling sun, planets and stars. Various gods and goddesses represent such cycles in different forms; it may be the solar turning of the year or universal turning of stars, within the pattern of the Weaver. This concept was well developed in both classical and Celtic mythology.

Contents of the Image

The Spindle/The Dragons/The Fourfold Cycle/The Four Seasons/The Four Creatures/The Centre/Minor Symbols

The Spindle
Tarot tends to work in a triple spiral, with a fourfold relative division or cycle of energies within each rotation (see Figure 3). The Wheel of Fortune

is the lowermost turning of a triple spiral defined by the images of the Wheel of Fortune, Justice and Judgement. These three Trumps are harmonics or levels of one universal concept: the threshold of polarity or relative states of being.

The Spindle, axis or Middle Pillar, is a triple sequence of cosmology/psychology found at the centre of the triple spiral. We may visualize the totality as an abstract sphere with three relative regions, though for practical work the image is usually represented as three spheres, wheels, or conceptual worlds.

In the Merlin Tarot and related cosmologies the Spindle is founded in the centre of the Earth and extends into the galaxy through the region of the Pole Star; it may also be directed, as a conceptual model, towards the Pleiades, which are visible from both hemispheres of our planet. This principle of direction and relativity is of far greater importance than seeking a precise correlation or 'factual' location. In truth, such 'locations' will vary from person to person, culture to culture, and over periods of solar or celestial time. The metaphysical centre, however, endures.

From the point or turning of the Spindle in Earth, its axis reaches through moon, sun, planets and stars; these are the Three Worlds shown by the Trumps Moon, Sun and Star. In human life the extreme poles of Above and Below act as an axis upon which all turnings, or cycles of change, revolve. This is reflected in miniature by our physical stance upon the relative surface of our environment, shown in Figure 5.

All cycles, such as Seasons, weather, birth, death and relative conditions of fortune, are aspects of one another: they are all linked by the centrality of our planet rotating around the sun. This central link is an undeniable fact of observed nature, not a matter of speculation or obscure philosophy. If we limit this concept to mere physical rotations, however, we miss opportunities inherent within our consciousness for transforming such cycles and rebalancing them. Such is the allegory found within the *Vita Merlini*, wherein Merlin travels around many cycles or turnings of the Wheel, from Seasons to stars, and is transformed by absorbing each relative stage within his understanding.

The Dragons

The Spindle is grasped by two Dragons at either extreme. These Dragons represent the ultimate polarities of creation and destruction: positive and negative, outgoing and ingoing. They appear in various forms and roles throughout the Merlin Tarot. At the level of The Wheel of Fortune, they symbolize energies which we simply cannot understand in our customary conditioned modes of awareness; the truth of the Dragons is discovered only through transpersonal meditation, vision, or more rarely, through direct revelation. Thus, the Dragons are 'outside' The Wheel of Fortune, and the greater part of their bodies is unseen. In a crude sense, they represent every power that we fear from our subjective state of ignorance; to an initiate or person who has changed the direction of their awareness, however, the Dragons represent every potential of liberation.

The entire sequence of Merlin's *Prophecies*, which reach far into the future of Britain in one section and relate the end of the solar system in another, is generated by the appearance of two dragons within a cave. [1, 3] There are several levels upon which this legend may be interpreted, but in our present context it means that the Dragons – interacting energies – generate all events until the dissolution of creation.

The Fourfold Cycle

In the Trump four small circles unite together within a fifth greater circle. This is the structure of the universe, as described by Taliesin the bard to

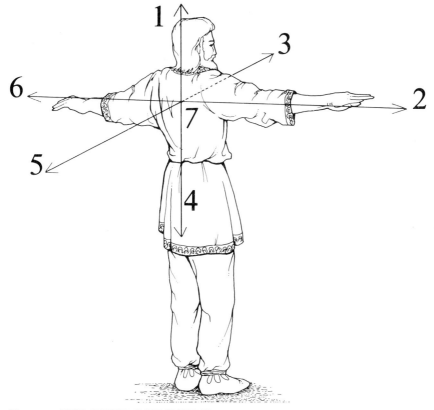

Figure 5: THE SEVEN DIRECTIONS

1. Above.
2. East (Before).
3. South (Right).
4. Below.
5. West (Behind).
6. North (Left).
7. Within.

the prophet Merlin. Within The Wheel of Fortune this pattern represents the planet Earth with its Four Seasons, four regions of East, South, West and North, four oceans, four winds, and central zone leading into other dimensions or worlds.

This last concept reflects yet again the four united by a fifth, or conversely the four generated by one. Each of the Four Quarters is unified by this mysterious central principle, which may encompass, reduce or originate. The mathematical sequences of the Tree of Life are based upon concepts of this sort, and though they may be interpreted in varying ways by different schools of thought, the underlying principles remain constant. The patterns of relativity are fundamental to magical art, metaphysics and the practical operation of a holistic world view.

The overall pattern is shown in the basic mystical circle or sphere (Figure 6), which defines an original cycle of energies as LIFE/LIGHT/LOVE/LAW.

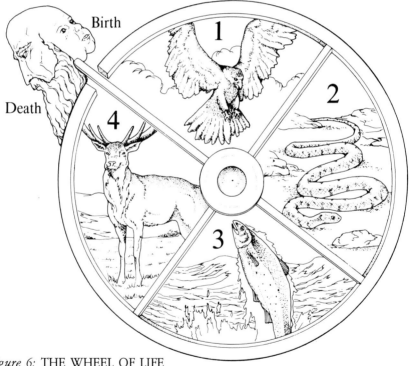

Figure 6: THE WHEEL OF LIFE

1. East/Life/Air/Dawn/Spring/Birth/Sword/Birds.
2. South/Light/Fire/Noon/Summer/Adulthood/Rod/Serpents.
3. West/Love/Water/Sunset/Autumn/Maturity/Cup/Fishes.
4. North/Law/Earth/Night/Winter/Age/Shield/Beasts.

These four create and reflect the Four Elements of AIR/FIRE/WATER/ EARTH.

Such relative modes of energy form and express themselves through all existence, all consciousness. We are nothing more and nothing less than reflections of a divine fourfold pattern. But esoteric or spiritual traditions suggest one interesting difference between humans and other expressions of universal being: we have an individual, spiritual heart or centre within each of us, around which the Elements rotate. In other orders of being, the centrality may be the planet, the sun or other great entities. In humans the spiritual centre resonates independently of such entities, though in most of us it is unrealized. Such an unrealized or unawakened centre tends to attune to organic or stellar centres, such as the land, the planet or the sun, but may become cut off from these entities through suppressive conditioning factors. This is the state of human existence at present, in which certain developing aspects of consciousness have dominated to such an extent that they have become suppressive and imprisoning.

Put more simply, our emphasis upon material science and the related concepts of materialist 'values' has led to a situation where our material knowledge far outreaches our inherent wisdom and understanding. This is reflected in personal and collective imbalance, and, further, in a planetary imbalance of both social welfare and subtle or Elemental energies.

There are, therefore, two possible routes to follow. The first is to re-attune our central energies or spiritual heart to the collective entities of environment, land, planet and solar system; the second is to de-condition our consciousness and redirect it to arouse our innermost seed of power. This second route is the human version of the two Dragons: land power and spiritual or star power. Ultimately, both should be united perfectly. In modern revivalist paganism, reflected politically by environmental issues, unity with nature is emphasized; but we need to realize that, in addition to the crucial need to reestablish such unity, magical and spiritual disciplines also teach the means to pass *beyond* the Wheel.

In terms of The Wheel of Fortune, it is the rotation of relationships or energies that gives the illusion of good or bad fortune. Like Merlin in his adventures, we may eventually understand that such conditions are relative, and are not so much understood as transformed. This is the essential difference between the tradition embodied in the West by Merlin and other mystical traditions. We seek to *transform* the world rather than *escape* from it. The only liberation is through transformation of consciousness; there is no spiritual élitism in which an elect are saved and the remainder damned.

When Merlin finally withdraws into spiritual contemplation, towards the close of his long life (in the *Vita*), he has related inwardly to the entire cosmos, and hands on his wisdom and powers to others. In another major variant of his legend, Merlin is absorbed into the land itself, where he remains until a time of desperate need or, on a deeper level, where he may be contacted by anyone seeking to learn from him.

The Four Seasons
The image is aligned as follows:

1. *Upper Circle:* Spring/Element of Air/Dawn/Birth.
2. *Right Circle:* Summer/Element of Fire/Noon/Adulthood.
3. *Lower Circle:* Autumn/Element of Water/Evening/Maturity.
4. *Left Circle:* Winter/Element of Earth/Night/Old Age.

Thus, the life of a human, the life of the year and the cycle of the Elements are related. When we are out of tune with the cycle of nature (either within ourselves in terms of health or in the deeper sense of the year and the land) we are ill, we have 'bad luck'. Vast imbalances of this relative situation result in wars, famines and incurable epidemics, and the individual is absorbed into a collective situation. The allegory of Merlin suggests that as he attunes to nature, so he passes beyond nature and begins to relate to higher spirals of the triple Wheel. This is no trite, dogmatic or easy process; he is first driven mad by grief and suffering. The teaching is that suffering must be experienced and transformed, rather than avoided.

Any relative event, good or bad fortune, experiences a fourfold cycle, with a life pattern of its own that corresponds to the Four Elements or Seasons: it begins, increases, matures and ceases. This is not as superficial as it might seem, for it gives us an initial overview and conceptual theme, leading in time to a deeper level of understanding. If we cannot see such relationships and cycles of energy at work, we crudely and selfishly assume that our *fortune* is bad.

There is a further, more dangerous, aspect of such limited vision, for we can also assume that if there is no relative pattern, we may be 'self-made' or generate good fortune through whatever means come to hand. This is one of the major illnesses of our culture, in which no ethical or spiritual concept balances our appalling and destructive greed. Collective negative conditions such as war or disease are frequently the painful exteriorizing of energies seeking to rebalance. This relates to the teaching described above in which our spiritual centres may be attuned to collective entities such as the land, planet or solar system, or may be individually awakened. The corollary is one of consciousness, in which we are either developing an increased awareness of our existence or are submerged in collective delusions.

The Four Creatures
Each of the Four Seasons or phases of life has a spiritual animal; this is a greatly simplified version of a symbolic alphabet of creatures. It seems

very likely that such naturalistic correspondences were an integral part of druidic philosophy. We have details of another natural alphabet in the correspondence between trees and letters (preserved in Irish tradition and in some forms of Ogham script) though this sophisticated system does not appear in the Merlin texts. [9]

In the *Vita*, Merlin relates to certain animals at particular times of the year, and gains an expanded vision of worlds, including descriptions of orders of creatures on air, land and sea. Spiritual creatures are found in primal traditions of magic and religion world-wide, and have a more subtle and complex function than might at first be assumed. So enduring is the concept of spiritual animals that it was preserved and transferred to Christian saints to help their credibility as replacements for pagan images.

Merlin is described as having an aged wolf for his companion in the depths of Winter; thus, we show a Wolf as spiritual animal for the cold season, the time of conclusions and endings, the unavoidable power of taking and death inherent in every year, every life. We should meditate upon the wolf as Merlin's companion; the wolf is the prophet's *friend*. This companionship is the key to a correct, balanced relationship with the catabolic or taking powers – they exist for our benefit and not merely to spite our whims and selfish desires. The totem of the Wolf appears also in the Trump of The Moon, where it has a similar meaning.

Merlin is described as riding a stag in Spring, when he seeks out his Flower Maiden wife, Guendoloena. Thus we have the Stag as spiritual animal of all beginnings, arising, openings, Spring-like energies.

The horse or mare is associated with the Great Goddess and her divine solar Child of Light, also known as Mabon, similar in many ways to the youthful Merlin. Thus we have a White Horse embodying the full surging power of midsummer.

The salmon is traditionally the carrier of wisdom and understanding; thus a Salmon leaps from the deep waters of the West in Autumn.

Each of these creatures may be meditated upon individually as a natural symbol, and a useful exercise is to draw up a list of connectives between the beast and its qualities, the Seasons, the Elements, and the legends or god-forms related to the animal. Such lists rapidly become very large, and the secret of using them is not merely to learn them by heart, but to be able to reduce them down to their essential concepts in meditation.

We encounter spiritual creatures repeatedly in the Merlin Tarot, both in major and minor images. The minor images, which are the Court and Number cards, derive from Elemental interaction, and are discussed in later chapters. There is also a connection between minor images and the Wheels, as all are formed from the concept of a harmonic or relative cycle.

The key to understanding spiritual creatures is that *they change and move around the Wheel*. They are not rigid correspondences devised to give a false sense of meaning or security to superstitious or ignorant minds.

The changes of animal, from one type to another, or their movement around the idealized map of the Wheel, depend upon our individual states of consciousness. Basic definitions offered in systems such as tarot are points of commencement; this is why spiritual creatures are traditionally allotted during initiation. They may act as anchoring symbols in visualization or inner journeys, for they enable us to commence and return to certain states or locations; traditionally, they act as guides upon the path, helpers, and indicators of power in operation.

Although the Four Creatures are placed squarely in each Quarter of the Wheel of Fortune, to emphasize Elements and Seasons fused with phases of the psyche or life cycle, a more subtle allocation might be as follows:
Stag: on the threshold between Winter and Spring (North East).
Horse: on the threshold between Spring and Summer (South East).
Salmon: on the threshold between Summer and Autumn (South West).
Wolf: on the threshold between Autumn and Winter (North West).
In the *Vita Merlini*, a system of psychological types, *personae* and god-forms is similarly allocated to the Quarters of the Wheel, and this concept appears in both the Trumps and the Court cards of the Merlin Tarot.

When spiritual animals are employed for the Number cards, a simpler elemental system is followed:
AIR = BIRDS.
FIRE = SERPENTS.
WATER = FISHES.
EARTH = BEASTS.

These concepts are developed in our chapters that deal in depth with the Court and Number cards.

Spiritual animals or creatures are not confined to a naturalistic cycle; they may be visualized through all Three Worlds, from expressed life forms to originative metaphysical images that embody universal power. The key to gradual changes of such creatures around the Wheel is that as they move, so they spiral upwards or downwards into higher or lower modes. Many of the creatures, such as dragons, serpents and salamanders, are supernatural in their form and function; others appear to be naturalistic but have many transcendent symbolic functions.

The Centre

Towards the centre of the image, the Wheel becomes less distinct; in centrality is dissolution and the stilling of cycles, opposites and relatives. Towards the core, the heart, the Spindle, are increasing reality and truth. If we reach that still centre within ourselves, we are gradually freed from interactions of the Wheel; ultimately, this liberation will extend to higher forms of the Wheel, shown by the Trumps of Justice and Judgement.

The centre of the First Wheel (Fortune) is in the Lunar World, the Sphere of Foundation upon the Tree of Life. To suspend and transcend the cycles of this Wheel we must first seek the roots of our physical, mental, emotional and sexual energies (see Figure 3). When these energies are redirected, however briefly or effectively, we move along the central Path of The Moon into the central Path of The Sun. The alternative is to remain circling around The Wheel of Fortune, with its rises and falls in terms of individual expression.

The centre of the Second Wheel (Justice) is in the Solar World, the Sphere of Beauty upon the Tree of Life. By moving towards the centre, the mental, emotional and spiritual energies are fused and directed along the Paths of Sun and Star. Most of us would regard this fusion and expansion of central consciousness as our highest transcendent goal.

The centre of the Third Wheel (Judgement) is originative universal being. It underpins and transcends all time, space and energy. The supernal Spheres of Wisdom and Understanding are the boundaries of this Wheel, while its centre is the Crown of the Tree of Life. Moving towards this ultimate centrality, consciousness ascends the Path of The Star and passes into the unknown.

Minor Symbols
At the circumference of the Wheel is a band of stylized stars. These represent the Zodiac, in which apparent patterns of stars relate to life patterns upon Earth. Two further symbols are found in the great circle: the 'Z' sign and small Spindle. Like many lesser symbols in tarot and other visual systems of inner transformation and education, these lesser symbols are incidental presentations of major concepts. They represent two modes and methods of transformation in magical and mystical arts: both methods are founded upon the concept of energies emerging from and returning to a still central non-location.

The first symbol, the 'Z' sign, is the lightning flash of spiritual fire. In the Mysteries it is not only a symbol of divine power in terms of creation, but of a secret path relating to spiritual sacrifice and redemption. We shall return to this important concept within Western esoteric traditions when we consider higher Trumps, particularly The Hanged Man, to whom this serpentine symbol relates. The 'Z' path cuts across all rotations and cycles, bringing transformation and energy from beyond any possible guidance, prediction or systematic definition. This is the terrifying power of pure spirit, vested traditionally in the Sons of Light or saviours.

The second symbol is a spiralling or rotating path shown by the Spindle or its higher universal form, the Distaff. This represents the spinning and weaving of creation, and cyclical patterns of creation and destruction that are understood by rising through the levels of the Three Wheels. Traditionally, the spindle is the path of the Goddess, while the lightning is the path of the God, but we should always realize that they are aspects of one another.

V JUSTICE

JUSTICE

WORLD The Solar World. Reaches into the Stellar World. Threshold between Solar and Stellar consciousness.

WHEEL The Second Wheel; encompasses and incorporates the First Wheel, Fortune.

BEINGS Archangels, angels; advanced innerworld communicators, saints or masters.

CONSCIOUSNESS   Transpersonal, transhuman.

PARTNER TRUMPS   The Wheel of Fortune and Judgement (as spirals or harmonics).

SPHERES AND PLANETS   *Spheres:* The 4th and 5th, Mercy and Severity. *Planets:* Mars and Jupiter.

ATTRIBUTES   Catabolic and anabolic energies within the solar system. Creation and destruction and properties of spiritual consciousness. The Goddess of Taking (Severity) and the God of Giving (Mercy). A perfect comprehension of the energies of adjustment.

GOD AND GODDESS FORMS   Mars and Jupiter. The Morrigan (Severity) and the Daghda (Mercy or Goodness). All negative and positive polar partners and images.

KEY PHRASES   Adjustment/balance.

MERLIN TEXTS   *PVM* The Goddess of the Land, balancing a forest in one hand and a city in the other; *VM* The king and queen hold a trial and judge Merlin.

DIVINATORY MEANING   Transpersonal energies of adjustment. Related to changes and interactions upon a spiritual level (just as The Wheel of Fortune relates to such changes upon a personal and collective level). May also relate to energies adjusting over long time cycles, similar to the Eastern concept of karma.

Justice always indicates essential adjustments that lead towards balance. It may be as direct as a court case or important decision, or it may be more profound in terms of deep adjustments in the individual.

RELATED NUMBER CARDS   Fours and Fives.

Fours: Truce, Generosity, Promise, Increase.

Fives: Loss, Retribution, Sorrow, Conflict.

Origins of the Image

Justice defines the boundary or relative region of energies of the Solar World. This includes our physical solar system, the Lunar and sub-Lunar world of our planet, and metaphysical attributes shown upon the Tree of Life and related symbolic maps (see Figures 1–3). Once consciousness has attuned to the Solar World, Justice represents extremes of energy, the two poles of Mercy and Severity.

The Solar World is traditionally the realm of immaterial but powerful entities such as angels and archangels, sacred kings, saints, enlightened ones, and innerworld masters and teachers. Such beings are frequently associated with balancing and adjusting forces; innerworlds are created from imagination and structured archetypes which are held together by a balance of power.

Whereas The Wheel of Fortune rotates according to Seasons (which might range from planetary to individual life phases), The Wheel of Adjustment or Justice rotates upon a higher octave; a working analogy might be that it moves at a far greater speed. The Third Wheel (Judgement) moves in a higher octave or spiral again, and may be said to be 'timeless'. Laws of this sort are redefined in modern physics through formulae describing the speed of light and its relationship to time and space.

The energies of Justice are a fusion of the Spheres of Mercy and Severity; building and breaking, anabolism and catabolism. These extreme poles of energy are centred upon the sun in terms of our physical/energetic solar system. The sun is traditionally said to be the manifestation or physical body of a spiritual entity, symbolized by the concepts of Beauty, Harmony, Centrality.

Without extreme limits of positive and negative energy – giving and taking – there could be no Solar World. It is the interplay between these extremes that enables entities to be defined or delimited. Once again, we find that it is a matter of concept relative to time: the solar entity emits both positive and negative energies through all dimensions attuned to its life cycle; simultaneously, the extremes of energy define and enable all patterns within their field, including the cycle of the Solar World itself. The entire view is not defined by discussion or calculation, for we may repeatedly find fresh philosophical positions or new mathematical models that are effective. True definition comes through changes of consciousness, for time, space and energy are relative matters moulded according to our degree of perception. All models are merely analogies or working models, not representations of final truth or ultimate reality.

An *entity* may be the sun, a planet, a region upon a planet, an angel, a blade of grass, a stone, an animal, a human, a nuclear structure such as the atom . . . any such entity is a relative state of energy in a cyclical form; the apparent balance that holds the form together is a direct effect of Justice or Adjustment. This Wheel encompasses the slower, form-generating Wheel of Fortune, and both lesser Wheels are encompassed and permeated by the Trump Judgement (see Figure 1). Thus Fortune encompasses and generates form, and Justice encompasses and creates force, while Judgement encompasses and originates all relative states simultaneously.

In their own archetypical realm, accessible to human consciousness through meditation and visualization, structured through symbolic alphabets such as tarot, the powers of Justice are transcendent; in our world they operate through rotation, the sequence of spirals broadly defined by The Wheel of Fortune. In magical and mystical arts it is possible for the transcendent power of Justice to transform human consciousness, and this transformation may be extended to the world of nature.

One of the most effective realizations of adjustment (Justice) is in magical or spiritual therapy and transformation, though such arts must not be confused with so called 'spiritual healing' or other activities in which vital energies are transferred in various ways. Through the operation of Justice changes arise within an individual or group; such changes are not bound by the mental/emotional/generative cycle defined by The Wheel of Fortune. Most genuine systems of initiation draw to some extent upon energies defined by the Trump Justice.

Contents of the Image

The Three Steps/The Two Trees/The Scales/The Owl/The Goddess of Justice bearing Sword and Cup/The Veil and Dragons

The Three Steps
The Steps in Justice are a higher form of those first encountered in the Trump of The Moon. The lowermost step bears the symbol of the Goddess; it may be read as a stylized distaff linking worlds together (the straight line uniting and bridging two curves) or as two dragons of positive and negative energy with a straight line of balance between them. This motif is repeated in the greater symbol of the Tree of Life. This simple but far-reaching symbol is cut into the lowermost Step; consciousness seeking to ascend these Steps must begin to comprehend relative patterns that run through all conceptual worlds – it is such patterns, in effect, that enable us to climb, change, transform. Energy may not operate without limitation. Just as the Steps of the Lunar World marked the triple climb into inner or imaginative consciousness, so the Steps of the Solar World (Justice) mark a triple climb into transpersonal consciousness.

The Two Trees
The lowermost Step is pierced by the roots of Two Trees that act as pillars on either side of the image; they are a naturalistic form of the pillars of creation and destruction, between which all entity resonates. Beyond the third Step, between the Trees, is a gateway to unknown supernal consciousness, the Stellar World beyond the Abyss. In cosmology this is the last step before leaving the solar system and reaching for the stars; any inherent imbalance at this stage will lead us back through the limiting Wheels of the Solar and Lunar Worlds.

It is at the third Step that souls are said to return to rebirth. This is the highest level of energy/consciousness that humans may attain; very few cross the Abyss into the unknown. Many souls, however, do not pass beyond the Lunar World, or the limits of The Wheel of Fortune, which touches upon the Solar World and acts as a threshold.

The Wheel of Justice is the highest boundary or delimiting pattern of energy known within human consciousness; beyond this pattern we leave transpersonal awareness and approach the transhuman. Much of the tuition of the ancient Mysteries was concerned with awareness after physical death. The Two Trees also represent extremes of choice – remembering and forgetting. Those who forget are reborn into the outer world; those who retain full awareness may remain in the inner dimensions, as transpersonal beings (adepts, saints, masters, wise-women, oracular heroes and similar forms or names for transpersonal consciousness or beings). Traditionally, magical arts and spiritual instruction are said to come from such beings in the Solar World, who have transcended physical death and relative personality, but retained individuality. A corresponding mode of consciousness is attainable in meditation, and through this mode and controlled visualization, contact can be made with transpersonal beings.

In the *Vita Merlini*, this concept is linked to orders of angels who convey messages or consciousness of divinity between the worlds or dimensions (a theme that reiterates the triple spiral found in tarot), and is broadly defined as follows:

Archangels: originative consciousness; The Star/Judgement.

Angels: creative consciousness; The Sun/Justice.

Spirits (*daemones*): formative consciousness; The Moon/Fortune.

All three orders may mediate to the sub-Lunar or Earth world, but generally through spiralling or threefold levels. The concept is not one of rigid hierarchy but of harmonic or organic metaphysics and cosmology/psychology.

The Scales

The symbol of the scales or balance, found in the astrological Sign of Libra, has been employed for centuries, possibly millennia, to represent a metaphysical condition of perfect equality. From ancient Egypt to orthodox Christian Europe, the scales were said to measure the weight of a soul after physical death. The balance should not be misinterpreted as a concept of purity set against impurity, or sin against holiness; this attitude is merely propaganda or ignorance. At its best, the orthodox interpretation of the scales or balance rests within a rationalization and

Figure 7: (opposite) THE DRAGONS, WORLDS AND IMAGES

I.   Lunar World (First Wheel).
II. Solar World (Second Wheel).
III. Stellar World (Third Wheel).

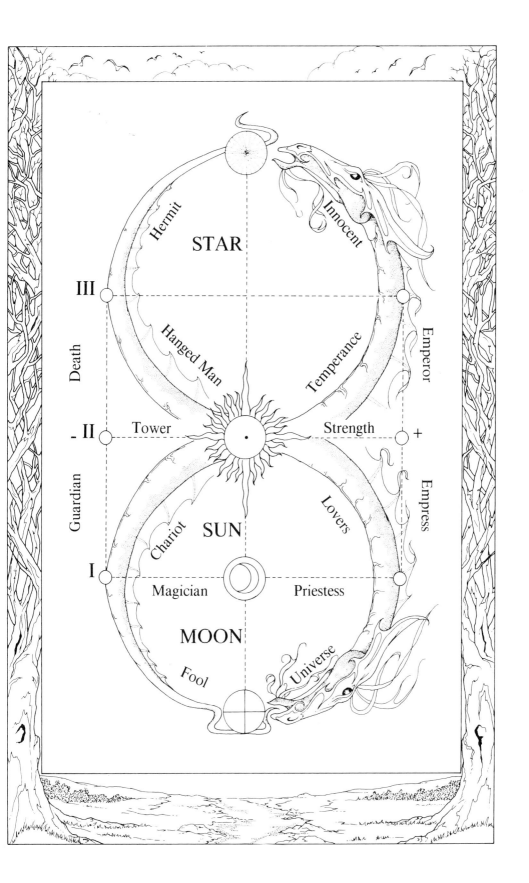

reduction of a universal law: positive and negative energies balance one another in a cycle of interaction – perfect balance comes only through central stillness.

Before taking the third step into the unknown we should be balanced in every way possible, otherwise we are destroyed by the power of supernal reality beyond the protective Veil. It is for this reason that so many guardian images are contained within the Trump Justice: first the Three Steps, defined to right and left by the Two Trees, then the weighing and balancing of the Scales.

Up to this level in the overall image, the symbols are of objects (Steps and Scales) framed by the lower part of the Trees, which stretch the full extent of the Trump. They reveal choices and energies that may be employed by each of us according to his or her ability – the Steps and Scales are both neutral, impassive symbols, though the Steps are linked to the Tree roots and the Scales provide a perch for the Owl. Beyond the Scales, the images take a living form, and represent powers beyond personality, and therefore beyond individual use: we may only relate to such powers by setting our personality aside, for they work upon us rather than we upon them. This should not be confused with a suppressive notion of meekness or abnegation, for it is a matter of understanding and will rather than submission or slavery. We may will to climb the Steps, and work to become inwardly balanced through meditation, but we offer ourselves unconditionally to the principle of perfect Justice.

The Scales or Balance have a further symbolic connection through their bow shape: the tripod upon which the Balance rests symbolizes the three Rays or Pillars of the Tree of Life fusing together at the point of perfection. If we see the image as a bow, it is our perfectly balanced intent that fires our spirit into the unknown; this is another way of defining the unconditional offering to universal Justice.

The Owl

The Owl is the bird of Athena or Minerva, or of more ancient goddesses of wisdom. It is also the spiritual animal of a dark and often frightening Goddess of the Underworld, who is the secret face of Athena. The Owl flies by night, and sees all; nothing may be hidden from it, and in this sense it is the totem bird of Justice.

In a lesser form, the Owl may appear in visualization upon The Moon, where it represents limited flight of consciousness; by the Trump Justice, however, the Owl has ascended to its rightful perch, acting for the Goddess of Justice. If we have any shadowy or superficially hidden imbalances, the Owl will reveal these to us before we meet the Goddess. The spiritual creature, as always, is there for our benefit and protection or guidance, not as a hostile or frightening image.

If we practise self-deception, the Owl is that area of conscience which sees all and declares the truth, even in the darkest night of delusion. It is also an oracular bird, seeing into the future and predicting or indicating any adjustment of the Scales that affects the outer world. The presence of an Underworld creature in a higher Trump is no confusion or accident; at the gate of The Moon we were able to rise along the Path toward The Sun or dive into the Pool. The journey downwards is a reflection of the journey upwards; an important magical and spiritual tradition involves this downward-seeking initiation. It must not be confused with concepts of devolution or corruption, for it involves a steadfast ethical and spiritual intent. The legend of the descent into the Underworld to benefit humankind with the wonders found therein, or the religious motif of a saviour descending into Hell and liberating the souls of the ancestral dead, are two extremes of this mystical tradition. [6]

The Owl symbolizes a state of consciousness upon the threshold of the Abyss; the unknown may be reached through the Overworld or the Underworld. Tarot in general uses an Overworld pattern, epitomized by the Tree of Life in its simple form; but the reflected Underworld pattern is indicated by the lesser symbols within the Trumps, and by certain enduring themes that run through the entire sequence of any tarot pack. As this is an extremely ancient tradition, it tends to be half-hidden, acting as an invisible but indispensable foundation for later systems and cosmic patterns.

The Goddess of Justice bearing Sword and Cup

Justice is blind; she adjusts by pure energy and sees no difference between any individual, soul, condition or entity that comes before her. Great or small, holy or depraved, all relative forms or entities are equally adjudged and adjusted according to their true state. She is a figure to both love and dread, for she adjusts according to our deepest need, which we may not consciously recognize. If we are unable to face this Goddess willingly, we return to The Wheel of Fortune, which is her instrument of adjustment in the outer or slower world, where illusions of fate, cause and effect, or 'karma' are generated.

Justice is a perpetual image at the threshold of life and consciousness: she is youthful and beautiful, yet aged; she is all-seeing, yet totally blind; she is ever merciful yet utterly severe. She holds the Cup of Blessing in her left hand and the Sword of Severance in her right; her gifts are only bestowed upon those who seek balance of the Scales, insight of the Owl and purification of the Sword. If this were not so, the blessing of the higher worlds or modes of consciousness would destroy us; their intensity or rate of energy would be unendurable. Justice is a goddess of equality, not of destruction. She stands before the Veil that hides truth beyond the Abyss.

The triple pattern of Scales, Owl, Goddess is a further motif or higher form of the Three Steps; we may find another harmonic of triplicity in the relationship between Steps, Goddess and attendant symbols, and the Veil.

The Veil and Dragons

In The Wheel of Fortune, the two Dragons were outside the Fourfold Cycle; they represented mysterious powers beyond our customary human intellect, emotions and generative drives. But in Justice we perceive the Dragons anew, with a transpersonal consciousness. Now they are almost fully visible as spiritual creatures upon the Veil that conceals the Abyss and our final leap into the void or unknown truth.

The double curve of the Dragons is identical to the symbol carved upon the first Step, that of positive and negative energies intertwined and balanced. These are the dragons seen by Merlin in his prophetic vision, reaching to the end of interaction, and therefore to the end of time. The full view of the Dragons is obscured by the figure of Justice; she protects us from this vision until we are perfectly balanced and ready to pass through the Veil.

In practical work with meditation, Justice is the zenith or highest point of consciousness while still in the physical world or body; beyond this point we need rare abilities of spiritual contemplation or power to transform as transhuman beings. For those of us who cannot cross the Abyss between relative consciousness and supernal reality, the Goddess of Justice acts as a mediator at the very zenith of the Solar World.

VI JUDGEMENT

JUDGEMENT

WORLD   The Stellar World.
WHEEL   The Third Wheel. Encompasses and incorporates the First and
Second Wheels, Justice and Fortune.
BEINGS   Archangels, supernal entities.
CONSCIOUSNESS   Transhuman, transcendent.

PARTNER TRUMPS Justice and The Wheel of Fortune as lower spirals or harmonics.

SPHERES AND PLANETS *Spheres:* The 3rd and 2nd Spheres, Understanding and Wisdom. *Planets:* Saturn and the Zodiac (or Neptune).

ATTRIBUTES Fusion of wisdom and understanding. The unknown limits and energies of the stellar originative universe. Absorption and emission of consciousness/energy into and out of the origins of being. The cycle of creation and de-creation in its primal universal condition.

GOD AND GODDESS FORMS The Great Mother and the Star Father. Saturn and Neptune (Matrona and the Zodiac). The ultimate polarities of being in the universe. Also images of space/time (3rd Sphere) and energy (2nd Sphere).

KEY PHRASES Understanding/wisdom/ultimate judgement/total comprehension/perfection of energies.

MERLIN TEXTS *PVM* Vision of the goddess Ariadne who unravels the universe and summons the ancestral spirits.

DIVINATORY MEANING May mean outwardly a matter of judgement in a situation, depending upon its position in the pattern of cards. Often indicates that a judgement must be made by the inquirer, often with profound or far-reaching effects. Also indicates collective or ancestral matters, such as national situations and seemingly unavoidable influences, but this level of meaning must be read only in association with all other factors.

RELATED NUMBER CARDS Twos and Threes.

Twos: Doubt, Choice, Freedom, Change.

Threes: Suffering, Intention, Affection, Effort.

Origins of the Image

Judgement defines the utmost circle or concept of universal entity, the stellar universe in physical relativity, or the multiverse of all existence. Unlike the lower harmonic Wheels or spirals of Justice and Fortune, Judgement has no spatial or planetary correspondence. Judgement is the depth of space and the energies of countless stars within that space/time/energy continuum.

There are three supernal Trumps: Judgement, The Hermit and The Innocent or Hierophant. These images are analogies for metaphysical states beyond the Abyss; but in most tarot packs and systems of relating Trumps to one another, these cards are given formal religious or worldly political meaning. Such orthodox interpretations act as very limited harmonics of universal concepts embodied by the three supernal Trumps. We shall encounter The Hermit and Hierophant in later chapters, but in our present context they are images which represent the extreme polarities that are encompassed and balanced by the Trump Judgement; The Hermit is consciousness withdrawing from universal existence into the unknown or void, while The Hierophant is the polar opposite, being consciousness emerging in a state of spiritual perfection to originate a universal truth or reality. Ultimately, such a truth or reality reflects right through into the Three Worlds defined by tarot, culminating in the material or consensual outer world or kingdom.

In the Merlin Tarot, the vision of Judgement is drawn from detailed apocalyptic imagery in the *Prophecies*. It is different in many ways from the customary Trump, yet both are founded upon similar concepts. The late medieval picture of an angel or archangel summoning souls at the last Trumpet (a typical instructional pun, for Judgement is one of the last Trumps or triumphs in the cycle of tarot) plays little part in the archetypes of consciousness; we do not require to be drawn back into the psychic trap of political religion.

Yet the images of Judgement upon standard tarot cards, no matter how suppressive, do draw upon an enduring archetype. When we meditate upon this deep level, even with a customary Trump image, we should pass beyond superficial nonsense regarding salvation and damnation, and tap into a state of perception rooted in a primal concept. An earlier and less suppressive image is that described by Merlin in the *Prophecies*, in which a weaver goddess, Ariadne, unravels the created worlds. She also summons ancestral spirits and withdraws into the unknown. The parallels between this vision and the later Trump are clear to see, but the visual form and purity of archetype in the Merlin vision generate a very powerful Trump image independent of orthodox propaganda.

This primal image is the foundation of later variant forms; we may trace their development historically in terms of literary evidence, culturally in terms of mythology, and magically or psychologically in terms of changes with specific collective and individual effect. As the sole purpose of tarot Trumps or triumphs is ultimate liberation, our primal image of Judgement may be more valid for the modern meditator or visualizer. The Trump is based upon a fusion of Celtic and Greek mythology, and classical and bardic or druidic cosmology.

Contents of the Image

The Sea/The Infant and the Aged Man/The Stellar World/The Veiled Goddess/The Opening into the Unknown Void

The Sea
The Sea is common to many Trump cards of Judgement and supernal archetypical symbols; it is the Sea of universal being. It takes relative form

as the interactions or depths of space and time, and the boundless ocean
of stellar energies; these three seas are ultimately one.

In both metaphysics and in magical psychology, the sea is *unified
consciousness*. We may regard it as an undifferentiated ocean of
consciousness in which all entities, from stars to crystals to subatomic
particles, swim and have their relative definitions or cycles of life and
death. The key to this concept is that all entities are relative definitions
of energy.

The sea is the Great Mother, 3rd Sphere upon the Tree of Life,
Understanding that encompasses and gives birth to all being. The Trump
of Judgement is divided traditionally into symbols of the Mother and the
Father – Sea and Sky. These enduring analogies help us to relate to
metaphysical concepts which are truly only accessible during altered
consciousness, and which cannot be defined adequately in verbal terms.

The Infant and the Aged Man

In regular Trumps of this image, we see a collection of people of all ages,
summoned by a trumpet-blowing angel; these are the elect or élite,
summoned to resurrection and paradise. In the vision of Merlin, the
goddess Ariadne causes the Four Winds to blast, and summons the 'dust
of the ancients' or ancestors to arise. All humankind, indeed all orders
of life, come to the last Judgement; otherwise it would only be a temporary
condition within one of the lesser Wheels.

Our combined image of an Infant and an Aged Man fuses the life cycle
of humanity, from first to last. We find this image in Merlin's vision of
the Apocalypse, for the presence of the goddess is preceded by that of
Janus, the god of gateways, who has two faces, young and old. This deity
still survives in our month of January, which looks both ways at the turning
of the year. Thus the Infant and Aged Man represent humanity, but also
the extremes of consciousness inherent within being or divinity. The two
heads appear back to back, emerging from one another, within Three Rays
of light.

The Rays are the extremes of the Spindle, or the Right, Left and Middle
Pillars of the Tree of Life. In very primitive symbolism, founded in the roots
of magical art, the three colours are red, white and black, the colours of
the Great Mother, representing blood, seed and matter.

In higher modes, these three colours will vary; upon the simple Tree
of Life they are black for Understanding or the Mother, red/gold for
Harmony or the Son, and white/silver for Wisdom or the Father. They
represent three strands of time, energy and space which weave the
universe – black for time, red for energy, white (clear) for space. The
definitions are not meant to be invariable, and other triplicities of colour
or meaning may be successfully employed in visualization, but red, white
and black are the traditional Three Colours. As we move lower down the

Spindle or Tree, colours open out into the spectrum, and other triple weavings or patterns become apparent.

The dual image of Infant and Aged Man is seen within the Sea, yet separated and defined by the Three Rays. It reveals differentiation or polarity out of universal consciousness. We find this theme repeated in the Trump in two further sets of relationship; the Sea and Sky, and the goddess Ariadne (the Weaver), and the unknown pre-originative state from which she emerges (represented by the vesica or lens-shaped opening through which the figure comes and raises her distaff).

It should be stressed at this point that the Merlin Tarot does not imply literal worship of images in the normal religious sense, though we are free to worship such archetypes if we choose to do so, for all worship is a matter of personal conscience and intuition. Images such as Trumps *reflect* and *embody* concepts which are beyond regular awareness. They are only truly apprehended in altered or meditational states of consciousness; there is no statement of so-called 'reality' in the vision of Judgement, but there is a powerful working image that stimulates and transforms our understanding if we choose to work with it.

The Stellar World
The stellar circle rises above the Sea; the stars are not limited by our card image, and extend upwards into dimensions which we cannot comprehend, moving out of our boundary defined by the uppermost limit of the picture. This circle or sphere defines the vast wheeling galaxies and clouds of stars which are the true life forms of the universe.

All other life forms derive from stars; poetically, they are the endless children of divinity, of God the Father seeding the womb of the Great Mother of space and time. The interaction between these two originative poles or extremes of energy creates our illusion of time, a seemingly infinite cycle of cycles. Although much of tarot is taken up with defining wheels and spirals, the aim is liberation of consciousness through organization and transformation of images; Judgement is one of the last images or higher Trumps in this process.

The divine masculine and feminine archetypes are defined upon the Tree of Life as Wisdom (2nd Sphere) and Understanding (3rd Sphere). The basic sexual division, with Wisdom as male and Understanding as female, should not be taken too literally; it is only a working model. Supernal polarities beyond the Abyss change according to our approach – which means according to our consciousness and the types of symbols or images by which we move our consciousness into different modes. In tarot we also find the higher Trump of The Hermit, which epitomizes understanding and wisdom, as a male image; conversely, The Hierophant should be a female image, corresponding to ancient forms of Sophia, the Goddess of Originative Wisdom. Later Trumps have rendered this concept down into that of a male hierarch in the role of Pope, thereby confusing the essential balance and grace of the system. We shall return to this theme when we examine the Trumps of Hermit and Hierophant in depth.

The stellar circle is that archetypical realm in which matrices and energy for the entire universe are first defined. We relate to this concept through imagery of limitation, but we should never assume that such limitation, employed solely for communication (circles, spheres, patterns), is anything other than a poetic or magical analogy. Conversely, we should not take the path of intellectual arrogance and presume that all symbols are mere illusions; archetypical symbols act as matrices for energies that we might not normally experience or generate within ourselves. This is our microcosmic reflection of the macrocosmic appearance of stars and worlds woven through space and time.

The Veiled Goddess
The veiled figure is the Weaver, called Ariadne in *The Prophecies of Merlin*. We cannot look directly upon her face, for she is the first form taken by the unknown, and we are not able to perceive such power or reality directly. The Judgement is within ourselves; only when we are truly ready may we look upon the Goddess, and this judgement is made through our innermost spiritual faculties rather than through will, curiosity or delusion.

In ancient mythology, the goddess Isis was veiled, as no human might look upon unveiled nature and remain sane. The Weaver is the highest form of universal Isis; she fuses being and non-being, she embodies the mystery of existence. Traditionally, these highest or most powerful images are feminine, though we should understand that they are a perfect fusion of male and female energies, god and goddess. Human consciousness has defined this level of universal entity as female for millennia, and such potent matrix archetypes are not easily set aside through mere intellect or discussion.

In her hand, the Weaver bears a Distaff which arranges and directs her triple thread towards creation. It is this Distaff, with its strands of time, space and energy, woven together, which turns the Spindle of created worlds below the Abyss.

The Opening into the Unknown Void
The vesica or lens-shaped Opening is a gate into the Unknown Void. The Veiled Goddess alone guards this gate; all paths lead to this supernal state in which existence and non-existence emerge from one another. Beyond the Goddess is Nothing; thus, to pass beyond her is to merge with the Void.

In a cosmic apocalyptic vision, such as that described by Merlin on which our Trump is based, the Weaver *judges* that her cycle of origination draws to an end; the power behind created cycles symbolized by the Three Worlds is withdrawn. The Distaff no longer spins the Spindle. This is the universal cycle referred to in many religions or esoteric philosophies. The crude assumption that we cannot experience such an event dissolves when we employ symbols in intuition or meditation; it is both a universal unweaving, and a truth encountered in the very depths of consciousness. Here is where the Trump Judgement should be understood, and not through trivial notions of an élite religious sect being judged and resurrected while all others are damned to Hell.

In mystical or genuine religious symbolism, the Opening is a higher form of that mysterious Cave mouth which we first encountered in the Trump of The Sun. It is the cave in which the saviour or redeemer is laid prior to resurrection; as an earthly Mystery, found in pagan and Christian mythology, it reflects a universal truth: all being returns to non-being, all being is resurrected through an unknown grace or will to existence. Below the moon, in the Lunar World, we find the wheels of birth, death and rebirth in nature; in the Solar World we find them in vast movements of the sun through space, with its lesser movements of planets in orbit, containing endless life forms and dimensions of energy. Each of these is a spiral or reflection of the life cycle of the stellar universe. Just as human forms are born from the womb, so are we reborn through the matrix of consciousness and imagination; the Son of Light is reborn in the womb of a cave, and the universe originates or dissolves through an opening or source which we as humans cannot comprehend. Little wonder, therefore, that the highest images of this concept are feminine.

The supernal reality, in which consciousness equals energy beyond rotations or conditions, is the true reality. All other worlds or states derive from it. If we can grasp some of the truth of this reality, we enter into the power of the last Judgement, for we begin to understand ourselves in original context rather than through relative reflections.

Images, such as Trumps, enable us to relate to and ultimately join with the higher consciousness which they embody; if we fill our imagination with such images in meditation and visualization, the higher modes of consciousness will gradually grow within our awareness. The last Judgement is the final fusion of polarized imagery, wisdom and understanding that we may achieve before passing through the source of consciousness and being into the unknown.

VII FOOL

THE FOOL

WORLD   Earth and all Worlds.
WHEEL   Travels through all Three Worlds, crossing all Three Wheels or thresholds. Relates initially, from an outer viewpoint, to The Wheel of Fortune.
BEINGS   Human.

CONSCIOUSNESS Internalizing consciousness, particularly that of mind or intellect in quest of truth.

PARTNER TRUMPS Polar partner: The Universe (The World). Ultimate partner or reflection: The Innocent (Hierophant). Harmonic forms: The Magician, The Hanged Man and The Hermit (in ascending order).

SPHERES AND PLANETS *Spheres:* 8th and 10th Spheres, Glory and Kingdom. *Planets:* Mercury and the Earth.

ATTRIBUTES Relates to all other Trumps through cycles of experience. Is a master Trump, fully mobile and transformative. Relates specifically to internalizing or catabolic Trumps and energies. The original spirit within a human being. Intellect or mind becoming self-aware.

GOD AND GODDESS FORMS The man/woman, primal humanity. The Child of the Great Mother. Mercury and Mother Earth.

KEY PHRASES Innocence/questing mind/traveller/perfect folly.

MERLIN TEXTS *H* The young Merlin as innocent prophetic child, who ultimately utters the *Prophecies*; *VM* The Youth of Three Disguises (who later becomes The Hanged Man).

DIVINATORY MEANING Inspiration, spiritual impulse. May also indicate naïvety, or foolish idealism, in relationship to other defining cards. Often indicates moments or decision of great change and opportunity hidden within apparently difficult situations. The mysterious liberating factor that cuts across form, especially when The Hanged Man also appears in the pattern.

RELATED NUMBER CARDS Tens (or Aces, see Figure 6) and Eights.
Tens: Disaster, Responsibility, Friendship, Opportunity.
Eights: Danger, Expediency, Excitement, Skill.

Origins of the Image

The Fool is traditionally regarded as the most important yet least significant of all tarot images. In some systems of tarot s/he is not given a number, being outside the regular order of Trumps. The Fool partakes of all images in the entire tarot pack, but particularly the Trumps; thus, there are 22 ways of defining The Fool. These definitions are given form by the Trump images, so when we consider the Trump of The Fool in its own right, we consider an overview of tarot as well as one specific image.

When a cosmic pattern of tarot is defined, we are looking at a map which acts as a working definition of the universe on one level of meaning, or of interactions between the *inner* and *outer* worlds upon another; both levels are represented by landscapes filled with images or symbols; both levels are reflections of one another. This is such an important and central obvious role of tarot that it is easy to overlook it or take it for granted. The Fool is an individual who travels through that landscape, both on a universal and human level.

Thus, The Fool is both originative divinity or pure being, and expressed humanity; s/he is a transpersonal androgynous entity, the root of consciousness becoming self-aware. Such self-awareness may be in the human sphere where the mind begins a long, slow process of reflection, assimilation and self examination; it may also be in the supernal or stellar sphere, where the unknown source of existence breathes forth or utters stars as reflections of itself. These ultimate extremes, and all reflections between them, are The Fool; though in the connecting images the role becomes very firmly attuned, polarized and specific. This specialization, of course, gives rise to the Trumps and their sets of relationships.

The Fool in the *Vita Merlini*
A strong role is given to The Fool in the *Vita*, as in many traditional wisdom tales or legends. Initially, Merlin himself is The Fool, and he retains this aspect through much of the text, asking seemingly naïve or ridiculous questions which centre upon himself, but which are always answered in deeper ways, thus directing his attention to links between his adventures and a natural universal cycle of relationships. But the *Vita* also makes specific changes to this general legendary theme, and The Fool is a very important *persona* or pivotal character in his own right.

The Fool in the Merlin Tarot is taken from an image found in the *Vita*; this image is also found in ancient ritual drama, perpetuated through folk ceremonies well into the nineteenth and twentieth centuries. He is a youth who changes disguises, sometimes appearing as male and sometimes as female. Eventually, he dies a ritualized death, which is described in the *Vita* as the Threefold Death, a theme which runs through Celtic myth, legend and ritual practice. This transformation of The Fool changes him into the higher Trump of The Hanged Man. In some tales, The Fool is reborn or resurrected after the Threefold Death.

In early Merlin legends, particularly those from Scotland, it is Merlin himself who undergoes the Threefold Death, but in the *Vita*, The Fool is given a separate identity as a youth. We may assume that originally, the central *persona* in the Great Story would have experienced the Threefold Death, but Merlin tends to take on some archetypes (Trumps) while apparently being central to, but not directly experiencing, others. The removal of The Fool from Merlin himself may be due to obvious religious overtones and the relationship between The Fool and both pagan ritual and Christian religion.

The Fool in Tarot
The Fool represents all men and women who collectively and individually travel around the Wheel. But s/he is most significant as an individual; no matter how many forms s/he takes, male or female, the spiritual individuality of The Fool is intact.

The mystery of the relationship between collective and individual consciousness, on both human and universal levels, is found in the interaction between The Fool and other Trump images.

As specific higher forms of The Fool are described in our chapters on the Trumps of The Hermit, The Hierophant/Innocent and The Hanged Man, we will concentrate at this stage upon The Fool within the human sphere of consciousness. This is the image usually found in tarot packs, legends, myths, religious images and other widespread representations of the archetype.

Contents of the Image

The Youth/The Staff and Bag/The Dog/The Path of Folly/The Cave/The Flight of Geese

The Youth

Our central character is a Youth of Three Disguises, found repeatedly in ritual drama or folklore, and very specifically defined in the *Vita Merlini*, in which the theme was drawn from oral bardic tradition. The Fool may not be aware of his ritual role – he forgets much between changes of clothes or life-cycles. He is usually portrayed as a ridiculous character – dressed ludicrously as a girl, wearing a wig – but humour enables us to understand a deeper truth behind the image. In the ancient Mysteries humour disguised yet simultaneously revealed reality that might otherwise be too difficult to bear. One of the most subtle dangers in esoteric studies, magical arts or meditation and spiritual disciplines is to take one's self seriously; in the Mysteries of Merlin there is no grave pompous male stereotype, no set of ego-inflating grades, and no reassuring claims to superiority or ultimate truth.

If we took our lives less seriously, we might be able to dissolve the demonic mask of the 'personality'; unless we achieve this self-dissolution willingly and naturally, we may encounter it as apparent confrontation or negative events, through the action of higher Trumps that cleanse and purify. Thus, The Fool prances happily upon his cliff-top; s/he is delighted to lose his self-image. This loss occurs in a higher spiritual form when The Fool undergoes the Threefold Death, becoming the Trump of The Hanged Man. The implication is consistent throughout tarot: transformation is essential for true expansion of consciousness, true spiritual development.

The Staff and Bag

The Fool always carries a rough Staff in tarot images; s/he is a traveller. This same Staff, worn smooth through long use, is carried by The Hermit at the end of his long spiritual adventure. Just as Merlin is a foolish madman who asks absurd questions at the opening of the *Vita*, so he becomes a wise man towards the close of the tale; these are the Trumps of Fool and Hermit.

A Bag hangs from the Staff; in some magical teaching traditions it is said to contain the four magical implements of Sword, Rod, Cup and Shield, by which The Fool will eventually learn to balance the Elements associated with each implement. In a higher Trump, The Fool becomes The Magician, as he discovers the contents of the Bag, given to him by his mother, and unpacks them upon the altar of controlled awareness, ready for use. The Bag is also said to contain letters of the alphabet, which are associated in mystical and magical arts with all the changes and reactions between elemental energies; thus, the Bag contains all of the remaining Trumps, or all the images and archetypes that The Fool might draw upon from within his protean self. The Bag, therefore, contains the entire universe; it is both a mystery and an obvious symbol of human consciousness; it hangs upon the Staff, which is a branch of the Tree of Life.

More simply, the Bag contains food and drink for the journey; in fairy tales it contains bread and wine that may be eaten safely in elfland or the Underworld. All such symbols have a basic meaning: *sustenance from a concealed or mysterious source*. The Bag is therefore a primal form of the Cauldron of Plenty, or the Grail; its highest archetype is, of course, the incomprehensible vessel of the universe, and beyond that the Opening or gateway of the void shown in the Trump of Judgement.

The Dog
As we discovered in The Moon, the Dog is an important spiritual animal. He guides the traveller to the Otherworld, protects him from attack and provides simple companionship. Conversely, the Dog may appear as a wild wolf or similar creature, and in some Trumps, this animal tears at The Fool's clothing. In the second context, we might take the wild beast to represent the paradoxical truth that it is our untamed savage folly that can lead us to enlightenment. This concept appears, transformed, in alchemical symbolism, in which the wild beast represents the breaking down of form or, in the case of The Fool, destruction of his ego image or illusions.

The Fool, The Moon and The Universe are all Trumps within the Lunar World: they form a triple relationship with The Moon at the axis or balance between The Fool and The Universe. This triplicity of Trumps, clearly indicated upon the Tree of Life, is very productive in meditation.

The Path of Folly
When we examined the three axis Trumps of Moon, Sun and Star, we found a Path that led, although spiralling, straight from Earth to heaven, or from planet to stars, or from mundane consciousness to transhuman

universal entity. The glyph derived from this path sequence may be drawn as a meditational aid: a pool or circle at the base, a straight line leading from the uppermost edge of the circle then becoming a spiral in the middle of the glyph, and a further straight line issuing from the centre of the spiral upwards to a star or burst of illumination. This continuous line glyph is one of the simpler maze patterns used in meditational work, and is a basic representation of the awakening of our energies, or Inner Fire. The three stages (Circle, Spiral, Star) correspond to three levels or centres of energy within our consciousness/organism, and the continuous line from which the glyph is assembled is our life-force, directed by will and imagination. More complex maps of our power centres are employed in detailed work, but this Spiral Path merges with the concept of Three Worlds (see Figure 8).

In The Fool, however, the Path seems to have come to a sudden end on the edge of a cliff. Does The Fool turn around and return, or does s/he

Figure 8: CIRCLE, SPIRAL, STAR: Three Worlds as human power centres.

leap over the cliff? Does he have any awareness of his perilous situation? In many Trumps, paths lead through gates, sets of pillars, or to veils and barriers which may or may not be passed. Certain images, however, have thresholds or situations where great *leaps* or apparently impossible transitions are required of the traveller. The Fool, and his higher form The Hermit, are examples of such images.

The Path along which The Fool has danced is a path of no return; the broken fence shows that the restraints and conditioning of his past have already been shattered; if s/he is to proceed, s/he must leap over the cliff. When s/he makes that irreversible leap, s/he may fall into the world below and be killed – or may live to tell the tale. S/he may even be carried upwards to the mountains beyond, through the miracle and grace of his spiritual inner being.

In a most direct sense this symbolic situation reflects our power of choice at threshold moments in life: do we leap or crawl back? Only The Fool leaps. If s/he falls unhurt to the outer world s/he is changed nevertheless. We all experience threshold leaps of this sort, from the merely trivial to the most shattering. Any new flash of awareness, any idea of change, any threshold crossed, is the power of The Fool within us. But most leaps are fairly small, and dependent upon situations with many interactions with relatively low thresholds; the degree of perfect folly in such situations is low. While we take small leaps endlessly, often jumping blindly around The Wheel of Fortune and missing paths that open out from it, the Great Leap epitomized by The Fool is seldom undertaken.

There are three types or qualities of folly;

1. *The folly of returning down the path.* Once the barrier or rail of conditioning and habitual illusion has been shattered, the path can only lead into the unknown. That which was safe before, which we assumed to guard us from change or accident, is now dangerous or deadly. In broad terms, our worst decisions and most self-destructive and poisonous situations are those in which we have seen the truth but refuse to accept it. This mode of folly ranges from personal wilful ignorance to international politics and pollution. In a mystical sense it is sin against the holy spirit to have seen beyond illusion yet refuse the truth of that vision.

2. *The folly of falling over the cliff.* Most of us make our decisions in life in a haphazard manner; we do not enter into a willed rejection of truth, nor do we fully leap joyfully into the unknown. We merely acknowledge that we cannot return, and thus fall inevitably over the cliff. The result will be change, life, death; ultimately, we all fall over the cliff of death. The cliff-top in The Fool is also a peak of rotation, the zenith of The Wheel of Fortune: most of us never pass beyond this threshold, which is built of our thoughts and feelings interacting endlessly.

In the folly of merely slipping over the cliff, the Dog acts as spiritual creature. He warns that the cliff is coming, for he is that persistent but seldom attended part of consciousness that always indicates the truth of any situation; on a deeper level, he guards mysteries of life, death and change, symbolized in Celtic legend by the hounds of the Wild Hunt that carry the souls of the dead into the Otherworld. Conversely, if we try to stand still and stagnate, it may be the Dog who bites us until we jump.

3. *The folly of the Great Leap.* This third folly is known to seers, mystics, initiates and, through inspiration, to all of us without exception. The individual does not turn back, stagnate or merely fall over, but leaps in full consciousness and knowledge that it is a leap utterly into the unknown. This applies upon all levels; physical, mental, emotional and spiritual. If these levels, usually and inaccurately regarded as separate, are fused together, the leaper reaches another world.

Here is where the mystery of sacrifice is first encountered: a Threefold Death of falling, hanging and drowning leads to the spiritual image or Trump of The Hanged Man. This, however, is the highest harmonic or level of the Great Leap, taken for all humankind. The Great Leap itself is not necessarily the great sacrifice; there are many kinds and degrees of sacrifice or exchange of energies and situations. Paradoxically, the Great Leap itself can only be undertaken in full willingness and understanding that it *may* be a leap of sacrifice obtaining utterly unguessable results. At this stage of development of consciousness we find the science and understanding of esoteric laws beginning to develop; an immediate relative of The Fool is The Magician, who we shall encounter shortly.

The Three Levels
The Trump is divided into three levels as follows:

1. Below: outer or everyday world.
2. Promontory or cliff-top: threshold before transformation.
3. Mountains: higher worlds or spiritual consciousness.

In cosmic terms the three levels of the image correspond to certain Trumps and overall relationships as follows:

1. Earth–Moon: Trumps of The Moon and The Universe or World.
2. Moon–Sun: Trumps of The Sun and The Wheel of Fortune.
3. Sun–Stars: Trumps of The Star, Justice and Judgement.

On the Tree of Life, The Fool may be first placed between Earth, or the consensual human world, and the First Wheel (Fortune). This location is our perpetual threshold of human life and folly. It corresponds to a path between the Spheres of Kingdom (Earth) and Glory (Mercury), shown in

Figure 2. It should be emphasized that The Fool, above all others, is a mobile Trump, taking the colouration and consciousness of each image or Trump upon and within himself in turn. Thus, in varied tarot systems The Fool may appear in different locations; his appearance will affect the relative position of all other Trumps. The three levels outlined above are actually unified by the presence of The Fool; it is his entity that generates all other Trumps across the levels or worlds. But conscious unity, in full understanding, comes only when The Fool is transformed into The Hanged Man.

The Identity of The Fool

We have touched upon the relationship between The Fool, The Hermit, The Hanged Man and The Universe or World. This relationship will be discussed within the chapters for each Trump, but it should be clear from the foregoing that The Fool has both a human and divine or transhuman aspect. In a human role s/he travels between the first and second levels defined above through repeated cycles of reincarnation. In his divine role, as the saviour or Son of Light at the heart of all religions or truth, regardless of creed or dogma, this being unifies the worlds. Such unification may be mirrored within ourselves, through the image of The Hanged Man or Threefold Death, a higher form of The Fool.

The Cave

There are two possible interpretations of the Cave, depending upon our quality of folly. If we choose not to jump but to crawl backwards down the Path, the Cave is the dwelling of unseen horror. It hides a monster, the ultimate expression of our fears embodied in a grotesque self-image. This monster is indeed the stuff of nightmares and irrational reactions, but we find it paraded all around us in images of the pseudo-self promoted by advertising, politics, religion and subtle propaganda and conditioning. In atavistic terms it is the horror that lurks in darkness, but when it emerges into the light it disguises itself as fashion, life-style, class, success, peer group, upward mobility and the delusion of integrated, balanced personality. On a national or international level, these delusions have their counterparts in politics, economics and warfare. As long as we pursue such ends, we are crawling deeper and deeper into the pit where horror dwells.

But that same Cave exists in another dimension, whereby all its horrific imbalanced energies are transformed; for those who make the leap of material folly but spiritual liberation, it becomes a Cave of hidden treasure, the gateway to the fabled Underworld oracle and a dwelling of the light within darkest, deepest earth. We might add poetically that for those who make the Great Leap, the Cave opens out into the universe as they fall, and the lesser worlds dissolve. The key to the paradox of the Cave is in the direction of our self-image, the quality and identity of fear at any threshold.

In the Merlin legends it is this Cave that undermines the tower of King Vortigern, which he tries to build as a rigid defence against change and the rightful rebalance of power. We shall encounter this image in more detail when we analyse the Trump of The Blasted Tower. It is upon high middle ground, such as the cliff in our present Trump, that such a false tower is usually built. It is destroyed in two ways; by a lightning flash from heaven, and by undermining from within a mysterious cavern below its foundation. In the Merlin Tarot this cavern holds two dragons, drinking from the secret Spring of life, death and prophecy.

The Flight of Geese
The distant Flight of Geese has several interwoven meanings:

1. On a very basic level of interpretation the Geese represent thoughts and aspirations winging their way into the unknown. Thus they show that the Youth in our image is already expanding his awareness, beginning to realize that there are further horizons.
2. In pagan augury, the shape, direction and nature of flying birds was of major importance: we find this clearly stated in the *Vita* where flying cranes are said to make letters in the sky. This theme is borrowed from classical sources, but reflects a deep-rooted belief in synchronous patterns, by which potential predictions, insight or farsight could be defined. Tarot is also used in this manner, of course. The pattern of the flight of birds in The Fool may be taken to indicate his future.
3. In European legend, deriving from pagan myth and religion, flocks of migrating geese were sometimes said to be the souls of the newly dead, flying to the Otherworld. In British folklore the sound of geese calling in flight was said to be that of the Wild Hunt; similar motifs are known world-wide. In this context we have the implication that The Fool will eventually become The Hanged Man (see Chapter 15), for his sacrificial death is closely connected to the theme of the Wild Hunt. As we shall discover, the harmonic images of Magician and Guardian (who is a form of the Lord of the Animals, Master of the Wild Hunt), through which The Fool becomes The Hanged Man and, finally, The Hermit, are developments of concepts symbolized in miniature by the Flight of Geese. Thus the flock of Geese in flight indicates unknown horizons, new dimensions, providing a sign that it is time to depart upon the Great Journey.

VIII MAGICIAN

THE MAGICIAN

WORLD   The Lunar World.
WHEEL   The First Wheel, Fortune.
BEINGS   *Daemones*, humans, ex-humans, ancestral spirits.
CONSCIOUSNESS   Human and collective or ancestral. May also relate to consciousness of other dimensions and beings, such as faery realms or elementals.

PARTNER TRUMPS   Polar partner: The Priestess. Harmonic forms: The Hanged Man, The Hermit. Relates also to the higher Trumps of Temperance and The Innocent (The Hierophant).

SPHERES AND PLANETS   *Spheres:* The 8th and 9th Spheres, Glory and Foundation. *Planets:* Mercury or Hermes, and Luna.

ATTRIBUTES   Hermes, the great initiator, through intellectual energies founded within controlled life forces. The organic growth of consciousness through individual effort. Educational traditions of magical arts and sciences. The questing intellect and collective sexual or foundational energies working together towards inner development and outer effects.

GOD AND GODDESS FORMS   Luna and Hermes. May also be represented by certain primal deities concerned with magical arts; the instructing or shape-changing gods and goddesses who educate humanity.

KEY PHRASES   Honourable power/imagination for life/living magical arts/glorious foundation of knowledge.

MERLIN TEXTS   *VM* Taliesin (inspired by the goddess Minerva) expounds the nature and pattern of the universe.

DIVINATORY MEANING   Usually indicates matters of mental energy, life forces, and the creative use of the mind and imagination. Often shows, according to position, those aspects of the situation which would benefit from imaginative effort.

RELATED NUMBER CARDS   Nines and Eights.

Nines: Misfortune, Endurance, Fulfilment, Means.

Eights: Danger, Expediency, Excitement, Skill.

Origins of the Image

In modern tarot interpretation The Magician is often given a divine originative significance; he is said to be the great juggler who sets creation spinning. Such an interpretation may derive more from literary sources than from the foundational traditions of magic, imagery and story-telling that underpin tarot.

All Trumps may reveal, through contemplation, a divine function. Any Trump, regardless of its initial imagery and role, may be penetrated until awareness reaches towards the root of universal being. This is an open secret, one of the great initiatory truths of imagination, of archetypes. Thus, it should come as no revelation that The Magician may be regarded as a divine image, for such a depth of interpretation may be applied to any Trump.

Tarot sets or packs should be rotated, with systems of arrangement that spiral in continual motion. Through this rotation, which is represented by the fundamental tarot concept of the Three Wheels, the Trumps merge into one another and transform. Thus, appearances change harmonically, but the innermost levels of comprehension, identity and truth are retained. This important concept lies at the root of all pairs, triads, relationships, marriages, balances and other sub-patterns that are discussed through this book and shown in the various illustrations.

In one system it is possible and valid to claim that The Magician represents divinity or originative being; in another, this same claim may be applied to The Fool, or to The Hierophant. All such definitions are both correct and incorrect, for tarot moves ceaselessly. It is our human consciousness that establishes harmonies, patterns, relationships; we use tarot as a system of inner development and expansion of consciousness. Without such well-defined sets of relationship, tarot becomes vague, enervated and trivialized.

The ordering of tarot Trumps derives from two sources. Individual understanding, meditation and intuition is the first; the second is the received teaching of active enduring esoteric tradition, which is not necessarily represented by any published sources. When individual understanding flowers within collective tradition, magical and mystical images come alive; tarot may be filled with transformative potency in this manner.

The Magician represents, on a human level, our efforts to relate elements of existence. In this context the Trump is very important indeed in our definition and use of tarot. It represents both individual consciousness juggling with symbols and energies, and enduring traditions of magical arts which assist and generate such efforts. Within the Merlin Tarot, The Magician is attuned to a very specific Western inner tradition that has remained unbroken for many centuries. Modern literature is merely a superficial emanation of such a tradition; the true magical instruction exists on inner planes or states of consciousness, and may be contacted through regular effort in meditation, visualization and ritual pattern making.

Merlin and The Magician

In very early sources, Merlin is not associated with magical arts, but with prophecy. His connection with magic developed gradually in literature, though certain primal magical acts are well defined in the *Vita Merlini* on the level of dramatic actions and adventures. The figure of Merlin has gradually absorbed many elements from tradition, and now acts as an imaginative interface for tuition from our collective consciousness.

In the *Vita*, Merlin is first driven mad by grief, then begins his long journey to spiritual maturity by asking foolish, self-centred questions. It is this act of questioning, so typical of both child and magician, that leads to his ultimate wisdom.

The questioning mind, the seeking intellect, is central to all magical arts. Such arts laid the foundation for modern science, though this is conveniently forgotten today. In magical arts, mental disciplines are applied to life energies for purposes of transformation. But there is also a deep collective anonymous tradition of wisdom within magic; this realm can supply energies necessary for early training and experience, for such energies are often not directly aroused within an individual until the later stages of inner growth.

The first quality, that of mind, is symbolized by Hermes or Mercury; the second quality, that of ancestral collective power, memory and intuition, is symbolized by The Moon. These two streams of energy and consciousness fuse together to form the Trump known as The Magician. Upon the Tree of Life we may allocate a path between the 8th and 9th Spheres, Glory and Foundation, Hermes and Luna (see Figure 2). This path of consciousness reaches to the threshold of the Lunar World, and thus may lead into the Solar World.

Contents of the Image

The Cave/The Sea/The Pig/The Magical Implements/The Magician/The Otherworld Islands

The Cave
For the first time in our ascent of the tarot paths, we are inside the Cave. In a superficial sense it is the cave of the human skull, holding the brain which is our physical organ of awareness. The brain, in which intellect and instinct are united (Hermes and Luna), is a physical form of a metaphysical reality. Esoteric traditions always teach that consciousness defines form or expression, and not vice versa.

Upon the Cave walls are ancient images and inscriptions carved and painted by the earliest primal magicians in prehistory. Primal cultures had highly developed magical arts, though we might not recognize some of these today. Some magical traditions are thousands of years old, with roots deep in the origins of humankind. Whoever dares to work magic in the Cave is supported and contacted by ancestors who have gone before; it is the Cave of initiation, education, and ancestral Earth power.

The Sea
Beyond the Cave mouth we can glimpse a sunlit Sea with clouds passing overhead. This represents a new dimension of awareness or, in magical terms, a new world. We pass from Earth to Water, lit by the Fire of the sun, inspired by the flowing Air of the Four Winds. It is through the skill of The Magician that we may learn methods of reaching such higher worlds, and of generating elemental changes within ourselves which

enable us to pass to and fro at will. Hermetic instruction (the forerunner of modern science, but really a fusion of art, science and mysticism) enables us to define relationships between consciousness and worlds or dimensions through which such consciousness seems to travel.

The Pig
Beneath the altar is a little Pig, creature of the Goddess, spiritual animal of the Underworld. In an old Welsh poem, Merlin has a little pig as his companion. In Celtic legends, a hero, king or magician is often linked with pigs. In the Merlin Tarot, the Pig guides The Magician, fusing powers of Air or mind actively with those of Earth or body.

The Pig stands between the supporting pillars of the altar; no altar may be raised effectively without the primal foundation of the Underworld to support it. This law of practical magic underpins all scared structures, from stone circles to cathedrals. As spiritual animal partaking of both upper and lower worlds, the Pig naturally belongs between the serpent pillars or poles of power. He stands exactly in the middle of primary forces, defined by the Directions of Above/Below/Right/Left/Before/Behind. The Magician occupies a higher level or harmonic of the same position, the magical centre of operation (see Figure 5).

One early legend, of importance to the Merlin tradition, is that of king Bladud and his pigs. In this allegory, an exiled prince contracts leprosy, and is forced to live as a swineherd. The pigs lead Bladud to a steaming, warm swamp, where he is cured of his affliction. He claims his rightful throne, and builds a temple to the goddess of the curative hot springs, dedicating an eternal magical flame to burn in her honour. The goddess is called *Minerva* by early writers such as Geoffrey of Monmouth, for she is a goddess of cultural development (originally a Celtic divinity with attributes similar to those of Minerva).

There are a number of druidic undertones to the Bladud legend, for he develops magical arts throughout Britain, and founds the first universities.[10] Later he flies through the air on artificial wings and crash lands in a temple of Apollo the sun god. All of Bladud's attributes, such as therapy, healing springs, magical arts and the worship of Minerva, feature in the *Vita* as well as in the *History* and folk tales. During the Creation Vision expounded by Taliesin (under the inspiration of Minerva) King Bladud appears as the guardian of sacred springs and wells. He is, incidentally, one of the line of British sacred kings, closely related to gods.[5]

The temple traditionally ascribed to King Bladud may be seen today, in Aquae Sulis, Bath, England. The goddess Minerva was amalgamated in this ancient worship site, by the incoming Romans, with the original Celtic goddess Sul or Sulis. The hot springs flow copiously now, even as they did in Roman and prehistoric times. We shall meet the goddess,

Minerva-like, when we examine the Trump of The Chariot in our next chapter.

The Magical Implements
Upon the altar supported by two serpents, which are a variant form of the primal red and white dragons, are four Implements. They are Sword, Rod, Cup, and Shield or Mirror; the symbols of operation, balance and interaction. These implements are the means available to human consciousness by which the Four Elements may be adjusted into relative states of balance. The ideal relationship is traditionally shown by the Circled Cross or Wheel of Life (Figure 6) which is a constant relative pattern of balance through the Three Worlds and Three Wheels of the Merlin Tarot.

In Renaissance tarot packs The Magician is often a juggler or conjurer; such skill is not based upon *controlling* the Elements, for the concept of 'control' of nature is one of the deepest-rooted vanities and most dangerous follies of materialism. Juggling is an art in which component parts in motion are *balanced*; only perfection of motion can keep balance, and any attempt at control through overbearing force generates destruction of the pattern. Yet a moving pattern of parts presents the appearance of a whole; juggling has many insights to offer in meditation and in actual practice.

The four Implements are given individual attention in a later chapter as the Four Aces of our Number cards, which represent Elemental energies and relative patterns through all worlds.

The Magician
Beyond the altar a smiling figure faces us, looking into the depths of the Cave. He is invoking, with arms upraised in a movement known to all humankind as the basic sign of magical art. The two burning lamps represent the pillars or gate through which energy passes between dimensions or worlds. The Magician is an image of paradox in operation, for although he looks into darkness (where we are), he is invoking light. In the sunlit realm behind him, powerful changes of weather seethe and flow across the Islands and water; these movements of natural forces within the environment or within awareness are directed by The Magician; he is intellect adjusting fundamental life energies into chosen patterns.

Through meditation upon this Trump we may grasp the secrets of magical art, which are secrets of inner transformation. Such arts work through reflection, reversal, polarity; a ceaseless dance of correspondence and relationship. That which seeks to exercise direct control is already moribund and doomed to destruction; but adjustment and balance, working through spiral patterns and harmonious intention, may be renewed and transformed. The eternal flames which burnt upon altars in ancient temples, or the lamp in a modern church or sanctuary, are reflections of this light perpetually renewed. Only by invocation in the Cavern may The Magician summon light; it arises from behind him, beyond the Cavern mouth.

The Magician is an image that both liberates and guards; as a guardian he is a lower harmonic of the great Guardian represented in another Trump. The Magician educates; we may not pass him without satisfying the strict demands of his artistic discipline and science. Only by passing through the darkness of the Cave may we meet The Magician and learn from him; every encounter with his power is concerned with breaking of barriers, crossing thresholds, death of world views and birth of heightened consciousness.

The consciousness of The Magician is first revealed to us by The Fool; we break our first barriers as fools, but to reach further requires a fusion of mental and life energies. The great Hermetic educational and scientific traditions (which founded modern science) are directly concerned with methods of liberation, in which we apply our intellect towards transformation. Through such traditions we learn very precise and detailed techniques for arousing our life energies and harmonizing them within the Three Worlds of Moon, Sun and Star.

In the basic Merlin legend, The Magician is not represented fully by Merlin himself, but by Taliesin, instructor of Merlin into the Mysteries of the cosmos and the orders of living beings that inhabit the Three Worlds. Taliesin gives Merlin a detailed sequence of Hermetic instruction concerning worlds, powers, elements, angels, spirits, Otherworld beings, and magical lands and islands. He represents mind or intellect applied to the raw power of Merlin's prophetic fervour, bringing it into an order or open-ended pattern which attunes to universal relative patterns of energy, time and space.

Such generation of patterns is the epitome of magical art and science; when Merlin finally learns the relationship between macrocosm and microcosm, he partakes of the knowledge of The Magician, and his wild, abundant powers are brought into perfect balance. This leaves him free to develop towards a deeper spiritual consciousness which is represented by the Trump of The Hermit. [11]

The Otherworld Islands
On the light-filled horizon we can just see the Blessed Isles, partly hidden by the figure of The Magician. These are the paradise islands of the Celtic Otherworld, as revealed to Merlin by Taliesin. Within these Islands is the Fortunate Isle, where the priestess *Morgen* and her nine sisters dwell. Morgen is given detailed attention in the *Vita* and is quite unlike the later corrupted image that became Morgan le Fey or Nimuë. Both of these literary forms represent sexual aberrations of the era in which they were

written, rather than genuine legendary tradition.

Morgen is a primal priestess of nature and light; she may change shape, fly through the air; she has great therapeutic power. Her Island is a realm of perpetual Summer and fruitfulness, to which the wounded King Arthur was carried by Merlin and Taliesin (according to the *Vita*, which is the earliest source of the legend). As we shall see in a later chapter, The Priestess or Morgen is the partner of The Magician; she balances his fusion of intellect and life energies with a fusion of emotions and life energies.

The passage of clouds and wind over the Islands suggests constant Elemental power in these primal imaginative realms; it also symbolizes the rolling away of the clouds or veil upon our limited perceptions. Through The Magician and his highly specialized art, we may part the veil that hides the Blessed Isles from our vision. Other images will assist our journey to those Isles and meet us when we arrive.

Who is The Magician?
We must distinguish between an archetype, Trump, or major image in its own right, and its inherent powers reflecting through a defined character, either in history, legend, poetry or fiction. Taliesin the bard embodies druidic cosmology in the *Vita*, teaching such lore under the inspiration of Minerva. There was also at least one historical Taliesin, an early Welsh poet, though like the name 'Merlin', 'Taliesin' was probably used as a title or honourable description. Thus Taliesin is not *The* Magician, but a human initiated into Hermetic or druidic traditions of knowledge and wisdom. He is a teacher who enlightens Merlin; Merlin in turn becomes a magician, bringing forth deeper wisdom which was not available to him as a wild seer or prophet. The mantle of The Magician is passed from individual to individual endlessly; it may never be lost, worn out, or retained by force.

We may each partake of the lore of The Magician, yet the power of the image is archetypical and constant, standing beyond human individuality or participation. In the *Vita*, Taliesin teaches in detail concerning Morgen and Bladud, who are both characters who fly, practise magical arts, and have direct connections with early Celtic religion and druidism. They are male and female divine images from an earlier culture; we might suggest that Bladud is The Magician, and Morgen The Priestess in tarot. Other names could be added from other cultures.

To understand tarot at work we need to appreciate two major concepts:

1. Tarot images are sets of archetypes with many branches or variants of expression.
2. Tarot systems work only through specific limitations. The limitation within a tradition or pattern gives tremendous energy; conversely, assertions of universality or reduction to catch-all concepts weaken the power of tarot, especially the Trumps. In some cases, a misapplication

of this magical theory will result in the inverse of a Trump arising – this is clearly found in the history of corruption of Trumps through orthodox religious suppressive conditioning.

Magician or Trickster?

One of the major paths to enlightenment is through humour; the face of The Magician is full of joy and good humour, discovery and enthusiasm. He is not a sombre, pompous 'adept' dictating occult dogma; such nonsense derives solely from human vanity wandering far from magical reality. To relate to The Magician we must become aware of the difference between humour as a spiritual or liberating power, and its inverse or shadow which is that of the malevolent trickster. This inverted image is often found in folklore world-wide; it occasionally manifests in the personalities of otherwise promising magicians in human society.

Anthropologists and commentators upon primal magical practices often confuse the initiatory tricks and paradoxes of practical magic with spite, malevolence and illusion. To understand fully The Magician and its profound background within development of human culture and civilization, we should not confuse it with the shadow of the trickster.

In classical mythology, the young Mercury or Hermes plays tricks upon other gods and goddesses; in Celtic legends such as *The Mabinogion*, a malevolent brother sets major changes in motion through spiteful action. [5] To understand such legends we must look deeper than superficial action; the trickery is often the beginning of sequence of change that leads to new worlds, eras or conditions. Such trickery is of a different, more powerful order than negative pettiness; much depends upon the relative viewpoint of the situation.

The Magician is an innovator; he works from states of perception which often seem paradoxical or even wanton to the slower awareness and pace of the outer world and our conditioned living habits. In our personal use of tarot we should meditate upon the *humour* of The Magician, and so develop the ability to laugh freely at ourselves rather than cruelly at others. Without this freedom through humour we may only meet the higher powers or Trumps through painful purgation and purification. This psychological and mystical truth was retained until fairly late in the orthodox churches; it took the form of a festival of folly in which all hierarchical roles were briefly reversed. Such festivals were drawn from earlier pagan tradition; eventually humour was utterly removed from Christian religion, which was a great loss to Western civilization.

In legends and folklore, however, humour was preserved in rather crude forms. The Fool is the subject of many folk rituals, butt of many coarse jokes, yet in his sex-changing role or his death and resurrection he preserves the most powerful perennial wisdom teaching. The Magician, one of the higher or more specialized forms of The Fool, presents us with more sophisticated and subtle humour. Perhaps his greatest joke, the one that causes him to smile in the Trump image, is that many years of magical training are finally discovered to be quite irrelevant. But this truth is only gained by experience, and not through discussion or mere playing with words; it is discovered only when we are able to live in the Fortunate Isle, where the outer order of the Elements is changed and many things are reversed or transcended.

IX CHARIOT

THE CHARIOT

WORLD   The Solar World.
WHEEL   The Second Wheel, Justice.
BEINGS   Angels, innerworld masters and saints (ex-humans).
CONSCIOUSNESS   Transpersonal, catabolic or catalytic. May include aspects of personal intellect.

PARTNER TRUMPS   Polar partner: The Lovers (see also Figure 4).
SPHERES AND PLANETS   *Spheres:* The 8th and 6th Spheres, Glory and
Beauty. *Planets:* Mercury and Sol.
ATTRIBUTES   Fusion of intellect or mind and spiritual awareness. The
energies of thought and mental discipline as a vehicle for transcendent
consciousness. Illumination leading to knowledge.
GOD AND GODDESS FORMS   Hermes and Apollo: Minerva/
Briggidda and Bel, the Lord of Light. Pagan goddesses of cultural
development, patronesses of solar heroes. Inspirers and teachers of
humankind on a transpersonal individual level that eventually benefits
many.
KEY PHRASES   Glorious beauty/harmonious thought/knowledge in
motion/higher awareness/inner teaching/vehicle of divine consciousness.
MERLIN TEXTS   *H, PVM, VM* References to Minerva as patroness of
knowledge and inspiration. Also references to transformative goddesses in
general.
DIVINATORY MEANING   Higher knowledge, scientific inspiration and
research. May also mean spiritual sciences and esoteric or Hermetic arts.
Enlivening energy within the psyche of the inquirer or the situation,
leading to a reasoned resolution inspired by insight.
RELATED NUMBER CARDS   Sixes and Eights.
Sixes: Transition, Balance, Joy, Benefit.
Eights: Danger, Expediency, Excitement, Skill.

Origins of the Image

The Chariot is a higher image of the energies or consciousness first
presented to us as The Magician. As we ascend the Spiral or Tree of Life,
we meet images and definitions of modes of consciousness. These begin
to appear in increasingly 'pure' forms, with higher harmonics or images
acting as the sources for those encountered upon lower paths or within
lower Trumps. The patterns of relationship are shown in our Figure 4 and
the reversal of polarity or apparent sexual role of each Trump is a key
concept in tarot. The Chariot is a feminine Trump, acting as a higher form
of the masculine Trump of The Magician

When we experience The Chariot, we meet for the first time in our
journey a fusion of specific ancient goddess forms and related concepts of
energy. The Charioteer is a female figure, deriving from a number of
goddesses well known in classical and Celtic culture. The concept of the
Charioteer as a male victor is a relatively late transposition, similar to other
alterations of gender and function which push tarot towards a suppressive
symbol system or religious orthodoxy, though never quite succeeding.

In the Merlin Tarot, the Charioteer is the archetype of Minerva, who plays an important role in the Merlin texts, and has variant forms in British or Western mythology from a Celtic and primal European goddess.

The name of a god or goddess is frequently a key to the function; Minerva, Athena, Briggidda, the Morrigan and other goddesses of war and cultural development are all closely related. While specific localized forms may have considerable variation, the deeper archetype and function remains constant. The political Minerva of the Roman Empire is a tailor-made image; she was imposed upon a wild chariot-driving war goddess of the Celts, just as she developed out of an Etruscan primal war goddess in Rome. When we use the name 'Minerva' in the Merlin Tarot, we employ it in a functional rather than Roman historical sense.

If we consider all variant forms of this goddess, we find that she represents culture and civilization utilizing wild energies of life towards creative, balanced ends. Thus she has savage, primal goddesses within her, yet protects and inspires selected heroes towards achievements that help humankind to develop collectively. We shall find a higher form of this goddess when we consider the Trump of Death or The Apple Woman.

Just as The Magician employs mind or intellect to balance and define the seething life energies of the Lunar and Earth Worlds, so The Chariot employs individual and collective consciousness as a *vehicle* (the Chariot itself) for solar or spiritual consciousness. We shall develop this concept as we progress through the Trump.

Contents of the Image

The Ford/The Heron/The Chariot drawn by Two Ponies/The Charioteer/The Distant Walled City

The Ford

We began our ascent of tarot paths at the still deep Pool of The Moon; higher Trumps, however, tend to have water that flows freely. The Ford enables us to cross a rushing river of consciousness in which many concepts, mysteries, theories, truths and rapidly changing thoughts flow without ceasing. In the realm of the mind this river represents intellectual development through time; it never stands still. If we follow it downstream it leads back to the collective Pool of The Moon, then flows down into the hidden Underworld where consciousness is reversed and transformed. If we follow the river upstream it leads beyond intellect to higher operations and modes of consciousness; ultimately, it leads to the source of being.

At this point in our inner journey or growth, several paths become available for the first time; these are shown by the map of the Tree of Life, and represented individually by the various Trumps that occur as images of the energies of each path. In one sense, the river is the limit of the First Wheel of Fortune, which flows and rotates around the Lunar World and into expression upon our Earth. Thus it flows from the emotions, represented by Venus (Victory, the 7th Sphere), to the mind or intellect, represented by Mercury or Minerva (Glory or Honour, the 8th Sphere), with its foundation upon the life force or generative roots of physical being represented by Luna (the 9th Sphere); this pattern is shown in our Figures 2 and 7.

The river or flow of consciousness passes through the Trumps of Magician, Priestess, Moon, Fool, and World or Universe, with The Wheel of Fortune as its threshold or defining zone. Beyond this defining zone it rotates into a higher spiral of the Second Wheel, Justice, with a further cycle of Trumps in the Solar World. In the various Trumps the river may appear as a stream, a pool, the sea, a spring, ice, a waterfall or any other naturalistic form relating to water.

The Chariot is the first Trump in our ascending sequence that we experience *across* the threshold of the river (The Wheel of Fortune, Lunar World), hence the flowing water at the boundary of the card. It is the threshold between the Lunar and Solar Worlds; if we are to reach into a higher cycle of Trumps centred upon the sun or spiritual centre of awareness, we must cross this threshold.

Under the flowing water we can see stones inscribed with curious letters or hieroglyphs; this is the primal alphabet of all knowledge, partly revealed by the flowing waters, yet partly hidden and obscured by the speed of their movement. While we may read fragments of this primal alphabet at the Ford, we can only learn its true contents and origins by experiencing the entire cycle of Trumps, the Great Journey or Story, from beginning to end. A fish leaps from the waters, representing individual awareness reaching briefly into the light of higher consciousness, yet partaking of the collective stream for its existence and reproduction.

To reach the land beyond the Ford, we must meet the Charioteer who has ridden out of the Walled City to greet us. She may turn us back if we do not have a proper claim upon her protection and inspiration. In Celtic tradition, a ford represents transition from one world to another; to meet a mysterious woman at a ford is to die or cross into the Otherworld. We shall encounter a higher form of this concept in the female image of Death or The Apple Woman, who mediates transformation across the Abyss of time, space and energy.

In our Trump, the Ford is that boundary beyond which the conditioned mind, regular thought processes, rigorous intellect, may not travel alone unaided or untransformed. The key word here is 'alone', for unless the mind or customary level of intellect is fused with consciousness higher than its usual cycle of thoughts and feelings rotating around sexual foundations, we cannot exist in higher Worlds. The Ford represents the death of one world view and birth of another.

The Heron

The Heron is one of the spiritual birds of the Great Goddess; she has many meanings. Patience, speed, silence, secrecy, solitude, all are typical qualities associated with the Heron. She is at home in both the air and the water, and spends much time perched upon the land watching the river or stream. In our image the Heron stands upon the near side of the Ford, where she acts as a guide or spiritual bird of the path forward.

The Heron spears single fish from the waters, and arranges them in the pattern of a Wheel. On one level this represents the understanding that relates individual ideas to one another; on a higher level, the spiritual bird and her circle of fish remind us that life, death and the Wheel are perpetual. This is a last clue or warning before we cross, for we leave one turn of the Wheel behind only to encounter a higher spiral and cycle of energies.

The Chariot drawn by Two Ponies

Horses in tarot and related picture images from esoteric tradition represent power in motion. The Ponies drawing the Chariot in our Trump are about to enter the river; the Charioteer may rein them in or allow them to cross. The Two Ponies show polarity out of unity; when they are pulling in balanced effort, they draw the Chariot forward. A similar polarity out of unity is found in The Lovers which balances The Chariot: two Lovers are blessed equally by the primal divinity Eros. Thus, there is a concept of triplicity, or power expressing itself through polarization, in each of these Trumps: The Chariot shows spiritual consciousness harnessing mental energies, while The Lovers shows spiritual consciousness blessing the emotional energies.

In The Sun, we encountered a divine Child riding upon the White Mare; in The Chariot a pair of Ponies draw the vehicle of illuminated consciousness. Both Trumps define paths leading from the Sun, Centre, or 6th Sphere of Harmony towards the formative and expressive Worlds – from creation towards manifestation. Both Trumps may also lead in the reverse direction. Whereas the divine Child may be born physically through the generative power of The Moon, the Charioteer remains in the inner worlds or realms of consciousness. She is expressed through reflection and mediation by the lower Trumps of The Magician and The Fool. While The Magician manipulates the energies to balance the Elements in the outer world, The Fool has adventures which lead him onwards, often under the guidance of a goddess similar to Minerva.

The Chariot is an enduring symbol of motion, attack and defence; it is often used as a symbol of triumph and glory. In many legends the sun flies through the upper air in a horse-drawn chariot; mystical visions describe divinity in the form of a glorious being in a chariot; such symbols incorporate solar mythology, but extend beyond it to spiritual perception. The Chariot is a major symbol of divine power in motion; it is a vessel, vehicle or enabling form carrying the force of spiritual or essential being.

In our tarot Trump, however, the pure archetype is modified by several related forms through tradition; the Chariot itself is mind or intellect drawn onwards by polarized activity; the mind is a vehicle for higher consciousness, and not an end in itself. Thus the Trump is also a human reflection of that mystical vision of a universal vehicle for divinity.

In simple magical terminology, our minds are inspired by the goddess, sometimes called Minerva, and our human awareness becomes transformed and amplified as a vehicle of higher transcendent consciousness – divine inspiration.

The Charioteer

Within the Chariot we see a striking female figure with long flowing hair, dressed in an ornate warrior costume. She carries a long spear or staff with three thongs blowing aloft in the wind. This spear is a lesser form of the universal Distaff carried by the Great Goddess in the supernal Trump of Judgement. In The Chariot, her weapon may manifest as a spear if we encounter the goddess in her war-like aspect, or it may be a staff or chariot whip if she appears in her role as patroness of culture and civilization. In either form the spear represents power under control and direction of guiding consciousness; the Charioteer directs Ponies and Chariot, and if necessary she defends the Ford, the road and the City beyond.

Upon her left shoulder is a circular shield bearing the face of a solar god who first appeared in The Sun. He is Bel or Apollo, or the solar king and druid Bladud. He represents the victorious sun, the pagan sun kings and gods and heroes, who were guided by the goddess. They in turn are natural or ancient primal aspects of a higher solar and stellar archetype, the Son of Light who unifies all such images as one being.

The hair of the Charioteer is red, a colour sacred to the goddess; she wears a torc around her neck as an emblem of nobility and power. She is a variant of Minerva, drawn from a primal goddess known and worshipped throughout the Western world. The goddess is patroness of all arts, sciences, all cultural growth. She brings balance and harmony into the minds of mortals; but she also has a war-like role acting as defender or destroyer. In The Chariot she destroys corruption through the cleansing and enlightening power of intellect in service to spiritual consciousness. She controls the Ponies and Chariot, hence her role may be to challenge our preconceptions of intellectual or scientific superiority before she allows us to develop further. In this last role the Charioteer is a reflection of the basic power of taking or red dragon; we shall encounter increasingly more direct and powerful expressions of this power as we climb upon the Ascending Path.

The Distant Walled City

The Chariot has travelled down a winding road through a fertile landscape to meet us at the Ford. This is the Solar World which we first entered through the axis Trump of The Sun; but whereas we perceived it as wild before, now it is cultivated and holds a Walled City. The path of The Chariot is that of development and pattern building; the cultivated landscape and constructed City are alternative forms of the spiral path over the moor and the Hill or Tor with its mysterious Cavern. We shall encounter a third alternative form in The Lovers, where we return to a naturalistic landscape, lush with the powers of attraction and beauty, with a rising hill and a single tower or monolith.

A vast spectrum of Hermetic arts and sciences has built the path upon which The Chariot travels; it is illuminated by the universal consciousness, symbolized to us by the sun and the image of a Son of Light in spiritual dimensions. The City is the enduring timeless Holy City, in which the Grail may be found at certain times. It is a pattern and a metaphysical location in which spiritual and physical energies are fused perfectly. This fusion declares itself to us as beauty, order, pattern, balance and transcendent meaning or truth. The City holds within its walls the Mystery of Light, and the Charioteer is the first of three guardians or threshold images which we encounter, either before we gain the right of entry to the City, or progress beyond it to the unknown. These three are The Chariot, The Guardian and Death.

X GUARDIAN

THE GUARDIAN
(The Devil)

WORLD   The Solar World.
WHEEL   The Second Wheel, Justice (connects Justice and the First Wheel, Fortune).

BEINGS Angels, the solar archangel, ex-humans, innerworld masters or saints, inner adepts of magical arts.

CONSCIOUSNESS Catabolic and transcendent.

PARTNER TRUMPS Polar partner: The Empress. Higher harmonic: Death.

SPHERES AND PLANETS *Spheres:* The 8th and 5th Spheres, Honour and Severity. *Planets:* Mercury and Mars.

ATTRIBUTES Fusion of intellect or mind with the solar energies of catabolism or purification. A guarding and inspiring power. Protector of life forms (moving outwards) and destroyer of falsehood or illusion (moving inwards). Mysteries revealed through destruction of personal illusions.

GOD AND GODDESS FORMS Hermes and Mars. The ancient Lord of the Animals, protector and healer of lesser beings. Powers of breakdown embodied as male god forms.

KEY PHRASES Honourable severity/purifying fire/Lord of the Animals/ Guardian of the Mysteries/Keeper of the Threshold/Initiator.

MERLIN TEXTS *VM* Merlin as Lord of the Animals, riding upon a stag.

DIVINATORY MEANING Energies of purification, disillusion and rebalance. May indicate restriction for positive ends, as it often shows the inner or spiritual truth of a situation, according to position. Marks thresholds which it is dangerous to cross, or beyond which the individual overreaches his or her abilities. More rarely indicates magical or spiritual initiation within a given situation; will often provide the key to solutions for difficult problems or personal negative areas in life.

RELATED NUMBER CARDS Eights and Fives.

Eights: Danger, Expediency, Excitement, Skill.

Fives: Loss, Retribution, Sorrow, Conflict.

Origins of the Image

We now meet the most misrepresented and misunderstood image in tarot: The Guardian or 'Devil'. Within the Merlin Tarot this Trump is redefined according to early imagery and the role of Merlin in the *Vita Merlini*. The primal symbolism and function of this image relates to specific god forms, and their function in both nature and human consciousness. These roles and divine *personae* were well defined in both classical and Celtic mythology, but later corrupted by religious political manipulation and propaganda.

We have risen the Ascending Path, encountering The Fool, Magician and Chariot. Each Trump relates to thresholds of altered consciousness which occur as a questing individual reaches within and beyond conditioned life habits and modes of awareness; such modes are summarized in tarot as the cycle of the First Wheel or Fortune.

The Fool represents every man or woman at the beginning of the inner journey, yet also holds the life force, pure spirit. The Magician represents an increasing application of mental abilities towards inner and outer transformation; the journey is no longer undefined, but set into patterns that enable the traveller to proceed and develop. The Chariot reveals a higher cycle of The Magician; forces higher than intellect fill the awareness for the first time, and the mind becomes a vehicle for spiritual or transcendent consciousness.

Through these three stages of ascent, the sex or polarity of the image has changed with each threshold; The Fool is androgynous; The Magician is male; The Charioteer is female, with a further polarized definition of forces through the symbols of Chariot and Ponies. As we might expect, the next level of image is male: The Guardian.

The Guardian is one of the first Trumps beyond personality as we ascend, or one of the first Trumps leading into personality if we descend the spiralling paths of tarot. Initially he represents an enduring power of nature, but this is only his anthropomorphic appearance and his most obvious functional role. This initial concept helps to define The Guardian through many worlds or levels of energy; he is a solar image, but attuned to the catabolic or breaking-down aspect of central solar or divine power.

All energy has a relative polarization – positive and negative, masculine and feminine, creative and destructive. The solar centre, represented by our physical sun at the heart of the Solar World and by our physical hearts within our bodies, is the location of an original stillness. From this still centre all cycles of energy emerge, rotate, relate. The quest for this elusive yet omnipresent stillness, source or seed generates imagery and cycles of consciousness found in tarot and in mystical or magical religious traditions world-wide. Today a similar but materialistic quest occupies much of the work of quantum physics.

If we are to work with The Guardian in a truly liberating context, the concept of polarity must be examined repeatedly and meditated upon in depth. The Guardian is a male solar image of the catabolic or breaking energies of existence; he is an agency of change. He is paired with The Empress, for she is female solar power that builds, increases, benefits. We may visualize The Guardian and The Empress on either side of the divine Child shown in the Trump of The Sun; they are the Father and Mother or Keeper and Tender of all life forms in the Solar World. In this last role we find ancient nature gods and goddesses, closely related to the Trumps of Guardian and Empress.

The Guardian is a male lesser reflection of the most powerful catabolic image: Death or The Apple Woman. She is paired with The Emperor; they are the lord and lady of the trans-solar realms, bridging the Abyss between solar and stellar life. Ultimately we come to another pair, and another reversal of polarization, in The Hermit and Innocent (Hierophant), acting as primal male and female images at the beginning and end of relative time, space and energy. The Hermit 'ends time' while The Innocent 'begins time'. Both emerge from the unknown source of being, the first and last divinity or apparent cause of universal interaction.

We must keep this overview in mind if we are to transcend and dispose of absurd notions attached to the Trump of The Devil or Guardian from the Renaissance period to the present day. When this image appears in the *Vita* and other early legends in a simple primal form, there are no connotations of evil or damnation.

Who is The Guardian?
The much popularized, little understood Trump of The Devil is a perversion or shadow inversion of the true image of The Guardian. Such shadow inversions thrive upon ignorance and superstition; they only have power over us through suppression and propaganda, rather than as forces in their own right. In short, there is a stereotypical 'devil' only if we allow such absurdity to dominate our imagination; true evil is only too evident in our world as the result of human greed and folly.

The Guardian is generally represented as The Devil in tarot, with a variety of vicious, superstitious and ridiculous images, ranging from phallic demons to enchained humans, extinguishing light, and inverted pentacles – all the trash and trivia of popular occultism deriving from medieval and later propaganda. Yet this nonsense comes through deliberate manipulation of the imagery of a pagan nature god – the devil is a relatively modern device. Many writers have dealt with this transition, but we need to reassess it briefly in the context of the Merlin Tarot.

The falsification of this Trump was central to the political psychology of state religion; the true role of The Guardian is as a great liberator and protector against corruption and ravening evil. In a world of nuclear pollution and destruction, widespread famine and disease in the midst of accumulated food and medical expertise, we have more than sufficient true evil of our own making. The childish notion of a 'devil' who 'tempts' us in order to steal our souls is outdated and degrading. Evil is the individual and collective responsibility of humankind, and not of a devil or tribe of imps and demons upon which we may conveniently locate and blame our greed and cowardice.

On a more subtle level than mere propaganda, we can understand in retrospect that the political Church closed and monopolized a potent technique of spiritual liberation. Such monopoly is reflected in the corruption of tarot images, which are nothing more nor less than symbols within our collective imagination that define an enduring Story of Life. The technique referred to was inherited directly from pagan philosophy and metaphysics and psychology; it was eventually corrupted and turned into a system of mental, emotional and perhaps spiritual slavery.

The way to liberation was embodied in pagan cultures by god forms such as Pan, or the Celtic deity Cernunnos; these were variants in nature of solar gods such as Apollo or Bel, the Lord of Light. The nature gods represented this vast solar life force manifesting upon Earth; more precisely, they represented its catabolic or terrible, purifying aspect. Certain feminine images of fruitfulness represented the polar opposite, the Flower Maiden who married the Herdsman. There are many variants of this type of mythical pattern, and our summary here can only be brief and general.

It is worth noting that the standard Trump of The Devil is not entirely negative. Two humans are often shown with chains around their necks; traditionally, the chains are loose, for our imprisonment by a devil or false god is an illusion. This does not imply that there *is* a diabolical entity who deludes and imprisons us, but that there is a superstitious delusion concerning a false diabolical entity.

The standard Trump of The Devil seems to negatively reflect The Lovers, in which a man and woman are blessed by the divine Eros or an angel. This is very revealing, for orthodox Christian and other Middle Eastern religions struck deep at the roots of sexuality and equality, creating guilt-ridden monosexual cults that still have drastic effects upon our planet.

If we approach the Trump from an esoteric Christian viewpoint rather than a merely propagandist one, we find that The Guardian is more than just an old nature god. He is that little understood brother or aspect of Christ, the bringer of retribution against evil, the purifier of corruption. He may bring a sword or spear before he declares peace, he turns over the tables of corrupt dealers in the Temple, and commands herds of swine, the magical Underworld beasts, to do his bidding. Even the heavily edited orthodox gospels retained these elements within approved accounts of the life of Jesus.

In short we cannot expect divinity to be incomplete; it has forms that destroy as well as forms that create. But when consciousness and will operate within this polarized pattern, the destruction becomes purification towards a higher end.

The Guardian is not a tempter, but a releaser from temptation; he guards the threshold of consciousness by which the personality, even its highest modes of spiritual balance and harmony, may be dissolved. To grasp this concept, we need to examine the Trump image in detail.

Contents of the Image

The Guardian/Crow, Wolf and Deer/The Oak Tree/The Path and Tower

The Guardian
In many ways The Guardian is disturbing, even terrifying, but he is not evil in any way. If we fear The Guardian it is because he is able to see corruption within us; his is a power of purification, a fusion of Severity and Honour, symbolized by the planets Mars and Mercury. He appears to us as Lord of the Animals, the wild Herdsman and Hunter, master of death and change in the service of balance and health. He will sacrifice an individual for the collective good, but in return liberates the individual from the collective dream and illusion.

Merlin takes on the role of Lord of the Animals during his mad journey through the seasons; he leads a herd of stags and goats (in the *Vita*) in a paradoxical motif of sexual and natural love, the marriage of male and female. This old legend is a confused reworking of courtship between the Lord of the Animals, Horned God or Guardian, and the Lady of the Flowers, Empress or Maiden. Both images appear in legends and in tarot Trumps; in tarot, however, the harmonic nature of the Trumps gives opportunities for the images to be understood on levels other than those of nature or the health of the land.

The value of the allegory, in which Merlin becomes Lord of the Animals for a season, is that the power of The Guardian may be realized within any individual just as it was realized within Merlin as part of his journey.

The Guardian is naked, yet clad in an all-encompassing cloak of green leaves and red flame. If he wrapped himself completely in the cloak we would only see a natural form of greenery and horns garlanded with Winter flowers and berries. If he reversed his cloak we would see a being wrapped in Fire, the Elemental power of purification or destruction. In the Trump image, however, we see both sides of the cloak, and the balance between them which is, of course, the form of a human. In this sense the male Guardian stands for all humankind, just as his counterpart The Empress is a female image that stands, on one level, for all humankind. But both are archetypes of higher energies; their role is not limited to being expressions of human collective imagination or nature worship.

The Guardian wears a horn, hung upon a cord. This is the legendary hunting horn that summons hounds to the chase, or souls to the long wild ride across the sky to the Otherworld. In Celtic legend and religion he is Cernunnos, the Horned One, shown in inscriptions and images from pagan culture. His name and role were preserved in various place-names and legends well into modern times, and he is famous as Herne the Hunter in William Shakespeare. This figure is also known as Gwyn ap Nudd, the powerful mysterious Lord of the Underworld, from Welsh tradition. In *The*

Mabinogion and other tales, he appears as a great dark herdsman who rules all living creatures, which come and go at his command and bow down at his word to feed.[5]

Such nature symbolism helps us to relate to the image, but we must also understand and attempt to encounter its higher levels. In the Solar World this same symbolism applies not only to life forms, but to thought forms, to consciousness. The Guardian transforms and purifies our awareness; he is a power that cuts away illusion. This is summarized upon the Tree of Life as a fusion of Mars/Severity with Mercury/Honour; catabolic solar power purifying and balancing the mind.

Just as ancient legends and rituals initiate us into mysteries of nature, so The Guardian initiates us into the mysteries of the nature of the Solar World. Indeed, he exists to protect us from approaching levels of consciousness which might destroy us or drive us mad; his highest reflection, in a feminine archetype, is Death. In the old legends she would be his Mother, the Great Mother of death and change to whom we must all return, even the gods. If we have understood and passed The Guardian and his test, death can hold no fears. If we are not able to understand upon this higher level of awareness, we return to the nature cycle of life, death and rebirth.

It is no coincidence that a primal nature god of taking, culling, herding, hunting, purifying, is found inwardly as a great initiatory power. One of the most effective ways in which humans become aware of higher worlds or experience altered states of consciousness is through thought or rational intellect fused with deeper transformative energies. This process transcends individuality, for deeper energies burn away illusions of personality. Just as The Magician touched upon The Wheel of Fortune, the most basic level of interaction, so does The Guardian touch upon The Wheel of Justice, which is the power of adjustment in the Solar World. Beyond this Second Wheel, personality and apparent cause and effect are found to be illusions.

In a simpler sense, we could say that unless we change and discipline our energies (Severity and Honour) through will and effort, we eventually but inevitably become subject to natural laws of taking or change, sometimes in the form of painful destruction or disillusion. The Guardian is one form for such forces.

His cloak of leaves and flames is fastened by a golden torc, symbol of royalty and of eternity; the meaning of the torc is identical to that of the double dragon: it shows polarity in unity. From his head grow branching antlers; these show that his power runs through many worlds, from human, to animal, even to the plant world, represented by the Winter garland that he wears. The antlers also have a traditional meaning connected to the branches of the Tree of Life, or the ramifications and networks of energy throughout the universe.

If we pass the test given to us by The Guardian – and it may be a different test for each person according to his or her needs – we are able to take our sexual energies and redirect them at will. The branching antlers traditionally show this esoteric teaching, for they are male emblems of generative power and virility, yet they are joined to the head, the location of consciousness. Each point of The Guardian's antlers reaches to a path upon the Tree of Life; this is the ultimate direction of our own vital energies.

The Guardian greets us right at the threshold of the card; we may not pass beyond without his blessing. He holds his right hand palm outwards, bidding us stop and consider before we seek to travel onwards to the distant Tower. On his palm is a scar or tattoo, in the form of a lightning stroke or 'Z' sign. This is both a warning of what may come to pass and a key to the nature of energy in universal life. In his left hand he holds a polished natural wooden staff or spear; this same implement is carried by other Trump images; sometimes it is crude tree branch, sometimes a spindle, sometimes a spear. It represents true will, the Rod of ritual magical art, the staff of divinity that supports the soul in time of need, and the distaff of the Great Goddess who ravels and unravels the universe.

Crow, Wolf and Deer

As The Guardian is Lord of the Animals, all living creatures are under his guardianship. Of particular significance are the Wolf and Deer, savage and gentle beasts together under one power. For The Guardian is both swift and merciless, yet he protects the gentle, and helps the weak to become strong. Perched upon a rock is a Crow, totem bird of the Dark Goddess; she is the higher form or mother of The Guardian, so her bird travels with him. In a more specific sense, the Crow or raven represents chosen heroes, blessed by the Goddess. King Arthur and other sacred kings of Britain have the crow, raven or chough as their emblem, and in some legends are said to live on in bird form. The raven is one of the guardian birds of the Island of Britain, deriving from the god-king Bran.[5,6] This legend refers to the role of powerful souls in the history and development of a tribe, nation, or land; to become such a hero, one must first be given over utterly to the power and role of Guardian.

The Oak Tree

The oak is the tree of kingship; it has many associations with primal gods, fertility, lightning, endurance, power. It is the tree which traditionally is used to show regeneration after death, for one oak produces thousands of acorns. In the *Vita*, the oak is associated with wisdom and great age, a motif found in other Celtic legends. Merlin outlives even the oldest oak, and becomes therefore the wisest man. He becomes, in fact, The Hermit, which is the highest Trump on the Ascending Path, and the highest harmonic of The Guardian.

The Path and Tower
A narrow Path leads to a distant Tower; we shall encounter one aspect of this structure shortly in the Trump The Blasted Tower, though this is not its sole aspect. The Guardian prevents us from approaching this awesome stronghold; he protects us from the devastating power that it contains. The Tower is the last *artefact* or human building that we find on the Ascending Path; and it may be blasted away by divine lightning. If we learn the lessons of the Guardian, we learn to transform ourselves through harnessing the taking forces and balancing them within ourselves. If we enter the Tower with his blessing, we can delve into its mysteries of energy, which are the ever-present dragons hidden in the hill below. The Guardian teaches the higher Mysteries of the Element of Fire.

XI TOWER

THE BLASTED TOWER

WORLD   The Solar World.
WHEEL   The Second Wheel, Justice.
BEINGS   Fiery or catabolic angels, the solar archangel. Innerworld beings concerned with purification and destruction.
CONSCIOUSNESS   Transpersonal.

PARTNER TRUMPS   Polar partner: Strength. Higher harmonics: Death, The Hanged Man.
SPHERES AND PLANETS   *Spheres:* The 5th and 6th Spheres, Severity and Beauty. *Planets:* Mars and Sol.
ATTRIBUTES   The blasting or breaking force inherent in the solar system and throughout the universe. The impersonal power of taking. Catabolism or catalysis causing change. Breakdown of form by force. The lightning flash.
GOD AND GODDESS FORMS   Mars/Minerva and Apollo. Gods of sudden and inevitable force (the bolts of Apollo, the spear of Minerva). Images of divine retribution or purification. Represented in early Celtic legends by the destructive power of The Morrigan, goddess of battles.
KEY PHRASES   Beautiful severity/release from form/purification by fire/destroyer of corruption/spiritual lightning.
MERLIN TEXTS   *H* A major motif in which king Vortigern builds a tower, undermined by the red and white dragons which are hidden in a cavern beneath its foundations. Leads to the *Prophecies* uttered by the youthful Merlin.
DIVINATORY MEANING   Breakdown and collapse of unhealthy, false or unnaturally rigid conditions. Destruction of illusions or delusions. May indicate material and physical breakdown or loss, depending upon position and other cards in the pattern. Sudden and often unexpected collapse or destruction within the query situation.
RELATED NUMBER CARDS   Fives and Sixes.
  Fives: Loss, Retribution, Sorrow, Conflict.
  Sixes: Transition, Balance, Joy, Benefit.

Origins of the Image

The Blasted Tower plays an important role in the early life of Merlin, when he discovers his youthful gift of prophecy. The text of the *Prophecies* is introduced (in *The History of the Kings of Britain*) by a scene drawn from tradition, in which the evil usurper Vortigern seeks to sacrifice the child Merlin to powers of darkness. The king has been advised that he must slay a child born of no mortal father, and that the blood of this child will uphold his fortress, which continues to collapse due to unknown powers. The allegory develops with Merlin challenging the false magicians who advised sacrifice; in a cavern beneath the mountain, red and white dragons are released by the presence of Merlin and the king. It is the release of these dragons and their battle that causes Merlin to see far into the future, even to the end of time.

   The symbols of tower, false king, magical child, dragons and powers are all central to the Merlin tradition. They form the foundation of specific magical, mystical and visionary techniques within Western esoteric tradition. While these symbols are part of the Merlin legend of growth and transformation, they are also poetic statements of universal energies. Thus, they are both individual and universal or transcendent truths that may be directly experienced within human awareness; they have many forms or modes of expression.

Ranging from the Biblical legend of the Tower of Babel to the Renaissance tarot Trump 'The House of God' or Blasted Tower, the image has always been a major key in the practice of esoteric disciplines. In modern tarot interpretation there has been a tendency to move away from the propagandist significance of the downfall of the damned or the Gate of Hell which formed the popular meaning of the Trump. Curiously, this is an example of a Trump where the orthodox and esoteric meanings are not widely separated, the main point at issue being the theme of cult élitism and threatening aspects of related propaganda.

The context of The Tower is clearly stated in the Merlin texts, using the visual image and associated symbols at least two centuries before they appear as tarot during the Renaissance.[1,4] In this early use of the imagery, The Tower has a complex and subtle role, not preaching damnation, but certainly associated with retribution or rebalancing of corruption and stagnation.

As a background to the *Prophecies*, The Tower is the setting in which corruption and delusion are shattered forcibly and instantly. The devastation releases energies, leading to a spiritual realization and prevision reaching to the end of time – which means the end of our solar system in human terms. The power of the dragons beneath The Tower acts in two modes simultaneously: for Vortigern they bring doom; for the young Merlin they bring realization and inspiration. The power is identical in both cases, but the results are polar opposites.

The outer significance of the Trump is shown by the destruction of Vortigern and his tower; the inner significance by the youthful prophetic vision of Merlin. These two aspects of The Blasted Tower are inseparable, opposite sides of the same mirror. We also find the motif of a tower in the *Vita*, where it is again linked to dramatic downfall and death.

In his role as Lord of the Animals, Merlin flings a set of stag's horns with great force, and kills a man looking out of a high tower. His victim is a lover or potential new husband of Guendoloena, the wife whom Merlin abandoned when he was driven mad by grief. This motif was originally connected to nature, to the cycle of the Seasons.

Conflict between the Lord of the Animals, the Lady of Flowers, and a rival lover has become attached to Merlin in his role as primal magician of the land. It seems no mere story-telling ploy that the Lord of the Animals and The Tower are brought together in the *Vita*; in esoteric tradition they are connected in a very specific manner. The ancient god of guardianship over life and death is a natural or imaginative form for abstract potent forces symbolized by The Blasted Tower. Both images represent the catabolic effect of energy, destruction of form, or purification. While The Guardian mediates this process to both life forms and consciousness, The Tower reveals a higher order of the same energy upon a cosmic scale.

Contents of the Image

The Mountain Path/The Tower blasted by a Lightning Flash/The Falling Man and Woman

The Mountain Path

As we reach into higher Trumps in tarot, mountain climbing becomes a feature of the imagery. The higher dimensions of consciousness, which correspond metaphysically to spatial and temporal concepts, require effort, risk and training. There is no easy, cosy way to expand or alter our states of consciousness; but unlike the physical sport of mountain climbing, we are not forced to descend once we have gained higher regions.

The general imagery of landscapes in tarot is defined as follows:

1. Lowlands and plains: the Lunar and sub-Lunar World.
2. Highlands and hills: the Solar World.
3. Mountains and peaks: the Stellar World.

This analogy should not be taken too literally, for there are many variants, particularly where the Worlds are shown in their own right by the symbols of Moon, Sun and Stars, and other major key images. Furthermore, we often find a triple division within any one Trump, particularly when the threefold pattern indicates properties or modes of consciousness inherent within the image. The triple division or spiral should be seen as a hologram or symbolic constant, rather than a firm map or detailed system of subsections.

The Tower is built upon a mountain peak, but it is not one of the highest peaks revealed in tarot. It symbolizes the highest point at which personality may remain within consciousness; beyond this peak awareness becomes transhuman. This theme is dealt with repeatedly in higher Trumps, and has already been touched upon in our chapters on Justice and Judgement. The Tower is one of three Trumps (The Guardian, The Tower and Death) that relate to the 5th Sphere of Severity and the Wheel of Justice.

The legend of Vortigern and his tower is a medieval retelling of the enduring tale of human arrogance, greed and false assumption of power or the right to power. It is not vengeance that leads to the blasting of The

Tower, but natural forces of rebalance and destruction; such forces are the breaking or catabolic energies of the Solar World.

The power of breaking may be expressed through human or environmental agencies, within consciousness, or upon a truly solar or stellar scale. The Path in our image has both danger and wonder, beauty and terror. As we climb the Path, we approach not only The Tower, but the hidden cavern containing two dragons. They are universal powers of light and dark, or positive and negative relative states of energy; they appear throughout the Merlin Tarot in many expressions.

It is the hidden cave or Underworld that causes Vortigern's tower to collapse; the same power generates Merlin's prophetic vision and, towards the close of his life, blesses him with the miraculous appearance of a curative spring from deep within the Earth. In most tarot Trumps a Lightning Flash blasts The Tower, while the earlier motif of a Cavern is modified to resemble the Gate of Hell yawning wide to receive the falling humans.

Despite the steepness of the Path, there are further heights in tarot, and the highest peak is yet far removed, in the Trump of The Hermit. The Path before us is a continuation of that protected by The Guardian, who acts as a great initiator into transcendent reality. We may try to approach The Tower without his instruction, but only at the risk of being blasted by energies too great for us to bear as humans.

In the Great Story, we might have been given instruction into the secret nature of Fire by the Guardian; this dangerous knowledge would help us to bear the terrible vision and confrontation of the Lightning Flash and Blasted Tower.

The Tower blasted by a Lightning Flash

The Tower, like all Trumps, may be interpreted upon three levels, either in a Lunar, Solar or Stellar context. On the first level The Blasted Tower simply states dissolution of form by force, of matter into energy. Still upon this first level, but merging into the second, we may apply the Trump to individual consciousness; The Blasted Tower now becomes an emblem of personality. No matter how well founded upon the roots of life, the personality may be blasted by events, changes of perception, and many other forces.

The personality, assembled out of interactions of intellect and emotion, fuelled by imagination and rigidified by circumstances and habit, may easily become a tyrant. Such is one of the allegorical meanings of the *persona* of Vortigern. Just as he steals the crown of the kingdom, usurping it from the true ruler, and tries to sacrifice the innocent child Merlin, so may our false temporary personality destroy our true balance and rule within our own sphere of consciousness.

On a daily or outer basis, The Blasted Tower symbolizes shock, disappointment, unforeseen disaster. When we consider the symbol in relationship to the Wheel of Justice rather than the Wheel of Fortune, it represents the changes of a lifetime, or of many lifetimes. The destructive energies of The Blasted Tower, the Lightning Flash of the inner and outer power of the sun, the arrows of Apollo, the sword of adjustment, all act rapidly. Whatever resists or persists beyond its natural cycle of change runs the risk of a sudden extermination. This destruction is the direct action of higher energies which might normally work through a diffuse cycle of interaction.

In esoteric or magical training, the student is taught to flow with natural cycles, to allow the rhythm of change and to employ it as an aid, rather than to fight against it. Beyond this first level, represented by Merlin's seasonal adventures, is a second level in which the initiate encounters such energies directly in their own dimensions; ultimately, we are taught to use such powers for rapid and deep transformation. Thus, The Blasted Tower may be sought intentionally; The Guardian teaches us methods whereby this initiatory experience may be survived successfully.

In the outer world we suffer lightning, earthquake, explosion. In the inner worlds we experience sudden devastating changes in our accustomed patterns of awareness. During our lifetime we are exposed to an interaction, a delicate balance of creative and destructive forces both inwardly and outwardly; when this balance finally tips in one direction beyond recovery, we die. But in the realms of consciousness it is possible to experience extremes of energy through imagination and will rather than be subjected to them unconsciously or unwillingly. This is the key to true inner development and the transformation of consciousness and entity.

The Lightning Flash represents a universal power of destruction, mediated through the solar centre. In a physical sense it is the undeniable blasting power of the physical sun, but as always in metaphysical traditions, this outer force is merely the embodiment of an inner truth. The Lightning appears in individual life when deep spiritual impulses cut across the conditioned, repressive, outer habits and destroy them.

The blast is impersonal, for it transcends mere personality, and renders form (even thought or imaginative forms) down into primal force. Unless we can relate to this phenomenon on a truly transpersonal level, beyond our self-limits, we experience it as an exterior agency of destruction; we are hurled from our false tower of usurped authority and icy self-delusion.

The Lightning may, therefore, be 'exterior' or 'interior'; this is the secret and Mystery of The Blasted Tower. The area immediately around the Tower is covered in ice and snow; this represents the frozen personality which has rigidified its Elemental powers. But on a higher level, it represents any formalized state that requires dissolution; many highly developed mystics, saints or masters may be struck by the Lightning; some seek it willingly through faith or through understanding.

The Falling Man and Woman

In our context of Merlin legends, the falling couple are Vortigern and his daughter. The usurping king snatches at his lost crown even as he falls; his vain daughter, rumoured to be his incestuous lover, still reaches for her mirror of self-delusion. These figures represent all men and women equally; the fall is not a fall from grace or a descent into hell, but a fall from high arrogance and overreaching imbalance.

In the orthodox development of tarot, these figures are damned through divine retribution; they are the races of mankind plummeting from the folly of the Tower of Babel, plunging into darkness, degradation and separation from God. In a more esoteric and Western Hermetic interpretation, they are individual entities being broken apart; coagulated energies of a lifetime are separated from the true essence of spirit by a flash of pure lightning; they then polarize in new directions.

This concept was developed widely in alchemy, where a sudden purging fire might separate the gross from the subtle bodies of the Great Work. In perennial metaphysics, we are taught that the spirit is reborn in a new expression or body, while the temporary personality or phantom is dissolved and recycled. The converse of this cyclical pattern is initiation or inner development, in which the personality is absorbed into our spiritual reality and ceases to exist of its own accord during the physical lifetime.

The recycling of energy occurs on the path of Justice or Adjustment, the highest Wheel, whereby individuals are ultimately returned to birth in the outer world. This tradition of reincarnation runs through religious and mystical teaching world-wide, and was only abandoned by political Christianity at a relatively late date in favour of more suppressive dogma.

The obvious actions of physical death and birth are extreme forms of transformation that may happen during outer life; in mystical and magical arts 'living death' and inner rebirth are crucial stages of development. Without such changes we are in danger of become passive victims of the Wheels, forgetting between each incarnation; alternatively, we may stagnate as usurpers or corrupters of our own inherent life energies, tyrants of self-image, such as Vortigern became before his fall. This last state is particularly tempting to so-called strong personalities, or to partly developed meditators and magicians, who attempt to draw inner power to themselves for self-aggrandizement. Such persons fear the blast of Lightning more than those who are unaware, and consequently suffer a greater loss when their illusions are shattered.

The Sun and Mars

The Blasted Tower is located upon the simple Tree of Life between the Sun and Mars, or the 6th and 5th Spheres, Beauty and Severity. Poetically, it is a severely beautiful realization of truth. In early religions this truth was represented by the deities of destruction, the bolts of Apollo, the lightning of Belenos, the spear of Minerva or Athena. When we move further back in human culture, we find that destructive and purifying deities are generally feminine; in simple magical terms, they draw back to themselves all forms that have been born into lower worlds, and render them down into primal energy.

It is at this level of consciousness that discipline and superficially disturbing concepts and images become vitally important for spiritual growth. We cannot grow without the corresponding elimination and purification, otherwise we become corrupt and poisoned. This is more significant on inner levels than it is in terms of bodily health, which reflects inner conditions.

The Lightning destroys in order to rebalance. The Trump is paired with that of Strength, which is the positive anabolic building energy of the sun, or Beauty and Mercy, the 6th and 4th Spheres. Only those of us who have failed to grasp the inner qualities and nature of life are afraid to meet the higher Trumps. The same Lighting Flash that brings ruin also brings liberation; it is, of its own inherent nature, the flash of spiritual illumination that transforms utterly and irrevocably.

Rotation of Trumps

It is at this stage on the Ascending Path that we can examine briefly one of the main teaching concepts associated with the psychology and metaphysics of the Merlin Tarot. One of the most valuable ways of working with Trumps in meditation is through rotation.

We have covered this concept repeatedly in context of the Three Wheels (Fortune, Justice and Judgement), and it may be used to make or draw circular or spiralling maps as aids to development of consciousness through new modes and regions. Some of the most important Trumps for individual work are those that rotate around the 6th Sphere, or the Sun, with direct contact to the axis or spiritual centre of Harmony.

Around this spiritual centre of balance, images revolve like rays of the sun, emerging from a radiant source and polarizing towards defined extremes symbolized by the various Spheres. The 6th Sphere is the only locus upon the Tree of Life connected to all others by direct paths; the sole exception is the Kingdom or outer world of the 10th Sphere, where the connection is mediated through Foundation of the Moon, or 9th Sphere. These connectives are always shown upon the Tree of Life, and appear in the cosmology of the *Vita Merlini*, which runs from heaven to Earth via the Solar and Lunar Worlds.

Having examined the axis or Spindle Trumps of Moon, Sun and Star, and the threshold Trumps or Three Wheels of Fortune, Justice and

Judgement, we have risen to an area upon the Tree of Life where we encounter the central rotation. In order of ascent and descent the cycle of Trumps is as follows:
The Sun.
The Chariot.
The Blasted Tower.
The Hanged Man.
The Star.
Temperance.
Strength.
The Lovers.
The Sun.

The axis Trumps are The Sun and Star, for they are the Middle Pillar or Spindle of the Worlds. If we begin an ascending and descending cycle as described, the Trumps merge harmonically into one another in terms of meaning and energy, passing through the midpoint or axis, emerging as polar opposites, and still merging together in the descending cycle. The direction of movement is for our benefit in practical work, and not necessarily a rigid law. We could just as easily pass around the circle in the opposite direction.

In the ascending part of the cycle, we rotate away from the cosmic Trump of The Sun towards The Chariot. This is the first modulation towards Severity or the powers of taking. It merges Beauty and Honour, the 6th and 8th Spheres. In this Trump, Minerva, the Charioteer, is the goddess of pure mind, health, control, cultural development, and purifying or disciplinary skills. She teaches both arts and sciences to humankind.

A further rotation brings us to The Blasted Tower, where solar catabolic power is encountered upon a higher level. Here are the cosmic forces of instantaneous destruction, symbolized by the Lightning Flash.

The last ascending rotation brings us to The Hanged Man, representing energy beyond time, and crossing the Abyss of energy, time and space. The Hanged Man is the highest level or harmonic of purifying and redeeming energy, working on both a human and universal level.

Then, from the axis Trump of The Star, we begin the balancing descending cycle, in which each catabolic Trump has an anabolic counterpart. These are examined individually in our later chapters. A simple diagram is often used in meditational instruction to help us grasp this radial concept. We may also lay out the Trumps listed above in a circle, following the order of rotation.

XII DEATH

DEATH
(The Apple Woman)

WORLD   The Stellar World.
WHEEL   The Third Wheel, Judgement (links the Second Wheel, Justice, and Judgement).

BEINGS Archangels, transhuman beings.

CONSCIOUSNESS Transhuman, supernal. Corresponds to both super-consciousness and collective or ancestral consciousness on its most comprehensive level.

PARTNER TRUMPS Polar partner: The Emperor (see also Figure 4).

SPHERES AND PLANETS *Spheres:* The 3rd and 5th Spheres, Understanding and Severity. *Planets:* Saturn and Mars.

ATTRIBUTES A feminine universal power of catabolic or inward-moving effect. Solar destructive and purifying energy fused with profound understanding. The ultimate dissolution of form and pattern, drawing energy back across the Abyss.

GOD AND GODDESS FORMS Mars/Minerva and the Great Mother. Death is a feminine figure, and all ancient goddesses of death, taking, dissolution and transhuman or total understanding partake of this image.

KEY PHRASES A severe understanding/The Apple Woman/ultimate transformation/purifying understanding/The Sun at Midnight/return to the Mother/comprehensive change.

MERLIN TEXTS *PVM* Connections with the goddess Ariadne who unravels the universe; *VM* The Apple Woman who seeks to kill or madden Merlin (a motif from pagan Celtic mythology).

DIVINATORY MEANING Initially means a change for the better. Implies that after dissolution and death comes new life. Often indicates total change and reorientation within the query situation. Can also indicate, by position and other defining cards, possible avenues of change and new beginnings. On a higher level of understanding, frequently indicates changes which arise from deep inner or spiritual drives, causing outer form or patterns in the personal life to dissolve. May therefore indicate areas of personal tension and inner conflict that can be resolved only by true change.

RELATED NUMBER CARDS Threes and Fives.

Threes: Suffering, Intention, Affection, Promise.

Fives: Loss, Retribution, Sorrow, Conflict.

Origins of the Image

The original image for Death is that of a taking or destroying goddess; in Celtic tradition, including our source text the *Vita Merlini*, she is often described as a mysterious woman who gives magical fruit. We have called her, therefore, The Apple Woman, and will refer to the Trump as Death or The Apple Woman equally.

The Apple Woman and two related feminine archetypes (a goddess of the land of Britain, and the Weaver or Ariadne) are described in detail in the *Vita* and *Prophecies*, but such images do not originate with our twelfth-century texts. The primal Goddess of ancient cultures was ruler of life and death, dissolution, transformation, purification and inspiration. Images of this archetype were of major importance in religion, magic and in mystical initiations. This role is preserved today in esoteric traditions in both East and West. Before examining the Trump in detail, we need to consider briefly the goddess images that have contributed to it.

The Goddess in *The Prophecies of Merlin*

In the *Prophecies* we meet with a Goddess of the Land; she transforms corruption and disease by taking them within herself, drinking of the springs of death and desire. She transforms from a maiden into a mature mother and summons ancestral spirits by walking across the land, holding the forests of the North in one hand and the towers of the South in the other; wherever she stands, flames are kindled around her feet. This powerful image is that of the ancient Goddess of Sovereignty, an archetype better known from Irish tradition. The details are precise and powerful, and so typical of enduring ancient religion and metaphysics that we may assume that they came intact from a traditional source.[1,6]

The Goddess of the Land represents feminine divine and natural power, but a second image appears at the close of the *Prophecies* in which we meet a stellar or higher form. This cosmic goddess is called Ariadne, the Weaver. In an apocalyptic vision, which forms the basis for our Trump Judgement, she is described as unravelling the solar system and sphere of the Zodiac. She de-creates Elemental reality or relativity, and withdraws behind a barrier or veil. This vision of dissolution is balanced by an extended detailed Creation Vision in the *Vita Merlini*.

The goddess controls death and dissolution simply because she is the giver of life; who but the creatrix may truly destroy and withdraw created life? This concept is central to mystical perception; in a lesser form it is crucial to human maturity and life adaptation. Through such understanding we learn to rise above cycles of giving and taking, and realize that life is more than a confusion of personal disasters or successes.

The Goddess in the *Vita Merlini*

We eventually learn, in the *Vita*, that a mysterious woman, once a lover of Merlin, laid out poisoned apples to entrap him. These apples, laid out under a tree upon a pleasant green, are eaten by Merlin's boon companions; they are either killed or driven insane.

The tale is rationalized and, like many major motifs, given almost as an aside to the main narrative; if it were the only tale of this sort we might be tempted to dismiss it, but tradition repeats the apple theme in other sources, sometimes in greater detail. The best example is that of Thomas Rhymer, a thirteenth-century bard and seer, and a proven historical character. Thomas partook of the love of the Queen of Elfland or Fairyland, and was carried off by her upon her white horse. During a visionary Underworld journey he saw a tree laden with magical apples. This fruit was under the control of the queen, who told Thomas that it could bring death or madness, and that he was not to touch it or eat of it.

The Fairy Queen sustained Thomas with bread and wine (which is, of course, the fruit of the land transformed) and he served her for seven years in the Underworld. He was blessed with the gift of prophecy, the tongue that cannot lie, and a cloak of woven cloth and green shoes. These were gifts marking both the blessing of the Goddess of the Land, and the prophetic vision that comes from such blessings. The theme is simple but profound: a feminine power enables higher modes of consciousness that transcend individuality; she does so by destruction of lower forms and recreation of these forms upon a higher level. [8, 11]

The similarities between this legend, the Apple Woman motif, and the general background to Merlin are considerable. Shared elements include: initiation under a tree/apples/further initiation underground/a female figure of great power/prophetic vision/relationship with the land. The overall legend is derived from a core tradition at the foundation of Celtic pagan and Celtic Christian belief; it takes many variant forms, but always refers to a specific original pattern.

The *Vita* also includes a number of other goddess images or *personae* who seem to embody the qualities of specific goddesses; these are dealt with in detail in our discussion of other Trumps, but include the following:
GANIEDA: sister of Merlin, embodies the archetype of Minerva.
GUENDOLOENA: wife of Merlin, embodies the archetype of Venus/ Flower Maiden.
MORGEN: archetypical priestess and goddess of hidden life force.

The Female Image of Death
The ancient Goddess, the Dark Mother who draws all life to herself, is the universal taking power in anthropomorphic form. Such forms are not products of ignorance or superstition; they are often combined with advanced metaphysics and philosophy. In magical and mystical training it is well known that such images *work* even though we may intellectually state that the energies behind the image transcend form or goddess shape.

The Goddess of Death and Change was eventually replaced in popular imagery by the medieval figure of a skeleton and scythe. The Goddess did not disappear, but endured in many tales, songs and folk rituals, and in the loose disguise of certain saints and aspects of the Virgin. The change was complex and gradual, and images such as the powerful Fairy Queen remained in collective tradition for many centuries.

The Goddess, however, was deliberately removed from the political Roman Church, thus enabling a long programme of suppressive conditioning connected to death, sin and damnation. Once the symbols and images had been corrupted, they enslaved rather than liberated. It is most significant that the skeleton is a male image, derived to a certain extent, but by no means exclusively, from the classical Saturn.

Certain attributes in the Trump of Death, however, may retain their original connection to the Goddess. These include reaping and the sickle (which was an implement of the ancient goddesses long before it was adapted to male jealous use) and the important concept of the dance. We might add timelessness and the obvious fact of physical death to the shared attributes.

The Renaissance image of a skeleton dancing and reaping heads with a long scythe can limit the Trump to a meaning of physical death, tied to suppressive religious notions of judgement, sin and resurrection. Interestingly, the Trumps of Death and Judgement belong together in orthodox tarot just as their feminine and earlier images belong together in esoteric tradition. The deep tradition underpins both sets of images, and endures despite debilitating and corrupting changes of gender and symbolic attributes.

The major difference, apart from those obvious changes described above, is that the ancient Goddess of Death and Change offers well-defined gifts of transformation and insight; these seldom appear in regular tarot Trumps and interpretations of Death.

Contents of the Image

The Landscape lit by a midwinter Sun/The Apple Tree/The Apple Woman/The Sickle/The Spider

The Landscape
When we look at the position of Death upon the Tree of Life, we find that it crosses the Abyss between Understanding and Severity. This metaphysical condition, bridging the abyss of time, space and energy, the rift between the created universe and supernal being, may only be represented by analogy. No picture image can directly show the nature of this metaphysical reality.

The Landscape, therefore, is timeless; there is no cycle of the Seasons in the Land of Death. The Sun stands still in the sky; it is the midwinter Sun at midnight, seen by initiates into the Mysteries as they died and were reborn while still in the physical body. The severity and purity of the Goddess generates a timeless consciousness, in which perfect under-standing bridges all relative conditions of space and energy.

Trumps that bridge and rise above the Abyss (Death, The Hanged Man, The Star, Temperance, The Emperor) reverse our superficial concepts of time and space. We could say that the Trump of Death is 'reversed', for we do not enter through the path that has carried us forward in our initial ascent; directions are reversed in Death. The low hills upon the horizon are not a further metaphysical realm or inner world, they are the boundary of the created universe that we have left behind. The still Sun only begins to move when we have crossed those low hills back into the outer world.

This paradox is found again in The Hanged Man, who is literally upside-down, suspended across the Abyss.

The Apple Tree

In the middle ground we see an ancient Apple Tree, before which the figure of Death or the Goddess stands. The Tree is of great age yet bears tiny young leaves and blossoms; it is eternally about to flower, timeless at the exact boundary of Winter and Spring. In the magical Circle or Wheel, this Tree grows at the point of transition, in the North East, where consciousness and the Seasons or Elements rotate from the closing of one cycle to the beginning of another. This is traditionally the location of ancestral spirits in primal magical arts, and the sacred entrance point into the Circle for powerful innerworld contacts, teachers or transhuman consciousness.

The Apple Tree is one of the simplest expressions of the Tree of Life; it is the Otherworld or Underworld Tree that reveals eternal potential, the fusion of ending and beginning in one paradoxical form.

Apples lie upon the ground beneath the Tree; these are the legendary apples of the Hesperides, or of Avalon, or the mystical fruit perceived by both Merlin and Thomas Rhymer. If humans take up this fruit and eat, they may be destroyed, poisoned, driven mad. The apples are the fruit of raw untransformed power. No mortal may consume the fruit of divinity safely; we may not aspire to higher consciousness without losing our humanity.

The quest for these apples occupies a number of mythological themes. Sometimes a hero (inspired by Athena or Minerva) must defeat or trick a dragon to approach the tree; when he finally gains the fruit and presents it to the goddess, she ultimately returns it to its original place. The story is not one of pointless effort, for it is the action of seeking, finding and delivering the fruit correctly that is important. The goddess, in other words, sets the entire scene to transform and develop humanity through her chosen hero. This concept appears in the legend of Thomas Rhymer, who volunteers to pick the magical apples for the Fairy Queen, who recognizes his gallantry by giving him bread and wine. The bold companions of Merlin, in the *Vita*, snatch at the apples and eat them greedily; thus they are driven mad and howling like wild animals.

The secret of the apples, the fruit of the Tree of Life, is learned through meditation upon and visualization of Death, the Apple Woman, the Fairy

Queen. If we look closely we see that one of the apples has a worm in it, for the cycle of energy runs through all created worlds, and death is as true for stars as it is for humans. Only the Tree and timeless Land of Death remain unchanged, and these endure until the Goddess unweaves creation at her moment of Judgement.

The Apple Woman or Goddess
The dark mysterious woman of the Trump is the archetype of all goddesses of taking; she is both beautiful and terrible. She is the power of death in life and life in death, creatrix and destroyer of relative form. In her hands she bears the fruit of perpetual life and rebirth, and the razor Sickle that cuts the thread of continuity. She is the terrible understanding that all existence, from wheeling stars to the merest atom is subject to change and death. She is the destroyer of hope and giver of hope; only through her effect upon our understanding do we approach the truth behind manifest relative creation.

The Apple Woman, at one with the land in which she dwells, is timeless. Both young and ancient, loving and killing, she is the Goddess of Death and Change.

The origin of the medieval 'Dance of Death', which became a grotesque, even ridiculous obsession, is the dance of the Lady or Weaver as she moves the threads of creation and destruction. Patterns retained in ritual dance speak directly to our deepest understanding through physical movement. Such ritual practices were repeatedly banned by orthodox religion, as they are guaranteed methods of altering consciousness. The result of this vicious suppression, combined with other manipulations of guilt, sin and perversion of imagination, was the inverted image of the Dance of Death, which contributed to the well-attested outbreaks of Tarantism or compulsive dancing in medieval times.

It is perhaps significant that Tarantism was said to come from the bite of the tarantula spider, when it was quite obviously not so. The image of a spider, however, is always connected to the weaving and dancing Goddess; furthermore the root word *tara* or similar forms is linked to concepts of circularity. There is an obscure word-play or relationship between *rota*, a wheel, and *tarot*, a cycle of images defining the Wheels of the universe. A Celtic god, Taranis, was Lord of the Wheel, as was the goddess Arianrhod (from *rota*) whose name seems related to that of Ariadne the spider or weaver. A number of other symbolic and broadly linguistic connectives may be woven around the words *tara*, *tarot* and *rota*.

The Sickle
The small Sickle carried by The Apple Woman is the origin of that long scythe wielded in later images by the 'grim reaper'. The lopped heads that appear in many tarot Trumps of Death are the fallen fruit of the Tree of

Life, altered into a negative grisly parallel connected to religious dogma. The classical god forms of Saturn and Chronos come from the Timeless Land, the golden realm of eternity; the change of sexual polarity renders a beautiful transcendent image into an ugly suppressive one. Eventually, we find that castration motif which so delights materialist psychologists, unable to see beyond their own organ obsessions.

The Apple Woman separates spirit and body with her razor Sickle, bringing consciousness to birth in her supernal or transcendent reality. She cuts away all unnecessary weavings of energy, and preserves only the seed of spirit in her vessel of understanding. In a simple alchemical analogy we might say that the Fire or Lightning of The Blasted Tower has shattered the redundant outer form or shell, releasing the ether or spirit which ascends to the Mother above the Abyss. She then cuts the spirit free of its deepest webs of energy, ready for birth. It is significant that this Trump preserves its true meaning in popular fortune-telling, where it is read as 'a change for the better'.

The Spider

The Spider weaves her web from Tree branch to roots; from Above to Below. This spiritual animal and sub-symbol, like all lesser elements in Trumps, is of major importance. She reveals the web that unites all worlds; she is the creature of the Goddess who weaves and unweaves. The spider is sometimes said to be the thirteenth Sign of the Zodiac, sitting at the centre of her web spun to sustain the pattern of the other twelve.

The web is the universe, but also any individual life form; the Spider has such sensitivity of touch that she is aware of all vibrations along her web. In an apocryphal legend, the spider wove a web to hide the infant Jesus from Herod's soldiers. We are told in folklore that this is why the garden spider (in Europe) has a cross pattern upon her back. This curious theme, long rejected by the orthodox Church, seems to reach back into a pagan legend of the Goddess and her Son of Light. In mystical terms the web of creation conceals the unknown redeemer, acting as a veil before the light of divinity or the power of being.

Another important aspect of the legend is that the infant Jesus was hidden by the spider to prevent his being carried away or killed by the tyrant king; in many legends of the Child, he or she is stolen away or lost. The spider thus enabled Jesus to grow to maturity and fulfil his destiny and divine role; she merges time and space with her web, and weaves interactions full of surprise and wonder.

Change and Death

During one lifetime, response to the power represented by Death will change. The power is both universal and individual, and in expanded consciousness greater and lesser levels work directly upon and within one another; ultimately, they fuse as one and all relative differences cease. Some of this changing response is described in the *Vita* in allegorical terms relating to Merlin's life and adventures.

The Apple Woman loves Merlin as young man, but he rejects her. She tries to poison the mature Merlin, but her fruit brings madness to his companions. The tale may be a confused remnant of an instructional mythic pattern showing that only through true innocence and perfect intent may humankind approach the Goddess. There is also some implication of the principle of reversal or reflection: the brash young Merlin rejects the Goddess (he is not ready for higher consciousness), and his rejection eventually leads to his madness through grief and suffering. The mature Merlin comes close to death through a possible misuse of Goddess power or the apples, but escapes when his greedy companions snatch the fruit and are driven mad. Ultimately, however, he cannot avoid his period of madness and reversion to nature.

The overall theme, found in various traditional sources, suggests a practical method of gaining prophetic insight. It seems likely that this technique was practised by seers, bards, druids and magicians; it is very different from the generalized techniques available today, which seem divorced from any enduring inner tradition.

Perhaps Merlin's sub-story of The Apple Woman simply means that adulthood is our most deluded period of life. We reject understanding and substitute self-image, habit, even dogma, in our convoluted attempts at survival; the hostility we experience is not that of the Goddess, but our own hostility reflected upon us. Reject love, risk poisoned apples – such fruits are deadly to the greedy or the unprepared. But if we accept the fruit or any of its many transformations (such as bread and wine) from the Goddess, she blesses us with gifts of timeless understanding. These gifts may appear in the outer world as prophecy, attuning to the land; death itself is a timeless moment of understanding when all relative interactions cease. Ultimately, we are the fruit.

XIII HANGED MAN

THE HANGED MAN
(The Threefold Death)

WORLD The Stellar World (crossing the Abyss into the Solar World).
WHEEL The Third Wheel, Judgement, crossing the Second Wheel,
Justice.

BEINGS   Saviours or redeemers, Sons of Light. Archangels, the solar archangel. Sacrificed kings and heroes. Innerworld communicators. The Order of Melchizadek or the Ancestral Kings.

CONSCIOUSNESS   Transpersonal.

PARTNER TRUMPS   Polar partner: Temperance. Relates also to The Fool as a Master Trump.

SPHERES AND PLANETS   *Spheres:* The 3rd and 6th Spheres, Understanding and Beauty. *Planets:* Saturn and Sol.

ATTRIBUTES   The fusion of the Great Mother and the Son of Light. The paradox of sacrifice and the inversion of time, space and energy. Redemption and transformation through understanding. Inversion of all customary modes of awareness. Universal comprehension and knowledge centred upon one individual entity.

GOD AND GODDESS FORMS   Saturn and Apollo. The Great Mother and her Son. All sacrificed gods, kings and heroes. Refers to Christ in orthodox Western religion, but encompasses a universal tradition embodied in various saviours.

KEY PHRASES   Beautiful understanding/universal harmony/sacrifice in full knowledge/keystone of the Arch of Heaven.

MERLIN TEXTS   *VM* The Threefold Death.

DIVINATORY MEANING   Sacrifice of outer form or habits or situation for a non-personal or transpersonal end. Situations or instants of paradox, when a new level of understanding is gained. On a higher level, the card represents initiation into the Mysteries of Light. Often indicates outer situations of apparent loss or difficulty which lead in time to growth and increased awareness that transcends personality.

RELATED NUMBER CARDS   Threes and Sixes.

Threes: Suffering, Intention, Affection, Effort.

Sixes: Transition, Balance, Joy, Benefit.

Origins of the Image

The Hanged Man is one of a small number of Trumps that have a special relationship to humankind; it relates both to our role and our understanding within the Three Worlds. In a religious sense, The Hanged Man symbolizes a unique bridge between divinity and humanity; in a magical or psychological sense, it shows practical means of relating human consciousness to transhuman or super-consciousness.

The Hanged Man appears in the *Vita* during a crucial scene in which a number of ritual patterns and concepts of magical and mystical tradition are embodied. This scene is one of the earliest literary sources of a motif known as the Threefold Death. The Threefold Death, which is widely known in Celtic legends, was at one time directly related to Merlin. In

Scottish variants of Merlin legends, a mad prophet suffers the triple death after predicting his own fate to St Kentigern. In the *Vita*, however, this motif is centred upon a youth, with Merlin's powers of prophecy being tested in respect of the youth's manner of dying.

Before examining the Trump in detail, we should briefly summarize the Threefold Death as described in the *Vita*, for this source material has important connections to both Christian and pagan mythology. It is also one of the perennial themes within religion, the magical arts, metaphysics, and mystical direct experience of altered consciousness world-wide.

The Prophecy of the Threefold Death

> To test Merlin's power of prevision, the king and queen sit in judgement over a deliberately contrived situation in which Merlin has to predict accurately. A youth is brought before them, and Merlin predicts that he will die by falling from a high rock. The same youth is presented a second time, in different clothes and with his long hair cut short. Merlin predicts that this youth will die a violent death by hanging from a tree. Finally the same youth appears disguised as a girl; girl or not, says Merlin, she will die by drowning in the river. Merlin is judged to be mad and inaccurate in his prevision; he is released from the court and city where the king has kept him enchained, and allowed to return to his beloved wildwood. Years pass and the youth grows into a young man. While out hunting he pursues a stag, following his hounds in a great fever of excitement, to the top of a high mountain. He falls from his horse over the edge of a precipice, only to catch his foot in a tree branch as he falls; he ends by hanging upside-down with his head immersed in the river below. Thus is the prophecy of the Threefold Death fulfilled, for the young man dies by hanging, falling and drowning.

We can see connections between this tale, summarized from the *Vita*, and the tarot Trumps of The Fool and The Hanged Man. Although we examine The Fool as a separate Trump in another chapter, we may draw together some of the connecting strands of symbolism now that we have ascended as far as The Hanged Man.

The Youth of Three Disguises described above is typical of ritual or folk drama; such dramas are usually part of ceremonies enacted at certain times of the year, linked to the cycle of the Seasons and the rising and setting of certain stars, planets or other signs. Originally they were part of formal religion, inseparable from pagan philosophy and metaphysics; today, they are curious but powerful remnants from a collective tradition that has endured for many centuries.

The central character in such ceremonies changes sex or clothing, a man pretending to be a woman. He may also die and be resurrected, and in some variants the ritual involves a dance in which geometric patterns are woven with footwork, positions, swords or sticks. This is the merest summary of such a traditional ceremony, and there are many variant forms according to country, locality, and presence or lack of religious influence from Christianity.

In the broadest symbolic sense this fool or changing person stands for all humankind, a man/woman that transcends and underpins sexuality and personality. He is, obviously, The Fool of tarot Trumps, an innocent dressed in woman's clothing undertaking a mad journey of no return.

If we follow the connections made so clearly in the *Vita*, there is no doubt whatsoever that The Fool eventually becomes The Hanged Man; this is firmly described without any ambiguity. We find that Merlin has the power to predict the Threefold Death accurately, though in other tales it is the prophet himself who is killed in a manner reserved for sacred kings or special persons. This reminds us immediately of another Merlin legend which features a tarot Trump: that of The Tower. The evil king Vortigern tries to sacrifice the child Merlin to bolster up his tower and his kingship with blood of an innocent. This tale demonstrates unhallowed, unlawful use of sacrifice. The Threefold Death, however, refers to an enduring Celtic tradition associated with sacrificial kings.

The Relationship between The Fool and The Hanged Man
Before moving on to the contents of the Trump, we should summarize concepts inherent in The Hanged Man and in his relationship to The Fool.

1. The Fool changes role or gender and traditionally stands for all humankind.
2. The Fool later becomes The Hanged Man, through the Threefold Death accurately predicted by Merlin.
3. The Hanged Man dies by falling, hanging and drowning, or similar triple means of death in other variants of the motif.
4. In religious and mystical tradition both Fool and Hanged Man represent sacrifices or procedures of sacrifice in which one individual stands for all humankind. The Fool is unrealized, unaware potential, but The Hanged Man transcends humanity through profound understanding, and merges with divinity.
5. The Hanged Man is resurrected. This is not overtly developed in the Merlin texts, though the *Vita* emphasizes very strongly and repeatedly that Merlin himself undergoes an inner resurrection and curative freedom from madness, as the result of mysterious powers from beneath the Earth issuing as a miraculous Spring. In the *Prophecies* we find similar regeneration and resurrection motifs connected to a Goddess of

the Land, and to Merlin's apocalyptic vision, which is the origin of our Trump Judgement.

Contents of the Image

The River/The Leaping Salmon/Mountains, Middle Ground and Spiritual Animals/The Hawthorn Tree/Bow and Arrows/The Hanged Man

The River

The Hanged Man is a Trump of inversion, though not in any negative or devolved sense. The image crosses the Abyss of time and space, connecting our central sun or solar system to the greater worlds of galaxies and the universe. In a human context, The Hanged Man fuses our spiritual heart or seed of individual being with the transcendent greater being; the microcosm at one with the macrocosm. Unification is realized through inversion or reflection; upon the Tree of Life, The Hanged Man bridges the Spheres of Beauty and Understanding, the Son of Light and the Great Mother of the ancient religions.

The Hanged Man is one of the higher Trumps upon the Ascending Path; yet it is also a fall or reversal, for Mountains that we have climbed are suddenly in the distance, the River of time and space flows in full spate out of the image towards us, almost threatening to wash us away. There is a mystery within this Trump which is revealed by *inversion*, by turning perception upside-down.

The River is the flood of created energies in the Solar and Lunar Worlds; it flows from a central solar source of energy to fill the lower spheres, which are the defining energies of the Solar and Lunar Worlds. While the picture of the Trump is painted in a naturalistic manner, the symbols should be read upon higher or poetical and metaphysical levels. Once again we come to the important concept within tarot that any Trump may be read upon three levels:

1. Lunar: World of Nature. Body, mind, emotions.
2. Solar: World of Soul. Mind, emotions, higher consciousness.
3. Stellar: World of Spirit. Spiritual and supernal consciousness.

The Hanged Man moves through all three levels, thus the Trump incorporates the Three Worlds and the Tree of Life within itself, while simultaneously acting as one part of the whole. The imagery moves from the River, which flows out into the lower spheres, to the high Mountains of the higher spheres. Both extremes of symbolism reach beyond the boundaries of our card image, and define between them a third area of Middle Ground. The Hanged Man himself merges all three levels or Worlds. This triple unity, inverted and defined by the Threefold Death, is within us all.

A physical act may have profound spiritual results; ritual magic is based upon this premise, and upon its creative inverse that a spiritual power may have transformative effect upon the physical world. Such theories are proven through experience rather than discussion; The Hanged Man symbolizes transformative experience from the most trivial level of personal self-limitation or sacrifice for a desired end, to the most spiritually profound level of transpersonal sacrifice with utterly non-selfish aims.

As we look at the River, therefore, we are at the boundary of the Solar World (the edge of the card) below which all created energies take increasingly complex and rigid forms and expressions. We have ascended and actually crossed the Abyss by the paths of Fool, Magician, Chariot, Guardian, Tower and the threshold of Death. The Hanged Man, however, inverts this sequence while retaining the understanding gained in the supernal sphere, the 3rd Sphere of the Tree of Life which is touched upon by all living beings at the moment of death. But as the key to The Hanged Man is found through inversion, we will shortly discover that all is not quite as it seems.

The Leaping Salmon
Leaping from the River is a Salmon, spiritual creature of all knowledge in Celtic legend. Salmon eat the nuts that fall from the sacred Tree into the holy Pool. In *The Mabinogion* it is the salmon who guides questing heroes in their search for Mabon, the hidden Child of Light. [5] This Child appears in our Trump The Sun; and the Salmon leaping against the flow of waters into the light is a perpetual symbol of consciousness reaching into higher worlds for knowledge.

Mountains, Middle Ground and Spiritual Creatures
The triple division of the Trump shows high Mountains reaching beyond the upper edge of the card; these are spiritual or stellar realms above the Abyss. In the *Vita*, these mountains are the giddy heights upon which the youth races his horse and hounds in pursuit of the stag. As we have seen in previous Trumps, each creature is one element of an allegorical alphabet or bestiary deriving from ancient poetic and magical traditions. The Horse is power in motion, life energies within the body or any other highly mobile form; the Hounds are questing or guiding creatures of the hunt, of the Underworld or Otherworld, representing wild nature serving an overview or overlord in pursuit of a mutual quest. The Stag is the spiritual creature of the Horned Guardian, the Lord of the Animals.

The hunt is an allegory of life, upon its most obvious level of meaning, but of an otherworldly or spiritual quest upon its more subtle levels. As the Stag is the spiritual creature of the Horned Guardian who preserves and enables the deepest secrets of transformation within and beyond nature, so the hunt is the foolish quest for the secrets of life. In this context we must remember that the hunting youth was once The Fool, and is shortly to become The Hanged Man.

There is a loose correspondence between the quest and the three relative divisions of the Trump; pursuit of truth and understanding must reach through all three levels, but at the highest peak there comes a total fall. The allegory of the *Vita* suggests at first that impetuous rash behaviour leads to a sudden downfall; this meaning is true only in the consensual outer world. The deeper meaning is discovered through understanding a law frequently employed in magical art or in metaphysical disciplines, demonstrated by sacrificial heroes, gods, kings and saviours in world religion.

This law, which has three levels of reaction, states simply that if we conduct the chase, the foolish hunt, the mad pursuit of life and its secrets *unknowing*, we come to disaster. The extreme of this concept is the blasting of The Tower, where false life-patterns are finally demolished. But if the same mad pursuit is conducted in full knowledge, it may lead to the Threefold Death, which is a totally different order of event to The Tower or to Death, yet incorporates and transcends both of those preceding Trumps. The potency and effect of the Threefold Death will vary according to the degree of knowledge and understanding of the victim.

We might also add that there is a further sub-level to the symbolism; that of Horse, Hound and Stag. Each represents one third, so to speak, of a human entity, separated out from customary patterns of consciousness by the shock of Threefold Death. The Salmon, however, represents fusion of consciousness into a new form in a new dimension. As in most tarot cards, we may read the sub-symbols of the Spiritual Creatures in their own right, telling a story which supports and brings further enlightenment to the major images within each card.

The Hawthorn Tree

A blossoming Hawthorn reaches its roots into the tumbled rocks, and down through hidden crevices into the River. The branches of this Tree reach up towards the sky. Like the ancient Apple Tree in the Trump Death, the Hawthorn is a primal Tree of Life, or Tree of All Worlds. It is traditionally the tree of sacrifice, associated with the Dark Goddess or Crone. It offers blossoms of great purity and beauty upon hard, painful, thorny branches. Even in present-day Britain and Ireland, it is considered unlucky to pick or bring hawthorn or May blossom into a house – though this is reversed at certain times or ceremonies. Such folkloric themes of ill-luck reflect ancient taboos or qualities of extreme holiness associated with certain objects.

In Christian tradition, hawthorn or other early blossoming thorn trees have become associated with the Crown of Thorns worn by Jesus at his crucifixion. The actual thorns used would have been of a different plant altogether, but it is interesting to see the fusion of Western pagan lore within an orthodox religious myth. During the medieval period in England, legends about the Glastonbury Thorn were added to this theme, with mysterious associations with Joseph of Arimathea and the Holy Grail. Such developments represent an organic fusion of pagan nature worship (for all the elements of sacrifice, thorn, blood, vessel, death and resurrection long predate Christianity) with an incoming Eastern religion based upon Jewish Messianic tradition. [11]

It is, of course, the pure symbol of a flowering thorn that is of value, and not any specific example in cult practice. All such legends of flowering thorns derive from an archetypical level as visions or poems embodying a paradox of joy and pain transformed to spiritual levels. Peace and beauty out of pain and hardness, Spring out of Winter, rebirth out of death, these are living elements of the hawthorn tree symbol.

We should also reflect that the Hawthorn supports The Hanged Man; it checks and halts his precipitous fall through Three Worlds; it upholds him (albeit upside-down) in his bridging, mediating position across the Abyss. The Hawthorn is, at the moment of death, his Mother – the Tree of the Great Goddess. Without this support or matrix, the victim cannot hang through the Worlds. As we might expect, the tree itself reflects triplicity in unity; its roots are in the Underworld, its trunk extends through the Solar World, while its crown of blossoms represents the Stars.

The tumbled rocks into which the Hawthorn is rooted embody the surfaces and planes or interaction and differentiation; these many facets and fragments merge into the flowing River. The waters from which the Tree drinks have come from a high upland stream, the source of the River, shown as a tiny waterfall in the mountains in several other Trumps. This stream commences as energy in the Stellar World, but becomes a boundless ocean of time and space, and also the watery seas of our outer world.

Bow and Arrows

Upon the rocks we see the victim's discarded Bow and Arrows; they represent his previous pursuits, which have been transcended by his harmony and understanding. The Bow and Arrows are will and intent, cut from the wood of the Tree of Life, and aimed at the highest peak of awareness or being. The meaning of this sub-symbol is that all acts of intent and will must be ultimately set aside through a transformation of consciousness; yet paradoxically we cannot gain that transformation without perfect will, intent and balanced aim.

The Hanged Man

In most tarot Trumps a curious posture is given to The Hanged Man: he is upside-down, with his hands and legs crossed and positioned in a very specific manner. One of his legs is crossed behind the knee of the other, with the foot of his straight leg tied to or tangled in a tree branch. In some Trumps his arms are also tied or folded behind his neck; in the Merlin Tarot they are spread open within the River waters as a sign of universal blessing.

Although variations do occur in specific sets of cards, The Hanged Man is a very consistent image deriving from a sacrificial vision, revelation or actual practice in religion world-wide. To understand the Trump more fully, we need to consider each aspect of the hanging figure in detail:

1. He is upside-down.
2. His facial expression is calm, peaceful and gentle.
3. His arms are outstretched in blessing in the River.
4. His hair mingles with the flowing waters.
5. His left leg is crossed behind his right knee. (We shall encounter a similar posture in The Emperor, where the right leg is crossed over the left knee of a seated figure upon a throne.)
6. His right foot is lightly caught, almost resting, in a cleft among the Hawthorn Tree branches.

The *Six Aspects* of The Hanged Man may be defined as follows:

1. *Upside-down:* The Man hangs inverted in comparison to our normal world view. His points of reference are reversed. Such reversal is typical of consciousness bridging the Abyss. From such a position of awareness, all time, space and energy interact in a different manner to that perceived in the outer or lower worlds. By reversing within himself all concepts of relative 'reality', The Hanged Man reaches instantaneously through all Three Worlds. Upon the Tree of Life this Trump reveals a fusion of the 6th and 3rd Spheres, or the Son of Light, Beauty, universal knowledge, and the Great Mother or supernal Understanding.

   The paradox of inversion increases with higher Trumps, all of which reach across the Abyss from originative to created worlds, from the Stellar to Solar and Lunar conditions shown by the Three Wheels. If we are able to attune to the beautiful understanding of The Hanged Man we may discover that he is, in truth, the right way up. It is our limited, reflected (reversed) world view that is the opposite of higher consciousness. Worlds are literally formed by reflection.

   By turning the entire card upside-down, a new understanding of the Trump is revealed. Over The Hanged Man's head flow the waters of creation, beneath him is deep sky filled with unseen stars. The Hanged Man is the only tarot Trump that may be genuinely used in reverse; the popular practice of reading tarot in reversed layout is both trivial and fruitless. Tarot systems of any sort have an inherent balance within them, and various patterns of relationship (such as cosmologies, the Tree of Life, or divinatory layouts) enliven this inherent balance and give it form. To cloud such a remarkable open system by applying negative reversals (demonic concepts) on the basis of casually upside-down cards is totally to misunderstand and misrepresent the spirit of tarot.

The Hanged Man, however, is a master Trump, a higher form of The Fool. He may be reversed, not for any spurious negative divinatory meaning, but to travel deeper into the secrets and revelations that he represents.

2. *His calm face:* In most versions of the Trump, The Hanged Man is smiling, yet he seems to have died a violent death. There is peace in his features; he contemplates or perhaps dreams the unity of Three Worlds in one. In his expression is the true concept of sacrifice – not agony and humiliation, but willed, knowing loss of chosen elements or aspects of being, sacrificed through transformation. The Hanged Man loses individuality, yet becomes unified with each and every life form and pattern of energy.

The Hanged Man is the archetype of all redeemers, mediators, sacrificial kings and heroes, and universal saviours. To the Christian he is Christ, to the Buddhist Buddha, to the pagan Lugh, Esus, Balder. To those bards who preserved Celtic tradition, he was the Youth of Three Aspects, the young eternal Merlin or Mabon, the Celtic Apollo. He underwent the Threefold Death – one death for each aspect, for each of three worlds.

3. *His outstretched arms:* His arms are open in blessing, revealing a giving and redeeming nature. If we are trapped within the torrent of waters, his hands are ever present to pull us free – if we have the courage to grasp them. While the Salmon leaping from the River represents knowledge and initiation, the hands immersed within the River represent grace and blessing from a higher power. If we invert the image, the Man's hands are seen upholding the waters that flow over his head.

4. *His hair flows out:* Awareness is frequently represented in mystical symbolism by hair. The flowing hair represents the consciousness of The Hanged Man, reaching to the ocean of being.

In this context we should briefly consider the Creation Vision from the *Vita*, for this gives insight into concepts which underpin all tarot and similar Elemental world views in magical tradition. Four Powers, Winds, Elements, Seas, Rivers, and realms of being all interrelate. This fourfold pattern is symbolized on Earth by the solar evaporation of water from the four seas falling as rain upon the high mountains. Streams are formed, which become rivers, and the sea is refilled through a constant circularity of changes. This natural cycle is traditionally regarded as evidence of a higher metaphysical cycle that permeates the universe. The hair of The Hanged Man, in the flowing water, encompasses all time, space and energy. Ultimately, it is woven through the Four Powers of Life, Light, Love and Law, and the Four Elements of Air, Fire, Water and Earth.

5/6. *The position of his legs:* The traditional posture of The Hanged Man has been subject to various interpretations, ranging from yoga to alchemy. In the Merlin Tarot it is related to the Four Elements, which are further demonstrated through the Court and Number cards.

In several Trumps in the Merlin Tarot a symbol known as the 'Z' sign appears, often paired with the Spindle. The apparently minor symbols are major keys within a Mystery; they act as educational and identity symbols for a specific school of initiation with a well-defined esoteric psychology, philosophy and metaphysics.

The 'Z' Sign

The 'Z' sign, lightning flash, or serpentine motion, is the key symbol for The Hanged Man. It is the flash of spiritual transcendent energy or consciousness that cuts across all cycles, patterns and preconceptions. The 'Z' sign reveals also a practical method used for many centuries in meditation, ritual magic and possibly in alchemy, for it relates to the arrangement and rotation of the Four Elements. We may summarize the method briefly as follows:

1. The Elements are set in rotation sunwise, in their natural order that follows the outer Wheel of the Seasons (East, South, West, North). This cycle is shown in Figure 6, and is one of the basic patterns in meditation and ritual pattern making, combined with the psychic structure of the Seven Directions, shown in Figure 5.

2. The rotation is amplified through the Three Worlds by the traditional technique of ascent and descent. In simple ritual this amplification is achieved through circle dancing. In advanced work it may be undertaken through visualization alone, but dancing (as we have suggested in our chapter on the Trump Death) is a major mystical and magical act. Such techniques have been forgotten in Western esoteric arts, but not entirely lost.

3. At the peak of the circling, which may be the high point of the ritual or the maximum energy of a lifetime, there is a sudden change in the pattern of the dance. It now moves through Air/Fire/Earth/Water or E/S/N/W. This new movement cuts across the centre of the circle, and then makes a reverse movement to the West or Element of Water. If we draw this new pattern across the Wheel, it appears as an oblique, serpentine, or 'Z' sign.

The Elements and The Threefold Death

How does this threefold dance and 'Z' pattern relate to the posture of The Hanged Man? To answer this we superimpose the Circle of Elements, or Wheel of Life, upon the Trump picture, with East or Air uppermost. This gives us the following outline of the Man:

1. His head (at the foot of the image) is in the Element of Water, in the West or lower quarter of the Circle.
2. His foot in the upper branches points to the Element of Air, in the East or higher quarter of the Circle.
3. His other leg crosses the centre of the Circle, from South to North, Fire to Earth, or right- to left-hand quarters.

This pattern, inherent in the image, is the 'secret' path of the Hanged Man. In some traditions it is known as the Path of the Thief, and initiation begins with the story that the man is hanging as a thief. What did he steal?

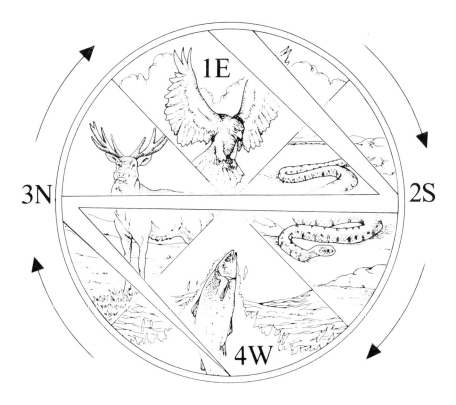

Figure 9: THE SECRET PATH OF THE HANGED MAN

Like Prometheus, he brought Light directly to Earth from Heaven to bless humankind.

The Threefold Death also represents this major mystical and magical teaching in Western tradition. It corresponds quite directly as follows:

1. The youth falls from a high Mountain; from supernal consciousness to outer expression. This fall corresponds to the Element of Air.
2. His foot is caught in the Tree branches, and his neck snaps with sudden shock. This releases his vital energies, corresponding to the Element of Fire.
3. Through his suspension from the Tree he is united with its roots. He merges with the basic matter of Earth, which comprises both the Tree and himself as outer forms.
4. His head is immersed in the River. This completes the pattern with the head or crown of consciousness within the Element of Water.

Thus the Threefold Death (which has several variants) may be related to the Four Elements. Most important is the fact that it represents an unusual or esoteric combination or rotation or dance of energies, which cuts across the Wheels. The Hanged Man does not die, but bridges the Wheels without being subject to them. (See Figure 9.)

The Dancer

If we reverse our card, The Hanged Man becomes The Dancer. He is poised perfectly between the Elements, arranging them in a new order. This secret order was concealed by The Magician, but is now revealed through sacrifice. The Waters flow over the head of The Hanged Man, Earth and Fire balance him right and left, while Air supports him. All concepts such as the Seven Directions (Figure 5) and the Three Wheels are utterly transformed by his Dance.

The Tree on which the Dancer is poised merges all Worlds and Elements, while he bridges all consciousness, and unifies it in a state of timelessness.

There is a further concealed pattern in the card, shown by one of the spiritual creatures: the upside-down leap of the Salmon. If we consider the hair, the fish, the bent knee, the Tree curve, and finally the waters overhead, we find a spiral pattern rotating around The Hanged Man or Dancer. The pattern is centred upon his navel; we shall encounter it again in a higher Trump (The Innocent or Hierophant) where a spiralling galaxy centres upon the head of the image.

XIV HERMIT

THE HERMIT

WORLD   The Stellar Originative World.
WHEEL   Beyond the Third Wheel, Judgement.
BEINGS   Supernal consciousness withdrawing from individuation. Also relates to certain innerworld beings who choose remain as guides or inspirers of understanding, rather than cross into the void beyond being.

CONSCIOUSNESS   Transhuman universal.

PARTNER TRUMPS   Polar partner: The Innocent (Hierophant). Also relates to The Hanged Man, The Magician and The Fool as lower harmonics.

SPHERES AND PLANETS   *Spheres:* 1st and 3rd Spheres, Crown and Understanding. *Planets: Primum Mobile* (Uranus in modern astrology) and Saturn.

ATTRIBUTES   Withdrawal of super-consciousness inwards towards its ultimate source. The comprehension of transcendent truth.

GOD AND GODDESS FORMS   Saturn and the Holy Spirit. Ideally represented by the Breath of Spirit within the Great Mother. All images that withdraw time and space: often mediated by ancient god forms such as the titans or dim figures from unknown cultures, but this is a property of human culture rather than an enduring set of god forms.

KEY PHRASES   Understanding truth/inward comprehension/light in darkness/withdrawal into spirit.

MERLIN TEXTS   *VM* Merlin withdraws as an ancient wise man towards the close of the *Vita*; this withdrawal is related to stellar observation (the passage of time and supernal energies).

DIVINATORY MEANING   Often indicates that the inquirer must look within for proper answers to his or her question. Shows that understanding can be found through meditation, and that guidance is possible even in the darkest situation. May also indicate the close of a life cycle or period, and a withdrawal of energies accordingly. On an outer level, represents a period of self-examination and assessment; may also indicate that action in the query situation should be taken cautiously or sublimated towards proper understanding. In the Merlin Tarot this Trump often appears in relationship to The Fool and/or The Hanged Man.

RELATED NUMBER CARDS   Threes and Aces.

Threes: Suffering, Intention, Affection, Effort.

Aces: Life, Light, Love and Law.

Origins of the Image

The Hermit is associated with the aged Merlin as the third of the Three Faces of Merlin; Bright Youth, Wild Man or Mad Prophet, Wise Elder. In popular misconceptions it is The Hermit or Wise Elder that has commanded most attention. This aspect, however, cannot be fully understood or even represented unless the other two aspects are integrated within the symbolism. In tarot, integration of all three aspects is through development via the Trumps of The Fool (Bright Youth), The Magician (Fool developing skill), The Guardian (Wild Man), and The Hanged Man (Fool transformed). We might add a basic correlation between these four stages and the Four Quarters of the Wheel of Life (Figure 6):

1. The Fool: Earth.
2. The Magician: Air.
3. The Guardian: Fire.
4. The Hanged Man: Water.

This sequence is not definitive, and may rotate or transform, but would be interpreted as follows:

1. *The Fool:* The human spirit upon Earth, a soul in the outer world beginning the journey of enlightenment. On a deeper level this stage represents the young Merlin, or the Bright Youth, within the cavern underground, where he confounds the usurper Vortigern and prophesies the future. Spirit within matter. Element of Earth, North.
2. *The Magician:* The human spirit emerging from Earth, a soul developing skills upon the inner journey. Now the Youth has emerged from underground, and appears in a cave summoning the Four Winds. He stands in the East, the traditional location for the altar of magical arts. Spirit rising above matter. Element of Air, East.
3. *The Guardian:* Transformative Fire, inner power awakening and purifying the soul. The Youth has become the inspired Lord of the Animals, filled with prophetic power. Spirit inflamed with higher forces. Element of Fire, South.
4. *The Hanged Man:* Consciousness immersed in the waters of understanding. The final cure of Merlin in a magical Spring; the ultimate sacrifice of love and compassion. Spirit dissolved in the unity of being. Element of Water, West.

Further attributes of each Trump are discussed in the relevant chapters, but we might add that The Hermit appears again in the North as a new turning of the spiral.

If we follow the Ascending Path, described in our cycle of Trumps, the transformations are further defined by The Chariot, The Blasted Tower and Death. These last three are feminine archetypes mediating catabolism, limitation and transmutation of form into force.

The Wise Elder
The Wise Elder of cautious habits, prudence, great experience and conservation of resources is a fragmentary archetype of the Element of Earth. In extremes he may become the miser or aged buffoon, as revealed in Shakespeare's play *Hamlet* through the character of Polonius. All images or Trumps should operate through Three Worlds, and if one image is separated from the totality, it may become a stereotype.

Extreme age, saturnine negative qualities, excess male-orientated wisdom roles, greed and conservatism are typical of exaggerated stereotypes fragmented from the Element of Earth within human personality. We might liken them to an aged King of Shields within tarot, or the jealous Saturn/Chronos or Giant Father in mythology. Such stereotypes are well defined in traditional wisdom, and should not be confused with the archetypical or magical images. The Old Man stereotype is frequently confused with Merlin or The Hermit.

The Old Man, however, corresponds only to a very limited material expression of the Third Face or aspect of Merlin, a superficial stereotype of the Wise Elder. In extreme examples it may lead to corruption, such as the literary invention of the Merlin–Nimuë story, in which a besotted aged Merlin is enervated by the seductive wiles of a young nymph or vamp. This false theme (as may be detected by simply reading early Merlin legends in which it does not appear) is a gross rationalization. It seeks to explain the mystery of relationship between a seer, prophet or magician, and the inspiration of the Goddess. In a non-sexual corruption of the Elder image, we have a bumbling old magician who forgets details and loses apparatus, yet may occasionally revert to his former powers. Each of the extremes described is inadequate and potentially dangerous if applied as a model for meditation upon The Hermit or aged Merlin.

To demonstrate further subtle differences between stereotype and archetype, both in human consciousness, life and metaphysics or magical art, we should examine briefly the role and requirements of a hermit. These will give us some indication of the higher role of The Hermit, as tarot, particularly the higher Trumps, work through analogy. The role of a hermit is as follows:

1. Withdrawal from the regular world in three stages: a) physical, b) mental and emotional, c) spiritual.
2. Removal to isolated locations, ascetic life patterns.
3. Special disciplines such as meditation, visualization, worship or magical arts.
4. Breakdown of habitual patterns of consciousness and behaviour.
5. Energy transformed (through the four means described) and channelled inwardly – a hermit seeks communion with essential truth, divinity, or the source of being; all other concerns are abandoned or transformed.

This short list shows that the attributes of a hermit are not identical with those of an aged man. An elder harbours energy and material assets prudently, while a hermit transforms and even disposes of such matters completely. Our comparison upon a human level may be extended into archetypical levels from which human interaction derives. The exterior role or *persona* of a Wise Elder may be absorbed within the archetype of The Hermit, and through this process exterior personality becomes a vehicle for transpersonal consciousness. But this is merely an interim stage, a balance established between personal life experience and transpersonal or inner understanding. Eventually, the way of The Hermit is to dissolve the personality utterly, and then to withdraw consciousness itself into the unknown.

The Hermit and the *Vita Merlini*

The Hermit in tarot stands upon a high mountain top; in the cosmology and magical psychology of the Merlin Tarot he stands at the summit of the Tree of Life or Spiral of Worlds. He represents the peak of both understanding and knowledge through experience. But this mode of inward-seeking consciousness is not static, for it finally withdraws into the mystery of original being.

This concept is shown upon the Tree of Life as a path or fusion between the Spheres of Crown and Understanding, the 1st and 3rd aspects of the Supernal Triad. The first three Spheres upon the Tree are Crown, Wisdom, Understanding; in religious terms these would be symbolized by the Holy Spirit, the Father and the Mother.

Towards the close of the *Vita*, Merlin withdraws into spiritual contemplation; he refuses to lead or advise assembled chieftains and princes (setting aside his role as druid or Wise Elder) for his long life and inner energies are finally directed towards contemplation and worship of divinity. This important theme underpins the conclusion of the text, and is more than a mere sop to orthodox religion. In Merlin's withdrawal we find connections to both Christian and pagan philosophical and mystical practices; such withdrawal still forms part of Eastern cultural fabric today, though decreasing in general use.

In short, a seer or holy man finally bids the outer world farewell, not as an inspired youth or madman seeking nature, but in full understanding. In tarot terminology we might say that after the triple death and mystical rebirth shown by The Hanged Man, all viewpoints are reversed, even while still living in the outer world. The theme of The Hermit was very popular in medieval culture, where actual withdrawal was practised as part of religious devotion. The image was perpetuated in Renaissance tarot, literature, magical arts and alchemy. Although the general tarot Trump of The Hermit is coloured by medieval orthodoxy, it derives from a much deeper enduring level, and it is to this level of consciousness that we should attribute the persistence of the image.

The overall symbolism of The Hermit refers to a transcendent or cosmic time scale, to universal experience and understanding. It is typified by simplicity, clarity and ultimate removal from manifest existence towards mysterious enlightenment, into the unknown. Within the *Vita* we find that Merlin retires to a special observatory built specifically for star-watching under the instruction of his sister Ganieda.

Contents of the Image

The Summit of a High Mountain/The Wren/The Hermit/The Crystal Lamp/The Sky

The Summit of a High Mountain

The highest Summit represents the peak of elevated expanded consciousness. This solitary Mountain top is the end of the Ascending Path that we have climbed upon the Left Hand of the Tree of Life. The Fool has now become The Hermit.

In a most direct sense the Summit is the end of any lifetime, with age and experience matured out of youth and folly through cycles of the Wheel of Life and Change. In a universal sense it is the overview or zenith of interactions between time, space and energy; from this point it is understood entire rather than in cycles or fragments. Traditionally, the Mountain peak is snow-covered, for it is at an altitude where sun's rays do not warm, and stars are seen direct in daylight.

The paradox of The Hermit is that while he looks back down the long spiralling path of ascent, he is also free to turn about and take his last step – but where does this last step lead? If he steps off the Mountain he does not fall, but passes upwards into the unknown, into unbeing beyond being. This mystical yet physical step is the highest aspect of the Great Leap taken far below by The Fool when he jumps over a cliff. Yet the last step and the first leap are one and the same.

The Wren

Even at this exalted level, a spiritual creature appears. The Wren belongs to all sacred kings; many rituals associated with it have passed into folklore from pagan ceremonies of ancient origin. The Wren represents the small that is great; a fusion of microcosm and macrocosm. The divine originative Spirit, as minute and insignificant as a wren, creates, traverses and comprehends the totality of all worlds.

In British folk ritual and song the tiny wren cannot be killed by an army of men with bows and arrows; it requires a huge cauldron (the vessel of the Underworld) to cook it; the spare ribs alone will feed all of the poor throughout the land. [12] At one time the wren was featured in the smallest British coin, the farthing. The wren also features in a legend about flight, kingship and power:

> The birds of the air held a competition to appoint their king. Whoever flew highest would be crowned supreme among the birds. Of the many who flew upwards only the eagle with his mighty wings and keen eye and great strength and endurance outflew all other birds. When he reached the limit of his strength alone in the upper

air, he began at last to descend, confident of his success. But a tiny wren, who had ridden unseen and unfelt upon the eagle's back, spread her wings and rose even higher than the highest. And so the wren is ruler of all birds.

The last spiritual creature, therefore, upon the Ascending Path, is the smallest and least significant. The great Wolves and Stags have been left behind on the slopes below, the Horse cannot climb icy rocks, and even Crows and Eagles may not fly so high. But the Wren, sacred bird of kingship, blessed of the Great Mother, accompanies The Hermit upon his solitary pinnacle. There is another paradox inherent in the Wren upon this Mountain peak, for in nature she lives only in low hedges. The spiritual creature again indicates a Mystery; that which is above is at one with that which is below.

The Hermit
An aged man, his face lined with understanding, stands supported by his Staff. He does not lean upon the Staff, for he is strong, but it gives him balance as he ascends. We first saw this Staff as a crude tree branch held by The Fool; now it is worn smooth through long service. It is also the Spindle of the Worlds, a branch from the Tree of Life, ultimately the rightful implement of the Goddess, the Great Mother.

The Hermit, a male image, is located in the realm of Understanding, that of the Great Goddess. This reversal of gender in images is of vital importance, particularly to our comprehension of higher Trumps. We shall find in our next chapter that a primal image for The Hierophant (usually rationalized into a Patriarch or Pope) is a girl Child of divine Wisdom, The Innocent. Thus an aged Hermit dwells within the Deep Mother, and a young Innocent dwells within the Star Father. This reflection and reversal of polarity disposes of all stereotypes and gives powerful insight in meditation.

The Hermit wears a black robe and hood, symbolizing withdrawal of energy from form. Astrologically, this relates to the planet Saturn and to myths of time and space. His cloak is the black of eternal night, the colour of the Sorrowing Mother. Its edges are ragged, worn by the long ascent, yet they also remind us of black crow feathers. The crow is the spiritual bird of the Goddess of Death, and is used in alchemy as a major symbol within sequences of transmutation. Without the blessing of the Mother through and beyond death, The Hermit could not have reached his mountain-top retreat.

The Crystal Lamp
The Lamp carried by The Hermit sheds light into the worlds below, leading any aspirants who follow, offering a sure sign that there is an end to the

journey. The light of The Hermit is small but steady, half revealed, half concealed – the light of Truth. Within any specific Mystery, religion, or initiatory system, the lamp is the specific promise that certain teachers or masters wait even upon the edge of the unknown to guide us onwards to our original home.

In the Merlin Tarot the Lamp is a crystalline sphere or egg in which two Dragons are encapsulated. The Dragons symbolize interaction between positive and negative energies throughout the worlds. The Hermit has risen beyond interaction, for he encloses the red and white Dragons within a sphere of light. The Lamp is of Crystal, for this is the mineral equivalent of light in the Underworld where primal dragons are born into expression and erupt through the dimensions of force and form.

The Crystal also represents the purified or crystalline body or energy-field of the initiate towards the completion of all transformations. At this last stage all energies are perfectly balanced and the Light of Being radiates forth; in a human this is only achieved through perfection of the relationship between the red and white Dragons. This is also the true meaning of the term 'astral body', the vessel of consciousness which shines like a star. The meaning used in popular occultism only relates to the phantom or emotional or thought form generated in any lifetime.

The light of the Dragon Crystal radiates to the worlds below; it is both a token of achievement and a symbol of that which may be achieved. In the medieval legends concerning Joseph of Arimathea, two vessels or 'cruets' are said to accompany the Grail, holding the blood and sweat, or seed, of Jesus Christ. This motif is simply a reworking of the imagery of red and white dragons, red for blood, white for seed; they appear in the Grail legends in an esoteric Celtic Christian form. The symbolism is perennial, and derives not merely from primitive ritual or myth, but from realities understood in heightened states of awareness.

The Lamp reappears in alchemy as the Philosopher's Stone, the eternal Lamp, or the mystic Egg. Whatever form this protean symbol takes, it always refers to perfection of energies and radiant light.

The Sky

The Sky to the left of the image, where The Hermit looks downwards, is filled with the light of the Crystal, appearing blue towards the outer and lower edges. This is the Sky of the created worlds through which he has passed. Behind him are the stars, into which he will turn and merge.

Beyond that last step is the Nothing out of which Everything is breathed forth. At the uttermost extreme of being, we approach the Crown of the Tree of Life beyond which Nothing may be found. The last words of The Hermit are an ancient paradoxical blessing uttered in theurgic ritual: 'Peace is a Secret Unknown.'

XV INNOCENT

THE INNOCENT
(The Hierophant)

WORLD   The Stellar Originative World.
WHEEL   Precedes the Third Wheel, Judgement.
BEINGS   Four Originative Powers or archangels. Divine universal being.

CONSCIOUSNESS Originative being.

PARTNER TRUMPS Polar partner: The Hermit. By reflection: The Universe or World and The Fool.

SPHERES AND PLANETS *Spheres:* 1st and 2nd Spheres, Crown and Wisdom. *Planets: Primum Mobile* (Uranus in modern astrology) and the Zodiac.

ATTRIBUTES The Crown of Wisdom. Perfect being emanating from an unknown source.

GOD AND GODDESS FORMS The Holy Spirit and the Zodiac or congregation of stars. The goddess Sophia or Holy Wisdom.

KEY PHRASES Perfection/innocence/truth/the Original Name.

MERLIN TEXTS *PVM* Relationships to feminine deities such as the goddess Ariadne, and the Maiden who purifies the Land. No distinct reference.

DIVINATORY MEANING Shows a spiritual originative power at work within any given situation or query. Indicates that a defined situation or pattern is enlivened by wisdom and truth; may be taken on a simple level as a positive indicator, dependent upon position and other cards. Often symbolizes powerful new beginnings in a life cycle or situation.

RELATED NUMBER CARDS Aces and Twos.

Aces: Life, Light, Love and Law.

Twos: Doubt, Choice, Freedom, Change.

Origins of the Image

In the Merlin Tarot we are directly concerned with relationships between, and restoration of, primal and effective images; but it is impossible to redefine certain Trumps without touching upon the political background or psychological purpose behind their current form. The Hierophant is one of those Trumps, like Death, Judgement, and The Devil, which has had its primal image overlaid by propaganda.

Within a Judaeo-Christian context, the Pope, High Priest or Hierophant can only be a stereotypical bearded mature male; this image may be perfectly acceptable within its own cultural limits, but tends to reinforce the monosexual imbalance within religion, tarot, and mystical or magical imagery in general in Western culture.

If we refer to both classical and Celtic mythology or legend, we find a wealth of imagery relating to feminine archetypes; within this storehouse of symbolism is preserved the means to rebalance tarot Trumps and related systems of inner development. In the Merlin Tarot The Hierophant reverts to a very potent archetype of The Innocent, represented by a young girl. This feminine image represents innocence or originative consciousness emerging from divine being. Perhaps variant Trumps showing a female

Pope (Pope Joan, La Papesse), which are often identified with The Priestess, actually originate in an ancient pagan and early Christian tradition; within the Eastern Churches and in Gnostic sources, wisdom was and still is known as Sophia, a feminine archetype representing divine consciousness.

Our Trump in the Merlin Tarot is partly drawn from visions of goddesses described in *The Prophecies of Merlin*, and from the broader base of traditions that allocated a goddess to the power of wisdom.

The Innocent balances The Hermit; they are a non-sexual pair, symbolizing mutually reflected supernal energies. While The Hermit represents consciousness moving inwards towards origination, or at the closing of a cycle of creation, The Innocent represents the birth of such a cycle, and the outward movement of consciousness generating time, space and interaction.

Understanding, the 3rd Sphere upon the Tree of Life, is the Great Mother, while Wisdom, the 2nd Sphere, is the Star Father. This male aspect of originative power is identified with the explosion of stars within the vessel or Mother of space and time. Any such terms of definition are merely products of language, and must always be regarded as relative; effective true relationship to the positive and negative energies of being (Father and Mother powers) can only be achieved through meditation or through symbolic units that transcend language. Tarot is an alphabet of such units.

When we meditate upon The Hermit, we find that this male image appears within the Sphere of the Great Mother; conversely, the tarot Trump for universal consciousness of the Father is female – The Innocent. This subject is one of the most significant and least understood laws of magical art, visualization and esoteric tradition, and requires some further elaboration.

If we employ *direct* god forms, such as planetary or cult deities allocated to the Tree of Life in any form or tradition of Kabbalah, we find simple male/female roles. These are shown upon our basic Tree of Life, with the appropriate deities shown for each Sphere (see Figure 2).

When these images or traditional god forms are fused in pairs, as in combining two Spheres, we generate a series of reflections and inverse polarities. This pattern of relationship is shown in the various figures that define connections between the Trumps.

The tradition that tarot Trumps relate to the Tree of Life is at least as old as the appearance of Kabbalah in Europe. It seems very likely that Trumps originally sprang from a visionary or poetic cosmology which was eventually adapted to the sophisticated glyph of The Tree: any argument need not be one of origins, for such patterns arise spontaneously within our awareness when we enter into meditation upon the nature of the universe. They are, in short, models or analogies or maps that have pan-cultural similarities. The cosmology that generates primal images (later to become formalized as tarot) pre-dates the Tree of Life in Western Europe, but both models fit one another very well indeed, particularly when we apply a sequence of Trumps such as that suggested in the Merlin texts.

The supernal Spheres, the first three powers upon the Tree, are beyond sexual role definition, but we need such definition as humans to enable us to react to images or archetypes that mediate the power and consciousness of these universal polarities of being. The reflective property of Trumps, such as a male Hermit associated with Understanding and a female Innocent associated with Wisdom, runs through all created forms. Nothing is male but it has a female aspect, nothing is female but it has a male aspect. Polarity establishes relativity of viewpoint; such reflection is taught, traditionally, as the creation pattern of all worlds.

The function of The Hierophant or Innocent is to mediate the divine will outwardly towards created worlds. It is an outward-moving image, power flowing from being towards and through infinite varieties of expression and interaction. The wisdom of originative being or divinity is mediated through perfect Innocence; this traditional teaching is found in the Biblical parable regarding entry into the Kingdom of Heaven. The parable reveals a profound truth embodied in the use of the name 'Innocent' by many historical Popes.

Just as the Supernal Spheres are beyond created polarity, yet have the triple powers of Crown, Wisdom and Understanding, or Being, Male and Female, or Holy Spirit, Father and Mother, so the two highest Trumps of The Hermit and The Innocent have a non-sexual emphasis, despite their gender as picture images. The sexuality of The Hermit has been transformed through direction of his life energies and consciousness inwards in spiritual enlightenment; the sexuality of The Innocent is latent and has not yet crossed the Abyss into polarities of creation and destruction, attraction and repulsion.

In this sense we may regard these two highest Trumps as the ultimate extremes of sexuality: The Hermit is an aged male, The Innocent is a young female. Neither is sexually active in a biological sense, for the male has moved beyond such modes of activity, and the female has not yet progressed towards them. This model of sexual polarity is an abstract or metaphysical law, but it has a natural reflection in human life cycles. The extremes of our lives correspond to archetypes which have a universal role as well as a reflection within human consciousness.

One final paradox arises in the higher Trumps: if we transposed polarities within the images at this supernal stage of the symbolism, The Hermit would become female (the Crone) while The Innocent would become a pre-pubescent male child. Further visualizations with the sequence that derives from this exchange are sometimes used in advanced magical or meditational disciplines.

Contents of the Image

The Circle/The Throne of Two Dragons/The Innocent/Galaxies

The Circle

The lower part of the Trump shows an abstract map of the universe; this cosmological pattern is the traditional Circle divided into Four Quarters. The map is not intended as a literal plan but as a relative or analogical key. Initially, it represents a cycle or spiral; ultimately, it is understood as a sphere encompassing all time, space and energy.

The fourfold division represents Four Powers, which ultimately reflect through the Three Worlds as the Four Elements. The Four Powers may be summarized as Life, Light, Love and Law; embodied by the Four Aces, they are conditions of pure consciousness, four relative powers extending through all existence from galaxies to subatomic particles. The Four Powers operate through the spiralling harmonics of the Three Wheels, and partake of a fundamental cycle in each of them. We usually perceive this cycle as Birth, Adulthood, Maturity, Death, but these relative modes may apply to any chosen subject, and are not limited to human expression.

In the outer world the Four Powers appear as physical interaction of the Four Elements, and as the Four Seasons. The significance lies in relative modes of energy, and not in lists of words used to describe them. In perennial traditions of magic, religion or metaphysics, the Four Elements appear in all worlds, from divinity to humanity, from pure energy to matter.

The Circle shown in our Trump is a matrix or archetype of the traditional Fourfold Cycle; it may be defined as Origination/Creation/Formation/Expression. It is inscribed upon a featureless plain, divided equally into two primal zones, symbolized by the colours black and white or silver. The plain itself floats in interstellar space; thus, an abstract symbol is shown floating within its manifest form. The flat plain with its inscribed pattern is one of the basic symbols of the Mysteries, revealing a matrix for relative order out of primal chaos.

In some tarot Trumps this is represented by the chequered floor pattern of a temple; whatever form it takes, the imagery is a simple analogy of states of existence which are beyond regular comprehension. The key to this part of the Trump is its relationship to topology, or to mathematical and philosophical forms such as the Platonic Solids. Such abstract forms represent an inherent tendency towards pattern-making within any world; the forms used in our perception are not necessarily ultimate or unchanging, but they work nevertheless.

The Throne of Two Dragons

A throne is both a symbol and physical expression of the Great Goddess. She is the Vessel, Cup or Matrix of all created existence. She is comprehension or understanding of all life, all time, all space. The pure concept of a throne is not related in any way to political 'authority', but to upholding, supporting, encompassing, sustaining and, on a more subtle level, to mediating. It is in this last role that the throne has become a symbol of worldly power rather than a sacred expression of an inner reality.

Once again we touch upon inherent reversals of polarity within tarot symbols; the orthodox Pope or Hierophant sits upon a throne (*cathedra*) which is the supporting matrix or mother of apostolic power. In the Merlin Tarot, we have a male Hermit upon a Mountain, for mountains are the primal realm of male divinities, yet associated with the Great Mother or feminine universal consciousness; likewise, the female Innocent upon her Throne appears within the imaginative dimension of the Star Father or masculine universal consciousness. The definition and limitation of these images, and their polar reflections and reversals, are properties of consciousness, and within esoteric training these properties are used as means of inner development.

The Throne, from which The Innocent mediates divine or originative will, is formed from Two Dragons, each in a serpentine or 'S'-shaped curve. This motif is reminiscent of the 'Z' sign that features in other Trumps, but the double Dragons balance one another equally, whereas the Lightning Flash cuts across all patterns. We might say that the Circle and Dragons represent primal patterns and powers, while The Innocent is an embodiment of the Lightning Flash in its first instant of existence. The Two Dragons may also be seen as two cups forming the Throne, one inverted, one upright. The balanced shape of the Throne holds The Innocent; the Dragons are universal power; black and white, male and female, positive and negative, life and death, opening and closing. They emerge from an abstract plan (the Circle) making its potential increasingly manifest.

We last saw the Dragons held in a crystalline Lamp by The Hermit, withdrawing into the unknown. Now they arise with increasing power, defining and enabling patterns of energy that will flow across the Abyss to take form as lower Spheres, Worlds, Trumps and, ultimately, as universal existence.

The Innocent

The Innocent is primal consciousness emerging from spiritual origination. Her wisdom is that of perfection before change; she knows all that there is to know, for she *is* all that there is to know. Her emblem of interlinked circles, worn on her breast, is a geometrical key to all worlds; it is the matrix for creation, which follows. The key shows the Four Powers within universal consciousness.

In her left hand The Innocent holds a white Wand; this is pure will, the measure of power within eternity, absolute and perfect rule. Once again we meet transposition of symbols: The Innocent bears a Wand or Rod, which is the male magical implement, while The Hermit bears a Vessel of Light, the female magical implement.

The Innocent lifts her right hand in a sign of blessing. In most tarot Trumps The Hierophant uses an orthodox sign found within the Roman Church; some modern Trumps employ another sign with the first and fourth fingers uplifted, which may have a pagan derivation. Traditionally, this second sign usually means that the sun and moon are equal in the sky, or that the Lord and Lady rule together; it may also be used to mean the horns of the moon, or the horns of Aries or Taurus. The blessing sign given by The Innocent has a different meaning to any of these, and may be summarized as follows:

1. The thumb and third finger form a circle, the sign of perfection or spirit.
2. The upright first and second fingers represent the Father and Mother, the God and Goddess, the polarities of power. They are the primary outgoing and ingoing archetypes that emit and modify power within the universe.
3. The fourth or little finger is the Child of Light; the Saviour, Redeemer, Mediator. He or she has passed beyond the circle of perfection (shown by the third finger and thumb) into the outer created worlds to bring blessing, illumination and salvation. We say 'he or she' as the Child of Light is androgynous, and may appear as either sex.

The blessing sign means 'Through the Child of Light receive the Blessing of the Father and Mother united in One Spirit.' It is also within itself a simple complete cosmology.

Galaxies
Behind and beyond the abstract geometrical plain and its inscribed Circle is the manifest universe. We see spiralling Galaxies, the greatest life forms that exist, the inhabitants of the Stellar World. The utterance of stars is associated with the 2nd Sphere of the Tree of Life, or Wisdom. This is where the Star Father declares his Name, which is symbolized by the Circle of the Zodiac. We see this emerging, rotating power behind The Innocent, like a halo. Her crown is made from all the stars in the universe.

XVI TEMPERANCE

TEMPERANCE

WORLD The Stellar World, crossing the Abyss into the Solar World.
WHEEL The Third Wheel, Judgement, crossing the Second Wheel, Justice.
BEINGS Archangels, saviours and Sons of Light. Special reference to the archangel or great consciousness of the Zodiac or the relationship between

the sun and other stars. May also include certain transhuman modes of consciousness deriving from human foundations (as in traditions of men and women who have become 'archangelic' or closely attuned to universal consciousness).

CONSCIOUSNESS   Transpersonal, transhuman, universal.

PARTNER TRUMPS   Polar partner: The Hanged Man (see also Figure 4).

SPHERES AND PLANETS   *Spheres:* The 2nd and 6th Spheres, Wisdom and Beauty. *Planets:* The Zodiac (or Neptune) and Apollo, Sol.

ATTRIBUTES   A fusion of stellar and solar energies. Perfect balance and harmony, giving rise to immaculate transmutation and balance of force and form. Concerned with the relationship between the sun or central consciousness, and the stars or relative sphere of existence. Crosses the Abyss between universal originative energies and solar created patterns and life forms. Traditionally is the Path of the Redeemer or Son of Light reaching into the created worlds.

GOD AND GODDESS FORMS   The Zodiac and Sol. Neptune (as Lord of the Universal Ocean of Stars) and Apollo as the God of Light. Also indicates a transcendent non-sectarian image for the Saviour or Being of Light. The image is androgynous.

KEY PHRASES   Beautiful wisdom/perfection of power/universal transmutation/The Bridge of Light.

MERLIN TEXTS   *VM* Implied in higher stages of the Creation Vision.

DIVINATORY MEANING   May simply mean temperance or balance within the query situation; forces or consciousness that lead to a harmonious result. On a higher level may indicate grace or power from unknown sources or through previously untapped inner resources. Occasionally indicates a direct spiritual influence at work within the query.

RELATED NUMBER CARDS   Twos and Sixes.

Twos: Doubt, Choice, Freedom, Change.

Sixes: Transition, Balance, Joy, Benefit.

Origins of the Image

Temperance is the balancing image to The Hanged Man. While The Hanged Man represents individuality tuned inside out, transformed and moved inwardly towards ultimate understanding, Temperance shows energy moving outwards. Power radiates from a universal source (Wisdom, the 2nd Sphere) towards a harmonious creative and ultimately individual expression (Beauty/Harmony, the 6th Sphere).

In a physical sense Temperance symbolizes a connection between the sun as centre of a world (the solar system) and all other stars, of which universal community (the Stellar World) it is a member. Temperance is the consciousness and energy that all stars hold in common. In a spiritual sense this image shows a divine originative source of being crossing the Abyss of time and space to manifest as the Son of Light, Saviour, Redeemer, Liberator or Prince of Peace.

In mystical exposition the path of Temperance is that taken by spiritual beings of a high order to reach the lower worlds such as the planet Earth. It is a perfect balance of universal energies. The symbolism of the Trump image is attuned to two prime concepts: a) Balance; b) Power.

The image may be seen as a matrix or imaginative source of illimitable power in meditation and visualization; such power should be routed through appropriate paths of balance, many of which are clearly indicated within the image. These aspects of the Trump hold within them seeds of many of the lower images or Trumps, suggesting and defining, archetypically, later development of images in their descent towards differentiation and expression.

Contents of the Image

The Threefold Division of Sea, Land, Abyss/The Salamander and Volcano/The Inverted Tree and the Path/The Winged Figure wearing a Woven Robe

The Threefold Division of Sea, Land, Abyss
Our card is an analogy of Three Worlds, of the macrocosm incorporating the microcosm. The lowest part is the manifest or sub-Lunar World (including the Trumps Moon and The Wheel of Fortune), the second the Solar or angelic World (including the Trumps Sun and Justice), and the third the Stellar or archangelic World (the Trumps Star and Judgement). The figure of Temperance spans all three Worlds; it also exists in a higher reflective state or spiral comprising the Three Supernal Spheres (above the Abyss) from which all other triplicities are reflected. These three Spheres, shown in The Tree of Life (Figure 2) are Crown or Spirit (*Primum Mobile*), Wisdom (the Star Father or Zodiac) and Understanding (The Great Mother).

In simpler terms, we could say that while the power of Temperance is universal down to the manifestation of matter, its true home is entirely spiritual. The act of bridging the Abyss is, in the case of Temperance, a profound extension of supernal consciousness towards the lower or less conscious worlds. While The Hanged Man crosses this bridge upon the Ascending Path, Temperance crosses it upon the Descending Path. They are, of course, two aspects, ingoing and outgoing, of the same power or consciousness.

The Sea represents created worlds formed and expressed below the Abyss; the Shoal of Fish within the seething waters symbolizes innumerable life forms in the universe. It has a particular reference, for us, to the life forms of the solar system, for we relate to that aspect or function of Temperance which reaches into the heart of our sun, and energizes the spiritual Son of Light or harmonic spiritual heart of our world.

The Sea also represents the 3rd Sphere of the Tree of Life, the Great Mother or Understanding, the originative Matrix within which all being is brought into creation. Thus the imagery has a double meaning: *universal* or connecting to the Spheres above the Abyss, and *individual* or connecting to the Spheres below the Abyss. In both levels of symbolism the lower part of the image is the Element of Water, firstly as the supernal, all-embracing ocean of time and space, and secondly as the ocean of created life. This concept is given careful attention in the Creation Vision of the *Vita Merlini*, where the relationship between divine power, the Four Elements, and the physical elements of the planet is described in detail.

The Land represents the Solar World, but also the stellar universe, of which the sun is a member, above the Abyss. This third of the image is primarily concerned with the Element of Fire. It is of equal and balanced proportion to the third allocated to Water.

A curving rift or gap separates Land and Sea; this is the Abyss, bridged by the standing figure of Temperance. Here we experience another of the paradoxes or inversions which are a feature of higher Trumps; to a being or highly energized consciousness in the Stellar World, outer or created forms are less substantial than inner or originative states. Hence the inversion of Land and Sea through the image, where the Sea is a symbol of created life, while the Land symbolizes an inner or energetic originative dimension. In other words, the spiritual reality is true, while the apparently solid material or biological spheres are merely relative and temporary.

The Salamander and Volcano
Here we see two symbols of energy, Elemental Fire in action. The distant Volcano erupting represents the universal explosion or 'Big Bang' of quantum physics; the Salamander, which is a mythical creature of transformative Fire, is a symbol of that same immense energy encapsulated in an individual life form. The Salamander is a legendary creature with a distinct physical nature, a manifestation of divine Fire; it has the remarkable power of transmutation, changing all that it touches into higher forms. This balancing and transforming power is shown again in the Chalices or Vessels held by Temperance.

The Inverted Tree and the Path
The Trump contains several sets of balanced symbols: the Path leads from the Volcano to the Salamander; universal energy leads to individual life

forms. The mythical Salamander balances the biological Fish; the Inverted Tree balances the Volcano. The Tree shows once again the inversion of reality that occurs in the higher worlds – our regular mode of existence is a reversal of transcendent consciousness; the reality of spiritual beings is a reversal of our reality.

Far below the level of Temperance, right at the lowest turn of the Spiral or the foot of the Tree of Life, we meet the Inverted Tree again, for it appears as the Underworld Tree which extends in reverse from the Kingdom of Earth downwards into the mysterious realms below and behind manifest creation. Paradoxically, it grows right into the stars, though it begins by growing upside-down within the Earth.

The Winged Figure wearing a Woven Robe

An androgynous being stands in all Three Worlds, crossing the Abyss, fusing the Elements into harmony. In traditional mysticism this is a great archangel, or operative entity that enacts and mediates the will of God. Images of this sort should not, of course, be confused with orthodox angels, as they are ancient archetypes of considerable power, and not merely outmoded aspects of formal religion.

Temperance holds two Vessels or Chalices; these are fundamental poles of energy, positive and negative. They merge and flow in a cycle of perfect harmony when directed by Temperance, who enables a perfect fusion or art and nature, positive and negative, will and energy, imagination and form. The relationship between the sun and Zodiac is inherent in this Trump – not merely as an outmoded world view, but as the principle of balanced centrality relating to a defined sphere of energy or activity.

Thus Temperance has both a universal meaning and a directly solar or localized meaning as the source of all saviour figures in human history. These Sons of Light cross the Abyss towards the outer or solar-rotating worlds to mediate spiritual light to those who remain in ignorance and suffering.

The Figure of Temperance is truly androgynous, both male and female. This perfect balance of the sexes is an essential aspect of the truth of the image, for all polarities are harmonized and made beautiful through the wisdom of its consciousness. In meditation or visualization we may choose to see Temperance as either sex if the pure concept of androgyny is difficult to uphold.

The Robe worn by Temperance, wrapped from a single unbroken sheet of weaving, suggests the 'Z' sign that has appeared in various forms throughout the Merlin Tarot. The woven fabric is, of course, the entirety of creation, given shape through the interaction of time, space and energy. We might say that while The Hanged Man represents Threefold Death, Temperance represents Threefold Life. The elements of both Trumps are similar: Tree, Fish, Mountain, and bridging or resolving Figure in human form. The Horse and Stag have disappeared in Temperance, but the Salamander is a higher form of the humble Newt first encountered at the very beginning of the tarot journey in The Moon. This reappearance of a transformed spiritual creature reminds us of the hidden connectives within the cycle of Trumps.

Traditionally, the great archangelic figures are crowned with light; they are the epitome of total universal awareness. Here, the Figure's wings merge with the sky, showing that this being reaches to all areas of the universe, both seen and unseen. We might say that Temperance may instantly fly to wherever he wills, as those wings touch all parts of eternity; but a deeper interpretation is that Temperance remains perfectly balanced at the centre of the Zodiac, with wings extending through all 12 Signs.

XVII EMPEROR

THE EMPEROR

WORLD   The Stellar World, crossing the Abyss into the Solar World, as does the partner Trump Death.
WHEEL   The Third Wheel, Judgement (links Judgement and the Second Wheel, Justice).
BEINGS   Archangelic, transhuman.

CONSCIOUSNESS Transhuman. Fusion of stellar and solar awareness.

PARTNER TRUMPS Polar partner: Death. Lower harmonic: The Empress (see also Figure 4).

SPHERES AND PLANETS *Spheres:* The 2nd and 4th Spheres, Wisdom and Mercy. *Planets:* The Zodiac (Neptune in modern astrology) and Jupiter.

ATTRIBUTES The Great Giver. The explosion of energy and potential life across the Abyss into the created or Solar World. Corresponds to the Father God. Wisdom and Compassion.

GOD AND GODDESS FORMS The Zodiac or Father God, and Jupiter. The ancient Sky Father, the universal seed or potency of being which manifests as galaxies within the vessel of space and time.

KEY PHRASES The Great Giver/the Compassionate Father/Merciful Wisdom.

MERLIN TEXTS *PVM* Vision of a white-haired man on a white horse, using a white wand to measure out dimensions of a river; *VM* Corresponds materially to the perfect king or emperor Rhydderch, the generous lord. Also inherent in the stellar creation described by Taliesin.

DIVINATORY MEANING Illimitable creative power. May simply indicate a period or opportunity of great benefit, according to other cards and position. On a higher level, often shows opportunities for relationship between, and fusion of, inner and outer life and consciousness (crossing the Abyss in a state of wisdom). On an outer level, may also indicate fatherhood or involvement in situations where a fatherly or beneficial role is undertaken successfully.

RELATED NUMBER CARDS Twos and Fours.

Twos: Doubt, Choice, Freedom, Change.

Fours: Truce, Generosity, Promise, Increase.

Origins of the Image

The Emperor is another image that has been altered through political psychology of both Church and state; it has accumulated an exaggerated and unhealthy degree of stereotypical male attributes. In The Hierophant, which represents a higher spiral or harmonic of The Emperor, we found an orthodox overlay relating to the Pope or exclusively male, rigid, dogmatic authority. The Pope was supposed to have spiritual authority over the temporal authority of an Emperor; in actual history, this theory was repeatedly corrupted and abused. But it masks a higher pattern perceived in contemplation, prophetic or religious insight, and in a rather ironic manner supported by modern theories of quantum physics, despite their origins within more primitive forms of logic and material physics now outdated.

The Emperor, a manifesting or outward-reaching harmonic of primal energy represented by The (female) Hierophant, is best defined by a very simple concept: the power of building. In a primal mythology, which is not necessarily a crude or inefficient system, The Emperor is basically 'He Who Gives', just as Death, his polar partner (shown in the Merlin Tarot as a female figure), is 'She Who Takes'. The next level of the spiral gives rise to The Empress, 'She Who Gives', paired with The Guardian, 'He Who Takes' (see Figures 2, 3 and 4).

In the *Vita Merlini*, the role of Emperor is taken to a certain extent by King Rhydderch, the epitome of a great powerful and generous ruler. We find that he is married to Merlin's sister Ganieda, who is an enabling, intelligent, female *persona*, similar to the goddess Minerva. Thus the primal symbolic partnership has become slightly altered as 'Minerva' is a harmonic image of the goddess shown by the Trump of The Chariot, but nevertheless part of the sequence of female archetypes that defines and energizes Merlin's adventures around the Wheel of Life.

The character of Rhydderch is a good example of the worldly emperor or king; ideally, such a figure should be inspired by and act as a mediator for the divine or transcendent image of 'He Who Gives'. Through gradual transformation of such simple primal imagery into the medieval and Renaissance tarot structures, we find that The Emperor (in general tarot packs) symbolizes worldly power on one hand, and the suppressive, orthodox, monosexual deity on the other. These two stereotypes, the ruthless ruler and the jealous male god, reflect one another and reinforce the imbalance in human society and individual consciousness. The balanced archetypes of an ideal king and divine Emperor will also reflect and reinforce one another – but they must be given context through their female partners and by definition of the roles that each pair and level of the spiral of symbols represents (see Figure 4).

As we have repeatedly emphasized in the context of the Merlin Tarot, the key to understanding this relationship lies in study and meditation upon the pairs, triads and harmonic spirals, rather than merely concentrating upon isolated Spheres, symbols or Trumps. Such relationships are clearly shown upon the universal spiral, or its more sophisticated expression, the Tree of Life.

Understanding and meditation upon The Emperor, therefore, is helped considerably by recourse to his female counterpart, Death or The Apple Woman of Celtic tradition. Just as Death crosses the Abyss of time, space and consciousness 'inwardly' towards originative or supernal states of being, reducing all expressions down to their deepest and simplest origins, so The Emperor crosses the Abyss 'outwardly', bringing originative power out into increasingly defined and complex patterns of creation.

In a cosmic sense, The Emperor embodies the energies of the birth of the solar system, though the image may also apply to the birth of any star pattern or set of stellar and planetary relationships. Traditionally, the Trump fuses the spheres of male deity: Jupiter or Jove and the Zodiac. This Zodiacal attribute of the second Sphere of the Tree of Life (Wisdom) was later redefined by the addition of Neptune to fit material observations of so-called 'new' planetary discoveries. Yet paradoxically, the archetype of Neptune, ruler of the deep ocean and bearer of the triple spear, may be applied on a universal level as an image of an originative outgoing or 'male' power which explodes into the dimensions of space and time. The triple spear represents time, space and energy, the inseparable constituents of our apparent universal reality.

In a metaphysical sense, The Emperor (fusion of Wisdom and Mercy) is an image of divine creative consciousness; it shows, in terms accessible to human imagination, the seeding or outgoing mode of universal being. This mode applies in all worlds, from that of material expression to the transcendent states of consciousness taught by mystical tradition.

Contents of the Image

The Threefold Division of Platform, Mountains and Sky/The Throne/The Emperor/Mouse, Ram, Lion and Eagle

The Threefold Division of Platform, Mountains and Sky

As in a number of other Trumps, the division of the picture symbolizes the Three Worlds or spiralling levels of the Wheel, Spindle, or Tree of Life. It is worth remembering, however, that triple divisions do not always mean the three overworlds of Stars, Sun and Moon, and that subsidiary elements of the symbolism, or overall position of an actual Trump upon the Tree of Life, will give further meaning to the divisions of any particular picture. As with all genuine magical traditions, the symbolism is fluid or plastic (in the true sense of the word) and not limited to a rigid rule-of-thumb system of interpretation.

1. The chequered pattern of the Platform, in the foreground of the image, symbolizes the polarity and relationship of energies in the created worlds. The Emperor defines these relationships as the results of his creative power; they, in turn, are lesser reflections of polarities that run through all existence, originating upon a transcendent or supernal level which sets the matrix or triple archetype for all that derives from it. This is shown by three supernal spheres of Crown, Wisdom and Understanding on the Tree of Life; they are androgynous, male and female in their respective polarity. The chequered pattern shows positive, negative and united energies through its alternation and overall unity. The chequered Platform supports the Throne of The

Emperor to our consciousness, but in meditation we find that it is The Emperor who creates the Platform as his Throne manifests into increasingly complex patterns of time, space and energy.

2. The Platform is at the edge of the Mountains, which form the next level of the image. On encountering The Emperor, our awareness extends into higher worlds or states; there is therefore a gap or void beyond the far edge of the Throne Platform; the Mountains beyond this gap are those same heights found in the Trump of The Hermit, who stands upon a higher harmonic level above the Abyss. A stream of water flows down from high in the Mountains, rising as a tiny spring, but gradually increasing to a roaring torrent. This is the River found in the Trump of The Hanged Man, and in other major images.

3. The Sky represents the originative or supernal world of spirit; The Emperor is a sophisticated image deriving from the primal Sky Father.

There is an overall elemental relationship to the three levels of this picture, and in some interpretations of tarot, a strong alchemical emphasis has been placed upon descending Trumps such as Temperance and The Emperor. In the Merlin Tarot, we find a proto-alchemy, suggested by repeated relationships of elements within the imagery. In The Emperor we find a serial pattern of expression, order and relationship. In the foreground we have a firmly defined chequered pattern, while in the middle ground is a Mountain range taking shape according to the laws of energy and matter in primal expression; above all is the Sky, the originative ethereal Element that transcends yet includes all Elemental patterns. The sequence, therefore, is one of expanding creation, from Sky downwards to increasingly complex and firmly defined entities or forms. This Elemental pattern is still some way from the ultimate fusion of energies that results in our outer world of planet Earth, but it shows the matrix pattern sought in alchemy, by which the relationship of Elements could be adjusted to harmonize and bring them closer to divine wisdom. Such an undertaking could only be achieved through the mercy of a god or being who was accessible to human awareness; concepts of this sort underpin all religious, magical and mystical systems.

The Throne

Upon the chequered Platform is The Emperor, seated upon his Throne, bearing the symbols of power. The Throne is a feminine symbol; the Great Mother (Understanding, the 3rd Sphere upon the Tree of Life) is the Throne and Vessel of the Universe. In medieval symbolism, a cathedral is also a throne, vessel or ship, for the power of God. Thus The Emperor crosses the Abyss in a vast explosion of energy, but is upheld and supported by a feminine-containing power or matrix: the Throne. This Throne is a lesser image of the great Vessel of Understanding, for it is the vessel of power within any stellar or solar system, or in a more specific sense the vessel in which any creative seeding or building operation is contained and enabled.

The Throne is a four-square shape, symbolizing its balance of the Four Elements or Four Original Powers. The back of the Throne, just visible beyond the seated figure of The Emperor, is carved in a series of squares, each one enclosing another. The Throne back, therefore, is a glyph of order, similar to the chequered pattern of the Throne Platform. While the Platform opens out beyond the borders of the image, implying endless development, the Throne back is an image of centrality, with each square leading inwards to a source that may never be seen, due to the paradox of endless division. Thus, the Throne is a symbol of expanding and universal consciousness or energy, upholding The Emperor. The beasts which seem to manifest out of the lower part of the Throne are a naturalistic expression of expansion and development of power; they represent the beginning of a change from energy to entity.

The Emperor

The seated figure is a mature male at the very peak of his powers. As he is a transpersonal or divine image, he remains at that peak in a state of perfect balance; as the image crosses the Abyss, he exists both in and out of our conception of serial time. The Emperor wear a traditional robe of office; his face is both powerful and generous, with long hair and beard symbolizing his maturity and potency. The Orb in his left hand is held directly over his heart or life centre; it symbolizes the sphere of being. The Orb, therefore, may be defined on three levels; it is the planet Earth, the Solar World or system, and the universal sphere of time, space and energy from which these lesser worlds are reflected.

In his right hand The Emperor holds a Rod or Sceptre. The Rod is an ancient male symbol in magic and religion, but it is far more than a mere emblem of sexual potency or generation. In its true form, the Rod represents the principle of relationship or relativity within the universe; it is an implement of outgoing power, connecting and controlling each stage of relative development or movement. It is the pure concept of the apparently straight line, which in metaphysical terminology is the will of God. Traditionally, the Rod is surmounted by an acorn, the seed of the great oak tree associated with the Sky Father, lightning, thunder and vast stretches of time linked by many life forms (trees growing from many seeds).

In the *Vita Merlini* and *The Mabinogion*, the oak tree is used as a symbol of life extending through time; Merlin outlives an aged oak tree, as does the oldest spiritual animal, the salmon. These aspects of legend echo ancient ritual and religious practices in which the oak was associated with principles of kingship, sacrifice and rebirth.

The crossed legs of The Emperor have a symbolic significance, for, like those of The Hanged Man, they relate to Elemental patterns and to ritual posture connected to magical art and changes of consciousness. If we compare the position of The Emperor to that of The Hanged Man, we find some obvious reversals: The Emperor is seated upright with his legs crossed outwardly, while The Hanged Man is inverted with one leg crossed behind the knee of the other. The general meaning is that while The Hanged Man internalizes consciousness, The Emperor externalizes energy.

Mouse, Ram, Lion and Eagle

We find three types and levels of beast in the image; they correspond to the three levels or Worlds into which the overall picture is divided:

1. The Mouse, holding a nut in its paws, sits right within the protective shadow of The Emperor's throne. This symbolizes that the power of The Emperor extends in mercy to all life forms, even the smallest and most humble. But there is deeper meaning to the Mouse also, for it is an animal that lives in holes in the ground. The Mouse is associated with the Underworld, and can live in both upper and lower realms; traditionally, mice are linked to the spirits of the dead. The power of The Emperor manifests right into the Underworld, and on into worlds which are utterly unknown to human consciousness. If we could see behind the Throne, we would perceive a tiny gateway or hole into which the Mouse runs to reach the realms below.

2. The Ram and Lion are both archetypical animals of rule, inception, power and kingship. They are also the traditional astrological Signs of Aries and Leo, or Spring and Summer, associated with strong anabolic and solar connectives. Aries and Leo are both Fire Signs, thus completing the Elemental pattern implied in the triple structure of the card.

3. The imperial Eagle soars high in the blue Sky above, king of the birds; yet we discovered at the Trump of The Hermit that one bird flies higher than the Eagle, and that is the smallest bird of all. The Eagle is associated with powers of great strength, clear sight, nobility and, of course, rulership of the Element of Air.

XVIII STRENGTH

STRENGTH

WORLD   The Solar World.
WHEEL   The Second Wheel, Justice.
BEINGS   Angels of building or blessing. The solar archangel. Innerworld beings concerned with positive or building energies and conditions.
CONSCIOUSNESS   Transpersonal.

PARTNER TRUMPS   Polar partner; The Blasted Tower. Higher harmonic: Temperance.

SPHERES AND PLANETS   *Spheres:* The 4th and 6th Spheres, Mercy and Beauty. *Planets:* Jupiter and Sol.

ATTRIBUTES   The anabolic or building power of the Solar World. The giving and creative force that supports all form and life in the various worlds.

GOD AND GODDESS FORMS   Jupiter and Apollo. The blessing aspect of the Son of Light.

KEY PHRASES   Merciful beauty/harmonious compassion/giver of strength.

MERLIN TEXTS   *PVM* Obscure reference to figure wrestling with a lion, not necessarily relevant; *VM* Indicated in the Creation Vision by profusion of creative force and beings.

DIVINATORY MEANING   A positive beneficial source of strength. May indicate power within a given situation, or may imply material benefit according to position and other cards. Often indicates creative or constructive possibilities within the query situation.

RELATED NUMBER CARDS   Fours and Sixes.

Fours: Truce, Generosity, Promise, Increase.

Sixes: Transition, Balance, Joy, Benefit.

Origins of the Image

Strength is traditionally shown as a Maiden or mature woman apparently wrestling with or controlling and subduing a Lion. Occasionally this theme has been rationalized to fit classical mythology and Strength has been represented by Hercules; if the image is given a male gender, no matter how superficially satisfying, we run the risk of missing many of its inherent subtleties and deeper levels of consciousness. Another alternative symbol might be Samson pulling down the pillars of the temple; but the further we define this Trump as crude power in male form, the closer it approaches its polar opposite, The Blasted Tower. In other words we have to approach Strength as a creative power, and not a destructive or overbearing entity.

Strength represents the anabolic or building energies of the sun; in a physical sense it is energy radiated through the solar system that enables life to grow and expand. Just as such solar energies are filtered through the atmosphere of Earth before they may be safely experienced by physical organisms, so is the power of the Trump filtered through lower images, such as the Trumps of The Empress, The Lovers, The Priestess and The Universe or World.

Strength is an immediate harmonic or reflection of Temperance, and this relationship is shown by their relative positions upon the Tree of Life.

In Temperance an androgynous figure mediates balanced energies from one dimension or state of consciousness to another; in Strength the image has polarized into a clearly defined female form. This polarization is the result of the relationship between Mercy (4th Sphere) and Beauty (6th Sphere): Strength is a beautiful and merciful power. The energies are firmly defined through contrast between the Maiden and the Lion; beauty controlling power, or harmony centralizing and having knowledge of abounding energy.

The polar opposite to Strength is The Tower, in which forces of catabolism or breaking down and purification are represented. While the Tower symbolizes solar destructive power (Sol and Mars), Strength symbolizes solar creative power (Sol and Jupiter). In both Trumps there is a deliberate juxtaposition of elements of imagery: seething Lightning and static Tower, lovely Maiden and powerful Lion. This juxtaposition is carried through the remainder of the imagery in both cards, shown by various symbols and the landscape. The Tower and Strength are ancient images, and occur in many religions, myths, legends and folk tales. If we were to work with a primal simple system of images, we might regard The Sun, The Tower and Strength as the triple pattern of power within creation.

Contents of the Image

The Twofold Division/Ground and Sky/The Maiden and Lion

The Twofold Division
An inversion of superficial experience or logic, typical of tarot, is very clearly stated in Strength. Natural Sky and Land form the right-hand portion of the image, showing day and lush scenery; the left-hand portion shows a night Sky filled with Stars, and Crystals growing out of bare earth. The two regions merge together within the central figures of Maiden and Lion.

The imagery reveals two aspects of life energy: the first, shown by Sky and Plants, is solar and biological; the second, shown by Stars and Crystals, is stellar and mineral.

Both aspects of growth derive from the archetypical image and mediation of Strength, through which raw, outpouring energy is harmonized into growing, expanding patterns. In a more obvious sense, the Twofold Division, in which both parts are equal, reveals that there is more to the material world than we normally assume, that there are stellar influences and Underworld powers constantly in operation within the outer form of nature. But this concept works equally on deep levels of imagination, consciousness and vital energy within us; it is not limited to exterior relationships or observations. The Maiden and the Lion have a particular reference to use of imagination in harmonizing raw energy. As with all Trumps, Strength has both an outer correlation and an inner function.

Ground and Sky

The level Ground upon which the Maiden and Lion stand represents the Solar World. It is the field of action in which energies operate; it is also their ultimate expression through interaction. More simply, the Ground in our Trump is a higher form of the Element of Earth, a level of energy which forms a base pattern or relatively stable state within any cycle. As the Solar World encompasses and generates life in the Lunar World (including the planet Earth) the Trump contains crystals from the Underworld, and Plants that reach from under- to overworld or the realm of Nature. The human and animal figures complete the unity of life forms (see Figure 1).

While the Ground represents the Solar World, the Sky represents the expanding, compassionate, all-giving energies of the creative Father; he is both the ancient Sky God who fertilizes Mother Earth, and the outpouring of universal energy which makes the sun.

The Maiden and Lion

Within this Trump, the Four Elements and various cycles of life are shown; the Maiden and Lion are archetypes of the human and animal kingdoms. They are not, however, actual created woman and beast, but images or matrices for energies that will eventually express themselves in polarized organic forms. We might say that the Maiden is the highest vessel of poise and balance in the Solar World, while the Lion is the highest vessel of raw natural force. The Lion is unmodified solar power, while the Maiden is that intelligence of beauty and compassion which polarizes and directs such unimaginable force.

This relationship between Maiden and Lion is also an analogy of human energy and consciousness; the astonishing power inherent within each of us may only be aroused and brought into full awareness through agencies of harmony and compassion.

When our inner power (the Lion) is awakened in a balanced manner (the Maiden), it becomes a powerful yet gentle friend, companion and servant, but if awakened without the harmonizing matrix this same inner power becomes a ravening beast. The matrix or Maiden is defined through our imagination working with patterns, such as those taught in esoteric traditions combined with inspiration and vision.

There are many legends concerning maidens taming wild beasts, or saints and holy men walking untouched among savage creatures; they are variants of a central image embodied by our Trump of Strength. Such imagery, however, is not merely a matter of holiness ethics or purity, for it reveals an exact, detailed, magical, meditational and alchemical process. The process, which has many variants but one unified central concept, results in beneficial transformation. It is significant that we may not experience the profound gifts of Strength until we have been purified by the catabolic action of The Tower. Only when pollution, illusion and self-inflation have been dissolved may we reform in a balanced state.

The Lion represents, on one level, the innocent but savage beast of power; the Maiden transforms this beast through her inherent grace. Yet upon a higher level, we might see the Lion as a spiritual animal of the Lord of Light, in whom the totality of illumination and power is vested. Individual human energies are the lesser Lion, while solar or divine energies are the greater Lion.

XIX EMPRESS

THE EMPRESS

WORLD The Solar World.
WHEEL The Second Wheel, Justice (connects Justice and the First Wheel, Fortune).
BEINGS Angels, the solar archangel. Innerworld beings and ex-humans.
CONSCIOUSNESS Anabolic or building solar energies embodied

within individual consciousness or collective consciousness.

PARTNER TRUMPS   Polar partner: The Guardian. Higher harmonic: The Emperor (see also Figure 4).

SPHERES AND PLANETS   *Spheres:* The 4th and 7th Spheres, Mercy and Victory. *Planets:* Jupiter and Venus.

ATTRIBUTES   Positive, giving, generous and blessing powers. Positive or healthy emotions within human consciousness. Life forces becoming attracted to one another and developing towards form.

GOD AND GODDESS FORMS   Jupiter and Venus, the deities who confer blessings. The Lady of Flowers (or of Nature). The Goddess of Giving.

KEY PHRASES   Merciful victory/compassionate goddess/the Lady of Flowers/giver of life.

MERLIN TEXTS   *PVM* A maiden vitalizes the land through mysterious forces; *VM* Merlin's wife Guendoloena.

DIVINATORY MEANING   Indicates a positive, giving state or condition. May relate to personal emotions or partners, or may symbolize a fruitful, creative or beneficial situation. Tends to indicate situations in which nurturing or cultivation are required to truly realize inherent potential, but this varies according to position and other cards in pattern.

RELATED NUMBER CARDS   Fours and Sevens. *Fours:* Truce, Generosity, Promise, Increase. *Sevens:* Dishonesty, Ability, Humour, Attention.

Origins of the Image

The Empress is the feminine counterpart of The Guardian; while he is an image of purification, protection and discipline, acting as a purging catabolic agency, she acts as an anabolic, giving and energizing force. Both are concerned with energies of varied life forms, thus both have a connection to ancient gods and goddesses of nature. We should be aware that these partners are clearly separated in their functions, yet balance one another perfectly. They are not identical to ancient god or goddess forms of Earth, such as the Earth Mother, but may be regarded either as forms that precede the Earth Mother, (in terms of increasingly manifest or defined energies) or as her divine Son and Daughter (in terms of abstraction or dissolution of forms towards primal force).

We meet The Guardian while taking an initiatory path, defined by the life of Merlin, which leads inwards or upwards through the spirals of the worlds; The Empress appears upon the path of exposition or mediation descending or spiralling towards the outer manifest world in which all other states of consciousness merge together. Thus she is symbolically aligned to ancient nature goddesses, but represents archetypes and patterns of life energy prior to manifestation as forms. In modern terms we might say that she is sexual energy without the generative or reproductive function taking form; this generative expression comes with the lunar Sphere or Foundation which appears at the next turn of the Spiral. We have dealt with lunar energies in the Trumps of The Moon and The Magician, but will shortly encounter them upon the Descending Path through the image of The Priestess.

Just as there are many aspects or areas to our outer illusory human personalities, yet such images are parts of one whole being, so tarot images define aspects of archetypical beings; essentially tarot Trumps are the varied cycles of 'personality' or masks of divinity, original being, or the primal God and Goddess. No matter whether we apply pseudo-scientific language or the poetic language of ancient Mysteries and religion, we need harmonic sets of images to help us relate to concepts which are otherwise difficult to encompass. Most important of all is the practical function of imagery in meditation and visualization; The Empress is a very important teaching and enabling image in this practical context.

As The Empress is an embodiment of the power of attraction or positive emotion, it is to her that mystics and magicians turn for education and enlightenment upon the truth behind appearances; her energies will rebalance and fulfil the soul. This is demonstrated by a simple example of the feeling of peace and joy brought about by the beauty of nature; intellectually we know that this emotional response is one-sided and that our reaction to the beauty and our satisfaction and delight are temporary; the same reaction may be found in a work of art or an emotional response to music. These effects derive from the power shown as The Empress. Her Mysteries are those in which we learn to harness and generate such energies from their inner source, rather than through outer reaction.

In the *Vita Merlini* The Empress is represented by the rather poorly developed character of Merlin's wife Guendoloena; her original role has been confused through rationalization of old tales and motifs that involved a Celtic nature goddess. A similar figure occurs in *The Mabinogion*, where a Flower Maiden called Bloduedd is created by magic; she too is something of a rationalization of a primal goddess of Spring.[5,6] This goddess, by whatever name we choose to call her, is a power of kindly fruitful blessing and sensation. Little wonder that by the medieval period her image was carefully rationalized and edited; she would have been regarded with some suspicion by monastic chroniclers.

In the *Vita* Guendoloena is divorced by Merlin in his pursuit of enlightenment; this confused motif suggests the insights of spiritual illumination in which consciousness travels beyond energies formulated by The Empress, and reaches to higher levels of the spiral of being. Significantly, Merlin plays the part of Lord of the Animals while relating to Guendoloena – in other words, he is filled with the power of The Guardian.[1]

The Flower Maiden, by whatever name we choose to call her, is not identical to the Great Mother, who combines within one goddess the powers of both life and death. The Empress, Flower Maiden, is a goddess of life exclusively, of the bounty of continuing life energy and of the more subtle aspects of those same energies within individual and collective consciousness and imagination.

With our meditations upon The Empress, we have now returned to re-encounter human consciousness in both single and multiple units. This may seem to be a rather obvious statement, but it is extremely important in our understanding of The Empress; she is one of the threshold images which interface between aspects of consciousness, both human and transhuman.

If we approach her from the human world, she is a goddess of the emotions; but if she is approached from the higher worlds (as we have travelled via the earlier Trumps of The Innocent, Temperance, and The Emperor), she is the matrix which reforms transpersonal or universal energies into polarized life forms. In other words, our thoughts and feelings are not merely generated through reaction, but are fragments of greater modes of awareness. Tarot Trumps help us to define such relationships and to work with them.

The relationship between worlds or states of existence becomes reflected into relationships between entities (including in human terms sexual or attractive emotions) through the archetype of The Empress.

Contents of the Image

The Threefold Division of Foreground, Middle and Sky/The Empress upon her Throne

The Threefold Division

As this image reaches towards the lower worlds or turns of the Spiral, we now find a Threefold Division with a slightly different emphasis to those of The Emperor or Temperance. The Division now manifests upon a lower harmonic, and represents the Solar, Lunar and sub-Lunar (Earth) Worlds. In our descent or outreaching to the manifest collective world, we now encounter the first Trump that connects directly to the world of nature without mediation through subsequent images or archetypes.

It is significant that upon this Descending Path the connection to the manifest or outer world is through the emotions. Here is one of the typical paradoxical teachings of the Mysteries or magical traditions; the energies, feelings or images generated through emotion, plus those images which cause emotional response, are forerunners of *entities* or life forms. This startling teaching is the converse of our usual approach in which emotions are generated through the reactions of entities to specific situations. The shared area between these two concepts is that of the imagination; it is the image-making ability that operates as an interface between inner and outer worlds. The Empress is mistress of this paradox of consciousness and energy.

In some esoteric literature this theory is found in a rather attenuated and confused condition when dealing with 'thought forms' or 'astral images'. These are reputed to be entities which originate in the human mind or imagination, energized by emotions and sexual impetus, but which somehow develop a degree of independence. The entire matter is clarified by a simple examination of the unfolding pattern of creation, as defined in the Creation Vision of the *Vita Merlini*, which may be summarized as follows:

Stages of Creation

1	Universal Origination	Divine or stellar being.
2	Defined Creation	Solar being or system.
3	Increasing Formation	Lunar diversity of life forms.
4	Multifold Expression	The outer worlds.

The Empress and her counterpart The Guardian are images which act as focuses for energy upon the threshold between Stages 3 and 4 of the above sequence. They may build up forms from energy, the function of The Empress, or break forms down into energy, the function of The Guardian. In the outer world of nature these functions or powers of anabolism and catabolism were given imaginative expression by early cultures as a god of wild animals (a hunter and culling god) and a goddess of fruit and flowers.

These figures appear in the life of Merlin as one of Merlin's own roles, Wild Man of the Wood, and as his Flower Maiden wife, Guendoloena. They appear again in Renaissance tarot as The Devil and Empress, or in the Merlin Tarot as The Guardian and Empress. Thus, our attitude towards, or understanding of, the concept of energies as entities is defined by the 'direction' in which we travel conceptually: if we reach inwards, we encounter The Guardian, who always dissolves illusory self-images of entity in the quest for truth; if we reach outwards conceptually, we encounter The Empress, whose bounty enables emotions, feelings and all positive sensations to take form through reflections of images – ultimately reaching into material manifestation.

In simpler terminology, this is how people become emotionally attracted and attached to one another. The rather vague esoteric theory of 'thought forms' is based upon reflections and polarizations of this type.

The Threefold Division of our card, therefore, first reveals a Foreground which is the boundary of the natural or outer world. We look over this threshold into a realm of highly energized and idealized images, living just behind expressed forms. This is the inner world in which our imagination and emotions play such an important part. It is the realm ruled by The Empress and her consort The Guardian; but in the present Trump we find only the female image in her individual aspect.

The Foreground is the sub-Lunar or outer World, but the Middle area of the card, merging imperceptibly with the Foreground, is the Lunar World. This area is typified by the flowing Stream and Waterfall, which originated in the higher Trump of The Emperor, in which the Three Worlds are Stellar, Solar and Lunar. It must always be borne in mind that these triple divisions are not hard and fast entities, but fluid sequences of reflection. In meditation our understanding of the triple division may actually become transformed from one level to another. If we follow the Stream, for example, it will lead us beyond the horizon of The Empress, and up into the realm of The Emperor.

The Sky expresses movement of the Trump from one world to another; all Trumps consist of a fusion of energies (or of Spheres in Kabbalistic terminology). The Empress is a fusion of the ancient sky power, or Mercy, with the emotions, or Victory. In the Sky we see a very clearly shining Evening Star, the planet Venus. Here the Sky Father (The Emperor) and the Maiden (Venus) are visibly related.

The Empress upon her Throne
A beautiful woman, crowned with a head-dress of stars and flowers, sits upon her Throne surrounded by the bounty of luxuriant nature. She is the goddess or matrix of all giving in life. All positive emotions are her children, she is the mother of every kindly compassionate warm feeling, she builds and generates cohesion and joy in the outer world of expression and form. Paradoxically, she is both virgin and mother, for her fruitfulness is timeless, a state of eternal Spring.

Victory (shown as the 7th Sphere of the Tree of Life) is found through a perfect relationship to the imaginative and energetic flow that appears in our consciousness as emotion and sexual attraction. Paradoxically, it is the fusion with Mercy (shown as the 4th Sphere upon the Tree of Life) that enables Victory within consciousness; there is no concept of strife or suppression in this archetypical realm.

The Empress sits upon a Throne inscribed with a carving of a Queen Bee; the symbol states that the seated figure is queen of collective energies, the archetypes of many ancient goddesses. She gives the sweetness and rapture of honey, and her power has a sting and pain within it that approaches ecstasy. Here, we are touching upon some very primal Mysteries, for the preparation of ritual drinks from honeycomb involved not only symbolic contents, but organic compounds derived from a fusion of the bee-sting, honey and alcohol. Every poetic or symbolic fusion in the imaginative world has a physical expression in the outer world; this is one of the principles of alchemy.

The Empress, seated upon her Throne, represents diffusion of cosmic energy into individual entities; she is the queen of the swarms of life, which move according to the rhythms and cycles of attraction and repulsion, life and death. In consciousness we experience such rhythms as emotions, but they are lesser reflections of great movements of the stellar beings, of the universe in which we exist and of which we are an integral part.

The Empress wears a flowing Robe, which merges with plants and flowers around her Throne; it is the veil or vestment of form which surrounds energy, and which may flow into different relative shapes at any moment of perception. She is an expression of the goddess Venus, who rules emotions, love and sexual power as an independent energy not confined to breeding, which is governed by the goddess Luna. Around her waist is the Girdle or Zona of Venus, symbolizing sexual energy and perfect victory over this most potent of life powers that leads to interaction. The Cord or Girdle of Venus symbolizes that there is a unity to each and every strand woven through the energies of relationship; they are all under the blessing of the goddess.

In her right hand The Empress carries a long Sceptre, topped with a crystalline Orb. In her the function of Rod and Orb, or organizing power and world-sphere, are fused into one implement. In our previous Trump, The Emperor, these emblems were still separate, though wielded by one centralizing figure.

The bird perched upon the Throne is a song thrush, symbolizing the heights and expressions of feeling through its song.

XX LOVERS

THE LOVERS

WORLD The Solar World.
WHEEL The Second Wheel, Justice.
BEINGS Angels, the solar archangel. Ex-humans and transhuman teachers, innerworld masters or saints.
CONSCIOUSNESS Spiritual energies reflecting as emotions. The

creative or anabolic life force of the solar being.

PARTNER TRUMPS The Chariot (see also Figure 4).

SPHERES AND PLANETS *Spheres:* The 6th and 7th Spheres, Beauty and Victory. *Planets:* Sol and Venus.

ATTRIBUTES Love as a spiritual power (rather than as a personal emotion). Emotions in their purest, most balanced mode or form. The perfect union of male and female energies within humanity, either collectively or individually. Inner energies moving towards life expression as polarized forms (male and female, positive and negative).

GOD AND GODDESS FORMS Apollo and Venus, the Lord and Lady of Light and Harmony. Also the mysterious Eros, who empowers the gods and goddesses.

KEY PHRASES Harmony and victory/beautiful emotions/perfect partnership/mutual reflection of truth/spiritual love.

MERLIN TEXTS *VM* Relationship between Merlin and his wife Guendoloena. (This motif is, however, confused or rationalized in the *Vita* and is better represented by the Trump image.)

DIVINATORY MEANING Love and relationships. Usually means positive, harmonious connections with other people (depending on position and other cards). May also mean a spiritual or transcendent power within the individual. Implies balance between male and female which may be outward- or inward-moving. Often represents inspired creativity, usually related to a lover or an idealized focus.

RELATED NUMBER CARDS Sixes and Sevens.

Sixes: Transition, Balance, Joy, Benefit.

Sevens: Dishonesty, Ability, Humour, Attention.

Origins of the Image

In this image, the emotions (which are *movements* or modes of energy within the human psychic/body complex) are perfectly balanced in their relationship to the spiritual centre or source of life. This was symbolized in traditional mythology by Venus, the goddess of love, and Sol, the god of light. But The Lovers is more precise in its symbolism, not showing Venus relating to Sol, but a pair of male and female figures being blessed by a veiled power or transcendent being. They are Venus and Sol within humanity.

At the root of this card is the concept of power or life energy emerging from a state of androgyny into sexually polarized entities. It shows a state in which flows of energy, which we call 'sexual' in the outer world, are still upon an inner, idealized level; hence a pair of perfect lovers, the original Adam and Eve in legendary terms. We may also refer this image to the curious tradition reported by Plato, in which humans were originally joined, male and female, as one androgynous or bisexual entity. Upon separation (physical expression) they ceaselessly sought their original partner of union, hence the ebb and flow and constant searching of human relationships in our manifest world.

Contents of the Image

The Threefold Division/The Robed Figure/The Lovers/Landscape, Stream and Path/The Pair of Pheasants

The Threefold Division

The Threefold Division represents the basic triad found repeatedly in tarot symbolism and in traditional glyphs such as the Tree of Life or the Spindle or Wheel of Being. It is a variant of the concept of the Three Worlds: the upper level represents the spiritual world, the middle the human world, and the lower the natural world.

In this image, which deals with polarization of energies towards physical expression and the converse flow in which physical and emotional patterns may be followed inwards to their transcendent source, the spiritual element is the Sphere of Harmony or the Sun (see Figure 2). The human element bridges the worlds, mediating between the inner power of the solar or central consciousness and life source, and the expressed natural world of living entities. In short, humans partake of both nature and super-nature.

1. SUN: Source of Life Power; Transcendent Androgyny.
2. HUMAN PAIR: Polarization of Life Force; Idealized Relationship.
3. NATURE: Expression of Life Energies; Interaction of Forms (Sexuality).

The development or progression towards multiple forms relating to one another, or conversely of multiple forms simplifying into one ultimate source of energy, should be considered and meditated upon in its larger context, that of the Three Worlds. When we locate this image within the overview of the Three Worlds (Star, Sun, Moon or originative, creative, formative) we find that it is in the Solar or Creative World (see Figure 1). Thus The Lovers does not generate physical expression; it is an idealized creative image. Upon the Tree of Life or the Spindle, the energies have to flow through the Spheres or matrices of the lunar (formative) levels, before they are finally expressed physically upon outer levels or in the manifest world as life forms. In human terms, The Lovers represents a process of *consciousness*, reflecting within our own microcosm of awareness and reaction a greater process of *interaction* that runs through all life.

In esoteric tradition, life in our world begins with the great consciousness of the sun, a living star that generates and vitalizes its own 'world'. This is apparent physically in the natural cycle of life which is derived from the relationship between our physical sun and planets, in our case the planet Earth. Without the sun, no life could exist in its present form. This physical, biological situation, however, is a reflection or expression of a metaphysical pattern. Upon this inner level, the sun is found to be a great being or divinity, and images immediately deriving from the solar being and leading towards the lunar formative and expressive realms (the Trumps of The Lovers, The Magician and The Moon) may be meditated upon in two related ways. The first is as ideal images generated by transcendent cosmic consciousness; they are, in short, the potent dreams of the source of all life and consciousness, within the Solar World that gives birth to lunar and Earth reflections. The second is that they are the microcosmic or individual reflections of this same process, found within the human psyche. In this context the images are used to lead our awareness inwards towards a unified source; this source is our own spiritual reality or centre, which in turn is a timeless part of that greater entity symbolized by the sun or Son of Light.

The Robed Figure

In the upper part of the image is a Robed Figure radiating light; the hands of this Figure are extended over the human couple in a sign of blessing. No face may be seen, for this being is both the source and fusion of individuality: the face is that mystery of Light which we may not look upon as humans. The Lovers in the image feel the presence and power of the being that blesses them, but look outwards, or perhaps towards one another.

Light from the hooded Figure begins to polarize into colours of the spectrum; this represents energies that harmonically separate into cycles of relationship. In very precise magical terms, the rays of light are inner powers which are liberated through disciplines that redirect the customary movement (emotion) of sexual attraction. These energies are present in the human being as a reflection or microcosm of universal cycles and patterns. When meditation and inner disciplines become effective, power centres corresponding to the Earth, Moon, Sun and Star are activated consciously. The Lovers is of paramount importance in this magical or mystical transformation and redirection of individual energies.

The Robed Figure may be regarded as the androgynous spirit of the central sun, or as the Son of Light, or as the Great Goddess of perfected love. In some traditions this figure is Eros, the ultimate power that directs even gods and goddesses in their relationships. In this context a spiritual Eros may be inferred, a primal power of separation, attraction and union that is shown by the triadic patterns of the Tree of Life, with their Spheres of male, female and androgynous divinities or universal polarizations. In the biological realm, this Eros becomes the erotic drive that leads to reproduction: the courting amorous Pheasants in the lower part of the image.

The Lovers

The man and woman shown are the original human couple, the ideal Adam and Eve of legend, the first man and woman described in tradition world-wide. In some Trumps they are shown looking lovingly towards one another; in the Merlin Tarot they touch hands as a sign of their perfect union, and look innocently outwards towards the world into which they are about to emerge.

Here, we find one significant difference between inner or magical tradition, and outer legend. The perfect couple is not cast out into the outer world (as in the story of the Garden of Eden) but is sent forth with blessing and harmony. As the first definition or polarization of life force into form, still upon a creative level, these primal archetypical humans pass from the imagination of divinity into the garden of an outer world. The Mystery of a restored or regenerated world is contained in this imagery, for by meditating upon the implications of two Lovers, their unity in separation, and the transcendent entity from which they emerge, we may find perfection and balance within ourselves.

The Lovers are garlanded with flowers, and stand unashamedly naked. They are in a state not of ignorance but of innocent perfection.

Landscape, Stream and Path

By the male is a flowing Stream, by the female a Path. Both lead to a distant Tor or sacred Mound, upon which a round Tower or upright standing Stone is located. Above this central locus rises the transcendent Figure of blessing, filling the Sky with its radiance. The imagery of the Landscape echoes the pattern of unity and polarity shown by the human couple, the courting Pheasants, and the transcendent Figure of power, but like many seemingly supportive or superficial elements of traditional symbolism, it contains an important sub-tradition.

The Stream flows outwards towards the unseen but imminent world of Earth. In Western esoteric tradition this stream is that of male polarity or seed, human sperm that flows ever outwards in countless millions to generate endless families, nations, worlds. It is a biological reflection of that great explosive seeding that utters forth across the Abyss of time and space, shown in the higher Trumps of The Emperor, Temperance and The Star.

Higher Trumps, however, have a high degree of polar separation, with outgoing Trumps balanced by separate inward moving images (Death paired with The Emperor, The Hanged Man with Temperance). We find that the lower Trumps begin to contain this polarity in ever more complex and inclusive structures of symbols.

Our human couple is a more obvious example of this pattern, for the Stream (seed) is balanced in the same image by the Path, just as the male is balanced by the female. To grasp this tradition, we need to meditate upon the fact that it is difficult (but not impossible) to wade upstream. The male Stream ultimately becomes a great River; in Underworld traditions it finally appears as a roaring river or sea passing through realms below the light of Sun and Moon.

While we are in the realm of The Lovers, however, the Stream is in its earliest stages of development, balanced by the Path of the female image. The Path is an alternative form of the traditional symbol for feminine power, which is, of course, blood. The blood and seed, male and female, are the human expressions of the two primal red and white dragons (see Figure 7) which define all worlds and all states of being, from the simplest organic forms to the immeasurable energies of time and space. Thus, the Stream is outward-moving life energy, while the Path is inward-moving, yet both may be travelled in either direction.

The Path, however, relates to an important esoteric tradition, found repeatedly in Grail legends, that the way to perfection, illumination and enlightenment is through feminine archetypes. In the corrupted Eden legends, we find a medieval tradition (probably from a very early source) that it is through woman that humankind may find the way back to the Garden, just as it was supposed to be through woman that we were cast out.

Despite an overlay of political and suppressive orthodoxy, this theme contains a great truth, which is at once spiritual and magical. On a magical level it suggests actual operations by which we may transform our consciousness through meditation, visualization and ritual pattern making.

The Pair of Pheasants
In the foreground we see a Pair of courting Pheasants; these birds represent final definition of polar energies into sexuality. They are before or ahead of our ideal human couple, thus physical mating has not yet been defined. Once the couple pass beyond the courting birds, they will emerge into the Lunar World, in which they will join together sexually, and eventually produce further humans through the process of childbirth.

XXI PRIESTESS

THE PRIESTESS

WORLD   The Lunar World (threshold to the Solar World).
WHEEL   The First Wheel, Fortune.
BEINGS   Humans, ex-humans, certain transhumans or innerworld teachers; *daemones* and nature spirits, elementals.
CONSCIOUSNESS   Human emotional and imaginative consciousness.

PARTNER TRUMPS Polar partner: The Magician. Higher harmonic Trumps: Strength, Temperance, The Innocent (Hierophant).
SPHERES AND PLANETS *Spheres:* The 7th and 9th Spheres, Victory and Foundation. *Planets:* Venus and Luna.
ATTRIBUTES Emotions and creative/reproductive energies. Tides of life power and swarms of life forms. Imagination forming or moulding reality in expression. A feminine anabolic and therapeutic consciousness/energy.
GOD AND GODDESS FORMS Venus and Luna, the goddesses of love and life, tides and feelings. All ancient goddesses relating to the positive emotions (attraction, love, sympathy, friendship). Goddesses or innerworld images connected to therapy, rebirth, transformation through the natural tides or cycles of the regenerative world (i.e. within The Wheel of Fortune). These goddess forms may also act as guides or initiators into the higher transpersonal consciousness of the Solar World.
KEY PHRASES Victorious foundation of life/love as a power/the Mysteries of the Inner Fire/the Muse/Queen of the Fortunate Isles.
MERLIN TEXTS *VM* Vision of Morgen and her nine sisters ruling the Fortunate or Blessed Isle and curing the wounded King Arthur.
DIVINATORY MEANING Relationship between emotions and foundational or sexual energies; often refers to mental and emotional health, matters of sexual attraction, reproduction, and creative work that employs the feelings. May also refer to insights into the inner Mysteries of life, either as maturity of emotions, or in the form of specific magical arts (such as meditation, visualization, prayer, or magical dance and music).
RELATED NUMBER CARDS Sevens and Nines.
Sevens: Dishonesty, Ability, Humour, Attention.
Nines: Misfortune, Endurance, Fulfilment, Means.

Origins of the Image

The Priestess, typified in the *Vita Merlini* by Morgen, is one of a small number of particularly significant images in the Merlin Tarot. While tarot cycles in general place emphasis upon all Trumps and more subtle emphasis upon their relationship to one another, specific packs or systems have a tendency to give more emphasis to certain key Trumps. In the Merlin Tarot, due to the ancient proto-tarot system upon which our modern pack is based, these key images are:

1. The Hanged Man.
2. The Guardian.
3. Death.
4. The Fool.

5. The Magician.
6. The Priestess.
7-9. The Three Cosmic Wheels (Fortune, Justice and Judgement).
10-12. The Three Worlds (Moon, Sun and Star).
13. The Hermit.

This is not to imply that these thirteen images are more powerful or important than the other nine, for, as we have emphasized all along, each Trump belongs to a pair, triplicity or even higher pattern of relationship, and is incomplete otherwise. The significance of certain Trumps or images is one of operation or practical application.

In the system of transforming consciousness which is epitomized by the Merlin tradition, the Trumps listed above play a major role in the initiation or catalysis of human awareness. In other systems we might find a slightly different list of Trumps, while ultimately all Trumps are present in a state of balanced, dynamic relationship.

The Priestess is one of the most important images in the Merlin system. We encounter her in the *Vita Merlini* as Morgen, a mistress of magical arts, therapy, shape changing and flight. It should be stated immediately that these abilities are obviously those of certain ancient goddesses, but they are also the essential qualities of transformation required of the imagination in pursuit of meditation, visualization and the magical arts.

In the Merlin Tarot, The Priestess is the female counterpart of The Magician. Both are founded upon an immeasurable source of life energy symbolized by The Moon; while The Magician polarizes this energy towards intellect, The Priestess polarizes it towards emotion. Each image represents one mode or direction in which energy may flow to gain further form or expression.[10]

The partner or counterpart to The Priestess in the *Vita Merlini* is possibly King Bladud, another figure who flies through the air, and who, in the *History*, is especially associated with magical arts and sciences. We might say, broadly, that The Magician of the Merlin Tarot is an archetype of which Britain's legendary druid King Bladud is a sub-image or mythical expression.

In one of the most important passages of the *Vita* we find Merlin, the bard Taliesin (who is another *persona* similar to the archetype of The Magician) and the Otherworld Ferryman Barinthus taking the wounded King Arthur to the Fortunate Isles. It is in these islands that our card is set.

The priestess or druidess Morgen has nine sisters, who are similar to the Muses of classical tradition, and might be said to be the tripled Triple Goddess: three times three. This becomes significant in our pattern of overall relationships in the Merlin Tarot, for The Priestess is that feminine archetype founded upon the 9th or Lunar Sphere. To reach her, the flow of power from Origination to Formation has passed through three worlds or levels, and generated nine Spheres or *locii* of polarized energy. Thus Morgen and her nine sisters represent the ancient ninefold unfolding of reality from its source of being.

The taking of Arthur, suffering from a deadly wound made in the outer world of conflict and pain, to Morgen, is an allegory that works upon several levels:

1. The ancient system of sacrificial kingship is dependent upon a magical or innerworld location, in which a goddess mediates the spirit of a king or hero to and fro between death and birth. In more sophisticated pagan variants, the goddess is represented by an order or sisterhood of priestesses, such as Morgen and her nine sisters. In Christian symbology, we have the Virgin Mary and the Conception announced by Gabriel, who is Archangel of the Lunar Sphere which governs tides, procreation, birth and death. In the Merlin legend, we have curious semi-material beings who live between the Earth and the moon and sometimes consort with human maidens and cause them to have children.

   Despite major differences in *realization*, there is an enduring and coherent thread woven through each of these allegorical or magical systems that represent the powers of birth and death, or of dissolution and salvation.

2. In a simpler sense, the allegory is that of natural healing, either of mind or body. The Priestess represents those organic natural healing powers of regeneration which are inherent in all living beings right up to the moment of final physical death.

3. The allegory may be worked as a practical system of inner spiritual and magical growth and rejuvenation; here is where we apply our imagination to a scene, such as the visualization of a Tarot Trump, and allow attuned energies to manifest naturally within our stilled and waiting consciousness. Morgen is The Priestess, mistress of this art of inner healing and growth.

Contents of the Image

Islands and Sea/The Two Trees/The Priestess/The Mask

Islands and Sea

The ground upon which The Priestess stands is the Fortunate Isle, the Avallach or Avalon, Island of Apples, or the Blessed Isle of Celtic legend. This is the eternal Otherworld, not remote or distant, but as near as life, feeling and imagination. The ancient traditions repeatedly advise us that the power of the imagination is the greatest power in the universe; it is, in fact, the power of being as it arises within human consciousness. The magical islands of tradition are found by passing through a veil or across an ocean, but also through another dimension.

Beyond the shore behind The Priestess is the Sea, the ocean of living consciousness and imagination, while further on are other Islands which represent further states of awareness, or in a tarot system, higher images or modes of awareness. The triple pattern found in most of the Trumps represents here three aspects or relative states of our imaginative power during the transitions from outer to inner life; this is the realm presided over by The Priestess.

The ground of the Island represents our foundation or formalized life energies. It is the Element of Earth upon which all beings interact with one another. But it is not the fully expressed Earth of the outer world, it is a primal archetypical Earth, a form of Earth just behind or beyond expressed outer manifestation. It is this Earth, the magical Island, that is ever fruitful, needs no intense labour, and bears repeated harvests. It is the *imagination* in terms of our individual or collective consciousness, or the Lunar Sphere in terms of metaphysics or magic.

Whatever is sown or seeded at this level will manifest in the outer world; whatever moves from the outer worlds towards inner being first reaches this Island. Both the Cave of The Magician and the Trees of The Priestess are upon this eternal Island or original Earth. In a more Christian mythology it is the Garden of Eden from which humanity was cast out into the outer worlds. As The Priestess is part of the cycle also expressed by the higher Trump of The Lovers, of which she is a polarized or harmonic image, meditation upon myths of this type is very fruitful at this stage of development and imagery.

The Sea is boundless consciousness, life and, in a physical sense, the sea of generation, waters of the oceans, body fluids, and the metaphysical sea in which our imagination and our spirits swim. In old fashioned occultism this may be loosely equated with the much discussed but little understood 'astral plane' in which life forms move prior to and after physical expression.

The Two Trees

The Two Trees are rowan, the guardian tree of the Celtic Otherworld associated with magical arts, fairy traditions and many ancient legends of sanctity; and the Otherworld tree of flames and crystal fruit. They are, in fact, one Tree. Its natural outer expression and its energetic inner transformation are reflections or inversions of one another. In a higher Trump of this spiral or cycle, Strength, the card was divided into naturalistic and crystalline areas. Now we find a similar bipolar pattern, but further expressed as Two Trees in growth. They are two extremes or pillars between which The Priestess stands to allow us to pass or to bar us from further movement into the inner worlds. One extreme is the organic natural body, while the other is the energetic and potentially spiritual or stellar form of that same body. We may see this polarity of Trees as two aspects of ourselves, but also as overt and secret faces of nature which must both be fully appraised before we may relate to the higher worlds shown in the tarot cycles.

The Priestess
The figure of The Priestess is that of a young but mature woman with hair shading from gold into dark red. Hers is that Otherworldly beauty that transcends yet includes sexuality. She wears a shimmering Robe and a Cloak made from the feathers of every wild bird in the land. This feathered Cloak (traditionally found in tales or early manuscripts describing druids or magicians) is her power of instantaneous flight; it is significant that this power is related not only to our imagination but also to creatures of the air in a specific environment.

In other words, The Priestess would be wearing different feathers in her Cloak if she represented a different land or part of the world. She might also be of the type and colour of that region, rather than bearing the magical or faery golden-red hair and colouration of Celtic archetypes. The images of tarot will manifest locally or geographically as well as universally. This is one of the great but quite obvious magical and spiritual secrets: the paths to enlightenment begin at home.

The feathered Cloak of The Priestess is fastened by a Pin or Brooch in the shape of mistletoe, reminding us of her druidic and ancient origins. She looks directly into our eyes; nothing in our imagination may be hidden from her, for she has the power of total empathy and fusion of consciousness. This is the secret of her therapeutic power, particularly if we seek to enact or mediate it into the outer world.

Around her forearms are spiralling Serpents of power, the ancient symbols of royal blood or Otherworld lineage. She appears to be holding something invisible towards us; whatever it is may be discovered in meditation or visualization. The object or meaning that she offers us will change as we change, but it has a constant reality and certain archetypical or primal forms.

The Mask
At the feet of The Priestess is a discarded leather Mask; masks of this sort are associated with Celtic water magic, or with ancient temples (such as Aquae Sulis, Bath, England) where ritual masks have been found by archaeologists. Masks were employed in rituals, worn by a priest or priestess to hide the intense power of divinity which flowed through them at peak moments. Nature wears a mask, but with our inner perceptions we may gradually see reality unmasked. One of the first images to be unmasked and to present herself to us in a true form is The Priestess.

XXII UNIVERSE

THE UNIVERSE
(The World)

WORLD The sub-Lunar or outer World, yet all Worlds.
WHEEL The First Wheel, Fortune, but also all Three Wheels.
BEINGS All living beings in the universe. Human beings on Earth.

CONSCIOUSNESS   Personal and collective. Also relates to the *Anima Mundi* or soul of the world in medieval metaphysics.

PARTNER TRUMPS   Polar partner: The Fool. Ultimate partner: The Hermit. Harmonic forms: The Priestess and Temperance.

SPHERES AND PLANETS   *Spheres:* The 7th and 10th Spheres, Victory and Kingdom. *Planets:* Venus and Earth.

ATTRIBUTES   The consciousness of the world or universe. The Four Powers and Elements within all life forms. Encompasses universal being in an expressed individual image.

GOD AND GODDESS FORMS   Venus or the Flower Maiden and the Earth gods and goddesses. Ultimately an androgynous being, often shown in alchemy and metaphysical imagery. By inversion, this is the divine androgyne, universal spirit inherent in matter.

KEY PHRASES   Victorious kingdom/perfection of Elements/universal being/divinity in matter/the universe within human awareness/manifest truth.

MERLIN TEXTS   *PVM* Vision of the Goddess of the Land; *VM* Aspects of the Creation Vision relating to the Four Powers and Elements.

DIVINATORY MEANING   May simply mean worldly or material concerns, especially in the context of other cards. Also refers to balance of Elements or energies within the individual (according to position) and indicates outer or outcome parameters. Is also a direct indicator of where the greatest power may be found in any situation, according to the position of the card.

RELATED NUMBER CARDS   Tens (or Aces) and Sevens.

Tens: Disaster, Responsibility, Friendship, Opportunity.

Sevens: Dishonesty, Ability, Humour, Attention.

Origins of the Image

This Trump has two names, but a single identity. On a macrocosmic scale, the image represents the entirety of the universe, not only in immeasurable physical dimensions, but in many interlinked inner worlds or states of consciousness. The Universe is complete being in all relative worlds or dimensions; in human terms, it has a special relevance as our outer or consensual world, the planet Earth with its life forms and related imaginal or inner worlds and dimensions. On a microcosmic scale, The World may also represent humankind, or one individual human, male or female.

A further and very important meaning to this Trump is that the entire universe is inherent in The World, which is to say, within any human being. The Trump shows an androgynous being, for this archetype both underpins and includes all relative sexuality and polarity. The World is balancing partner to The Fool, who represents an individual soul beginning the great adventure, while The World represents all souls at all stages of development. Yet, paradoxically, The World is a complete entity, and not a collective or assembly of beings. The World is also a polar partner of The Hermit (as The Fool is to The Innocent); for the ultimate internalizing power of consciousness, The Hermit, is a mirror image of the maximum externalizing power of being, The Universe or World (see Figures 3, 4 and 7).

The image arises from a fusion of the 7th and 10th Spheres upon the Tree of Life – Victory and Kingdom, or Venus and Mother Earth. Thus, it has a special relationship to our feelings and expanding emotions, just as The Fool has a special relationship to our thoughts or developing mind. There is a further mystical yet practical level to this relationship, for emotions are one of the main routes by which our Inner Fire is aroused. Generally, we experience this in a sexual manner, but in magical and mystical disciplines, carefully defined images are enlivened through visualization, and specific emotional responses generated. Thus, we may employ our emotions to alter the energy patterns of our world; in the simple sense, balanced emotions and pure imagery will inspire and enable us to live together and create a happy planet, but this must first be achieved within the individual.

Upon the Descending Path or Right-Hand Pillar, The Universe is an image of manifestation. Swarms of energies finally become formed and expressed as entities, and take on material form through cycles of the Four Elements in the outer world. In this sense Victory or the emotions are energies of consciousness prior to physical definition. We may understand this to mean both primal energies in an idealized creation sequence finally coming to expression as human beings, and as conditions of consciousness that define and influence reincarnation and life patterns. In this last sense we should remember that this Trump connects also to The Wheel of Fortune, which is the threshold or boundary of the Lunar and material World. The image is not exclusively related to humans, of course, but emotions within our framework of consciousness/body are our most obvious energies encompassed by The World.

It is in this Trump more than any other that we have the Mystery of the Virgin and Whore embodied. In esoteric Christianity we might rename our image and call her Mary Magdalene. Her secret is timeless renewal, a fusion of the Four Elements that enables Inner Fire to radiate both outwardly as sexuality, and inwardly as Victory over sexuality. The Trump is a resonance combining the Earth Mother of fertility and death with the Flower Maiden of sensuality and birth; the archetype is so potent that its Elements spin with immeasurable speed; the resulting androgyne is both world and universe, mother and child, whore and virgin. The secret of this Mystery is one of the great initiations or revelations of consciousness; how to fuse purity and passion, how to comprehend polarity as unity without losing one fraction of its dynamic power in the outer world. We use sexual symbolism, but the inner meaning reaches far beyond sexuality.

To illustrate this Trump, we can turn to a traditional exercise which has been used (in various forms) in magical and mystical tuition for millennia. It is called:

Constructing the Universe

1. Draw a circle.
2. Draw a second circle with its circumference touching the centre of the first, its centre upon the lower circumference of the first.
3. Draw a third circle within and below the second likewise.

These three interlinked circles are the Wheels or Spirals of Judgement, Justice and Fortune. The areas enclosed by them are the Worlds of Star, Sun and Moon.

4. The Two Dragons are discovered by following the line from Earth, at the nadir of the lowest World, in a serpentine manner passing through the centre of the Solar World and emerging at the crown or zenith of the highest World. We may make two serpent or dragon paths through the Worlds in this manner – left–right and right–left. These are the great Dragons defining the Worlds and Tree of Life, shown in our Figure 7.
5. The Trump The Universe contains all the foregoing stages in one image. The Three Rings in the card are time, space and energy; but they are also the Three Wheels and the Three Worlds.

Contents of the Image

The Androgyne/The Three Rings/The Four Creatures/The Four Power Centres

The Androgyne
The central figure of our Trump may be male or female; unlike The Fool, who seems to change roles, this archetype expresses all roles simultaneously. The gender is both male and female at the same time, but there is more than mere bisexuality in the symbolism. The Androgyne combines the physical organs of erect penis, vagina and full breasts with a face and figure that may be a young female or male. There is no definable age to this image, which is both eternally young and immeasurably old, for The Universe includes yet transcends time.

The higher modes of sexuality, or Inner Fire, are demonstrated by Three Power Centres. These are shown in our image as a crescent Moon (the genitalia), a blazing Sun (the heart) and a shining Star (above the crown of the head). Thus the figure is not only a fusion of physical gender, but a fusion of the Three Worlds of energy: Moon, Sun and Star.

In magical arts and esoteric disciplines, students are taught to redirect their sexual generative energies into arousal and refinement of the power centres, which are often dormant or imbalanced in habitual life. This art is very dependent upon emotion and purified imagination; sexual fantasy will imbalance our power centres.

In some traditions, particularly Eastern, there are further centres or *chakras*; many Western sources define seven such centres relating to the Seven Planets. In the simplest master pattern, however, we find Three Centres for the Three Worlds with, of course, a fourth location at the feet, which paradoxically is both the highest and lowest power centre – the Kingdom.

The Veil which hides and yet reveals the genitals of the Androgyne is an 'S' shape, as described in the exercise given above and, of course, relating to the serpentine sign of The Hanged Man. It is a Veil of power, not of confusion. It suggests that if we can solve the Mystery of directing our inner forces upon a lunar level, then the other Worlds will harmonically become available to our consciousness. In human terms, this means a redirection of our sexual and emotional drives from outer projection to inner balance. The Androgyne, after all, is biologically present in every man and woman; this sexual potential, or residual balance of gender, indicates our inner potential of balance.

We encountered a Veil before the face of the Goddess in the Trump Judgement; now we see its final expressed mystery, for it reveals secrets of sexuality, yet seems to hide them. The Veil shows a serpentine or undulating path of energy which must be established to understand the relationship between the Four Elements, obviating the cycles of The Wheel of Fortune.

The Three Rings

The Androgyne seems to be within, yet unbounded by, Three Rings; the area of these Rings defines the figure, and separates it from the cloud background and Elements. Traditionally these encircling definitions are the essence of *triplicity*. In modern esoteric texts (combining theories from stellar physics with ancient metaphysics that long pre-dated any modern theories), the Rings are defined as time, space, and energy or events.

The Three Rings are the supernal Spheres of the Tree of Life: Being, Understanding and Wisdom. Yet they are also the Three Worlds of Star, Sun and Moon, and the Three Wheels of Judgement, Justice and Fortune. The triple pattern that runs through tarot and the Merlin cosmology reflects an inherent triple relationship that causes events, time and space: three qualities or quantities, three relative definitions, three modes of consciousness. The weaving together of these three makes The Universe.

The Rings, or relative fields of definition, are not rigid or locked together. If we look closely at the Trump, we will find that the spatial relationship between the figure and the Rings is difficult to define. The figure seems to be coming forward out of the frame or field defined by the Rings, yet the hands and feet are clearly in contact with each Ring.

The figure's left leg is bent behind the right knee, reminding us of the symbolic posture of The Hanged Man, in which patterns shown by a human figure relate to the mystery of the 'Z' sign or Lighting Flash. This shape motif is repeated in The Universe in the Veil over the Androgyne's genitals, and the position of arms and legs relative to the Rings.

The relationship between The Fool, The Hanged Man, The Hermit, and The Innocent, Temperance and The Universe is completed by our examination of this Trump; and the entire story of these images is the entire universe, or Spindle of the Worlds, in terms of *changing human consciousness*. This concept is important, for Trumps have not only a coherent cosmology/psychology, but a number of world views that harmonize with one another.

We could, for example, say that the Trumps Moon, Sun and Star define the totality of the universe, but they would do so without the presence of human consciousness. Similarly we might say that Judgement, Justice and Fortune define the totality of the universe; they have a relationship to human consciousness, but could be visualized without human interaction. The master Trumps, however, which are The Fool, The Hanged Man and The Hermit, and The Universe, Temperance and The Innocent, are intimately related to changing modes of consciousness: their highest forms are The Hermit and The Innocent, in which transhuman consciousness passes to and fro from the void.

Between these extreme poles of consciousness and energy, we find the transformative Trumps which make up the remainder of the 20 major images. They are harmonics or specialized reflections of the basic triplicities revealed in the sets of Trumps listed above. This theme of triplicity is, of course, found in the structure of the Tree of Life, and the cosmology of the Three Spirals that underpins it as a symbolic map.

The Universe or World seems to be stepping out of the Three Rings, for it seems apparent and evident to our perception, yet it is in perfect contact with each Ring through its head, hands, and feet. Here is another aspect of the esoteric teaching regarding the power centres, and the essential divinity of the human body. If we knew how to realize our potential, we would find that we are in touch with the universe; many physical aspects of ritual, in both movement and special positions (such as the disciplines of yoga) are related to this metaphysical proposition.

The image also represents the final stage of manifestation; a complete divine/human figure steps out of the metaphysical fields of power that have created the universe – and now the world begins. Behind the figure, we see the vertical Ring as a Vesica or lens shape; this is the traditional symbol of the Gate into the Unknown. When we encountered this Gate in the Trump Judgement, it led into the void. In The World, however, it leads into the Underworld, or the realm of eternity beneath the Earth. In this role the Androgyne is the Great Goddess who incorporates both male and female, and whose temple is always underground. Yet we may see the figure also as a blessed youth of light, who declares unity and victory of all Elements in spiritual being. These two perceptions do not oppose or cancel one another; they are essential results of the androgyny of the Trump.

The Four Creatures
The background of the image is one of seething clouds and wind, blown by Four Creatures who define each corner or Quarter. These are both the Four Elements and the Four Powers. In the apocalyptic vision of Merlin (in the *Prophecies*), Four Winds blast together as the solar system is dissolved, and their resonance reaches to the distant stars. In the balancing Creation Vision (in the *Vita*), Four Original Powers create the Worlds, and are reflected upon the planet Earth through the action of Four Winds.

Although the Four Creatures have a relationship to astrological Signs, we find them in a very primal mode in our Trump. The Eagle is the creature of Air; the Man is the creature of Water; the Lion of Fire; the Bull of Earth. They are Signs in a proto-astrology, rather than in any later mathematical system of correlations. They relate to the Four Seasons, Four Ages (in a life cycle), and, more subtly, to the Four Power Centres defined in the Trump. This last correlation requires further examination:

The Four Power Centres
The Androgyne is both a universal entity and an idealized human being. As mentioned above, it reveals a very simple map of the Power Centres, or locations of energy, which relate to the Three Worlds and their various attributes. These Centres also have a broad correspondence to primal powers or Elements, though each Centre has all Four Elements within its power cycle.

When we consider these correspondences, we must not confuse them with more complex and sophisticated relationships of the 12 Signs to parts of the body, which played a major role in the development of astrology as a science. The connections given in tarot and in primal systems of magic reach back to simpler (and in some ways more effective, though less detailed) power symbols.

Feet: Earth;   Bull.
Genitals: Water;   Human.

Heart: Fire;   Lion.
Head: Air;   Eagle.

When we use the images in this manner, we must see the Creatures as sources of power, rather than detailed intellectual correspondences. This Elemental theme is our final use of spiritual animals within the Merlin Tarot, for we have now come full circle in our journey through the Worlds.

THE FIRST TRIAD OR STELLAR WORLD
(The Numbers One to Three)
Introduction to the Number Cards

In the following chapters, I have presented the Number or Elemental cards as a progression from Ace to Ten, dealing with each cycle of the Four Elements in turn. So we have a section on the Four Aces, the Four Twos, and so forth. The effect is to spiral around the Wheel of Life towards expression or physical manifestation. But it is not a rigid progression, for there is no such thing as 'ultimate manifestation' distinct from, or opposed to, 'pure spirit'. However much we may use such terms to help us grasp the flow of energies and patterns, we must always remember that they are only convenient phrases that describe the indescribable: all energy, all being, all matter, is spirit.

The Merlin tradition, like all primal traditions, is particularly good for our modern constipation of perception. It teaches us repeatedly that all energies and entities, all forces and forms, all spiritual powers and living creatures, are within one another. Until we free our perceptions of the rigid materialist delusions of the eighteenth and nineteenth centuries, we cannot begin the task of regenerating ourselves and restoring our world. The Merlin Tarot shows the world pattern, cycles and rhythms that may flow through us in this transformation.

A dualistic separation of spirit and matter is really a variant of materialism: ideas of spiritual evolution and abandoning the gross body or material life are deeply ingrained in modern thinking and language, even for non-religious people. This is our inheritance from orthodox Christianity, which was, ironically, the direct source of materialism and atheism. Once the natural world is deemed unholy or sinful, and divinity becomes a distant rather than intimate realization, the abuses of scientific materialism can develop and eventually flourish. In our culture we have abandoned the orthodox religion, but are still the heirs of its terrible conditioning.

The perennial philosophies and magical arts never separate spirit and matter: the land, the body, is as holy as a god or goddess. There are no spiritual masters or highly evolved beings ruling in a hierarchy, only interconnected energies and entities.

In tarot this interconnection is well represented by the Elemental Number cards. They reveal a relative cycle of the Elements and Directions, modified by, and resonating through, each Sphere, World or polarity of the Tree of Life (Figure 2).

In the progression of numbers towards Ten, I have used certain keywords and repeated patterns, but have not stuck rigidly to these. Each number section contains a series of ideas, insights, relationships, and meditative suggestions and exercises. I feel that this is a better way to present the Number suits than to plod rigidly through them and generate increasingly complex strings of correspondences. Forget correspondences, and find instead *relationship* and *inspiration*. That is how tarot can work for us, if we pass beyond the initial stages of becoming familiar with the seemingly large and diverse number of images and ideas shown in the cards. Eventually, we may find that the deck of cards is not as large as we had thought.

This is the paradox of tarot: the more you understand it, the smaller and simpler it becomes, yet the number of cards and the immense complexity of their relationship remain the same.

The Elements and Directions have a general relationship as a holism of fourfold energy and consciousness. This holism is both universal and planetary, collective and individual. Number cards in Tarot tend to work through a pattern as follows:

1. AIR: Energies of spirit and mind. Origination and Inspiration, LIFE.
2. FIRE: Energies of spirit and soul. Creation and Illumination, LIGHT.
3. WATER: Energies of spirit and emotions. Formation and Fertility, LOVE.
4. EARTH: Energies of spirit and body. Expression and Reflection, LAW.

The sequence from Air to Earth, Origination to Expression, flows through the Three Worlds, with Earth as the expressed Kingdom of the Lunar World, Water as the Lunar World, Fire as the Solar World, and Air as the Stellar World (see Figure 23, p.326). But this idea is only an aid and should not to be taken too literally; it certainly is not dogma or static revelation.

In each World the Four Elements rotate and interact; each World has its polarities (Spheres and Triads) and its inherent numbers. The progression from Air to Earth, Origination to Expression, gives us locations and relative Direction when our consciousness and energies are set free from conditioned patterns, as we begin to seek the holism of being. Such seeking is often described as a change of Direction: our consciousness moves inwards rather than outwards.

The flow inwards passes through the Three Worlds: our outer attention and body is the Lunar World; we move further in to the Solar World, and at the seed of being within is the Stellar World. But the Three Worlds interpenetrate each other, there are no hard boundaries. In the Merlin cosmology, the Stellar World includes the Solar and Lunar (see Figure 1), while the Solar World includes the Lunar. For us the Lunar World includes our body, our ultimate Earth. The ultimate Earth is simultaneously the Stellar World and spiritual and planetary and material being.

In practice, be it of meditation, insight or divination, we tend to use the number cycle very simply. The numbers are powers of each Ace, modulated or polarized by a Sphere of the Tree of Life. Thus the Four Aces at the Crown of the Tree are the Four Powers of *Life, Light, Love* and *Law*. In the 2nd Sphere (Wisdom or the cycle of the Zodiac) the Aces become the Twos, and their Fourfold Cycle is uttered again, but in the polarity of the Star Father, of Wisdom, of the One becoming Two and so forth. These basic correspondences are helpful as indicators for meditation and interpretation.

The relative pattern must not be taken dogmatically, for it is a holism, not a hierarchy, an inspiration and not a rigid teaching. Each Element or Quarter of the Wheel of Life has within it a relative cycle of all Four Elements, and each of these has its fourfold cycle. The progression is infinite, and Elemental holisms are 'proven' today by computer fractal images and so-called 'chaos mathematics'. We shall return to this subject again as we move through the numbers, for Elemental holisms, or self-uttering and mirroring patterns, are at the very foundation of perennial wisdom teachings concerning creation and manifestation.

The best way to relate to the Number cards is to work with them in meditation, visualization, and related (lesser) arts such as divination and farsight. Any or all may give us insight and understanding. There are several ways of developing and training with the Number cards, and it is not difficult to work out patterns and methods of relating the numbers to one another for yourself. Two basic patterns, however, should be thoroughly developed and practised before any experimental work. These are:

1. The Numbers (from Ace to Ten) (see Figure 10).
2. The Elemental Cycle (around the Wheel) (see Figure 11).

In the first pattern we work with each suit in turn, beginning with the Ace and progressing through to the Ten. In the second pattern we work around the Wheel of Life, beginning with the Four Aces, then expanding

Figure 10: THE EXPANSION OF NUMBERS

through to the Four Tens. The second pattern is usually worked with after some training with the suits and the first pattern.

The Number Cards as Spiritual Creatures

In the Merlin Tarot, emphasis is given to spiritual creatures for each Element, as the Creation Vision (from the *Vita Merlini*) begins with Four Powers and gradually expands into orders of living creatures, showing how the Powers are within all living beings. Renaissance tarot images tend to show the suits as objects or implements: Swords, Wands, Cups and Discs. These are the Four Implements of Sword for Air, Rod for Fire, Vessel for Water, and Shield or Mirror for Earth. The Implements are present in the Merlin Tarot and appear in the Aces, but not in the images for other Number cards. In the Merlin Tarot, the Four Powers are embodied by Birds for Air, Serpents for Fire, Fishes for Water and Deer for Earth.

The creatures are not limited to natural forms, however, nor are they restricted to actual birds, serpents, fish or deer. In the sacred land, they

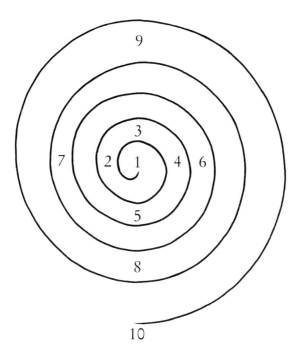

Figure 11: THE ROTATION OF NUMBERS

appear outwardly as specific living creatures, but have many connectives and counterparts across the orders of life and in other worlds. The creatures of Air are all living beings that have an airy quality, the creatures of Fire are living beings that have a fiery quality, and so forth. It is a valuable meditational and visualizing exercise to associate creatures with Elements, and this is exactly how our astrological Signs were originally intuited and visualized.

The Signs of the Zodiac are a living alphabet of creatures that embody the power of the Elements. Their location in stellar patterns, often confusing to the modern mind and frequently misinterpreted as ancient ignorance, is derived from visionary experience and intuition concerning the power of specific star groups. This was understood in an Elemental context, for the Elements are the Four Powers. In magical and mystical traditions alike, these powers are Life, Light, Love and Law (see Figure 6).

In the Merlin Tarot, however, the four suits are intentionally simplified into basic creatures: Birds, Serpents, Fishes and Deer. This theme of creatures relating to the Elements, Directions and Seasons is found again in the Court cards, which we will explore in Chapter 28.

Patterns of the Creatures

On the cards themselves, the numbers Two to Ten are shown as simple interlaced creatures, in the style of ancient Celtic designs. These interlacings and patterns are not merely formalized decoration: when we use them in the expanding number cycle from Ace to Ten, the polarities and groupings of each number have specific powers. Their *shape* often defines a meaning or energy from the card just as much, or even more, than the keywords used in meditation and card reading.

The Numbers, Triads and Worlds

Once you have gained some familiarity with the numbers and their key energies, many insights can be found by working with the Triads. These are shown in Figure 12. Each of the Three Spheres of a Triad has a cycle of numbers inherent within it. But the proper relationships are found through the triple pattern of the triad.

Thus the supernal or originative Stellar Triad consists of Crown or Being (the Four Aces), Wisdom (the Four Twos) and Understanding (the Four

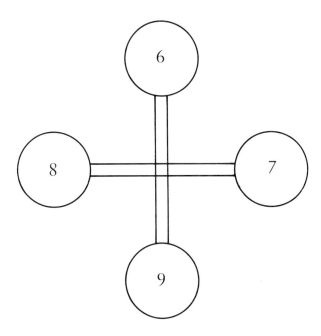

Figure 12: THE TRIADS OF NUMBERS

Threes). This is reflected into the creative Solar Triad of Mercy (the Four Fours), Severity (the Four Fives) and Harmony or Beauty (the Four Sixes). The formative Third Triad, in the Lunar World, comprises Victory (the Four Sevens), Glory or Honour (the Four Eights) and Foundation (the Four Nines). With the Four Tens we have the Kingdom, the expressed or manifest outer universal world of substance or matter, specifically our planet Earth. This is the final cycle of the Aces, appearing as the Four Elements, Four Planetary Directions, and so forth.

By meditating upon the Triads and Worlds, it is possible to attune to the flow of the number energies. This type of meditation is far more productive than separating the numbers and studying them or memorizing them individually. The entire pattern of the Worlds, shown throughout tarot (of any sort or tradition) is about *relationship* and *polarity*. The Stellar Triad shows us universal *originative* polarities; the Solar Triad reveals these becoming *creative* forces in the realm of the spiritual heart and higher consciousness. The Lunar Triad *forms* them into the subtle substance of mind, emotions and life energies before birth or *expression* and manifestation.

This sequence, from Origination to Expression, is a harmonic development of the Four Aces, and is found in all cycles, all entities, all energy patterns. There is no such thing as 'inanimate' matter in the Merlin cosmology – or in any other perennial wisdom teaching. All energies and entities have consciousness, be they stars, sun and planets, the land, or the creatures of the land. Bearing this in mind, let us begin our journey through the numbers from One to Ten.

The Four Aces

Aces are cards of original or primal power; they are the beginning and end of each Elemental cycle or suit, the empowering spiritual creature of each Element (in the Merlin Tarot), and the implement, hallow or Mystery of each Element and Direction. The primal power of the Ace manifests through the numbers, eventually coming into outer expression with the number Ten, shown as 1+0.

When working with Number cards, we should be aware of the Ace inherent within each one, for the power of the Ace is present in each number, but with a varying effect or form according to the number itself. Some of the more subtle aspects of tarot reading are related to this idea.

More valuable than tarot reading, however, is meditation on the power of an Ace flowing through the cycle of numbers. The numbers should never be regarded as isolated entities or forces in their own right; they are relative vehicles and patterns for the power of Ace, the Element, and the Direction from which they derive.

The relationship between Number cards and Sacred Space (Figure 5) has hardly been touched upon in the modern tarot revival, yet the perennial wisdom traditions always related the Elements to the Directions. In both the Creation Vision and the Apocalypse of Merlin, Four Powers, inherent in the universe of being, manifest as four winds, four rivers, four planetary zones and Four Directions. In the Apocalypse of Merlin (found within the *Prophecies*), four great winds blast together at the ending of the universe, as the goddess Ariadne unweaves manifest creation. These four winds are the Four Powers of spiritual being that are at once the Elements of Air, Fire, Water and Earth, and the universal truths or Powers of Life, Light, Love and Law. The Four Aces reveal these Powers to us, acting as keys or gateways in meditation, visualization, insight or farsight. They also act to arouse and balance the Elements and Powers within us.

The Aces as Spiritual Creatures
The spiritual creatures of the Aces are the Eagle, Dragon, Salmon and Stag. These are living beings, not 'symbols' of something else. Except for the

Dragon, the creatures are found in the land. In nature, the Dragon is represented by the Serpent, Snake or Lizard. This Elemental representation does not preclude or contradict any biological knowledge of species, but works in a magical or poetic manner rather than a literal one. We shall consider the Elemental aspects of the various creatures as we progress through the numbers.

The Ace of Birds
Element: Air; Direction: East; Suit: Swords or Arrows; Power: Life; Keywords: Dawn, Spring, Beginning, Flight, Birth, Morning
The Ace of Birds is the Eagle; our image shows an Eagle bearing an Arrow to a Nest. The presence of the Ace of Birds causes powerful and disturbing new openings, beginnings, changes. It is a card of great but unrealized potential, of *originative* energy.

Depending upon other cards present in a pattern, the Eagle can bring benefit or difficulty, life or death. Affiliation with this creature and achieving a balanced relationship to its power are difficult – Air is a *difficult* Element. The difficulty arises when the originative power manifests through expressive outer circumstances, and appears as a disruption. But spiritual power will blow where it chooses, and we may not stand against it.

The effect of false resistance to spiritual change is shown by the Trump of The Blasted Tower (pp.136–45), in which breakdown or catalysis comes as a blast of lightning and a roaring wind. The power of Air, however, should not be considered as negative or suppressive. It is the inspiration of the spirit reaching the soul, it is the breath of life, of vitality, of being itself.

In most tarot decks the Ace of Air is shown as a Sword, first of the suit of Swords. Our Ace uses the Arrow, implement of flight, accuracy, and of penetrating to the heart or centre of its target.

The Ace of Serpents
Element: Fire; Direction: South; Suit: Rods or Wands; Power: Light; Keywords: Summer, Noon
The Ace of Serpents is the Dragon, the creature of Fire and Light. It is also represented by the Salamander, born of fire, and appears, sometimes as a Lizard or Serpent, in certain cards. The Elemental powers and beings were sometimes described as four orders of supernatural being: Sylphs for Air, Salamanders for Fire, Undines for Water and Gnomes for Earth. Regrettably, this has been weakened by modern fantasy literature and cartoon images, but still forms the remnant of the old fairy Otherworld tradition.[8]

The Dragon is the power of Light within the Earth, and it is the arousal of dragon power that causes Merlin, as a youth, to utter his prophecies.

In one sense, the Dragon is the Element of Fire, the burning flame, while in a higher octave it is universal Light, the energy of being. The presence of the Dragon in a tarot pattern shows a balancing, affirmed power, an energy increasing in potency.

The implement of Fire is the Rod or Wand, or occasionally the Spear. In Christian religious dogma we find the archangel of the South, Michael, reputedly subduing the dragon with his spear. This is a corruption of an ancient god-vision, in which the god of light (Bel or Lugh in Celtic mythology)[6] is associated with the dragon power. Early chapels to St Michael were located upon the great hilltop shrines to Bel, the god of midsummer, the South and radiant light. This theme is also found in England as St George and the Dragon, connecting to the classical myth of Perseus and Andromeda.[12]

If we strip away the intentionally corrupting propaganda, we find a potent vision: the god of light and the dragon in balance with one another. The implement of balance is the Rod, and the image of god and dragon should show them interacting, much in the manner of the oriental ying-yang emblem.

Meditations upon the Dragon Ace bring arousal of our Inner Fire and Light, hence the use of the Rod for harmony, balance and control.

The Ace of Fishes
Element: Water; Direction: West; Suit: Cups or Vessels; Power: Love; Keywords: Autumn, Evening
The Salmon is the creature of Water. In Celtic tradition the Salmon is the primal creature of deep wisdom, the great fish swimming in the waters of eternity. Although our modern minds tend to see fish as cold creatures, there is a long association of the fish with sexuality and fertility. The teeming shoals of fish in the mother ocean are manifestations of the Vessel of Love and Abundance.

The traditional implement of the West is the Cup, Cauldron or other Vessel. It signifies the Mystery of Love, of filling and emptying, of fruitfulness, of Autumn and evening. When the Ace of the West appears in a tarot pattern it reveals Love, either in a personal context or in a deeper spiritual sense, depending upon other cards present. It can indicate creativity, personal emotion, or the unbending strength and energy-source of the Vessel of the West.

The Direction of West is also associated with perfection and ideal spiritual vision, the Blessed Realm. The Vessel may also be the Grail, the Mystery of spiritual redemption and regeneration. There is a further association with physical birth and death, the vessel or gate between worlds. The Ace of the West often enables human fertility and situations involving fruitful interaction.

The Ace of Beasts
Element: Earth; Direction: North; Suit: Shields or Mirrors; Power: Law;
Keywords: Winter, Night
The Ace of Beasts is the Stag, king of the wildwood, lord of the four-footed
creatures. The spiritual creature is strongly linked to Merlin as Lord of the
Animals, referring to his period of madness in the forest, when he ran with
the deer. This nature-aspect of the wild god also transforms into the
goddess of the North, the Mother of the Land.

The traditional implement of Earth is the Shield or Mirror, and in our
image the Stag's antlers frame a black Mirror, which shows the fivefold
pattern of the Merlin cosmology. In this pattern the Four Powers are unified
by a central fifth. Within this we find a further pattern of four-in-one (or
five), and so forth.

The presence of the Ace of Earth in a tarot pattern reveals manifest or
expressed power, often concerned with outer or material circumstances.
But its deep power is that of Law and Wisdom, the Mystery of Night and
Winter. Thus it can indicate a force or restriction that leads to liberation,
the Winter that precedes Spring, the wisdom of endings that bring
beginnings. In the Celtic calendar night preceded day and Winter
preceded Spring, so all cycles began not at dawn, but in the darkness.

The ultimate vision of the North is of the goddess Ariadne (or
Arianrhod in Welsh tradition, Lady of the Silver Wheel). She is the Great
Mother of the Stars, and her power is felt most strongly at night and in
Winter.

Working with Aces, Trumps and Number Cards

Some powerful visualizing and meditational exercises can be developed
working with the Trumps and Aces. The basic method is to meditate upon
a chosen Trump, and then visualize it in the centre of the Elemental Circle.
The power of the Aces flows through or in and out of the Trump, and the
Trump itself will resonate according to each Quarter. We can work the
Trump around the Quarters, so to speak, then return to the centre with
a balanced holism of the Four Powers expressed through the Trump.

This is not an 'advanced' exercise, for Elemental working and the Four
Directions are at the foundation of the Merlin Tarot, just as the Aces are
inherent in all other cards. While they manifest as the numbers for each
planet or Sphere of the Tree of Life (Figure 2), such as the Four Twos, Four
Threes and so forth, the Aces also work through the Trumps.

A more complex but very fruitful sequence is to work with a selected
Trump and the Aces, visualizing the Trump at the centre of the fourfold
Circle as before. We then introduce into the meditation and visualization
ideas of the numbers associated with that Trump, according to their

Quarter. These connections are shown in the summaries at the beginning of each chapter on the Trumps, and in Figure 18.

An example would be as follows: the Trump of Strength is visualized in the centre of the Circle. How does each Ace or Direction work through this Trump? What are qualities or relative powers of Strength and the Element of Air, or Strength in the East, then in the South, West, North and back in the centre, resonating to all Four Elements? We can meditate upon the relative power and energy of the Quarters resonating through the Trump in the centre of the Circle, and then move towards communion with the Trump as a universal power merging with its reflection within ourselves. Working through the cycle of Aces and Directions will enhance this change of consciousness.

Next we can meditate upon the related numbers. For Strength these are the Four Fours and the Four Sixes (see Figure 3). We introduce the numbers through meditation on their keywords or inherent associations and energy. There will be two numbers in each Quarter: East appearing as the Four and Six of Birds, South appearing as the Four and Six of Serpents, West appearing as the Four and Six of Fishes, North appearing as the Four and Six of Beasts.

The keywords are:

East:　　Truce and Transition
South:　Generosity and Balance
West:　　Promise and Joy
North:　Increase and Benefit

These are the powers of numbers associated with the Trump Strength, that has the keywords *Merciful Beauty*.

If you work with this method, remember that Trumps will have two sets of numbers associated with them, but that the same numbers will resonate with multiple Trumps. The Sixes, for example, resonate within the Trumps of The Sun, The Star, Strength, The Blasted Tower, The Lovers, The Chariot, The Hermit and Temperance. The Tens resonate within the Trumps of The Moon, The Fool and The Universe or World.

The Aces resonate through all Trumps, all numbers, and all People or Court cards. The Aces have a primal resonance, however, with the three originative Trumps of The Hermit, The Star and The Innocent.

Using only Aces and Trumps

A simple and powerful way of using the Merlin Tarot for inner work or tarot reading is to use a reduced deck consisting of the Trumps and Four Aces. The Aces play a strong role in this method, for they empower and highlight the patterns of the Trumps. Any of the tarot patterns found in Chapter 30 may be worked with this simplified deck, and it is also very effective in methods such as choosing random groups of cards for meditation.

Let us now move on from Ace to Two, beginning our expanding spiral around the Wheel of Life.

The Four Twos

The 2nd Sphere of the Tree of Life is that of Wisdom. Traditionally, it is the Zodiac, the stellar patterns relating to our own solar system. The 1st Sphere is the *Primum Mobile*, or first movement of originative being, the Breath of Beginning, or the nebulae in which universes are born. Divine Wisdom is often understood as the Star Father, the polar partner of the

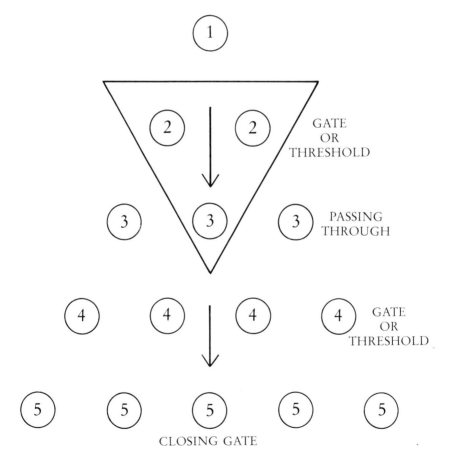

Figure 13: THE POLARITY THRESHOLDS

Dark Mother of space and time, Understanding, the 3rd Sphere. It is, in sexual terms, the explosion of stars in patterns, the universal seeding of the Deep.

Twos are the power of each Ace and Direction in transition, the second card of any suit is an image of Thresholds. There is a tendency for the even numbers to reveal thresholds and gates and the odd numbers to reveal crossings or movements. The odd and even numbers, however, may be either *giving* or *taking* in their function. The general rhythm of this polarity is shown in Figure 13. Movement inwards across the thresholds (decreasing towards the original Ace) is often catabolic or breaking down, while movement outwards is anabolic or building up. The decrease or increase of the numbers obviously states this, but the situation is more subtle and inter-connected than we might think at first.

As the numbers rise from Ace towards Ten, so their potential becomes increasingly expressed and materialized. This increase means that the potential of each number seems to enlarge, but the increasing number also limits energy into form. We find this repeatedly in our lives: a choice of two only possibilities seems limiting, while seven or more seems rich. But with only two choices the potential paths beyond the dual threshold are innumerable; with a seven or higher number, the number itself imposes its character, its Elemental pattern, and its limitations and cycle of reiteration upon us.

Twos are thresholds stripped of all further manifestations; they are the deep crossings, the ultimate thresholds in life, moving outwards from the Ace Direction or inwards through the unifying power of the Ace towards the centre of being.

The power of an Ace moves into that of a Two, generating a gate. The passing through that gate is shown by the Three, while the Four presents a further threshold/gate that is sealed or concluded by the Five.

The Two of Birds
Doubt or Uncertainty
The Suit of Air, Direction East, is the power of Life, and is a suit of constant motion. The Two of Birds (Two of Swords in Renaissance tarot) is a vehicle of uncertainty, of rhythmic polarity that may at times alter its pattern. It may return to its Ace, or it may act as a threshold into a Three or another number. Regarding a human situation, it often represents a pattern in which the outcome seems impossible to predetermine.

There are two ways of considering this image: if we seek rigid results and fixed outcomes, then the Two of Birds is a 'difficult' card, two birds peering at one another's backs with their necks interlocked, neither knowing where to look or what will happen next. Mostly they fear coming apart from their uncertain union. If, however, we see the Two of Birds as a source of unlimited potential, the first threshold from the potent Ace of Air, we may time the rhythm of the twofold energy pattern, and step through. To do so requires courage: all Air cards are concerned with courage and inspiration towards movement, be it physical or spiritual.

In the context of the cycle from North to East, night to dawn, the Two of Birds is the doubt that comes at the very brink of daybreak, at the point of stepping over. The fear inherent in the Air cards is a fear of the unknown, which blows through them all in various expressions.

If we use a keyword system for our initial experience of the numbers, we can relate them to the Elements and the Tree of Life. Thus, the Two of Birds is the Wisdom of Air: *Doubt! All life is uncertain; all is relative.* The power of Air is often one that breaks us down, leading to that terrible freedom when all known patterns, all secure situations, are blown away.

The Two of Serpents
Choice
With this Two we find will – it represents the polarities of either/or, positive/negative, yes/no. In Renaissance tarot this is the Two of Wands;

it represents the two pillars of any choice, any balancing or polarizing situation. These should not be understood as antagonists, but as mutually connecting relative opposites, each defining and enabling the other. The choice is an act of will, of stepping through from one side to another, one world to another. Here the Ace, the primal Dragon of Fire and Light, empowering the Rod, radiates through first polarization. Gates and thresholds have not only a right and left, but an inside and outside. The inside is the Ace; the outside, the Three and the subsequent numbers.

In life situations this card shows there is a choice that can be made. In our progress around the cycle of Twos we are now coming towards fruition: change involving breakdown and renewal/doubt or uncertainty as to the direction of the newly inspired energies/choice is realized.

The keywords for this card are the Wisdom of Fire: *Choose well between right and left.* As for darkness and light, they depend upon one another. With the Two we cross from the primal light of the Dragon Ace of the South into the polarized light of the outer world, the Three. One light is darkness to the other, yet each is light, and could not shine without darkness.

The Two of Fishes
Freedom
This is the most kindly Two, if we may use such a term. In Renaissance tarot it is the Two of Cups. Cups or Fishes, Vessels or life forms, the Two of Water defines an easeful threshold. We swim through it comfortably toward the Three; it gives us a sense of release, of freedom. There is a further implication here of the emotions, associated with the Element of Water. In the Merlin Tarot, Beasts indicate the spirit and physical body, Birds the spirit and mind, Serpents or Dragons the Inner Fire of the spirit and soul, and Fishes the spirit and emotions. Law, Life, Light and Love are all spiritual powers, but they flow through the body, mind, soul and emotions in human expression.

Our keyword for the Two of Fishes is the Wisdom of Love: *Freedom.* Love frees the spirit and soul, acting as a gateway through which we pass towards the number Three. It also frees the soul towards its spiritual origins, and with this directed love, we pass within to the Ace of Water, Love, perfect being.

The Two of Beasts
Change
In the North the Element of Earth is often felt to be the culmination or ending of any cycle, be it a day, a year or a lifetime. But the Wisdom of the North is concerned with change arising out of darkness, night, stillness. The ancient Celts counted time by nights and moons, rather than by day or suns. The cycle of the year was calculated from darkness to light

to darkness, usually from November to November in terms of the modern calendar. There are some powerful insights to be gained by working with this concept. It is based upon a truth: from light we move towards darkness, from darkness we move towards light. This is the planetary situation, and therefore our human situation as beings upon, and of, the planetary being. Change may manifest at dawn, but it begins at the point of relative rest, at midnight, in darkness.

The Two of Beasts (Two of Discs or Shields in Renaissance tarot) shows change arising out of the potential of Earth, the Direction of the North (see Figure 6). It can be a change of substantial power, and acts as a gate towards major transitions and movements of energy in any cycle, be it our own lives or that of any relative situation. It is the gate through which the power of the Ace passes towards outer expression: and through which our awareness passes as we move consciousness/energy towards the Ace in meditation and visualization.

The keyword for the Two of Beasts is the Wisdom of Earth: *All things change*. Even within the apparent solidity of matter is the energy of perpetual change.

The Four Threes

The 3rd Sphere of the Tree of Life is Understanding, the Dark Mother. This is the universal Great Goddess in her dark aspect, the Mother of Sorrows, the Great Deep of Time and Space. The planetary attribute is Saturn, but we should look to the older goddesses rather than the male god-form. The 3rd Sphere completes the supernal Stellar Triad, Star Father, Deep Mother, or Crown, Wisdom, Understanding.

The Twos are gates or thresholds through which energies and entities pass; the Threes are whatever is found beyond the gate. They are simultaneously the territory beyond Two, and the act of passing beyond and between a gate. Regarding consciousness/energy, Threes are what we become by moving beyond Two: through *change* towards *effort*, through *uncertainty* towards *suffering*, through *choice* towards *intention*, through *freedom* towards *affection*. A valuable exercise is to work in meditation or association with the relationships between Number cards: in all Number cards *movement* and *directions* are important – the flow of ideas, keywords, energies, moves inwardly or outwardly. It also moves in a circular or spiralling pattern, around the Wheel of Life, the Directions and the Elements. Working with relationship and direction in the numbers is the key to understanding their power; isolating cards and allocating rigid meanings to them is fruitless.

The relationship between Two and Three is our first gate and crossing for each Direction and Elemental suit. Because Three, like all odd numbers in the suits, has a concluding, limiting power, Threes also represent a locked or temporarily static state, the first to be encountered since the emergence of the Aces towards expression. Conversely, movement from Three to Two is the last liberation in the tarot cycle, moving from relative form (the numbers) towards formless power, the Aces.

There is an interesting relationship between the Number cards and the Tree of Life, *Axis Mundi*, or Three Worlds. We may follow it through the Spheres of the Tree, from the 1st to the 10th (the Four Aces, Four Twos, and so forth.) But there are other inherent patterns in the numbers that span areas of the Tree of Life. Here, at Three, is good place to examine this important relationship, as we have emerged through the gate of Two toward Three, Understanding.

Ones or Aces correspond to the entire Tree of Life as the Four Originative Powers of Life, Light, Love and Law, and the Four Elements of Air, Fire, Water and Earth. They also relate to the unfolding pattern of Triads on the Tree, from Origination (Air) to Creation (Fire) to Formation (Water) to Expression (Earth) (see Figure 1). These are the Zones of Star, Sun,

Suffering

Effort

Intention

Affection

Moon and Earth, shown by the Trumps of the Middle Pillar (Star, Sun and Moon). The Aces represent the fourfold rotation or cycle of energies around the *Axis Mundi*, the Pillar of the Worlds.

Twos correspond to the Right- and Left-Hand Pillars of the Tree of Life, to the basic polarities between any two Directions (Above/Below, Within/Without, Right/Left, Before/Behind, North/South, East/West), and any two Spheres, (Mercy/Severity, Wisdom/Understanding and so forth as in Figure 2).

Threes correspond to the Triads or balanced (sealed or completed) power patterns of the Tree. They also reveal the Three Worlds of Star, Sun and Moon (see Figure 1).

The triple pattern was frequently at the foundation of ancient ritual, myth and magic. Even using the word 'foundation' leads us to the 9th Sphere of the Tree of Life (3 + 3 + 3), which is the pivot of the Lunar World, the Moon, realm of the Ninefold or Triple Goddess.

The Three of Birds
Suffering
Air cards are frequently 'difficult'; the power of Air is that of changing winds, wild inspiration, tumult. The energies of the Air suit are those of ecstasy and agony. We frequently misunderstand that spirit (the breath of being) brings drastic change, and if we resist this spiritual transformation, we suffer. The suffering arises from unresolved forces within ourselves.

The Three of Birds is the Understanding of Air, *the Suffering of the Mother*. It has resonances of giving birth, for from Two to Three is the movement of birth, but the birth and suffering are often upon the level of the spirit, reaching into the mind and soul. The higher numbers tend towards physical manifestation, while the lower numbers tend towards inner and metaphysical dimensions, though we should not take this idea too literally.

Because the Ace of Air is a power of dawn, beginnings, life, arising, flight, freedom from form, its passage through the numbers will generate difficult situations and inner responses. The suffering of the Three, however, should not be a fruitless experience. It is the inner suffering that leads to understanding, to realization (in the sense of 'being-made-real').

The ancient augury pattern for this power shows when a pair of mating birds or a flock of birds tussle with another type of bird in the air. Watching the movement of birds in flight gives deep insights into the Air suit. The collective wheeling of large flocks, for example, still a mystery to modern science, reveals the power of the Ten, where many together suddenly break into ones, then re-form as one unit made of many.

If possible, we should enlarge our experience of the Merlin Tarot by observing the movements of the creatures found in the various suits and

Trumps. This simple meditative act will bring deep insights, and eventually replace the use of keywords, written attributes and illustrations. This is a major part of the living Merlin tradition, the one represented in the *Vita Merlini* and other tales and poems in which the prophet, wild man, seer or seeress, gains spiritual insight by relating to the sacred land and the living creatures of the land. [3]

The Three of Serpents
Intention
Serpents/Dragons are creatures of Fire in the South. In geomantic or planetary terms, they embody the fire within the Earth, the light of the land. In human terms, they are the Inner Fire and light, the spiritual power inherent within our bodies. There is an unfortunate tendency for modern meditators to separate the so-called 'higher powers' from the body, but in the primal traditions there is no such separation. Hence the Serpent or Dragon that is a creature of Fire and Light.

The Suit of Serpents (Wands) is concerned with will and increasing energy. The keywords for the Three are *The Serpents of Understanding* or *Understanding Fire*. Here the uncertainty of the Two, in which polarities were constantly alternating, is left behind. Through an intentional act of understanding, seeking to cross, seeking comprehension, the Two becomes Three. The converse direction is where we choose to leave all intent and known patterns behind, and (intentionally) enter the Two, the state of uncertainty that marks the threshold towards the Ace, the primal Dragon of Fire and Light.

In Celtic mythology, the goddess Brig or Brigid has the Serpent as her animal. She was the goddess of both inner and outer fire; her skills were therapy, smithcraft and poetry. These arts are all involved with different qualities of Fire. Three is the Mother number, with implications of giving birth; Brigid, a triple goddess, eventually becomes identified as the Celtic St Bride. In this form she was said to be the midwife to the Virgin Mary, and to be the foster-mother of Jesus.

This is a significant reworking of an ancient myth of the Great Goddess and the Child of Light. Three is the Mother number, and Six ($3+3$ or 3×2) is the number of the Sun and the Child of Light. Nine ($3+3+3$ or 3×3) is the number of the Moon, and the incarnation of spirit into matter. The cycle of Threes resonates with the Trump of The Star, the cycle of Sixes resonates with the Trump of The Sun, and the cycle of Nines with the Trump of The Moon. There is a wealth of meditational material in these connections.

The Three of Fishes
Affection
Fishes, the suit of the West, of Water, of Love as a spiritual power, are

frequently cards of the emotions. They show the transition and relationship between our feelings and the deeper spiritual powers flowing from the Ace (Cup or Vessel) that is the universal power of Love.

In the Ace of Fishes we see the Salmon leaping upstream, and the Cup or Vessel. In the Two we see liberty or freedom of movement through Love flowing from the Ace. In the Three we find the Understanding of Water. The *affection* in our keyword is not a weak or temporary emotion, but that steady and constant timeless affection that is more powerful than personal emotion or romantic love that seeks gratification. It is that deep affection seen between mother and child, an unconditional state of love. In another expression, which works through time, it is that deep affection that grows between friends or partners who have spent time together and shared many experiences.

The Three of Beasts
Effort
The number Three and the Element of Earth give rise to the Three of Beasts or Shields, a card in which the changeability of the Two is stabilized and temporarily paused. The keyword is the Understanding of Earth: *Expressive Comprehension, Effort.* The effort is initially made to move beyond the choice of the Two, but soon becomes the effort of unlocking the Three towards the Four. Threes in the North are triads of power working through manifest patterns; in life situations they show right effort towards a graceful or wise end.

We will now move into the Second Triad or Solar World, and consider the numbers Four to Six.

THE SECOND TRIAD
OR SOLAR WORLD
(The Numbers Four to Six)

The Four Fours

The 4th Sphere upon the Tree of Life is Mercy, with the planetary attribute of Jupiter. This is the Giving God, the benevolent power resonating across the Abyss, the first life and energy to emerge into the Solar World as creative power.

In out-dated literary occultism, mainly from the nineteenth and early twentieth centuries, there is a complex style of working through planes and levels of manifestation, often using the Tree of Life, images of worlds, and related patterns as the model. In the Merlin Tarot, we use the Creation Vision (from the *Vita Merlini*), but this medieval literary source is not the origin of the Vision. The pattern of the Three Worlds, the Sacred Directions and the Four Elements united by a central and universal Fifth, is inherent in human awareness; many traditions world-wide use variants of this Vision. In other words, it models or presents our deepest insights and intuitions into the universal holism, the nature of being. The Creation Vision, which is the heart of the pattern making and Trump relationships in the Merlin Tarot, is not an intellectual construction to satisfy or support superficial ideas of order, hierarchy or obsessive correspondences.

Four is a good place to pause and consider the rift between intellectual occultism and real magic. Real magic comes from enduring organic traditions, preserved in religion, in temples and in the tales, songs and practices of ordinary people. 'Occultism' is the product of an élite, intellectual and often power-hungry minority over a short period, probably no more than 200 years.

By comparison, Renaissance 'high' magic was closer to ethnic and classical roots than Victorian occultism, and the sources of many images and practices of Renaissance magic are found in the primal shamanistic, bardic and Underworld traditions in Europe. The Merlin tradition, mainly emphasizing prophecy and the sacred land, is one such source. Thus the progress from Ace (an unknown, potent, primal, first magic in the ancestral seed of time and being) to Two, marks the separation of cultures and streams of power and expression in the ancient world. It also indicates the unresolved differences between technological civilization and the organic or environmental consciousness.

Atlantis, Egypt and Rome were all polarized towards unstable extremes, as is modern Western culture, while primal cultures polarized towards conservative, regenerative, but vulnerable patterns. These extremes are the Twos in the Number cards expressing themselves culturally. Eventually the dominant technological societies destroy the primal ones, and then proceed to destroy themselves. The technology (dividing knowledge, Two) of Atlantis and Egypt was of stellar magic; the technology of Rome was, ultimately, statecraft and politics, while that of modern civilization is mechanical and electronic. This abbreviated picture (into which many

Truce

Increase

Generosity

Promise

other civilizations could be fitted) shows a devolvement from a magical technology of spiritual forces through social and political statecraft into an increasingly materialized culture, in which the creation of exterior entities – machines – is the ultimate triumph. Nature, the land and the planet are ignored, abused and destroyed through this devolution. All such societies, of course, (and Atlantis, Rome and the modern West are only models or examples) rely on coercive forces, ranging from brute oppression to subtle manipulation and conditioning.

As the power of the Aces moves through from Three to Four, we have our first step in *mirroring* or generating a harmonic of the entire cycle. Four is the beginning of the Second Triad of polarity, or of relationships (see Figure 12). With four revolutions or spirals, the Aces work through from an originative or universal power state towards creation, the appearance of entities that will eventually express themselves as organic and inorganic forms.

The Four of Birds
Truce
The Four of Air (Birds or Swords) mitigates the turbulence and cutting power of the Ace. In other words, it takes the *suffering* of the Three, and reduces it *mercifully*. The keywords are *Merciful Air* or *Spirit of Compassion*.

In societies where close-contact manual weapons were commonplace, we find a curious archaic form of warfare in which the combatants seldom sought to wipe each other out. The rules, widespread in ancestral cultures, by which war-like situations were resolved without slaughter, were those of Truce and Championship. Indeed, the Romans ultimately defeated the Celts by refusing to follow the old collective rules of combat, in which truces were honoured and a few champions would fight rather than entire armies be laid waste. The Romans politicized their expansion and became dirty fighters.

Modern 'truces' tend to be mere political manipulative scenarios, our inheritance from the Roman-style civilization in which outward legalizing, hiding inward martial force, replaced nurturing social concepts. A military truce, once a time for wise consultation or sowing of crops, or rest before single combat, has become a veil over covert aggression.

The Four of Birds has many implications beyond outer conflict and truce, of course. It represents a *breathing-space* (Air in the Four Directions), a giving-pause during which the turbulent, irresistible force of the Ace is balanced briefly by the number Four. The next major location or state of balance is the Six of Birds. As a gate the Four of Air offers each of the Four Directions, and a truce in which to survey the territory and make a further decision.

In life situations this is an important card for awareness of potentials, or rhythm. If we are not able to perceive it, it can slip by too easily and suddenly turn into the Five.

The Four of Serpents
Generosity

The Four of Fire (Serpents or Rods) is a card of giving without cost. It is that generosity which asks no return, and when we encounter it in life it is the building, giving power that aids us in any situation or pattern. It works on a physical level as the Four Elements building, balancing and regenerating the forces within us, and on a personal or emotional and mental level as the vast potential of power into which we may tap if we truly choose to do so.

Its keywords are *Fire of Compassion* or *Merciful Dragon*. It represents that potential of giving that comes from a total selflessness, an established energy attuned to the universal power of Mercy, the giving gods and goddesses.

It is that merciful power to which people pray, through the images of their various religions, when they seek intervention and kindliness from fate. But the secret of the Four of Fire is that it has to flow *through us* and *out of us*. If we seek simply to draw it towards us, we misunderstand its nature. As a double gate (2+2), it offers many choices (the Gate of Gates, the Choice of Choices) when it comes into our life situations. If we are merely receptive or greedy, we can confuse and poison ourselves, for the building or nourishing power of the Four has to be balanced by the breaking and eliminating power of the Five.

The hinge between Four and Five is the number pattern of our current situation in Western technological society. We have taken and received so much, generated so many greedy potentials and situations out of the merciful Earth, that we can only be balanced by the vigorous taking force of the Fives. Fours relate to the Trumps of The Emperor and Strength in the Merlin Tarot, while Fives relate to the Trumps of Death and The Blasted Tower. Our contemporary Trump at the close of the twentieth century is The Blasted Tower.

The Four of Fishes
Promise

The Four of Water (Cups or Vessels) is a card of what are sometimes called 'higher emotions', though in primal wisdom traditions the ideas of 'higher' and 'lower' do not involve antagonism or dualism. Its keywords are *Promise of Mercy* or *Creative Compassion*. As a double gate, the Four of Water (West, evening, fruitfulness, giving and receiving) is the expansion, the flooding tide, of the affection that we encountered flowing through the Three.

Its promise is that of spiritual mercy, the promise of a giving power that will compassionately respond to our needs. This is a subtle idea, for *needs* and *wants* are often confused in the Fours, Sevens and Nines. If what we need in a life situation is a total undercutting, breakdown and devastating change, then that is what eventually comes to pass, but beyond it is the Promise of Mercy. No being is separated from the holism of the Three Worlds, from being itself. This Creative Compassion or compassionate creator or creatrix is the power to which supplications are made for the welfare of others. The key to such prayers and contemplative or mediating acts is that power flows through ourselves towards others; we are a vessel that simultaneously receives and gives out. Many compassionate spiritual abilities are realized through the Four of Water: healing; empathy; transpersonal love; forgiveness and taking away, washing or dissolution of soul-burdens.

It is at this threshold, the Four of Cups or Fishes, that we first find sexual energies in humanity. It is the promise of expansion, of material increase (Four of Earth), of procreation that will eventually be realized through the following greater numbers. But this is not sexuality in a personal or gratified sense, it is that flow of energy in which personal focus is washed way, and through which the compassionate powers are established upon levels on which personal sexual gratification becomes meaningless.

As the power of the Ace of Love flows towards expression in the Tens, it works through collective levels of power (for most of us in human life). But for an individual to attune to other modes or levels involves moving away from the collective dream, the natural drive towards sexual reflection and reproduction, yet retaining full sexual potency and power, amplified beyond our usual experience of such energies. There is no sexlessness in spiritual reality.

The secret of this law, with its very practical possibilities, is in the law of harmonics, of octaves, for the Four of Water is a higher octave of the greater numbers such as the Seven, Nine and Ten.

The Four of Beasts
Increase
The Four of Earth (Beasts or Shields) is a card of growth; its keywords are *Merciful Earth*. It is the further gate or threshold after the effort of the Three. Four Beasts form the first true increase of a herd, for two pairs may breed on, generating offspring in polarized patterns with many potentials. The 4th Sphere upon the Tree of Life is Mercy, the planet is Jupiter, and the god and goddess forms are all those of *giving*. The nature of an Ace or primal power will flow through the Four and attune it, but as a double gate (2 + 2), Four is the greatest giving power that we may experience. It flows outwards, towards or into increasing manifestation.

Above the Abyss, in the Stellar World of originative powers, the numbers rotate either inwardly or outwardly, towards or from the Ace. This is shown in the First Triad (Figure 12). Below or across the Abyss, there is a tendency for the Triads to be more directional, increasingly polarized. Thus the Four gives outwardly while its polar partner the Five takes inwardly. They are resolved and balanced by the Six. In human circumstances the Four of Beasts enables increase in any existing situation; it gives power to it and expands it. Keywords for all the Fours are *expansion* or *opening*, while for the Fives they are *contraction* or *closing*.

The Four Fives

The power of the Fives is difficult. On the Tree of Life they are the vehicles of each Element or Ace flowing through the 5th Sphere. The polarity is Severity or Taking, and the effect is catabolic, breaking down. The planetary attribute is Mars, and the gods and goddesses are those of strictness, severity and purification. Although Mars is usually assumed to be 'war-like' and 'male', this is a very modern post-Christian

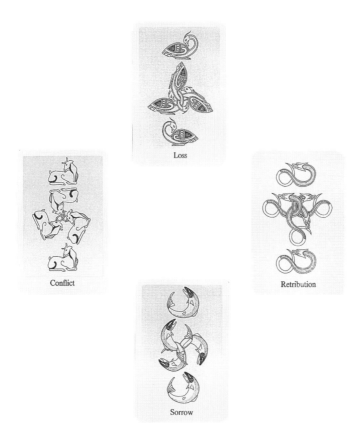

Loss

Conflict

Retribution

Sorrow

interpretation. The 5th Sphere, Severity, is on the feminine or left-hand polarity of the Tree of Life, and its power is embodied by a range of goddesses of taking. These include the universal Death Goddess found in all pre- or non-Christian cultures, and the important warrior-sister goddesses who define the development of inner growth and cultural or civilized societies.

In classical terms we should look to Athena and Minerva for models of this power, or to the Celtic goddess of death and sexuality, the Morrigan. The Trump of Death in the Merlin Tarot acts as a vehicle for various goddesses of taking, and for the fusion of the power of Severity with that of universal Understanding, the Great Mother. Trumps are always fusions of two Spheres, and may embody many divine forms, rather than one specific god or goddess. As the Merlin Tarot is based upon the Celtic and early classical imagery of the bardic tradition, the divinities tend to be from those sources. The numbers are impersonal direct potencies, the expansion or contraction of the Four Aces through the Worlds; the Trumps are simultaneously visionary gateways and actual entities of energy/consciousness.

An unmodified or unbalanced Five will break any entity or pattern down to a possible point of no return. But Five also brings the possibility of returning to Four and beginnings.

The Five of Birds
Loss

The Five of Air (Birds or Swords/Arrows) is a card of *movement*. The power of Air becoming Five blows patterns and situations away. Its keywords are *The Taking Wind* or *The Birds of Loss*.

As an Air card, the Five of Birds is often related to loss or abandonment in early phases of a situation, but it may also appear as a power in collapsing patterns. The conflict of the Five of Beasts can lead to the loss of the Five of Birds. Separation and breaking up of established patterns (Earth) bring a bleak beginning (Air). The Five of Birds is a number in which we are not even aware of the beginning, only that known patterns or situations (Fours) have been spirited away by the Taking Wind.

As Five is the number of humanity, the reflection or microcosm of the universal pattern, we express the power of Five into the Lunar World, which is the holism of our planet and its life forms. We are working, at the close of the twentieth century, through a collective cycle in which our destructive fivefold power is paramount: we have tapped into a stellar force of destruction, the fission of the atom. But we express it into the Lunar World without the mediating harmonizing power of Solar consciousness.

Esoteric tradition teaches that the fabled fall of Atlantis was through the summoning of a stellar being (not our sun) into the substance of the planet, an improper or imbalanced pattern of power. We see this repeated and materialized today with our nuclear potential. Interestingly, the tradition of the Atlantean fall long preceded the manifestation of nuclear fission and nuclear weapons, which use the heavy or stellar metals, such as uranium and plutonium. The reaction itself is the fission (catabolic breakdown) of matter, releasing stellar/solar energies. This terrible reality leads us to the Five of Serpents.

The Five of Serpents
Retribution
The Five of Fire (Serpents or Rods) is an active power of rebalance; it counteracts the increase of the Four. This is generated by the Aces of Life and Light flowing into the form of Five, in which the double gate is sealed by a fiery power, which consumes any further expansion. The keywords here are the *Purifying Fire* or *The Flaming Pentagram*. Any entity or energy seeking to pass through the Five is rebalanced by its consuming flame. There is a connection here to the angelic order of Kerubim, the flaming beings of purification associated with the 5th Sphere of the Tree of Life. As the Merlin Tarot and Merlin tradition do not use extensive angelic names and attributes, we do not need to pursue this branch of correspondences in detail, though there is a wide range of books that give the lists as preserved in Kabbalistic and Gnostic teachings.

Retribution is a complex idea, too often used as propaganda. In the purest sense of the word (from the Latin), it means *assigning back* or paying back tribute – retribution is the balancing return for either good or evil. Popularly, we colour it with notions of retribution for evil or for infringement of authoritarian rules, but this is the most superficial and propagandist level of the power of the Five of Fire. Inwardly, it involves an act of will (Fire cards frequently define will and creative forces of consciousness): we *choose* to invoke the power of Fire in the number Five, to seek rebalance. In this sense retribution has a therapeutic connection, as the cauterizing fire, the surgical laser, the healthy Inner Fire that leads to vitality and purification of the blood.

Five is the number of humanity, and the Five of Fire represents energies of balance or health, and of collective change. At present we have to face the retribution arising from our corruption and pollution of the sacred land, the Mother Earth. Imbalances in the planetary ecology are mirrored in imbalances in our souls and bodies – stress syndromes, mysterious incurable diseases. The Five of Fire is the power that will enable our cure.

The Five of Fishes
Sorrow
The Five of Water (Fishes, Cups or Vessels) ends the promise of the Four. It is the Fifth Vessel that pours out its contents, emptying the accumulated flow of energy from the Ace of Love. The Direction of West is frequently

associated with longing, sorrow, and that mysterious grief for our lost paradise or primal world. The card may represent personal sorrow in a direct situation, but more frequently defines the deep sorrow of the soul.

The keywords here are *Flowing Away* or *Ebb-tide*. The Five Fishes are the shoal of promises that vanishes into the ocean, the paradise over the horizon. These are not vague romantic longings, but true representations of our loss, our separation of the true perfect world from the corrupted world that we have imaged and built through our increasing power of materialization. The power of Five at work in humanity is a restricting or destructive power unless balanced by spiritual insight and harmony (the Sixes). Perversely, while we plunder, destroy, pollute and degenerate our sacred land and planet, we know and ignore the deep sorrow of our loss.

The Five of Beasts
Conflict
The Five of Earth (Beasts or Shields) shows tension or conflict. It marks the maximum increase of the Four to a condition in which a balancing force of decrease must appear. The conflict can be between opposing forces or interests, but they have grown out of the Four. Five is the closing of the gate of Four. The keywords are *Earth's Severity* or *The Breaking Earth*. Any gardener knows that the Earth gives and takes equally: to have vigorous growth there must be a cycle of decay. This applies to human life just as it applies to the land and the planet.

In the Element of Earth, the Power of Law or Liberty, and the Direction North, we realize Five as the number of humanity. Five closes the gate of Four, limiting its outpouring power. Humanity limits and defines the Four Elements, expressed as human entities and united by the spiritual Fifth. Here is a deep Mystery, for Five is the conclusion and spiritual union of a cycle. The Creation Vision reveals Four Powers united by a Fifth, an image that is mirrored right through into manifestation of the planet, and into the shape of humankind. Yet Fives as numbers are difficult and limiting and destructive powers in our lives. The truth here is that spirit flowing outwards towards expression seems beneficial to us, while its movement inwards towards origination or being is often unwelcome.

The conflict of the Five of Earth is that adjustment of pattern, of energies and entities seeking the balance of a new cycle or further pattern. To find this the old pattern must first be broken down. It can revert to Four or move on to Six. As we move down the Tree of Life towards expression, the potential paths of movement inwards or outwards tend to increase (see Figure 11). In this summary of the numbers we are working with the direct flow of the Aces towards Ten, but extreme polarities such as Five and Four may also change into other numbers. Five may move to Three, Four, Six or Eight, while Four may become Two, Five, Six or Seven. There is a vast range of fruitful meditation upon these connections, which gives insight into the Number cards and their potential in our own lives.

As we are working with Five, the power of taking, this the place to remind ourselves that though a Four can flow directly to Six or Seven in terms of beneficial expression, its balancing power may be realized in the Nines or Tens of Air, powers of extreme breakdown. Five is the number of humanity, and if we address its power within ourselves, upon its own level or state of consciousness, there will be less outer disaster or severe limitation in our expressed lives.

The Four Sixes

Six is the number of Harmony and Beauty on the Tree of Life. It is the sun, the heart of the Solar World, the central being of our solar system. All that we are, all that we may be, is of the sun, moon and Earth. The moon and Earth (the Lunar World) are of the substance of the solar system (the Solar World). As the sun is itself a star, it is our harmonious

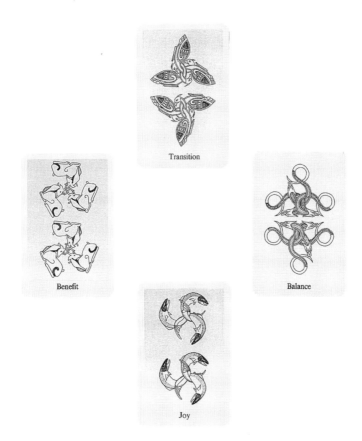

Transition

Benefit

Balance

Joy

connection to the Stellar World, the universe of being. A resonance of that connecting tone is found in our own hearts, and Sixes are concerned with such heart connections, balances and centralizing powers.

Upon the *Axis Mundi* or pivot of the worlds, the Middle Pillar of the Tree of Life, the 6th Sphere occupies the central location. It is the realm of the physical sun, and of the solar divinities, the gods and goddesses of Harmony, Beauty and Redemption. Six is the number of the Hexagram, two harmonized triangles of power, united in perfect balance, 3 + 3. In Earth the Three embodies effort, and a double Three shows this effort reflected. The Hexagram shows the fusion of Worlds, the Stellar and Lunar Worlds as triads or triangular poised patterns, merging as the Solar World. Thus 'effort' brings 'benefit' in our outer worlds, but only if the inner dimensions of energy are harmonized. The Divine Child, the Son or Daughter of Light, is at the heart of the Hexagram, the centre of the Four Directions.

The Six of Birds
Transition
The Six of Air (Birds, Swords, Arrows) is a card that tends to modify the turbulent, changeable effect of the Ace of Air. Six is a harmonizing number, and the Six of Birds shows movement from one state to another, a balanced transition. There is also a sense of movement towards sanctuary, safety or settlement in the Six of Air.

Keywords for this card might be *Beautiful Flight* or *Harmony of Birds*. This second key phrase brings us to the musical attributes of the number Six.[13] A sequence of bird-song is an air transition, sound as defined shape. Music consists of shapes within shapes in Elemental cycles that resonate within our consciousness, and even into our physical substance. The Six of Air might, in a rather restricted classical music scenario, be interpreted as a fugue and variation pattern. In fundamental tones or empowered musical calls, it is the overtone or harmonic sequence inherent in any emission of sound. The Six of Air is where 'chaos' and 'order' are found inherent within one another; harmonized flows of shape, energy and music, within the holism of the worlds.

The Six of Serpents
Balance
The Six of Fire (Serpents or Rods) is a number of poise, of balance. The keywords might be *Illuminating Beauty* or *Perfected Fire*. As Serpents and Rods are vehicles of the true will or spiritual intent, the Six embodies this will and its Fire energies in a condition of balanced power. This is not resting or static, but energizing and active to such an extent that is perfectly poised over the centre of being. One key model here is that of the spinning-top or gyroscope. We might visualize the Six as a wheel with six

spokes or as a resonating sphere of power in perfect alignment.

Balance comes from a correct relationship between the giving and taking powers (the Four and Five). This is how it seems to us as humans in the manifest world, but by turning our attention inwards, we find that balance (Six) may be understood as emitting the positive and negative poles from its still centre. The physical representation of this is our sun – its light and heat are essential to the pattern of energies, the flow from darkness to light to darkness that generates our living world. The solar power is equally creative and destructive. Balance (the Six of Fire) is the pattern of the solar system, the planets, the orbits, the relationships. In mystical sense, it is the harmonizing and redeeming will of the Son or Daughter of Light, enabling life for all beings within the holism of the Solar World.

The Six of Fishes
Joy
The Six of Water (Cups Vessels, Fishes) is a card of flow, of giving, of receiving. The joy that it contains is a selfless joy, often found as the ecstasy of spiritual enlightenment. As a Water power, it harmonizes the flow of the Ace from the West, transforming its power of Love into beauty and sharing. The keywords here are *Singing Harmony* and *Sea of Beauty*.

The joy of the Six of Water is a sharing joy, it is that joy of union that comes with sexual ecstasy and mystical ecstasy. The two joys have been wrongly separated due to orthodox religious conditioning in the West, but they are the same joy. All spiritual powers are sexual, all sexual powers are spiritual.

In creative sense, it is the joy of creation, in which the giving power, the flow of the Ace, is shaped and harmonized by the Six into a beautiful pattern, to be given freely to others, that they might see the inherent beauty of it. In a sexual sense, it is that joy of souls mingling, rather than isolated gratification or selfish sex, that joy that can lead to spiritual realization, or may lead to the incarnation of a joyful soul.

The Six of Fishes holds many insights into the harmony of spiritual sex and the calling or singing in of souls into the vessel that leads, through the Nines, towards physical birth. It is also that unconditional joy that comes with the conception of a child, but we must be able to distinguish between this sacred feeling and selfish gratification or stereotypical breeding for selfish or socially conditioned reasons.

The Six of Beasts
Benefit
The Six of Earth (Beasts or Shields) is a beneficial power. Its keywords are *Harmony of Earth* or *Beautiful Land*. The power of Six is solar and centralizing, and often acts as a healing and redemptive force. As the Ace

of Earth resonates through the number Six, it confers a beautifying and blessing power upon situations, entities and energies.

We might also say that the Solar World, to our fivefold consciousness, seems to separate out into the Stellar World (above) and the Lunar World (below). This is the idea of the Three Triads of the Tree of Life. The benefit of the Six of Earth is often through shape, pattern or form. We may use the Earth shapes (geometry) in meditation, for they act as keys to a change of consciousness that we might not otherwise find. Harmonious form is found in all magical arts, pattern making, geomantic and geometric pattern making. In the realm of shape and pattern making, modern computers are restating the Elemental flow patterns taught for millennia in spiritual and magical arts.

By a typical inversion of the scientific mentality, these are popularly known as 'chaos' patterns, but they are the number patterns of the Elemental Dance. The simple geometric shapes and the Platonic Solids work directly upon our consciousness/energy. This is a property of the Six of Earth, the Beautiful Land. But they are not rigid structures, for within them are found the Elemental flow patterns of all other numbers. This has been called 'chaos' by modern materialist writers because it seems to break up the old rigid world view of mechanistic physics. In truth it is beauty, flow, living shape.

The reiterative Elemental pattern has always been taught in all mystical or spiritual traditions world-wide. The Creation Vision of the Merlin tradition is a classic example of this teaching attuned to Western consciousness. A simple diagram of the reiterative Elements is shown in Figure 14.

The numbers Seven to Ten are the Third Triad or Lunar World, with the expressed Kingdom or planet Earth. We will examine this last spiralling of numbers in the next chapter.

Figure 14 (*opposite*): THE REITERATIVE ELEMENTS

THE THIRD TRIAD OR LUNAR WORLD AND PLANET EARTH
(The Numbers Seven to Ten)

The Four Sevens

The 7th Sphere is that of Venus, Victory or Triumph. It is particularly a Sphere of the emotions, and of sexual energies working through emotion. The goddess Venus and the mysterious Eros, who is simultaneously a universal Power and the god of sexual love, are defined within us as Triumph.

There is an interesting aside into the origins of formal tarot cards here, for, as mentioned earlier, it seems likely that they derived from images first designed for Petrarch's *Triumphs*, hence the name *Trumps* or *Triomphi*.[4] (As I have discussed, this only marks the appearance of printed or distributed cards and repeated illustrations, and not the origin of the images themselves. The origins of tarot itself are in the cosmological and poetic images used by bards and story-tellers, including those found in the early Merlin texts upon which the Merlin Tarot is based. The Merlin images and cosmology, clearly those that we recognize today as tarot, pre-date the first known tarot cards by at least three centuries. The *Prophecies* and *Life* of Merlin are therefore the earliest formal texts containing descriptions of tarot images and a tarot cosmology. They only carry, however, that which as already in circulation, which may be traced conceptually and thematically back into Northern European and classical mythology and cosmology.)

In the context of the number Seven, *Trumps* or *Triumphs* are images that stimulate our feelings. They cause our consciousness to move, generating emotion. The Victory or Triumph is not a gloating or superior or enforced conquest, but the surge of feeling, of recognition, the emotional peak that comes with the fusion of energies of the 7th Sphere.

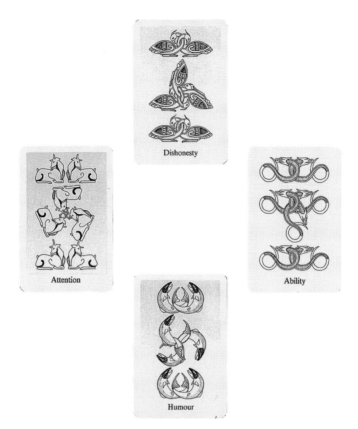

Thus, the Number cards of the Sevens are often concerned with human emotion.

Seven is also the number of Sacred Space: the Seven Directions are Above, Below, Before, Behind, Right, Left and Within. The Directions East, South, West and North are often aligned as Before, Right, Behind and Left (as in Figure 5), but the primary Direction of consciousness (Before) will vary as we turn towards each planetary Direction, as we stand at the centre of the Circle. We shall return to some of the concepts of Sacred Space shortly.

The Seven of Birds
Dishonesty
The Seven of Air (Birds, Swords, Arrows, Direction East) is often a card of self-deceit. The mind talks itself out of truth, and the turbulent power of Air disrupts the emotions. In broader terms, it is a card of complex movement. It can, therefore, indicate intentional dishonesty, in which the thought and will generate a false situation or false emotions.

Keywords here are *Original Victory* and *Dawn of Feeling*. These crucial modes of *beginning*, the Ace of Air flowing through into the number Seven, often appear as impulsive patterns of emotion. These are dishonest not through will or conscious choice, but because they are followed willy-nilly without any reflection or attention (the Seven of Earth) to bring them into balance.

Just as we live in an age of the destructive Fives, we respond emotionally to our situations with a potentially destructive Seven. It is found collectively as the dishonest emotions of patriotism and nationalism, particularly where technological warfare (Swords) is excused by emotional appeal (Seven). The Seven of Air is a power of propaganda and mass-appeal, a cutting mind steering the emotions of many. It may be a simple event, or it may be those long-term programmes laid down by manipulators of religion. It can also indicate spiritual dishonesty, in which deeply reasoned, lucid systems of belief intentionally cover the true living feelings. In this sense it represents the vital spiritual power of the Ace sealing the triple gate of the Six. Such a sealing can only be temporary (i.e. bound by a time cycle) for the Ace will always regenerate itself, and cut back to the Six or move through its cycle of Sevens towards Eight.

The dishonesty of the Seven of Air is in many ways the 'opposite-opposite' of the Seven of Earth. This is shown upon the Wheel of Life, for after the grace of the Seven of Earth comes the potential dishonesty (temptation) of the Seven of Air. We must always remember that we tempt ourselves – no outside agency can ever do so – and so we are always responsible both for our own temptations and our response to them. The Sevens are cards of the feelings, the emotions, of power energies that tend to reflect themselves in increasingly glamorized or potentially deluding patterns. Yet the Elemental Cycle and the Directions of the Four Sevens hold perfect balance and all the necessary powers for our return to grace.

The Seven of Air is an essential inspirational and disruptive force; it originates the tension of power that is used creatively by our ability, moved towards form by a generous humour, and reflected or expressed through grace, care and attention.

The Seven of Serpents
Ability
The Seven of Fire (Rods or Serpents, Direction South) reveals the increasing manipulating or organizing power of will. Whereas in the Six this power was spiritual, creative will or intent, it now moves forward to fuse the intent and the feelings. The ability is not a conditioned or trained ability, but that natural feeling for any act or activity that brings it to a victorious conclusion. It is the light of ability in the South reflected to and from the mirror of attention in the North.

Keywords here are *Victorious Fire* or *Triumph of Illumination*. The

Seven Wands or Rods are the markers of Sacred Space upon a ground-plan, the layout of the sacred land or geomantic zone. They represent the ability of human consciousness to define, perceive and relate to Elemental, planetary and stellar forces. While the Seven of Earth manifests and reflects the Directions in various forms (from spiritual to imaginative to physical), the Seven of Rods marks and defines their relative locations and potentials.

Other keywords for this card are *Fiery Serpent* or *Loving Dragon*. This aspect of the Seven of Fire refers to energies within ourselves and within the sacred land: the human emotions and their equivalent geomantic forces, those of hidden fire or energy within the land. There is, again, a powerful sexual movement to the Seven of Fire; it can show sexual ability, which is balance and loving relationships of the Inner Fire. This same Fire flows through the land (sometimes called the Green Fire, though this is merely a convenient symbol as the colours may vary from place to place and time to time) and is the equivalent of sexual energy aroused, related, balanced and made fruitful.

The Seven of Fishes
Humour
The Seven of Water (Cups, Fishes, Direction West) reveals the Ace of Love flowing through our feelings. It is that sense of humour which is spontaneous and deep, bringing clear laughter, free of personality or pose. Keywords here are *Star of Laughter* or *Triumph of Feeling*. Laughter is a powerful spiritual declaration – when we truly laugh, we allow the inner Love to manifest directly through our body, through our voice. Real laughter is always spontaneous, surprising, never planned.

Humour is a hallmark of a clear soul (as the Seven is clear in the sense of being sustained and washed by the Element of Water). The ability to bring humour into people's lives is a spiritual gift. By this we should not accept or devise vicious comedy or intellectually contrived wit, for these are lesser aspects of true humour, comprised of mixed numbers or Elements, which are often in imbalance when themes of cruelty are present.

The Seven of Water is also the sexual laughter that rises unbidden in ecstasy: the Seven Cups or swimming Fishes are the union of male and female, and the climax of energies that leads to further life. The union may be understood as two intersecting triangles (Six) with a perfect point or seed of fusion and origination in the centre (Seven). The Seven, however, does not ensure fertility, but forms the energetic emotional sexual conditions in which a soul may be attached to parents. The further stages towards physical birth are in the Eights and Nines.

There is sometimes a sense of self-delusion to the Seven of Water, often where romantic choices and images are taken too seriously, or accepted without any proper attention to their effect. The Seven of Fishes or Cups is, in this sense, rising towards or filling with the unstable dishonesty of the Seven of Swords or Birds. The humorous heart, however, will always clarify delusions, for a balanced emotional pattern is one in which we cannot take ourselves seriously.

The Seven of Beasts
Attention

The Seven of Earth (Beasts, Shields or Mirrors, Direction North) embodies the Ace crossing from the harmonized energies of the Six and expanding towards expression or manifestation. The Seven of Beasts or Shields has moved beyond the triple gate of Six, and focuses its energies upon *formative victory*. This card has the power of building, of defining, of structuring, in readiness and preparation for a further step or steps towards Ten. Its keywords might be *Attending the Earth* or *Venus Reflecting*.

Venus is also the morning and evening star, the definer of the thresholds crossed between night and day. Attention to the rising and setting of Venus over the horizon, and to the rising and setting of her powers within ourselves, brings a pattern, a rhythm. The Seven of Earth is concerned with patterning the flowing energies of the emotions and sexuality, the attractive forces of nature. By giving our attention to these forces consciously, rather than being unconsciously dominated by habits moulded from these forces (or conditioned into us by circumstances), we find the *Victory of Earth*, which is, in its highest spiritual form, *Grace*.

The grace of Seven, of spiritual Earth, is a much abused idea. Orthodox region is deeply interwoven with ideas such as 'triumph over sin', with the rejection of sexuality being praised as a spiritual act, a way of 'gaining grace'. If we pay proper *attention* to this propaganda, we free ourselves of many related ideas that have persisted through into the post-Christian era. In New Age philosophy, if such a term may be used in its widest sense, we frequently find emphasis upon 'higher consciousness' and 'rising to the Light'. This is merely a variant of the old propaganda in which the natural powers of the Goddess were remorselessly denied to ordinary people. The perennial wisdom, of any land or religion, always teaches that Earth, the body, the land, is sacred.

There can be no rising into light, no false victory over matter, in terms of antagonism or dualism. Meditation upon the Element of Earth, Venus, and Seven in the North (the Seven of Beasts of Shields) can give us the graceful insight into this truth.

The other northerly insight of the Seven of Shields or Mirrors is into the significance of the star group the Pleiades, the Seven Sisters. As already discussed, these play an important role in the turning of the Wheel of the Seasons for all primal peoples the world over. The Celtic and European nocturnal and lunar calendar employed the rising and setting of the Pleiades, in May and November, as its major turning-points. In the Merlin cosmology and psychology, lunar and stellar patterns are more important than the solar Seasons. The Seven Sisters are also said to be the original home of humanity in many primal traditions. In esoteric tradition they are said to be the octave or matrix of our sevenfold basic planetary system.

Whatever the accumulated traditions, people all over the planet paid (and still pay) close *attention* to the rising and setting of the Pleiades. When they rise in one hemisphere they are setting in the other. This is an important meditational subject. The major festivals of May and November were defined not by the sun, but by the Pleiades. May is the festival of rebirth and light, while November is the festival of death and darkness. At both thresholds, the ancestral spirits are contacted, the rising or setting of the Seven Sisters creating powerful geomantic and collective tides that enable such contacts.

The Seven of Earth is that pattern of Sacred Space enlivened when we face North. Traditionally, the Shields, Mirrors, Crystals or Lenses of Earth are located in each direction: Above is the Mirror of Night; Below is the Mirror of the Underworld. Before us in the North is the Mirror of Winter and Earth, Behind us is the Mirror of Summer and Fire. To our Right is the Mirror of Spring and Air, to our left is the Mirror of Autumn and Water. Within is the Mirror of Truth, Being, the Ace of Law and Liberty.

The Seven Beasts Together
One way of working with the Seven of Earth is with Seven Beasts, which may appear in a variety of forms. They may begin, for example, as the Four Creatures of the Aces in each Quarter. Above are the angelic or spiritual beings, specifically our individual angelic link or messenger. Below are the Underworld beings, with an individual fairy or Underworld ally, co-walker or companion being. Within is whatever spiritual form being or creature we resonate out of ourselves during any phase of our lives (see Figure 15). This variant of the Seven Directions, as Seven Living Creatures, is a powerful pattern for meditation, visualization, ritual dance and ceremonial magic.

The Four Eights

Eight is the Sphere of Mercury, or of certain aspects of Minerva and Athena. In broad terms, it is the power of cultural development, of society, civilization, and structures in which collective patterns of humanity relate to one another. More precisely, this 8th Sphere forms the mental communicative world, the thoughts and exchanges that pass between entities. A key concept here is *communication*.

The traditional name for the 8th Sphere is Glory or Honour. Both Victory (7th Sphere) and Glory (8th Sphere) seem to have militaristic

undertones at first glance, but this is, in some ways, a modern misinterpretation. The Victory, as we found with the Sevens, is within our own feelings, the triumph of clarified, balanced emotions energized by the Elements. The Glory of Eight is a perfect intellect, an active, swift, communicative mind. The aim of martial arts (developed through the relationship between the powers of Five and Eight manifesting through Ten) is not merely to defeat opponents, but to bring spiritual enlightenment and balance to the warrior. The glory and honour of propaganda and militaristic cant are travesties of the true meanings.

There is a fourfold pattern in the Spheres Six, Seven, Eight and Nine (see Figure 16): Six is originative spirit *creating* through the soul, the sun or Beauty/Harmony; Seven is creative spirit *forming* through the emotions, Venus or Victory; Eight is creative spirit *forming* through thought, Mercury or Glory; Nine is originative and creative spirit *forming* a body, the moon or Foundation. Ten is the *expression* and sum of all worlds, the fusion of spirit and matter, the Earth or Kingdom.

Figure 15: (opposite) THE SEVEN CREATURES AND SEVEN DIRECTIONS

Figure 16: (below) THE FOURFOLD BALANCE

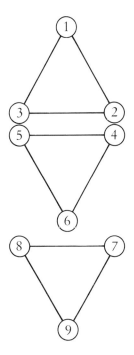

While Sevens work through the feelings and sexual attractions, Eights work as thoughts and intellectual attractions and activities. Honour is a concept deeply seeded into the power teachings of the 8th Sphere, for an arrogant, dishonourable mind can create havoc with its surroundings. It is our lack of honour that has caused modern science to wreak destruction upon the sacred planet, the arrogant pursuit of 'science for science's sake' with an intentional amoral detachment from the ethical humanitarian and environmental reactions to experiments and inventions.

The weaknesses of Sevens tend to be emotional and sexual; there is often insufficient critical analysis. This over-emotionalizing often leads to deluding images that can imbalance our energies and create loops or seemingly irrevocable cycles and life patterns. Much of the popular notion of 'karma' is about such emotional loops, and not really karma in its original sense at all. The weakness of Eights tends towards intellectual arrogance and lack of feeling, leading to a dissociation from other life forms.

With Seven and Eight we emerge into the arena of human consciousness

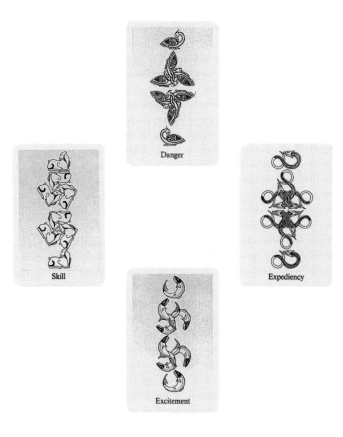

and energy forming as specific entities, yet we must be aware that the laws or patterns of these greater numbers hold good in all conditions, all energies and entities. Eight or Mercury is the interchange of communication, that is, not only ideas and thoughts in our minds, but any energetic interchange that carries specific messages.

The Eight of Birds
Danger
The Eight of Air (Birds, Swords, Direction East) is a card of uncertainty and potential destructive or disruptive energy. It represents that danger that may be passed through, but has to be addressed, either in potential or in reality, come what may. As an Air card the Eight opens the Four Gates to the Four Winds, and the blast of their coming together disrupts our accustomed patterns.

In the Apocalypse of Merlin, found in the *Prophecies*, Ariadne, the Weaver Goddess, unravels the solar system, causing the ordered cycle of the planets and Zodiac signs to disintegrate. She then withdraws her presence into the originative crack or source from which the worlds were emitted, and the Four Winds come together with a blast that is heard by the distant stars. This is the cosmological vision of the Eight of Air, in the Stellar and Solar Worlds.

In the Solar and Lunar Worlds, however, the effects of the Eight are modified by relative patterns. That which is dangerous for one individual or group is safe for another. Skill plays a great part in the relative danger of any situation.

Keywords here are *Encircling Wind, Ceaseless Change, Restless Motion.* The danger can equally come from within as from without. It is the danger that comes from uncentred restlessness, from seeking ceaseless change for no reason. It can, under extreme circumstances, break out as violence in the individual or group, creating a danger to others. As Air cards are concerned with the mind and mental activity, the Eight of Birds may also be a card of mental disturbance, imbalance and confusion.

As we move through the larger numbers, their power must be cycled or balanced around the Wheel. Thus the Eight of Air is balanced by the other Eights, either from within ourselves or through external encounters. The simple glyph of the equal cross within the circle is a powerful aid to insights on this balance: Air and Water, Fire and Earth (see Figure 16). The relationships may be cyclic or spiral, as in the Wheel of Life. They may be across the Circle (E–W, S–N) in either direction, or they may follow the serpentine lightning-flash or 'Z' sign pattern. This last pattern is the empowering movement of The Hanged Man (see Chapter 15).

The Eight of Serpents
Expediency

The Eight of Fire (Rods or Serpents, Direction South) is the fourfold pattern of Twos, the pillars of the Four Gates. Because the pillars represent polarity, the Eight is a card of constant interchange of energies. It moves with great rapidity, and will take whatever action is necessary to rebalance and enable the intent of the mind. Expediency means taking whatever action is right at any moment; its negative possibilities spill over into dishonesty, dishonour and politics.

Keywords for this card are *Creating Possibilities*, *Glory of Wands*, *Wisdom of Serpents*. Wisdom (Two) is a higher octave of Glory (Eight), just as Understanding (Three) is a higher octave of Victory (Seven). But while Wisdom and Understanding tend to be universal polarities, the Star Father and the Great Mother, Victory and Honour are teeming with sexually polarized interchanging beings. These are the swarms of potential life often described in creation myth, in esoteric teachings and mystical cosmology.

The Eight of Fire is a card of *interchange*: the danger of the winds of Air causes balancing, expedient action to be taken. Fire cards, Serpents, Rods, are all concerned with will and intent. Again we have the keyword for the 8th Sphere, Honour or Glory, to remind us that the intent must be unselfish for the power of the Eight to flow fully.

The Eight Rods of this card are the four fingers of two hands, or the upper and lower arms and legs. There is an eightfold pattern in the manipulative extending bones of the human skeleton, which manifests the universal pattern and elemental being in human form.

The Eight of Fishes
Excitement

The Eight of Water (Cups, Fishes, Direction West) is a power of fluid motion. Keywords here are *Forming Glory* or *Cascade of Energy*, *The Swimming Shoal*. This last phrase uses the image of a seething shoal of fish, endlessly turning and forming patterns out of their living movement and relative positions, a whole entity as a shoal, yet many excited individuals.

The Element of Water flows through the gates and forms complex interacting patterns. In fluids these flow-patterns are of infinite variety, and form part of the 'new' mathematics and physics that uses computer generated models and fractal systems. The fluid dynamic patterns are those of the Elements: each Element has within it relative patterns of all four (see Figure 14).

The excitement of the Eight of Water may be mental, emotional or sexual, or an interplay of all three. The Eight (thought, communication) causes the mind to seethe with possibility, with anticipation, to be restless and full of expectation. It often involves thought leaping ahead of itself, looking forward to a specific event, manifestation or meeting.

As Eights tend to be cards of mental activity and communication, they often reveal our inner responses to outer situations. The Eight of Water, being the infinite flow of potentials, is also a card of reproduction, though not always in the physical, sexual sense. It is involved with the thought processes of artistic creation, the excitement of forming a work, an image, a project of any sort. It is also a card of co-operation, of many potentials flowing together, the excitement of working with and relating to others.

The Eight of Beasts
Skill

The Eight of Earth (Shields, Direction North) embodies the power of the Ace through mind working with substance. Keywords are *Glorious Expression* or *Honourable Mind, Earth Skills* or simply *Quicksilver.* Eight is 4x2, or 2 + 2 + 2 + 2. Thus, it represents the Four Gates of the Quarters, and offers the definitions or skill to work with their energies and forms.

There is a further implication in the Eight of Earth, for it reveals manipulative skill. This honourable skill is that of the fingers working upon substance. Its converse, of course, is dishonourable manipulation for selfish ends.

In Greek myth Mercury (the 8th Sphere) was the inventor of the lyre, a stringed instrument with cosmological significance. [13] While the human digits are ten, the fingers are eight in number. Our thumbs are the expressive digits of Earth, making the Right and Left Pillars of the Kingdom or 10th Sphere, and without them the fingers cannot work. But the eight fingers are the fast-moving, skilful manipulators of substance, of form, of inventive techniques and communicative devices. The eight fingers are also the Eight Rods or Serpents in the Eight of Fire, Fire and Earth being complementary opposites or polar reflections of one another.

The Four Nines

Nine is the Foundation of the Tree of Life, the spiritual power of the Lunar World. The foundational power is that of the Four Aces immediately behind or within our manifest world. The Moon is the sphere of gods and goddesses of fertility, tides, birth and death. It is also the realm of the *daemones* or intermediary spirits, and of certain ancestors and teachers of the human race.

In modern psychology, the Lunar World has some broad correlation to the Jungian idea of the unconscious, at least as far its collective pool of images and energy is concerned. But we should be cautious in making comparisons between modern, essential, materialist systems of therapy and

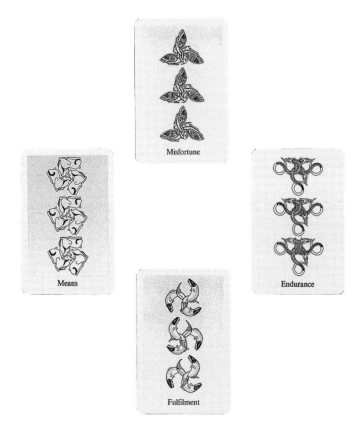

Misfortune

Means

Endurance

Fulfilment

the spiritual and magical traditions. The Lunar World includes countless orders of existence, life forms, entities and types of awareness that are simply not understood or admitted into materialist psychology.

The Mother of Birth and Death is found in the Moon – she is that aspect of the Great Mother that is concerned with the passing to and fro between physical existence. The world of dreams and half-formed entities is also that of the 9th Sphere, the great Ninefold Womb of all being and unbeing upon the planet Earth.

The Nine of Birds
Misfortune
The Nine of Air (Birds, Swords or Arrows, Direction East) is a power of taking or breaking. The Eight, Nine and Ten of Air are difficult and unavoidable powers; they may be balanced, but not cheated or escaped. As Air approaches outer expression, so it becomes more dangerous, complex and cutting or blasting.

The Nine of Air is 3x3 or 3 + 3 + 3, the Mother of Mothers, with keywords such as *Bringer of the Whirlwind, Birth of Sorrow.* This card is frequently associated with pain, with birth pangs and death pangs. The pain may be physical, mental, emotional or spiritual. Spiritual pain is the Sorrowing Mother of all Being (the 3rd Sphere), physical pain is the birth or death of any life-phase within our organism. This too, is a type of motherhood, whether you are male or female. Air cards are often concerned with therapy and imbalance, and the greater numbers can indicate occurrences or periods of physical illness as well as mental and emotional disturbance.

As Air is such a mobile Element, there is often surprise or suddenness associated with its greater numbers. This is the storm that breaks unexpectedly, the whirlwind that rises from the calm sea, the sudden accident. Its misfortune is associated with cutting and separation, loss and diminishment.

Air is the Element of Origination, primal Spirit or First Breath. When it manifests within an increasingly material holism, the spirit can be, in relative terms, destructive. But the misfortune or cutting away of one cycle or being is the beginning and birth of another. One important key to this card is that it is the power of separation that brings beginnings. But within its storm, at the moment of flight or loss, we cannot perceive what or where or who the beginning might be.

The other Nines – the endurance of Serpents, the fulfilment of Fishes and the means of Beasts – help us, however, to contemplate and understand this power. The misfortune of the East is balanced by, or takes from, the fulfilment of the West, flowing between means in the North and endurance in the South (see Figure 17).

The Nine of Serpents
Endurance
The Nine of Fire (Serpents or Wands, Direction South) is the firmly founded will and strong intent. Its endurance is that of the Three of Fire (intention), tripled into expression and manifestation. Keywords here are *Enduring Fire* or *Immutable Foundation.*

The Nine embodies the Fire and Light power emerging in its last step towards manifestation. It is the connecting force, the intent to remain in a structure, a shape, a pattern. In human terms it is endurance of will, in which we hold ourselves together through all misfortunes. There is a further aspect of imagination in the Nine of Fire, for it represents the will creating images in the inner light, the imaginative pool out of which dreams are made substantial and expressed as outer patterns. The technique of empowered and guided visualization is a perfect example of the Nine of Fire: the will generates and reinforces images, while the images give us further power to perfect our will. But this is not a closed system or dogmatic in any way.

We must be wary of confusing the endurance of the Nine with obstinacy

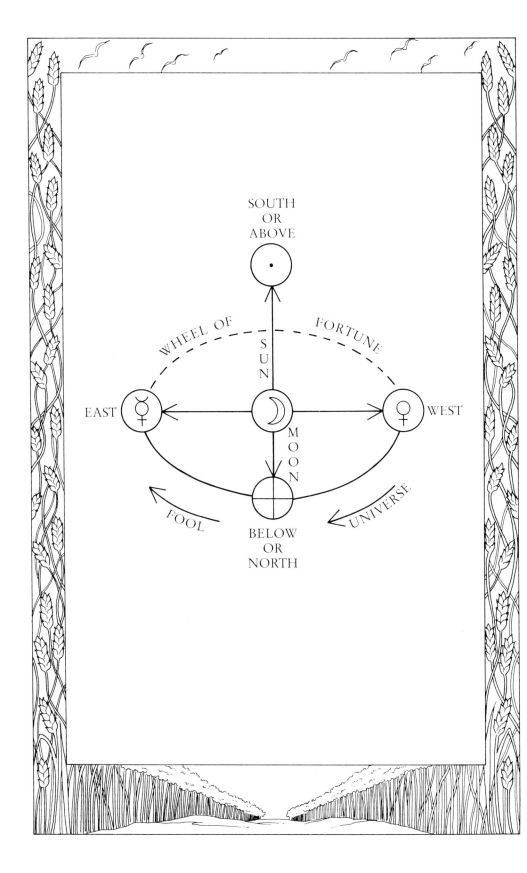

SOUTH
OR
ABOVE

WHEEL OF FORTUNE

SUN

EAST ☿ ☽ ♀ WEST

MOON

UNIVERSE

FOOL

BELOW
OR
NORTH

or rigidity. The triple Three is a pattern of foundation, but it does not last forever. Its immutability is often that of regeneration, for any of its three Threes can regenerate a further cycle, just any two Threes or all three Threes will work towards an end, towards Ten in one direction or One in another.

There is sometimes a sense of burden and weight with the Nine of Fire, knowing that the intent will carry us through a difficult situation and imagining the potentially good outcome. By such imagination, using the inner light creatively, we can influence the outcome of situations (the power of the Rod). The 'secret' is always to work from the Ace outwards, and not to seek the direct power of the Nine or Ten without the deeper insights of spiritual reality.

The Nine of Fishes
Fulfilment
The Nines of Water (Cups, Fishes, Direction West) is a card of great blessing. It has physical, emotional, mental and sexual content; it can be the fulfilment of an emotional union, of sexual union, or of a long and productive life. It is a card of fecundity, of production, of reproduction. Its keywords are *Fountain of Full Moon, The Giving Mother, Waters of Life and Love.*

In a sexual and fertile sense, the Nine of Water can be the fulfilment of the womb, the pregnant mother at the outset of her nine-month wait to give birth. It is also the successful birth after the pain and endurance of the Nines of Air and Fire. Upon inner levels, it is the perfection of a full heart, the satisfaction and recognition of a balance and completion. There are strong undertones of giving in this card – the Nine Fishes swim in a sea of plenty, the Nine Cups are outpouring and ever refilled.

With the Nine of Water, the fusion of will and imagination in the Nine of Fire becomes fluid and flows out into expression. Thus, it is the realization, or making real in manifest terms, of that which we have imagined. Empowered visualization will bring physical results, though they are sometimes unexpected. Fulfilment often comes from surprising sources or directions, and an ideal may be embodied in many different shapes. The greater numbers tend to define forms, but also to increase the number of entities through which energy may be encountered.

The Nine of Beasts
Means
The Nine of Earth (Beasts or Shields, Direction North) shows manifesting energy and ideas taking shape. The power of the Ace of Earth here enables

Figure 17: (opposite) THE NINEFOLD POWER PATTERN

the means towards expression. It is the last step before physical life, and the first step after it. The Nine of Earth is the ninefold inner body that enables the outer form. When the Nine of Beasts appears in tarot patterns, it can suggest means ranging from the most subtle energies to simple physical means towards a chosen end.

Keywords for this number are *Founded within the Earth, The Ninefold Womb, Expressive Moon*. All means towards realization are here: dreams, seeds, life patterns, sexual fertility. These are also the means towards spiritual truth: inner birth, vision, wisdom teachings, and the movement of sexual energy towards subtle ends rather than gratification or physical fertility.

As 3x3 this is the body of the Goddess, the foundation of the all being, the thresholds or crossroads between the Worlds. All Spheres merge at Nine, the Foundation. But the Earth itself and physical matter in the universe are the outer body of the Goddess, and the Foundation or lunar powers form the subtle body and regenerative force that keeps the outer body in manifestation – and which also demanifests it. The movement between inner and outer is constant and simultaneous.

The Lunar Sphere is centred on the Triad formed of Glory, Victory and Foundation. With the Trumps of The Wheel of Fortune, The Universe, The Fool, The Sun and The Moon, we find a potent Ninefold power pattern (see Figure 17). This may be used in meditation for each cycle of Nines in turn.

The Four Tens

Ten is the Kingdom, the expressed manifest world. For us this is the planet Earth, the Earth Mother. But Ten is also *all* manifest being, so it is all matter/energy in the universe, all entities and energies that appear 'materially'. There is no separation between spirit and matter, but the Ten is a number of expression as far as our consensual world is concerned. The truth of Ten is that it is One emitting Nine.

The customary versions of the Tree of Life in Kabbalah and in modern interpretations have an unfortunate tendency towards the idea of fallen matter, probably as a result of Christian influence. But the Merlin tradition and the Merlin Tarot do not assume that the body and the land and planet are separated from spiritual being; in it they are mirror images or harmonics of the holism. This is why the traditional pattern of the *Axis Mundi* (the Trumps of Moon, Sun and Star) is so important in the Creation Vision: all Three Worlds interpenetrate and partake of one another. The Kingdom, the sacred planet, our own bodies, are the manifest living being.

With the Kingdom we come that planetary vision within the universal

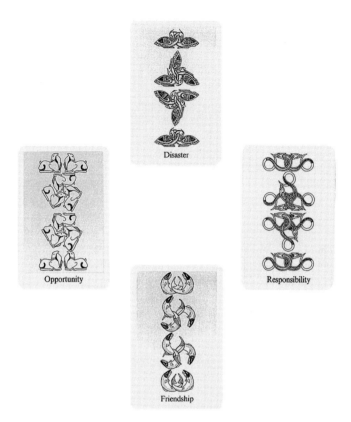

vision (see Figures 1–3 and the two instructional cards of the deck) that was central to the Merlin tradition. The Earth was a mirror of the greater universe, a central entity (as far as our awareness is concerned) within the Three Worlds of Moon, Sun and Star. This is not an ignorant geocentric vision, for our ancestors knew perfectly well that the planet was not the centre of the physical universe. It is, rather, a world view relating to our physical perceptions as beings upon the surface of the planet. This is also meditative truth: wherever we are is the Kingdom, the centre and circumference of being. Although Kingdom is the traditional word, from Jewish mysticism, we might also use the terms *Sacred Body* or *Holy Earth*.

Tens are cards of interaction, and if we combine them in various patterns, they reveal the so-called 'laws of karma'.

The Ten of Birds
Disaster
The Ten of Air (Birds, Swords, Direction East) is the ultimate cut. It is the manifest departure of the flock (the collective entity of any body or

situation) and the fall of Ten Blades upon matter. Keywords here would be *Collapsing Form*, *Cutting Free*, *The Bitter Wind*. In the Ten, the Ace of Air manifests right through into substance and brings a complete separation, dividing any form or pattern into its constituent parts.

In human terms, this power is often seen as a disaster. It has a special emphasis upon mental and emotional situations, disastrous life events. It can also, of course, indicate physical disasters and natural disasters, and must be interpreted in context of other cards and through the inherent nature of the question, if it appears in a tarot reading.

As a meditational aid, the Ten of Air helps us to contemplate and understand the inevitability of cycles, of beginnings inherent in endings. It is the breaking power, the cutting edge, that liberates through disaster. This effect will be greatly strengthened if it is association with certain *taking* Trumps, such as Death, or The Blasted Tower. The higher Air cards must be understood from within, for if they are encountered as outward forces, they are almost always felt to be hostile or antagonist to our temporary self-interest. If we can turn this situation round, and find their inner meaning, the antagonism or conflict, which is essentially within ourselves, flies away.

The Ten of Air is the transition between night and day; it marks the end of dark comforting night and the dawn of a harsh morning. It often indicates collective disputes and irresolvable difference of opinion, in which acceptance is the key rather than further conflict. Acceptance, is not, however, a meek and diminishing act, but comes from an understanding of the power of Ten, from the knowledge that we must move with it rather than against it.

The Ten of Serpents
Responsibility
The Ten of Fire (Serpents, Rods, Direction South) is the bundle of a manifest will. This implies not only responsibility for our own actions and intent, but often also for the lives and interaction of others. The Ten of Fire is the effect of the intent, imagination, will and energy within the outer world, where we cannot and should not avoid responsibility for our own actions.

Keywords here are *Expressed Intent*, *Manifest Power*, *Action and Reaction*. The Ten of Fire, Rods or Serpents is the complex interaction of will, the so-called 'cause and effect' relationship. If our intent is aligned from the Ace, the perfect will of Light, the Ten will be a potent force of balance and control. But if we are separated from the Light within, the Ten of Fire becomes either a burden or the seeming effect of energies and forces *upon* us rather than through us. Whatever we cannot or will not take responsibility for within ourselves seems to come towards us from outside.

This card is also the Earth Dragon, in the sense that we are collectively and individually responsible for the sacred land and planet, and for the forces and other lives upon and within the Earth. The Ten of Serpents can represent the relationship with the subtle fire forces of the land, or it can, in its polar role with the Ten of Beasts, represent work with the land in terms of tools, systems, patterns and projects. These all partake of the Rod, the enabling implement, and the Dragon or Serpent, which is energy expressed in a living form, the power that coils around the Rod.

The Ten of Fishes
Friendship
The Ten of Water (Cups, Fishes, Direction West) is a power of collective Love. It is the inherently friendly nature of our collective existence, our sharing, interacting, creating and living together. It may also refer to specific friendships, depending upon the context of other cards such as the Trumps and Court cards.

Keywords here would be *Great Sharing, Collective Creation, Children of Earth*. The card has a further implication of interchange, of flowing to and fro, of the exchange of energy between people. As a Ten it may refer very simply to the material of our ordinary friendships, but it has inherent within it all the other numbers from the Ace, or power of universal Love. Thus it can refer to that deep spiritual friendship that manifests outwardly, yet does not necessarily include romantic love, sexuality, or other spheres of energy associated with the Element of Water.

As a Ten this card also embodies the essential caring and respect that we should have for our land, for all living creatures on it. We are all fish swimming in the ocean together upon the Mother Earth as she swims through Mother Space, even though hostility divides us against ourselves.

The Ten of Beasts
Opportunity
The Ten of Earth (Beasts, Shields, Direction North) is the ultimate Earth of Earth. It is the planetary body, our own body and all matter/energy. Its keywords would be *Sacred Body, Holy Earth, Perfected Kingdom, Earth Mother, Regenerating Substance*. Tens are numbers of substance, the ultimate expression of all numbers.

The Ten of Beasts offers substantial opportunity, all the material and spiritual opportunity of the world itself. As an Earth card, involved in the manifest body, it has an interesting temporal pattern. We are born into this world as tiny infants, with a lifetime of opportunity ahead of us. As our outer physical body grows and matures, however, the opportunities often seem to peak, and restrictions become increasingly evident in our life pattern. Then, towards the close of a life cycle, the restrictions fall away, and the opportunity of death comes to us.

In a simple sense, the Ten shows opportunity in any situation. It is the Ninefold Gate plus One, the last threshold crossed. All that there is here, and we need only to transform our perceptions to find the opportunities that the Earth Mother offers us.

There is often a special emphasis upon *material* opportunity when this card appears in a reading, depending upon other factors and particularly upon Trumps in association with the Ten.

With the Four Tens we have completed our spiralling expansion of numbers from the originative to the expressive states of being.

Summary of the Number Cards

While Trumps give imaginal expression to complex energies or modes of consciousness, numbers or Elements define basic interactions. Such interactions are derived from four universal Elements or Powers which underpin existence: Air, Fire, Water and Earth, or Life, Light, Love and Law. Rotation of these energies (which are relative conditions or phases of one originative being) creates a relative cycle of Three Worlds and Three Wheels.

There are, therefore, two ways in which we may understand the Number cards in tarot. They may first be pure or abstract formulae for energies, known intellectually through mathematical analogy. This corresponds broadly to Pythagorean and Platonic theories of number. Such theories were widespread in ancient cultures, and underpinned Hermetic science and philosophy. To a limited extent they persist today in modern esoteric philosophy, but advanced work with such theories is now found mainly in the realm of physics, with no overt or intentional metaphysical correlations.

The second way in which Number cards may be understood is as simple direct indicators of energies manifesting as circumstances. This elemental Cycle formed a major part of the medieval and Renaissance world view, and is clearly inherent in tarot generally. It corresponds to the Wheel of Fortune, while the higher understanding of numbers corresponds to the Wheel of Judgement. Justice partakes of both conceptual models, being the transition or balance between the higher and lower orders or powers of number.

In the Merlin Tarot, the Number or Elemental cards use symbols of creatures rather than the customary Swords, Wands, Cups and Coins. The overall emphasis of the Creation Vision from which the Merlin Tarot is drawn is upon an interacting set of worlds, teeming with orders of life. Celtic tradition, which forms a major part of the Vision, contains a natural magical world view, often described as 'shamanic' in modern literature.

It is from this tradition that we draw the suites of Elemental and Number cards, following the interlaced patterns which were so essential to symbolists in Celtic art. In simple terms, the interlaced patterns of Pictish and Celtic art represent a vision in which energies and worlds are woven together. This vision is clearly found in the Merlin texts in poetic descriptive form. We may see aspects of the Weaver's pattern through four orders. These orders or modes are represented in the Merlin Tarot as follows:

AIR: Suit and Court of Birds, Swords or Arrows.
FIRE: Suit and Court of Serpents or Dragons, Rods or Wands.
WATER: Suit and Court of Fishes, Cups or Chalices.
EARTH: Suit and Court of Beasts, Shields, Discs or Coins.

Basic meanings are derived from the simple process of a cycle of Four Elements through Three Worlds. The numbers One to Nine correspond to Nine Spheres, which are triads of polarity in each of the Three Worlds: positive/negative/balanced or male/female/androgynous. This tripled or ninefold pattern gives rise to the familiar Tree of Life. The 10th Sphere is the outer world or Kingdom, in which all polarities are inherent, and which is an ultimate reflection of the 1st Sphere. Such is the simplest metaphysical origin of the decimal system.

The Number cards, One to Ten, reveal prime interactions of Four Elements through Ten Spheres (see Figure 23). A table of single word attributes would read as follows:

| | **Birds** | **Serpents** | **Fishes** | **Beasts** |
Aces	*Air/Life*	*Fire/Light*	*Water/Love*	*Earth/Law*
2	Doubt	Choice	Freedom	Change
3	Suffering	Intention	Affection	Effort
4	Truce	Generosity	Promise	Increase
5	Loss	Retribution	Sorrow	Conflict
6	Transition	Balance	Joy	Benefit
7	Dishonesty	Ability	Humour	Attention
8	Danger	Expediency	Excitement	Skill
9	Misfortune	Endurance	Fulfilment	Means
10	Disaster	Responsibility	Friendship	Opportunity

Upon a deeper level of meaning, the Four Suits broadly correspond to the Worlds as follows:

AIR: Originative/Stellar World.

FIRE: Creative/Solar World.

WATER: Formative/Lunar World.

EARTH: Expressive/or totality of Worlds.

Each World, of course, is a harmonic of the Fourfold Cycle (described in the *Vita* as the Four Powers uttered by Divinity). We may visualize a 'vertical' rotation (the Three Worlds or *Axis Mundi*) and a 'horizontal' rotation (the Three Wheels); both are rotations of the Four Elements from different modes of consciousness or energy. A third rotation is, of course, found around the outer perimeter of the Tree of Life, which shows the Four Powers centred upon the 6th Sphere of Beauty or Harmony (see Figure 2).

When allocated as cycles of energy expressed into human activity (the standard interpretation of Number cards), we must assign direct meaning to the numbers according to life patterns and reactions. Thus the AIR of the Stellar World, which is *pneuma* or originative spirit, becomes expressed as Air, or the changeable, energetic Element, most transient and most vital. Air cards, therefore, have a tendency to have changeable or disruptive expressions – hence the traditional use of the two-edged sword or keen arrow. In the Merlin Tarot flying, rapidly moving Birds represent this energy. Bird omens were an essential aspect of life in early times, and bird omen sayings are still widespread in folklore today. When we hear old rhymes such as 'One for sorrow, Two for Joy, Three for a girl, Four for a boy' (referring to magpies), this is merely a crude form of tarot or spiritual creature number symbolism.

FIRE, the creative light of the Solar World, becomes the peak of balanced energy in a human psyche or situation. Fire cards tend to have a strong and positive set of meanings. Hence the traditional staff or Rod or Wand (implement of perfect balance and control). In the Merlin Tarot the radiant and energetic Serpents or Dragons represent this energy. Dragons are the mythical creatures of hidden or living Fire. The red and white dragons are the primal images of universal being first defining itself by polarity or number.

WATER is the formative element, in which all energies are nourished and defined prior to expression. It corresponds to the Lunar World or dimensions immediately behind outer form. We now find less difference in meaning between the higher and lower levels of the number symbolism, for the Lunar World is that of the foundation of life, and contains the thoughts and feelings by which we habitually exist. Water cards tend to have meanings connected to human relationships. The traditional Cup or Vessel may be the universal Great Mother, the Grail, or a simple life form containing consciousness. In the Merlin Tarot this energy is represented by Fishes, standing for life forms found within all waters. They are generally hidden beneath the surface, within the greater world yet apart from it, just as our thoughts and feelings swim beneath the surface of consciousness.

EARTH is the expressive Element, the ultimate reflection of the Spirit or Originator of all being. Thus it is both the highest and lowest Element simultaneously: all Three Worlds converge within Earth, which is both ending and beginning. Traditionally, the Shield or Mirror (often trivialized as the Coin) represents number sequences for this Element, for it is a surface, a plane and a reflective substance, the final phase in the relative Fourfold Cycle of Elements. In the Merlin Tarot, Beasts (four-footed life forms) are the spiritual creatures of Earth, represented particularly by the Stag.

In the *Vita Merlini* and other Merlin texts used as sources, Merlin relates specifically to Birds (which fly through the air and form mystical letters), Serpents or Dragons (which cause his *Prophecies*), Fishes in the Creation Vision of various realms or orders of life, and Deer in his role as Lord of the Animals.

Such symbolism derives from a deep-rooted ancient and remarkably effective magical 'alphabet', comprising life forms within the world or environment. Higher life forms, the spiritual beings described in esoteric traditions, are likewise the inhabitants of higher worlds, forming their own alphabet or symbolic set of characters. Human awareness is able to reach through the Three Worlds in spiralling pattern of ascent and descent, represented by the relationships between the tarot Trumps. But the rotations of consciousness on any one plane or level are generally defined by the Court cards, which have a particular reference to the outer or sub-Lunar World, but may also refer to characteristics of innerworld beings.

In the next chapter we will meet each of the People or Court cards of the Merlin Tarot, and consider ways of working with them.

THE COURT CARDS
OR PEOPLE

Introduction to the Great Court Circle

The Court cards revolve around the Wheel of Life, and have a general relationship to the Directions and Seasons of the year, as shown in Figure 18. This should not be taken literally, but as a poetic or holistic guide to relative qualities and types of person. Providing you do not fall into the trap of using rule-of-thumb attributions – everyone born in November must be a Page of Beasts, everyone born in July a King of Dragons, and so forth – the Great Court Circle can give penetrating insights into People that appear in tarot patterns.

As the relationships are within or of a holism, rather than a linear sequence, I have simply begun the following sequence in the North and travelled around the Circle. As each type of Court card appears for the first time – Page, Warrior, Queen or King – some general information is given. We then progress to the specific type for each Quarter and Element, occasionally comparing them to their polar relatives (see Figure 18).

If you wish to draw up tables of comparison or correspondences, there is ample information here to do so, though the basic Table on page 308 should be meditated upon first, using each card in turn. As always with tarot, true insights come from working directly with the images, and not through learning long lists or making futile attempts to develop

Figure 18: (opposite) THE GREAT COURT CIRCLE
1. Spring/Birds/Air.
2. Summer/Serpents/Fire.
3. Autumn/Fishes/Water.
4. Winter/Beasts/Earth.

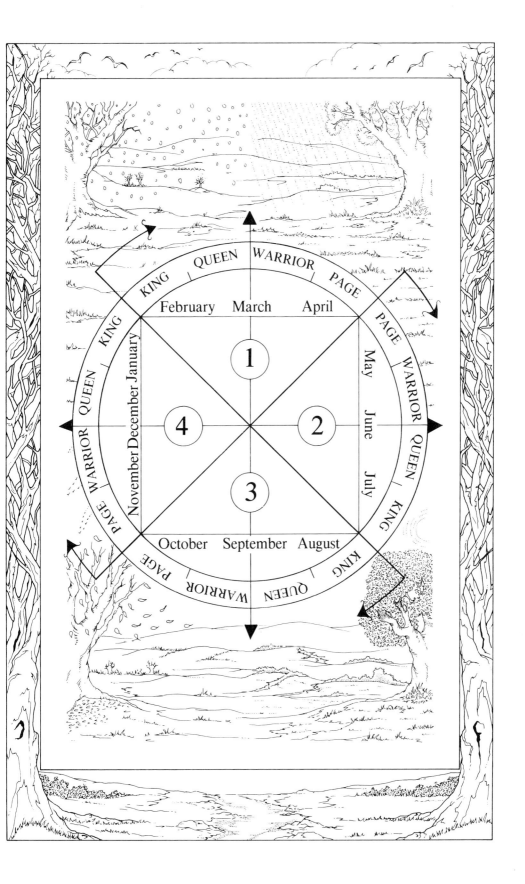

'complete' patterns of reference. The completion is in ourselves, always, and never in lists, tables or inventories.

Court Cards and Trumps

When you are using a full deck of tarot cards, the Court cards represent actual people. The interpretations that follow here will help you to work with the Court cards or People of the Merlin Tarot, and also have a general connection to any other tarot deck. The only possible exceptions to this would be highly specialized modern decks that have abandoned perennial traditions and images in favour of intellectualized systems.

The deeper levels of the Court cards, however, touch upon primal gods and goddesses. Thus we might feel the power of a certain god or goddess inherent within or actively working through a human being. Understanding these primal deities is very helpful in working with Court cards, but we must be cautious and not assume that they are 'archetypes' in a psychological sense, or that they always equate closely to Greek or Celtic or Norse myth. The connections are, undoubtedly, there, but this is because all such systems or patterns, whatever their origin and development, work with variations of primal gods and goddesses, whatever we choose to call them.

The student often experiences an initial confusion between the deepest levels of the People or Courts and the Trumps, as they seem in some ways to overlap one another. Some examples will serve to define this in the Merlin Tarot, bearing in mind that we use an older Trump pattern and interpretation than those of Renaissance and post-Renaissance decks in which the cosmology and divine beings have become confused or dogmatized. The Trump of The Empress and the Court card of the Queen of Fishes may seem similar, for example, as does the Queen of Birds and the Trump of Death. The Trump of The Emperor seems similar to both the King of Fishes and the King of Serpents. Indeed, in simpler usage of tarot, it is common to do away with the Courts and Numbers, and work only with the Trumps, which are then given a dual level of meaning, for they may either be people or powers.

Much of this initial confusion is clarified with practice, however, for the Queen of Cups, say, appearing with the Trump or power of The Empress will be powerfully reinforced and energized, but if she is linked with, say, The Blasted Tower, her *persona* is counter-balanced or even broken down in whatever situation is shown by the remainder of the cards. Tarot is all about relativity and context, and not about precise rigid interpretations that can be automatically combined with one another. The Queen of Cups will always have something of the goddess Venus within her, for it is her inherent power. But she will be empowered, limited or transformed by

Trumps of any kind, as they act as forces flowing through and modifying her inherent nature.

Pages always represent young children, yet they all have a deeper correlation to divine children, and to the Trumps of The Fool and The Hanged Man. These last two Trumps relate to Pages or Warriors, for they are the eternal fool or redeemer/sacrifice that is ever-young within any human being. They are also powers in their own right, and the images of the Trumps are merely our way of giving them a human-like form, drawn from our collective imaginative store.

Another way of looking at this flow between people, deities and the images used on Court cards is to consider the basic pantheon as defined upon the Tree of Life. Court cards often tend to embody the gods and goddesses of the Spheres in very primal Elemental aspects, stripping away the cultural names and specific attributes. Trumps, however, which are not Elemental *personae*, are images of the paths or fusions between Spheres. Much of this has been discussed in our earlier chapters on the Trumps and their relationship to one another, the *Axis Mundi* and the Three Worlds.

Once you have worked with the deck and meditated upon the cards, following their cycles of connection to one another, any initial confusion that may occur will be clarified inwardly. In short, while Court cards or People frequently cross the boundaries between human *personae* and mythic *personae* or deities from assorted pantheons, the Trumps are a unique set of powers as images, and never human personalities.

The Four Powers as Court Cards

In the Number cards we explored the powers of the Four Aces expanding and rotating through the numbers One to Ten. A further image or model that repays meditation and visualization is to regard the Court cards as gods and goddesses of the Four Powers before each Ace, and inherent within all numbers. Thus, before the numbers of Air, we find the Page, Warrior, Queen and King of Air. These are the Four Powers manifesting to human vision as primal deities: Earth of Air, Air of Air, Water of Air, Fire of Air. Their numbers (1 for Air, +2 for Fire, +3 for Water, +4 for Earth) total 10 or 1 (1+0).

When the Elemental cycle is presented as Fire, we find the Page, Warrior, Queen and King of Fire as primal deities before the power of the Dragon Ace, and so through the Court cards for each Element.

Conversely, we may work with the mirror image of this idea, which is that *personae* indicated by the Court cards arise after the number Ten of each Suit. If we work with this reflection, they are the images of human personalities and Elemental types through which the Ace and expanding spiralling numbers manifest in terms of life energies and interactions.

When we work, in meditation, through the numbers from Ten back to the Ace, we approach the Four Powers by dissolving aspects of the personality, a time-hallowed meditational tradition found world-wide.

Let us now move on and meet each Person around the Great Court Circle, beginning in the North. As always with tarot, you will benefit from having the cards in front of you as you read the descriptions, and should aim to rely on your own meditations and insights rather than constantly looking up 'meanings' in a book.

BEASTS

BEASTS

BEASTS

BEASTS

People in the North

The Page of Beasts
Earth of Earth, Male or Female, Keyword: Amenable
The Page of Beasts or Shields is usually a child or younger person. Pages tend to represent individuals before or up to puberty, Warriors tend to represent individuals from puberty to approximately 30 years of age,

Queens and Kings, individuals from 30 years onwards. These definitions are very flexible, however, depending entirely upon the inner state of the individual, and not upon physical age.

The keyword for the Page of Beasts is *amenable*, as he or she is of the *expressive* Element of Earth within Earth. This means *plastic* in the original sense of the word, a being that may be shaped and developed. Pages of Beasts tend to be direct, uncomplicated children, mirroring their circumstances and other people around them. Because of this mirroring quality, a Page of Beasts can often innocently reflect truth towards the more complex and confused adult. In the card we see a modest Child holding a mysterious Disc in which the stars are visible.

The Season for this Page is, broadly speaking, late Autumn and early Winter, the Direction North of North West. This is the basic Earth power after the fruit of Autumn, the child of Winter. These Seasons and Direction imply simple waiting, nourishment, development in sleep and Earth-potential. There is also a deeper implication of the natural wisdom of the organism, the waiting soil, the fallen nut, and the watching Fox, shown in the card. This is not conscious, but the innate or inherent power of the Element and Season within the individual. For this type of Page, the coming Spring will eventually cause a blossoming into Warrior status, the inspiring and unstable time of sexual opening and increasing awareness.

If the card indicates a child, as it usually does, it is a being of tremendous potential. The *impressions* made upon and within the Earth or *plastic* soul and mind of this child will be of great influence when he or she emerges into Spring. By comparison we might briefly consider the Page of Birds, of the Element Air, who is wilful, difficult, and not particularly amenable towards or reflective of surrounding people. Earth and Air are 'opposite-opposites' just as Earth and Fire are 'balancing opposites' (see Figure 19 for polarities across and around the Wheel).

The Warrior of Beasts
Air of Earth, Male or Female, Keyword: Ambitious

In the Merlin Tarot the Warriors may be male or female, as was the custom in ancient Celtic culture. But this is not a false pseudo-historical derivation, for it refers to an inner condition rather than to actual combat training or bearing of arms. The Warrior tends to be the status of the young male or female adult, though it can remain present for a lifetime within anyone. There is a broad correlation here to the development of sexuality and the stages of early adulthood, in which many skills of both inner and outer life are learned as increasingly powerful energies manifest through the body, mind and emotions. The skills balance the inner energies – this is warrior training. In this deeper sense we are all warriors, though many people only develop the minimal, socially conditioned, inner skills during

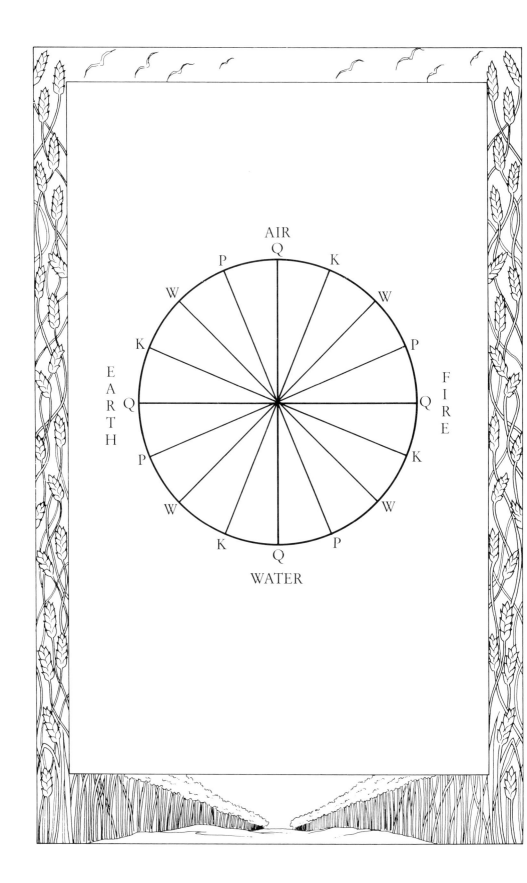

their teenage years, and after that remain relatively static.

The threshold between Warrior and Queen or King status is that obscure but potent crossing point in life at which the individual either slows down and rigidifies, or continues to grow and develop. It can occur during the late teens and early twenties, and many aspects of education and social conditioning tend to freeze the individual at this time. It can also occur in the mid thirties, as people approach the stereotypical false threshold of their middle-life. Both potential thresholds may be happily crossed by people with inner direction, through meditation, visualization and farsight.

The Warrior of Beasts or Shields has the keyword *ambitious*, being of the *originative* Element Air within Earth. The power of Air stirs the potential of Earth into realizing the possibilities of new forms. The ambitions of the Warrior of Beasts range from the most banal to the most extreme, depending upon the factors of imagination and discretion or judgement. This card represents a young man or woman who seeks to benefit from changing his or her circumstances. There is often a corresponding drive to work hard: the Warrior of Beasts will toil and strive for a chosen ambition, determined to bring it to harvest.

The Season of this *persona* is late November, and the Direction approaches true North. The Warrior travels out of the great November threshold marked by the Pleiades (*Samhain*, marked in the modern calendar by what were originally ancestral festivities such as 5 November and Halloween). He or she has seen the harvests that can be obtained in the world, and is determined, with the coming Spring, to work towards such a harvest for the coming year. This is an ambitious person who understands Earth and Winter to be times of labour and preparation for the future, and often has a single-minded attention to specific goals.

In the card we see a Warrior riding upon a huge shire or heavy Horse, the great workhorse of the land. The Warrior seems small, but it is the Horse that is large. The beast offers the power of endurance, strength and connection to the Earth, the living power that works the land. The ambitious Rider is the mind (Air) working with the body (Earth). There is often a desire for material benefit in this type of person, and the ambition is usually self-orientated, though it can be found in altruistic forms. The Mask indicates inner power expressed and modified through outer forms. In the simplest sense this Warrior is often concerned about his or her 'personality' or presentation to others. Originally, Warriors worked for the protection and benefit of all people in the land.

Our image shows the earliest phase of this Warrior of Beasts, still bearing

Figure 19: (opposite) POLARITIES AROUND AND ACROSS THE WHEEL

the last Sheaf of Corn. The other spiritual creature is the Mouse, providing for the future by storing the seeds of the past.

The Queen of Beasts
Water of Earth, Female, Keyword: Practical
In the Merlin Tarot, Queens are female, and are equal polar partners with the Kings. The Queen is usually a mature woman, with a physical age from the late twenties or early thirties onwards. The *inner* maturity, however, is what defines a Queen or King as distinct from the life-phase of Warrior. Some individuals may merge both phases successfully for several years, others may find a conflict of phase, in which they oscillate between the mature phase of King/Queen and the less mature phase of Warrior. The emergence of a woman as Queen in tarot always occurs after a certain amount of life experience.

It is worth remembering that the tarot frequently 'chooses' the correct *persona* or Court card, and that they rise within a reading without prejudgement or expectation. Thus, during a lifetime, a particular person may be defined as Page, Warrior and then King or Queen. The sequence does not always follow on through the same Element, and an individual commencing as, say, a Page of Water, may eventually emerge as, say, a King of Fire. The crossing between Element or Directions is enabled by the life powers (Trumps) that come into operation during the life cycle. It can also be radically enabled and empowered by will and intent, working directly with inner transformative exercises and energies.

The Queen of Beasts or Shields has the keyword *practical*, as she is of the *formative* Element, Water, within Earth. She is able to make specific forms out of potential substance, is able to both nourish and define. Her power is that of practical wisdom, the teachings and experience of mature woman on the human level. On the inner level this also involves applied wisdom, the techniques and experiences of spiritual reflection.

In our card she holds a Mirror made from a green Stone, the Stone of Wisdom. Her spiritual animal is the Bear, the creature of the North, of Earth, and of primal Motherhood; here it is shown as a maturing Bear Cub that she protects and rears. Her Direction is somewhat East of North, and her Season is that time between the midwinter solstice and the (old date of) New Year.

On the deepest level, the Queen of Beasts is empowered by Artemis, in her form of the Bear Mother, the Earth Mother. Our image shows the entrance to an Underworld Cave-temple or Long-barrow in the background.

The King of Beasts
Fire of Earth, Male, Keyword: Reliable
Kings in tarot are always male, revealing mature men with considerable power and life experience. There is no value judgement or hierarchy, by the way, in the Court cards – a King is not 'superior' to a Queen, though both King and Queen have greater life experience and maturity than the Warriors and Pages. The Warriors and Pages, from their less defined but more immediate energies, may reveal truth to the Kings or Queens, and may inspire, exhort and catalyse them. As shown in Figures 6 and 18 the key is always one of *interaction* and not of hierarchy or age and gender-defined false authority.

The King of Beasts or Shields has the Direction of North East, and approaches the major threshold of the year, between death and life, Winter and the dawn of earliest Spring, midnight and the beginning of the dark morning phase of a new day. His keyword is *reliable*, as his strength is the strength of the Fire hidden but active within the Earth. He is a mature, dependable and wise male, one upon whom others can, and often do, lay their burdens. But he holds up the Mirror of the Elements (in the card as in life) and teaches that we must all learn balance and strength from within ourselves.

On a deeper level, the King of Beasts is the Earth Father of Winter, the Horned Man. In our image he is crowned and garlanded with Mistletoe, the herb of mysterious sacrifice and regeneration, death that creates life. Thus the King may be relied upon to initiate into the Mysteries of death that brings life, Winter that brings Spring, night that becomes day. His spiritual animal is the Badger, a nocturnal beast of terrible strength, an intelligent, devoted family creature, bearing the alternate light and dark colours of midnight and first dawn, grey, black and white.

The King of Beasts is the primal male ancestor of Earth, and by looking into his Mirror we may contact our own ancestral wisdom. In human terms, he is the older man whom we often instinctively trust, rely upon, and ask for help and advice.

The Threshold of Spiralling Transition
Between the North and the East is the point of spiralling transition, the threshold between one cycle and another. It is the threshold between death and life, ending and beginning. It is marked in the classical wisdom traditions by Janus, a silver-coloured god with two heads, looking simultaneously to Winter and Spring. He is the god of portals, gateways, passing in and out. His power is in the eternal centre, the unknowable out of which all known polarities emerge. In the Merlin cosmology Janus is porter or gatekeeper to Ariadne, the Weaver Goddess who creates and unravels the pattern of the universe.

In the Court cards we find two Kings upon this threshold, the King of Beasts and the King of Birds. They are the Winter Kings of Earth and Air respectively and, as 'opposite-opposites' or 'rivals of one watch', are the ultimate partners. This polarity pattern is repeated at each Cross-Quarter of the Court Circle: there are two Summer Kings in the South West, Fire and Water; in the South East there are two Spring Pages (Air and Fire), and they are balanced by the Autumn Pages of Water and Earth in the North West (see Figure 18). The Cross-Quarter thresholds mark the four great turning-points of the ancient year, with the rising and setting of the Pleiades in May (*Beltane* or May Day) and November (*Samhain* or Halloween), balanced by the thresholds of August and February (*Lughnasadh* or Lammas, and *Imbolc*).

The People of the East

BIRDS

BIRDS

BIRDS

BIRDS

The King of Birds
Fire of Air, Male, Keyword: Severe

The King of Birds, back to back with his rival/partner the King of Beasts, is a mature male. Within him the *creative* Fire radiates through the *originative*, inspiring, changeable Element of Air. He is characterized by the keyword *severe*, for the cutting power of the Sword of Air reaches its ultimate phase of creative control and will in this *persona*.

Severity in this King is just rather than unjust, and as a human being he is often involved with matters of justice, discipline, civic and personal order. His Direction is at the threshold of the year, associated with the month of February and the ancient feast of Imbolc. The King of Birds or Swords brings vitality and beginnings out of the cold of Winter, and epitomizes the clean cutting power of a new blade. He may also be that type of inspirer and teacher who enables us to see the value of severity and discipline within ourselves, ranging from the skills of the mind to the spiritual arts. Most of all he teaches us what we must lose, leading us to peaks beyond which we cannot retain a concept of false selfhood.

In the card we see the King of Birds seated on a Throne of Glass upon a high Mountain top. He carries the Sword of the East, and his spiritual creature is the Eagle. As a deeper power, he fuses certain primal god forms, or perhaps (like all Court cards) he represents a god form out of which later deities known to history have become defined and differentiated. He is, for example, the kingly power of justice to which the supplicant applies, even at the risk of self. He is also a power of flight and communication, swiftness, accuracy. In our image there are flocks of Birds flying across a Winter Landscape: they are the messengers of the King of Air, heralding swift movement, the beginning of Seasons, and the power of individual thoughts transforming collective consciousness.

The Queen of Birds
Water of Air, Female, Keyword: Serious

The Queen of Birds or Swords is an older woman, the feminine counterpart of the King in many ways. Her *formative* energy, often associated with the emotions, works through the *originative* power of Air to give a *serious persona*. Thus she will criticize emotional outbursts, and will tend to use the Sword, her mental discipline, to balance emotions within herself.

In the card she holds Sword and Scabbard equally in prominence: her formative, feminine energy balances the originative Sword. This is one of the Grail Mysteries, that the Sword and Scabbard should never be separated or regarded as superior to one another. As a deeper image, the Queen of Birds is the stern but fair feminine power, able to both give and take. Her Direction is the East, her Season early Spring, in which the frost can still cut off the budding leaf. Just as the King is upon the aery threshold of the Mountain tops, where the heights aspire to light and Air,

298 *The Complete Merlin Tarot*

so is the Queen upon the high Cliff-tops of the Sea, where Air and Water meet.

Her spiritual creatures are sea birds, and in the foreground of the image we see a Nest with two Eggs in it. The Queen guards with Sword and Scabbard the potential life about to emerge from the Water of the Egg into the Air of Spring.

The Warrior of Birds
Air of Air, Male or Female, Keyword: Combative
The Warrior of Birds or Swords is a young man or woman in whom the *originative* Air is doubled, giving rising to a turbulent and changeable nature. This person is enthusiastic, highly active, always rushing, often argumentative. He or she may be buffeted to and fro by the winds of energy within, rushing from one enthusiasm to another, ready to fight and defend ideals and beliefs.

The keyword here is *combative*, and the urge to combat may either be exteriorized or remain as an inner conflict. The Season is Spring, and the Direction is due East. In the card we see the Warrior, youth or maiden, riding a spirited white Horse that is free of Reins, though Reins are present. The Warrior draws a Bow, shooting ahead of the gallop. The spiritual creature is a Swift or Swallow, with darting flight and shrill cry.

Upon a deeper level, this is the androgynous god of beginning, rising energies, intense feelings and powerful ideas. It can also be the young warrior god or goddess, riding to right imbalances. There is a further correlation here with the young Diana or Apollo, god and goddess of the hunt, of prophecy, music, archery and healing.

The Page of Birds
Earth of Air, Male or Female, Keyword: Difficult
The Page of Birds or Swords is a child or younger person, usually below the early teens in age. This person has the *expressive* Earth within the *originative* Air, and can have inner conflicts that will only be resolved with maturity and experience. Sometimes it is a child wise beyond his or her years, but lacking the means or experience to relate to such wisdom.

The Direction is South East, a child of Spring moving into Summer. The keyword is *difficult*, and the difficult nature can show in several different ways. It often manifests as obstinacy, a kind of inner strength and wilfullness. The Page of Air can also be the intelligent child, perceptive beyond his or her years, to whom less intelligent adults (such as schoolteachers) have no adequate response. Such Pages are often inspired (Air) by a wise teacher (Earth), if they are fortunate enough to meet one. They often have demanding natures and special needs.

Our card shows the Page armed with a large Bow, as yet undrawn, also a full Quiver of Arrows and a sharp Dagger. We see that the Bow is just about to come off his/her shoulder, indicating readiness for action.

The People in the South

SERPENTS

SERPENTS

SERPENTS

SERPENTS

The Court of the South consists of Fire People, people with a summery quality, powerful will and great radiant energy. There is often a charismatic or sexual aura about people in the South, due to the potency of their Inner Fire. In this significant area of energy we must be aware that spiritual enlightenment, charisma and sexual power are all one; they derive from differing patterns or direction of the Inner Fire. The Element of Fire is associated with creativity, and People of the South are often superb creative artists, for they combine the inner power with the will and discipline and balance of the Rod and Dragon.

The Page of Serpents
Earth of Fire, Male or Female, Keyword: Diligent

The Page of Serpents or Rods is a child or young person full of potential, bursting with energy. The *expressive* Earth combined with *creative* Fire makes this child confident and willing to work very hard if necessary. The keyword is *diligent*, and the diligence will be applied in any work, from ordinary daily activities to creative expression.

The card shows the Page about to run, bearing a short Wand or Staff, the token of the messenger who carries a given authority. Whatever this person undertakes will be done in an unassuming, efficient manner. The spiritual animal is a baby Dragon, just beginning to emit its first flames, experimenting with its Inner Fire.

The Season for this Page is May, and the Direction is South East. The Page stands upon the threshold of Summer, for May Day, marked by the Pleiades and the feast of Beltane, is the beginning of Summer. Thus the Page of Serpents is the young god/goddess of the new Summer, ready to run to the heights of the full southern Sun, shining upon the Hilltops of our image. We see that the Page is already in the Uplands, and ready to run higher, up the Slope rising from left to right (East to South).

The Summer child is often a redhead, though we need not be too literal when this card appears in a tarot pattern. The fiery *qualities* of the redheaded boy or girl are indicated here, if not an actual *persona* with red hair. In very early times, dating back to the megalithic culture from which the Celts inherited much of their stellar and Underworld lore, the redhead was a sacred person, often chosen as king or queen. But the way to Queen or King begins with a Page or young soul.

The Warrior of Serpents
Air of Fire, Male or Female, Keyword: Perceptive

The Warrior of Serpents or Rods is the enlivener and protector of the Summer land, a person from the early teens to late twenties with endless vitality, ceaseless activity and ability. The *originative* power of Air and *creative* Fire give him/her intuitive insight (not necessarily born of experience, but arising spontaneously). The keyword here is *perceptive*, for the Warrior is able to see to the heart any person or situation.

In the card, the masked Warrior rides upon a healthy chestnut Horse, the beast of Epona, horse goddess of the South. The Warrior of Serpents carries a long Spear at rest, for he/she knows instinctively how to control aggression or combative energies within. The Mask is an ancient emblem of the South, and the Warrior is still masked because he/she is potent but inexperienced; the inner light is masked by the outer form. With the Queen and King the outer mask is removed, and the face shows the light within.

The Direction is approaching due South, the month late May or early June, leading to the Summer solstice when day is longest. The spiritual animal is the Serpent, sacred to the Fire deities such as Apollo or the Celtic Brig or Brigid.

The Warrior of the South is often a skilled facilitator, able to pierce the heart of situation and bring it to balance with the necessary action. If s/he couches the Spear or throws it, the results are dramatic, but the preferred action is often to mediate and simply show potential rather than to impose it.

The Queen of Serpents
Water of Fire, Female, Keyword: Skilful
The Queen of Serpents or Rods is a powerful mature woman, often of great sexual attraction. We must, however, be cautious in using the term 'sexual attraction', for it does not necessarily mean stereotypical glamour. The Queen of Serpents is, however, a person of *formative* Water and *creative* Fire, hence she may be powerfully sexual. The energies may also be routed into creative work such as art or music, or into a career, a lifetime dedication to developing, nourishing and bringing into being something of value.

The Direction is West of South, just beyond the peak of midsummer, and the Season the months of late June and early July. The Inner Fire is very strong in the Queen, and her fusion of fiery and watery nature can lead to powerful impulsive urges. Usually, she is able to balance these with her will and experience. The keyword is *skilful*, for she is the Queen of Rods, able to mediate, balance, control, manipulate and direct energy.

Our card shows the Queen seated upon a serpent Throne, in the mountainous Uplands towards which we originally saw the Page about to run. Behind her is a dormant Volcano, which may erupt at any time. Her wand is a fusion of the Staff or Rod and blossoming Flower – traditionally this is a violet-coloured bloom, showing formative lunar powers harmonized with creative solar fire.

In her hand the Queen of Fire bears a tiny Lizard, basking in the full sunlight. Her spiritual animal is the Cat. In our card, the hair of both Cat and Queen is red, flame-coloured.

The King of Serpents
Fire of Fire, Male, Keyword: Decisive
The King of Serpents or Rods is a mature male, one in whom the potential of inner and outer being is well harmonized. As Fire of Fire, he is powerful, creative and well balanced. He is an individual of very strong will and ceaseless energy. He may also, rarely, be a highly empowered spiritual

being, but we must always exercise caution in this interpretation, as false 'gurus' often try to present themselves as Kings of Fire. The genuine Summer King lacks pretension, only having inner light and harmony. As a rule, this type of person does not seek us out, but we may find him if we are drawn towards his energy.

The Direction is West of South, the ripe time of Summer, as July turns into August. At the very threshold of the Quarter, where the King sits back to back with the King of Fishes, he is *Bel* and *Lugh* in the old Celtic mythology, the god of light, fire and high places. The August festival of Lammas (Lughnasadh) is named after this major deity.

In the card, the King is shown seated upon a dragon Throne, at the shore of burning golden Lake. He is crowned with a Dragon and Flames, and his Robe is of gold and flame pattern, partly revealed through the parting of his red Cloak. In his right hand he carries a long pointed Staff of spiralling pattern, and his left hand is held open in a sign of welcome. His face, like that of all the Kings and Queens, is unmasked. Just beyond

FISHES

FISHES

FISHES

FISHES

the Throne is a golden Tripod with a Salamander, the legendary Fire creature, within its basin.

The keyword is *decisive*, as all decisions made by the King are balanced and fired or empowered from within. He is able to decide on proper action without debate or reflection, and works directly from inner enlightenment and creative power. Coiled upon a rock at his feet is a Snake, the spiritual animal of sacred Fire within the sacred body, be it the human body or the body of the land or planet.

The People in the West

West is the Direction of the feelings, of Love, of the Element of Water. It is also the Direction and power of fertility in all senses, either as the spiritual Love that generates the universe, or as the collective or individual fertility of motherhood. The People of the West live in and through their emotions, and are often giving and forgiving individuals. Upon the higher octaves of the West, emotion is transformed into spiritual power, selfless love, compassion, even sacrifice. The Court of the West is concerned with purification, cleansing, regeneration, nourishment and support. These, too, are the qualities of the People.

West is the Direction of the Fortunate Isles, or Blessed Otherworld, the setting sun. People of the West can often enter that Otherworld through their sensitivities, feelings and spiritual insights and devotions. They can also communicate this vision and the presence of the spiritual world to others (the power of the Cup).

The King of Fishes
Fire of Water, Male, Keyword: Jovial
Back to back with the King of Serpents is the King of Fishes. These Kings of Fire and Water support one another and are partners upon the thresholds of the Autumn, both being involved in high levels of energy, one of Fire and Light, the other of Water and Love.

The King of Fishes or Cups is a mature male with considerable life experience, and he has not been hardened or embittered by his life. The *creative* Fire within him is modified and made gentle by the *formative* water, his main Element. The keyword for this person is *jovial*, which means more than merely good-natured or jolly. The god Jove or Jupiter was the ancient All-Father, the giving god from whom all bounty and kindness flowed. He is associated with compassion and mercy upon the Tree of Life (see Figure 2), and one of the most constant factors in the King of Fishes is his compassionate, giving nature. As King, however, he is able to temper this with the power of Fire, and does not let his kindly feelings control him or carry him away, as is true with the Warrior of Fishes, whom we shall meet shortly.

The Direction is West of South, and at the beginning of August, the theme is of first fruitfulness and beginning of harvest. The Water Element gives a particular emphasis to feeling and emotions, the fruits of creativity, 'fatherhood' in both the spiritual and material sense.

In the card we see the King at the Sea-shore, the realm where all Elements meet and where Water predominates. He sits upon a granite Throne that is clearly washed or even covered by the tides at times, for there are Sea Creatures around it and lodged upon it. This gives us some insight into the King's nature, for even the highest tide that washes his Throne will not carry him away. His face is smiling and welcoming, kind and compassionate. In his hands he bears a glass Vessel. His spiritual creatures are the Crab, the tenacious beast that crosses between land and water, and the Dolphin, the highly intelligent and friendly animal of the ancient sea gods.

The King of Fishes' hair is plaited, unlike that of his Elemental polar opposite, the King of Birds, whose locks blow wildly in the wind. Plaiting hair is an ancient magical technique, for it involves twisting or sealing up power. In our image the plaited hair indicates that the King chooses to restrain his full power out of kindliness, but he can, like the sea-gods of old, unleash the storm if he chooses. In human terms, this individual is full of hidden depths (Water) and deep currents, seldom revealing his true strength, working through gentleness rather than overt acts of will.

On a deeper level, we may link this King to certain primal water deities, to the speed and intelligence of the dolphin, sea-friend of humanity, the jovial or all-giving power, with the potential for great storms.

The Queen of Fishes
Water of Water, Female, Keyword: Loving
The Queen of Fishes or Cups is a mature woman with deep sexual and fertility powers. These may manifest as actual motherhood, or through a creative line of work. This woman is often in love, giving her heart freely, revealing the power of love to those involved with her. As a mother she is devoted and protective, as a lover she is both fulfilling and demanding.

The *formative* power of Water is redoubled within her, and everything in her life is about nourishment, sexual exchange, giving and receiving, feeling, passion. Her keyword is *loving* in all senses. As she grows older, the sexual side of her nature may be less apparent, but it never fades away. Many Queens of Water become spiritually dedicated later in their lives. In earlier cultures they might have become saints or holy women, replacing the bodily love with the spiritual, and realizing that they are indeed one Love. The older Queen of Cups may also become the mother of an extended family, the grandmother in a spiritual or physical sense of many younger people, all treated equally as her children.

The Queen's Direction is due West, the time of the Autumn equinox and the great tides. She is also associated with Venus, the evening star, and the power of the lunar cycles. These forces tend to be strong within any woman represented by this card.

In our image, we see her sitting upon a huge shell Throne with the Sea washing around her. It seems as if the Waters flow up and become her Robe, embroidered with a pattern of tiny fishes. In her left arm she cradles the Horn, the magical implement of fertility, or vitality, of sexuality, of summoning. Her spiritual animal is the Seal, reminding us of the ancient traditions that seals are the People of the Sea, often associated with the Fairy Realm and the magical singing of the West that lures men into the unknown.

Upon a deeper or mythic level, she may be identified, to a certain extent, with Aphrodite in classical myth, but the Queen of Cups is also a Sea-Mother, so she combines the sea-functions in one figure.

The Warrior of Fishes
Air of Water, Male or Female, Keyword: Idealistic
The Warrior of Fishes or Cups is a young man or woman filled with dreams, visions and high expectations of life. The *originative* power of Air stirs the *formative* Element of Water, causing the Warrior's emotions to be highly developed. The keyword is *idealistic*: often an ideal will replace simple human love within this person. With experience, such idealism is often modified, but is never completely abandoned or lost.

The Direction is North of West, after the Autumn equinox towards the close of September and early October. In the card we see the young man or woman riding upon a white Horse, sign of idealism and purity of intent. The Warrior has let go of the Reins (for a dream will be more empowering than common sense or control of energies), and offers a Cup to the sky. The Horse wades through the incoming Sea proudly, and although the Warrior has a Shield (sign of approaching Winter in the North), he/she does not bear it up, and carries no other arms. In the distance we see Whales rising from the ocean; these spiritual creatures indicate the tremendous power of the Element of Water that resides within the Warrior, mostly hidden, yet surfacing from time to time for Air.

The Page of Fishes
Earth or Water, Male or Female, Keyword: Pleasant
The Page of Fishes or Cups is a young person or child, probably before the age of puberty. This is a responsive, easy child, very attached to parents,

and able to make friends with others (in contrast to the Page of Birds, who can find making friendships difficult). The *expressive* Earth and *formative* Water make this Page a generally good-natured person, as Water and Earth merge imperceptibly into one another. The keyword is *pleasant*.

The Direction is North of West, in October, just before the threshold that crosses into Winter. In our card the late Autumn Landscape is set by the Sea, but the Tide has yet to rise, for this Page is Earth of Water. Again we see the Crab as a spiritual creature, and in the distance a flock of Sea Birds come to land. The Page holds a copper Bowl (Venus) from which a tiny Fish leaps. The small Fish is his/her personal creature, for if it is nourished and allowed to grow, the Page will begin to move around the Court Circle and change *persona*.

Summary of the Court Cards

The People of the Merlin Tarot have many relationships with one another, around and across the Circle. While the emphasis upon Directions and Seasons may seem odd at first to the modern mind, it is a type of understanding that we have deep within us. We inherit this directional poetry or intuition from our ancestors, but also have it of our own nature, due to our location upon the surface of the land and planet. If you work with the hints of Direction and landscape, Seasons and Elements described in this summary of the Court cards, you will find that many intuitions concerning the cards begin to arise spontaneously.

In tarot readings of any sort, you will eventually gain rapid insight into the human personalities represented by Court cards. The cards always choose themselves, and if you predefine people you will often generate confusion. In meditation and visualization, the relationships between the cards, either within or across the Courts and Elements, bring many insights and levels of understanding. It is worth repeating here that it is best to work without notebooks and without repeated reference to textbooks. Once you grasp the wholeness of the Wheel of Life, and its relationship to the Court cards, the meanings of the cards will leap out at you.

Talking to the People

A valuable exercise is to *talk* to the People. After stilling your awareness and undertaking some preliminary meditation, it is possible to hold an imaginative conversation with any of the Court cards. You may select a card, or turn one or more up at random, and hold a conversation with the Person. However we might rationalize this method, or interpret it, it works.

An interesting beginning might be to ask each Person to tell you their story. Then, once you have some acquaintance with the People, you may ask them questions. You may seek the answer in meditation, or lay out a tarot pattern as shown in Chapter 30 for your reply. The Kings and Queens are often helpful mediators of inner or ancestral wisdom.

An interesting variant is to ask a question of say, the King of Beasts. Then ask the same question of, say, the King of Birds, and see how the answer varies. These exercises may seem like children's games, but there is great wisdom in the imaginative play of a child.

Finally, it is important not to become too obscure or complex. If you feel that the imaginative methods described add to the complexity of your tarot work, simply leave them alone. You will soon find, from direct experiment, which combinations of tarot work best for you.

The Court Cards
Court cards in tarot, Page, Warrior, Queen and King, represent the Elements within or through the human psyche. Thus, they are frequently used to define psychological types, and such systems of Elemental psychology far pre-date modern materialist theories. The entire *Vita Merlini* holds a strong emphasis upon psychological types and phases, either directly described (as the Elements and orders of beings in the Creation Vision), or through the adventures and experiences of Merlin or subsidiary characters.

The simplest way of regarding the Court cards or People is to show them upon the Wheel, with The Fool in the centre (see Figure 18). In other words, the cards are not firm individual categories or types, but phases of one primal or original being: The Fool who is both male and female, human and spirit. Once we have grasped this cyclical nature of Court cards, we may also use them in the more limited popular sense, to define actual persons in tarot patterns.

In meditation, The Fool represents the innermost self, the true transpersonal individual. The Court cards or People represent aspects of personality (sometimes called 'sub-personalities' in modern psychology). Most of us tend to express ourselves through one or two basic personal roles, and these basics are typified by the Court cards.

In tarot pattern making, the *personae* are automatically defined in a reading: they choose themselves, so to speak, and do not require prejudgement. Cards arising in this way often give considerable insight into the nature of individuals, for the tarot cycle will occasionally show a living person as a Court card which he or she does not expect, yet which reveals inner qualities and tendencies. Some individuals may have very simple *personae*, while others have many active levels of personality.

The Court cards also show the cycle of a lifetime, from Spring or beginning, to Winter and death. Thus a fourfold life pattern (birth, adulthood, maturity, old age) corresponds to the Court cards as well as to the broader cycle of the Four Quarters (Spring, Summer, Autumn, Winter).

In the Merlin Tarot, a seasonal annual rotation, which is an analogy of Elemental energies and life phases, has been followed in the arrangement of the People. These images should be seen as fluid aspects of the inner being, and not as rigid types which form a closed system or 'complete' map of the human psyche. The Wheel is therefore collective or individual, seasonal or defined by any chosen time cycle.

We each have all of the People inherent within us; if we are able to balance them perfectly, we become The Fool or pure being. The magical/psychological technique which derives from this law is simple: if we aim to realize our inner being through insight, meditation and right living, then this inner being will gradually adjust the cycle of *personae* through which we express ourselves. Life experience tends towards this end, in a rather haphazard manner, but active will and intent speeds the balancing process remarkably. The tarot People form a simple map which helps us with this process of transformation.

Table of Court Cards or People in the Merlin Tarot

Page (male or female)	Element of Earth	Child
Warrior (male or female)	Element of Air	Young adult
Queen (female)	Element of Water	Mature adult
King (male)	Element of Fire	Mature adult

Table of General Attributes

	BIRDS/ Swords	DRAGONS/ Rods	FISHES/ Cups	BEASTS/ Shields
KING:	Severe	Decisive	Jovial	Reliable
QUEEN:	Serious	Skilful	Loving	Practical
WARRIOR:	Combative	Perceptive	Idealistic	Ambitious
PAGE:	Difficult	Diligent	Pleasant	Amenable

METHODS OF DIVINATION, FARSIGHT AND INSIGHT

Before proceeding to examples in which cards are laid out and interpreted, we should briefly consider each of the three categories within which such applications of tarot are found. The categories are: 1: Divination; 2: Farsight; 3: Insight. Each category may be seen as a mode of consciousness; each mode of consciousness corresponds to functions of the individual psyche, the collective or ancestral consciousness, and the Three Worlds of Lunar, Solar and Stellar relativity. The Three Worlds generate and enfold all life, all aspects of consciousness and energy, from material substance to metaphysical entities; such is the foundation of the world view of tarot.

The three categories listed above are not rigid, and are not offered as being definitive; they provide general definition for practical work. Each of the three may have lower or higher harmonics of energy, by which they merge with one another. The degree of fusion or separation depends upon the intent and skill of the reader, meditator or magician using tarot images.

The Three Wheels

The Merlin Tarot is based upon the ancient but effective pattern of the Spindle or Tree of Life; three spiral levels are found within this pattern, which are formalized as the Three Wheels or Three Worlds, without any suggestion that they are separate from or inaccessible to one another. The expressive realm of Earth (the planet in one sense or material substance in a universal sense) partakes of all three turns of the spiral, for it is the ultimate location or summation. Thus, traditionally we are taught that lunar or formative/generative energies, solar or creative energies, and stellar or originative energies fuse together to express the universe. In human terms, such fusion is reflected microcosmically in the individual, or collectively in the consensual or outer world of humanity within the environment.

We may apply the cosmology shown within tarot to form patterns for divination, farsight or insight in addition to using single, paired, triadic or other number combinations of images (cards). Three levels or degrees of consciousness are defined by the Trumps Moon, Sun and Star, with three threshold Trumps of Fortune, Justice and Judgement.

Thus, so-called 'divination' may reflect energies or interactions upon three levels:

1. *The Wheel of Fortune:* events in the outer or consensual world of human and environmental relationships.
2. *Justice:* events in the inner creative world of spiritual energies.
3. *Judgement:* events in the cosmic, stellar or supernal world. (In divination this third mode may also represent collective consciousness, or long-term cycles of events involving nations, races and metaphysical cycles of development.)

In actual practice with tarot, it is essential to develop *intent*, and to combine intent with intuition, through which the Worlds may be defined and apprehended. This skill only comes through repeated meditation upon tarot and the patterns of relationship inherent within any tarot system. The three categories of divination, farsight and insight may be briefly defined as follows, providing we bear firmly in mind that the relationship is harmonic rather than divisive.

Divination

Divination may extend from superficial or trivial prognostication, which is essentially a misuse of tarot and a squandering of the user's energies and consciousness, to far-reaching visions of the future on a national or even global scale. Either extreme of divination may be encapsulated within Trump images and combinations of Trumps with minor images (the Number and Court cards). Tarot works equally well upon an exalted level as upon a trivial, and fluctuations of response or levels of significance are due to the reader or pattern maker, and not to the symbols themselves. This quality of tarot cannot be overemphasized, for the same set of symbols will reveal something pointless and trivial to one reader and something profound to another, while retaining throughout its symbolic individuality and character of pattern. In other words, we cannot reduce tarot to generalizations, yet we may find more than one specific level of symbolism in any chosen tarot pattern.

Various methods of divination are described shortly, but before any use of these is made, we should define some of the properties or behaviour of tarot in actual divinatory practice.

Tarot cannot work for us as humans to divine matters upon a cosmic or universal scale. There is no point in asking questions relating to the life of the solar system and expecting tarot patterns to provide an answer; such questions are matters of metaphysical or mystical vision rather than of mere divination. We may use tarot Trumps or patterns in meditation to aid our understanding of reality, but this is not a matter of divination or prediction, as it relates to higher modes of consciousness.

The broader the range of the query, the more archetypical will be the responding pattern of symbols. A crude example should demonstrate this operational matter. There is little or no point in asking 'Will there be war?', as war and conflict are an enduring aspects of human suffering in the outer world – wars express our imbalance, ranging from individual to collective energies and follies. The reply to such a general (pointless) question will be cards which symbolize the energies concerned in an archetypical and broad manner; it will be difficult to define a meaningful temporal answer.

For precise divination we need to ask if there will be a conflict of defined nature between specified parties within a selected time period. Only such a firmly attuned, precise mode of forming questions will generate detailed answers; it will result in some identical cards to the more vague question discussed above, but there will be supportive elements in the pattern which will enable the reader to be more precise in interpretation.

The divinatory power of tarot operates only in the context of questions that relate to matters below the Abyss (see Figure 2). The Abyss, which is physically the distance between our solar system and any other or, metaphysically, the distance between human consciousness and divine or originative consciousness, is one of the paradoxes of mystical perception: it is a barrier of seemingly insurmountable proportions, yet there are well-known ways of crossing it in either direction. Divination is not one of the Paths across the Abyss, though a higher mode of divination, that of prophecy, may bridge the Abyss occasionally.

There is another way of expressing the law of divination in connection with tarot: the cards may reveal insights into both inner and outer events/energies, but they will not reveal deeper truths other than through meditation. The quality of revelation is entirely dependent upon the consciousness and intent of the individual using the tarot symbols; more insight or truth may be gained through a short period of right meditation than through many hours of tedious sequences of laying out cards for divination.

There is a qualitative difference, for example, between the appearance of the Trump The Hanged Man within a life query, and the same Trump as a spiritual principle. The first is an indication of power in operation (below the Abyss), working within a temporal inner or outer situation, through a cycle of interactions. The second is that same power in its own right, in its own world or true identity, regardless of the innumerable harmonic situations that may reflect its energies in selected states, places or persons.

Farsight

Farsight is traditionally employed to overlook situations at a distance from the observer. This does not usually involve a predictive or divinatory function; the pattern of tarot symbols is generated to define a current interplay of factors or energies in a known location. A typical example would be one in which the tarot reader seeks general information on the status of a distant friend; a question of this sort may be answered through symbols extending into the material, mental, emotional and spiritual levels of the situation defined within the query.

More complex situations may be overlooked by farsight with tarot patterns, but it is often difficult to obtain factual material responses to queries involving such situations. The more complex a situation, such as one with a large number of persons or potential interactions, the more abstract the response will be. This is simply because tarot always tends towards truth; in this matter we touch upon one of the most important aspects of tarot in connection with divination, farsight and insight.

Tarot always works towards the true heart of any query, even if this is counter to the formulated question that is uppermost in the mind of the seeker. This quality can be very frustrating for beginners with tarot, but with some practice becomes an invaluable factor for the individual who seeks enduring insights through work with tarot symbols. A general rule, never to be side-stepped, is that while we should define each question as fully possible, we should never limit or force the answers by imposing conditions or preconceptions upon them. It may seem initially that we impose such preconceptions by detailed formulation of the query, but the inherent tendency of tarot symbols to gravitate towards the heart of any matter will frequently cut through this initial structure.

In this context it would be extremely difficult, if not impossible, to use farsight for trivial matters such as industrial or military espionage; the symbolic language of tarot simply does not relate to such matters in direct terms, or in sufficient serial detail to be of any value. In personal, mental, emotional and spiritual matters, however, tarot can and does provide unfailing responses to defined questions involving farsight.

Insight

Insight, which takes up the majority of this book, is the result of higher functions of tarot. These functions interact with human consciousness through the disciplined arts of mediation, visualization and contemplation. Our descriptions of the individual Trumps deal mainly with insights into the symbols and their relationship with one another, and with deeper insights into their function as a holism or model of the universe. Insight comes from work with tarot over periods of time, yet the actual moments of insight are timeless.

It is typical of tarot work, for example, that a highly energized sequence of insights will arise in the earliest stages, and that effort and discipline will be needed to fix and relate to these insights, bringing them through into regular awareness. The converse, that unrewarding effort and discipline must be undertaken before any results occur, is rare indeed in work with tarot; but discipline must be part of any use of tarot, otherwise the results return, so to speak, to inner or unconscious dimensions.

Insight plays a major role in both divination and farsight, and requires a fine degree of application and control. A typical example might be a situation in which a Trump appears in the context of a question and its answering pattern. Perhaps the reader cannot grasp the relationship of this particular Trump to the overview or pattern that arises – it seems to be out of keeping – and cannot give a satisfactory divinatory or farsighted answer. To reshuffle the cards and create a new pattern is often equivalent to trying to force an answer. We are at a loss to read a symbol, so we try to dispose of it; in such cases it often reappears. If the Trump in question is meditated upon briefly *to a defined depth or degree* it will often reveal its meaning within the apparently difficult context or placement in the pattern of cards.

The matter of a defined depth or degree of meditation is important; tarot and similar psychological/cosmological systems have clear worlds or realms of definition, not because people believed that the universe was made of three sections or anything so absurd, but because the organic triple division was employed to help human consciousness develop and expand without risk of loss of focus or, in extreme cases, imbalance. The threefold pattern does have clear analogies and correspondence with a physical relativity (the Worlds of Moon, Sun and Star), but it is at its most valuable to us as a model of deliberate control and balance. If the meditator breaks through into the higher contemplative levels of a Trump, he or she reaches beyond the temporal situation in which a question or answer may be employed. The Trump is thus encountered in its own archetypical state or world, rather than in relationship to a human expression or situation. The threefold pattern helps us to limit our consciousness intentionally just as much as it helps us to expand it intentionally. The key lies in the matter of intent, for this is voluntary use of consciousness, rather than involuntary or habitual use.

Under specific circumstances, access to a deeper level of insight will help a tarot reader to interpret a card or pattern, but in normal matters of tarot reading (for divination or farsight) it is not necessary, and may even be counterproductive to answering a temporal relative question. None of the foregoing theory should give us an excuse for neglecting the deeper aspects of tarot in favour of the more superficial functions, however. It merely suggests that we should apply the appropriate degree of meditation, concentration and visualization to our use of tarot in any form.

Tarot works through *relationship*, and not through random collections of images in juxtaposition, as is frequently stated or assumed. There is no 'chance' in the layout of tarot cards, even though it appears that statistical elements or chance movements define the order in which a run of cards appears. Only experience of tarot will prove this paradoxical statement.

Results from divination, farsight and insight will vary enormously. The variation is more noticeable in the lesser arts of divination and farsight; the closer we work with the world of expressed interactions (the everyday world), the more variable will our collections of defining symbols (cards in layouts) become. Some card sequences are utterly clear as soon as they are laid out, others may require lengthy meditation. The art is greatly enhanced and made more rapid by regular meditation upon the Trumps in their own right – the more trivial the reader's relationship to the symbols, the more random and chaotic their appearance will be in any attempts to generate a meaningful pattern for any chosen purpose.

A skilled meditator with experience of tarot will be able to generate accurate patterns of divination and farsight with a very small number of cards. Many methods in publication tend towards large sequences of cards, but these are not necessary. Our basic *Three Rays* method, outlined in the next chapter, can be worked with as few as four cards, though it may be expanded to seven or twelve if required.

TAROT PATTERN MAKING

In literary methods of tarot work, particularly those derived from nineteenth-century cartomancy, we often find extremely complex methods of randomizing, ordering and laying out cards. Such methods coexist with simpler, possibly traditional layouts such as the well-known 'Celtic Cross'. The entire subject of randomizing, shuffling and laying out is central to the minor arts of tarot, and may under certain circumstances run over into the major arts. We may define the minor and major arts as follows:

MINOR ARTS: 1. Divination, 2. Farsight, 3. Personal insight.

MAJOR ARTS: 4. Meditation, 5. Visualization, 6. Contemplation, 7. Pattern making and story-telling.

This definition covers seven arts, all of which are encompassed by the highest art, that of pattern making or story-telling.

Dissolving/Clearing/Shuffling

To establish a working relationship between ourselves and the tarot, we must first examine and meditate upon the actual process of shuffling and laying out cards, for this has a symbolic content that is often ignored or trivialized. When we randomize a tarot pack we are *dissolving the universe*. Conversely, when we lay out a pattern after randomizing the pack, we are *creating the universe*. When the pack lies dormant, it is the universe in potential. This is an important concept fundamental to tarot either as picture symbols or as images within a mystical tradition, yet it is frequently ignored, and further confused by various theories regarding statistical correlations, or temporal suspension. Tarot patterns are primarily *magical rituals* rather than attempts to isolate sets of meaningful symbols in any coincidental order of appearance.

In other words, it is the pattern or layout that is important in tarot, and not the ever-changing presentation of symbols within that pattern. This is sometimes a difficult concept to grasp, for the cycle of images (cards turned up) is always the focus of outer attention and interest; but on inner levels it is the matrix or pattern that creates the appearance of those specific orders of cards. This paradoxical theory will be unacceptable to anyone who believes that tarot works through statistics or random number sequences, for it defies superficial logic.

Once we have understood the principle of *creation and dissolution* with tarot, much confusion over handling and reading sets of cards disappears. The process of shuffling or randomizing cards is an outer ritual, an expression of the metaphysical reality that dissolves the worlds; all previous combinations and interactions are separated, and the elements or energies are present in potential. This potential state is a randomized pack, face down, cleared of any associations.

When the reader lays out cards according to a cosmological pattern, he or she enacts an ancient magical ritual, a minute reflection of divine creation. There are two ways of developing this concept in practice. The first is that a willed pattern, regardless of its tradition or origin, will give meaning and insight to any random cards that appear within it. This is perhaps the most acceptable rationalization in modern psychological terms. Even if this alone was all that occurred in tarot work, it would be a valuable and effective system of symbolic insight and experiment. There is, however, much more to tarot than may be rationalized in personal or psychic terms. The second development, of creation or pattern-making concepts, runs through esoteric traditions using tarot images.

Before entering upon practical work with the Merlin Tarot, we should examine further the concepts outlined above, and their practical application.

Dissolving
The act of dissolution or disassembly is an essential first stage to any successful tarot work. The reader/meditator should commence by balancing and stilling his or her awareness. This is a basic meditational exercise, and should be undertaken in its own right, unconnected to any religious, magical or meditative school or cult. It is the primal act of meditation – just as poetically the universe originates in the void, so consciousness originates out of nothing. A stilling and meditative clearing of consciousness should be undertaken before any operation with tarot, be it divination or further meditation.

Next we make a *physical representation* of this inner act of stillness; this is where the magical ritual of tarot is outwardly evident. We shuffle or randomize the cards, and when we do so we are (consciously or even unconsciously) ritualizing the dissolution of the universe. Sets of interaction between the Four Elements are separated or stilled, reaching inwards to potential being, ultimately stemming from non-being. The non-being is truly found within our deepest selves, that point beyond which all consciousness dissolves; the potential being is represented (for the duration of the ritual) by the tarot pack or cycle.

It is possible, in theory, for an experienced meditator to 'clear' a tarot pack without shuffling, but the physical ritual of dissolving any previous order within the cards is central to tarot symbolism in practice. One of the most effective ways of clearing a pack, particularly during a session of pattern making, is as follows.

Clearing

1. The pack is divided and laid out face down into seven groups or packets in a single line. This is done by holding the pack, and building the seven packets sequentially, working from one to seven, left to right, laying down a single card upon each position until the pack is reduced to one remaining card ($7 \times 11 = 77$), which may be placed anywhere. There are various metaphysical and mathematical correlations in this procedure, relating to the Worlds, Spheres and planets, with the remaining card representing The Fool, but these concepts are not essential in any way to the practical operation of clearing a pack.
2. The seven packets, now containing all of the pack fully randomized, are placed upon one another, working from left to right, and recombined into a single pack. This sequence will clear any connections between cards, either physical/statistical or energetic/intuitive.

Shuffling

The reader holds the pack of cleared cards and defines a question, attuning his or her previously stilled awareness to the subject. This is a meditative process, and not a matter of force, wishing or will power.

The pack is then shuffled in the normal manner, but slowly and steadily. A steady pace (quite different to the fast shuffle of card games) allows the reader to stop easily at any given point in the shuffling sequence. Steady rhythmic shuffling is a physical reiteration of the turning of the Wheel (for both the cosmology and psychology of tarot are based upon Three Wheels or Spirals of consciousness). With practice and meditation upon tarot, a reader will know intuitively when to stop shuffling and lay out cards. With continued use, this inner sense becomes highly developed, and in some cases the cards will seem to 'kick' or lock immovably at the right point in a steady shuffling process. If shuffling is too rapid, this intuitive process may be disrupted when the cards run beyond the point required.

There is no point in expecting your cards to act physically in a manner which obviates general laws; we are not suggesting any dramatic psycho-kinetic event. The 'kick' results from a fusion of meditative consciousness with ritual pattern making. Some people never experience a 'kick' from the cards, yet always stop shuffling, intuitively, in the best possible place for the purposes of their reading or layout of patterns. Intuition is the key to the moment of pausing and laying out, rather than mathematical number sequences or rigid rules of practice. The formalizing, or pattern making, comes *after* dissolution, shuffling and intuition. Thus, we fill a pattern (the method of layout chosen and applied by the reader) with consciousness symbolized by images chosen intuitively. With practice the general term 'intuition' may be replaced by recognized levels of consciousness reaching through the Three Worlds and their thresholds formed by the Three Wheels.

Systems of Divination, Farsight and Insight

The Merlin Tarot may be used in the same way as any other tarot pack, according to systems or methods preferred by the user. But there are a number of previously unpublished methods of use which relate specifically to this pack, and to the Mysteries of Merlin. Reversed cards are not used in any of the following patterns.

The Three Rays
In this simple but effective method of using the cards, the primal symbol of the Three Rays or Three Strands is employed. The triple pattern represents the basic polarities of positive, negative and balanced, or male, female, androgyne. In druidic tradition and mystical perception, three rays or primal qualities of divine consciousness interact to form the created worlds through their rotation in a Fourfold Cycle. This symbol is shown as the Three Strands from the Distaff of the Weaver Goddess in our Trump Judgement. The rotation or spinning of Three Rays or Strands forms the Three Worlds and their limits or thresholds, the Three Wheels. But as always, we should see this pattern of Worlds and Wheels as three turnings of a triple spiral, reaching from origination to expression, or from Crown to Kingdom.

The Three Rays pattern is shown in Figure 20, and can be worked using only four cards. The cards are cleared, shuffled, and the first four laid out face down in the pattern and order illustrated. They are then turned face up displayed and read as follows:

1. Represents the seed, heart or root of the query.
2. Represents positive aspects or energies within the situation.
3. Represents negative aspects or energies within the situation.
4. Represents the fusion of the first three cards, and the result or outcome or basic answer to the query.

Figure 20: (opposite) THE THREE RAYS

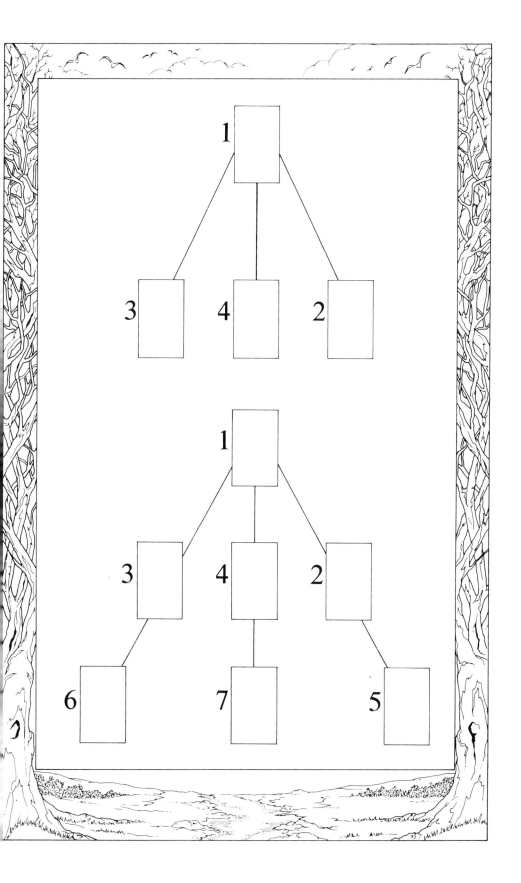

A more detailed development of this pattern is to repeat the layout three times, until twelve cards are displayed. The three sets of cards (3x3 Rays/but 3x4 cards) may be defined as follows:
1st set: Past relating to the query.
2nd set: Present relating to the query.
3rd set: Future relating to the query.

Alternative Pattern of Three Rays
A more sophisticated pattern based upon the Three Ray concept uses seven cards as shown in Figure 20. This employs only one cycle or layout (as opposed to the pattern of one or three layouts described above), but has a more complex and comprehensive interpretation.

Positions 1-4 represent inner spiritual and transpersonal matters; positions 5-7 represent outer temporal and personal matters. Position 4 acts as the central or pivotal point between personal and transpersonal consciousness.

1. Seed or root (transpersonal).
2. Positive.
3. Negative.
4. Resolution, balance, or centre.
5. Positive (personal).
6. Negative.
7. Outcome.

This sevenfold pattern within Three Rays has a broad correspondence to a septenary pattern of Moon, Sun, Star and planets or polar Trumps as follows:

1. Star (spiritual consciousness, deepest impulses and energies, Trump of The Star).
2. Jupiter (transpersonal positive, giving energies, Trump of The Emperor).
3. Mars (transpersonal negative, taking energies, Trump of Death).
4. Sun (fusion of transpersonal and personal central harmonious balancing energies, Trump of The Sun).
5. Venus (positive emotional, giving aspects of personality, Trump of The Empress).
6. Mercury (negative analytic, intellectual aspects of personality, related to image of Minerva, Trump of The Chariot).
7. Moon (fusion, outcome, generation of events/consciousness from all of the foregoing, Trump of The Moon).

Any card may appear in any position, of course, and the meaning of each card is analysed in our respective chapters, with key phrases or tables summarizing the qualities of the images where appropriate. But in patterns such as the sevenfold system, there is an obvious implication that a Trump appearing in its own position (e.g. The Emperor in position 2) has a strengthened effect, while a Trump appearing in its polar opposite position (e.g. Death in position 2) has a cancelling or negative effect upon the consciousness/energies of that position.

We could extend this conceptual model and include the Court cards, for they express Elemental energies as *personae* in abstract, ranging from god forms to psychological types, and have a concrete function in card reading as symbols for actual persons or personalities. Thus, a Queen of Birds in position 5 (an analytical, stern, active person in the position of The Empress) might modulate or even conflict with the basic energies/consciousness of the position.

Much of this subtlety of reading comes with practice, and once the basic attributes of each card have been *learned* (rather than read from books or lists), the reader soon develops a style and feeling for the relationships defined.

If we examine the major glyph of the Tree of Life, we can see that certain Trumps are harmonics of one another, and this harmonic relationship may also be applied to reading card patterns, and to the conceptual model described above in which Trumps have positive or negative accentuation according to the position in which they appear.

The Spindle
In this method of laying out tarot, the Spindle is used as a pattern. Card positions are allocated according to the Trumps of the Spindle as shown in Figure 21, and seven cards are laid out in order after clearing and shuffling the pack.

The three divisions of the pattern broadly represent:

1. The origin of the query.
2. Energies at work in the query situation.
3. The outcome of the query.

Positions on the Spindle

The Upper Third
A: The Star.
B: Judgement.
C: Justice.

These positions, named after the Trumps that define the energies/consciousness of the upper third of the Spindle, represent (A–B) spiritual impulses/transtemporal or transpersonal situations and energies. They may also indicate (B) collective or world movements of consciousness, far-

Figure 21: THE SPINDLE

1: Stellar cards: reveal the origin of the query.
SPIRITUALITY.
A: (Star position) Deep spiritual impulses or
  patterns of transformation. Consciousness/
  energy upon transpersonal and trans-
  temporal levels. (May also indicate matters
  of planetary consciousness, collective
  changes over a wide area of humanity.)
B: (Judgement position) Far-reaching changes,
  including physical death, total alteration of
  life, and profound decisions or events.
C: (Justice position) Creative and destructive
  energies/qualities within query situation.

2: Solar cards: reveal the energies in the query
situation. INDIVIDUALITY.
C: (Justice position) Positive or negative
  energies (defined by card arising on this
  position).
D: (Sun position) Major central factors or
  decisions. The heart of the query.
E: (Fortune position) Career, life work. True
  spiritual marriages or partnerships.

3: Lunar cards: reveal the outcome of the query.
PERSONALITY.
E: (Fortune position) Changes in life, work,
  fortune, circumstances.
F: (Moon position) Sexual matters, family,
  home, children. Also unconscious
  foundational aspects of personality within
  query.
G: (World/Universe position) The physical
  outcome or pattern of the query. Outer
  activities, temporal relationships or partnerships. Manifestation of consciousness/
  energies defined in higher positions of
  the Spindle.

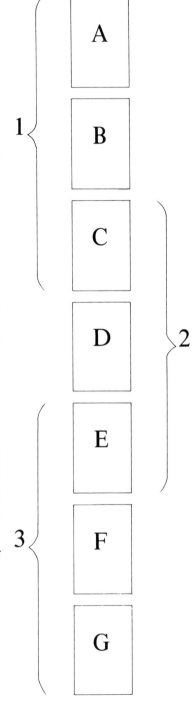

reaching changes that effect the individual or situation of the query, and may indicate effects carried over from the distant past. They correspond to the Stellar World, with *Justice* (C) acting as a threshold to the Solar World.

The Middle Third
C: Justice.
D: The Sun.
E: The Wheel of Fortune.

These positions, named after the Trumps that define energies/consciousness in the middle third of the Spindle, represent (C) the interaction of positive and negative energies at work in the query situation. They indicate (C–D) creative and destructive forces or patterns of consciousness in life, and indicate some powerful long-term life situations, though others are indicated by the upper third of the Spindle. Position D represents the heart of the query and inner core or heart of the person or persons concerned. Positions D–E major decisions, individuality, and matters of career, life work, marriages and partnerships. The middle third relates to the Solar World, with The Wheel of Fortune acting as a threshold into the Lunar World.

The Lower Third
E: The Wheel of Fortune.
F: The Moon.
G: Earth (The Fool or Universe).

These positions represent (E) daily changes of fortune in life and work situations and immediate short-term circumstances, also the emotional and mental condition or impulses of the querent or subjects of the query; (F) natural life factors, biological and health conditions, inherited tendencies, the dream or unconscious life; (G) personality, family, home, place of work, temporal or temporary relationships and situations. The lower third generally indicates the outcome of the query.

We may see a broad correspondence to the planets in the seven positions of the Spindle as follows:

1. Uranus and Pluto (1st Sphere on the Tree of Life and the Abyss with its mysterious bridge).
2. Neptune and Saturn (2nd and 3rd Spheres).
3. Mars and Jupiter (4th and 5th Spheres).
4. Sol (6th Sphere).
5. Venus and Mercury (7th and 8th Spheres).
6. Luna (9th Sphere).
7. Earth (10th Sphere).

Seven cards are sufficient for a very detailed reading in response to a query seeking divination, farsight or insight through this pattern.

The Creation of the World

This method of laying out cards (ritual pattern making) is based upon the mystical cosmology contained in the *Vita Merlini* and the *Prophecies*. It is similar in many ways to the popular Celtic Cross method of pattern making, for both derive from the Wheel of Life, Circled Cross or Elemental

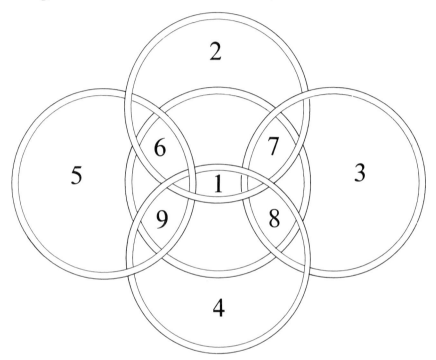

Figure 22: THE CREATION OF THE WORLD

Original Powers
1. Origin and seed of query. TRUTH.
2. New beginnings and changes. LIFE.
3. Source of maximum energy or potential. LIGHT.
4. Nourishes, strengthens and purifies. LOVE.
5. Manifestation or outcome. LAW.

Archetypical Personae
6. *Merlin:* Insight or prophetic awareness (spiritual influence).
7. *Guendoloena:* Positive emotions (lover).
8. *Ganieda:* Intellect, rational thought (sister, enabling influence).
9. *Rhydderch:* Outer activity.

cosmology/psychology of esoteric tradition. The symbolism is based upon a cycle or relationship of four rings (modes of energy/consciousness) united by a fifth representing unity or spirit and truth.

The layout uses nine or ten cards (see Figure 22). The order of laying out and turning up the cards is as follows.

1. *Centre:* Origin and seed of the query.
2. *Air:* New beginnings and energies of change. Power of Life.
3. *Fire:* Maximum source of energy within the query situation. Power of Light.
4. *Water:* Means of nourishing, purifying and maturing. Power of Love.
5. *Earth:* Manifestation or outcome of the query; form and definition of energies involved; may indicate opposing or balancing forces tending towards stabilization or resistance. Power of Law.

(Further attributes may be built through meditation upon the Fourfold Cross or Wheel of Life.)

Personae

To the basic fivefold pattern we may add four *personae*, described in the *Vita*, having parallels in various Trumps, and also found in variant forms as Court cards throughout tarot.

6. *Merlin:* Male anabolic energies/consciousness in spiritual or inner dimensions. Transcendent awareness.
7. *Guendoloena:* Female anabolic energies/consciousness in Nature. The power of positive emotions and sexuality.
8. *Ganieda:* Female catabolic energies/consciousness. The power of the intellect, serving higher consciousness and cultural or human development.
9. *Rhydderch:* Male activity manifesting in the outer world.

Thus the four *personae* represent broad images of energies, but may also stand for human individuals, depending on the cards that appear in their positions and the nature of the reading.

6. *Merlin:* Prophetic and higher consciousness.
7. *Guendoloena* (the wife of Merlin and polar 'sister' of Rhydderch): Emotional and sexual energies.
8. *Ganieda* (the sister of Merlin and wife of Rhydderch): All harmonious powers of the mind.
9. *Rhydderch* (a mighty king): Worldly matters of all sorts.

The *personae* complement the Elements defined by cards appearing in the basic fourfold pattern and stand at the Cross-Quarters, squaring the Circle by adding the human Elemental psyche to the natural and superhuman powers. It is worth noting that this layout is summarized completely in

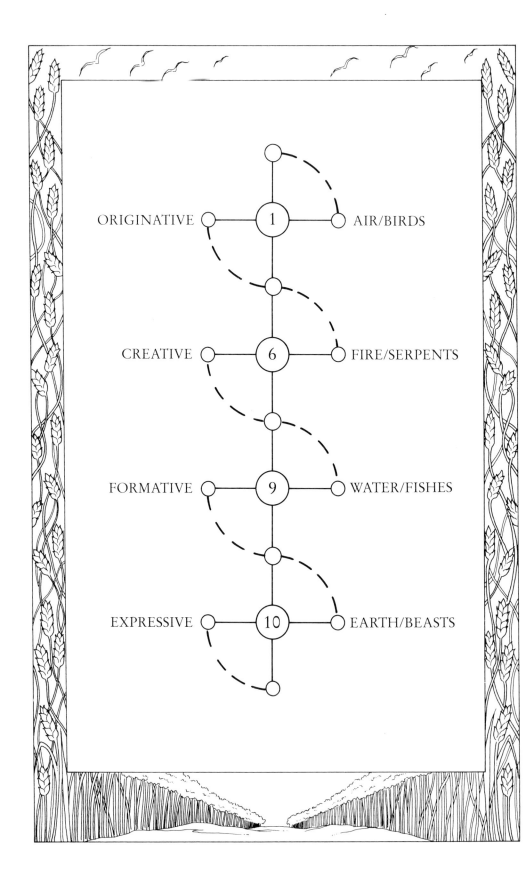

the Trump card The World or Universe, where the Elements and Worlds are defined, and the human modes of consciousness or *personae* are fused into one androgynous figure.

The four *personae* also correspond to a certain extent to the 1st–6th Spheres upon the Tree of Life, or levels within any one individual consciousness.

Finally a tenth card may be drawn (if required) as a summation of the entire matter; this is placed over the first card in the centre of the pattern. Paradoxically, this last card also represents The Fool, and may reveal surprise elements in the query situation or within its resolution.

The Ferryman

Despite connections between Merlin and King Arthur in fiction, there is no doubt that Merlin legends (as preserved in dated sources) pre-date Arthurian material. In the major Merlin sources there is little connecting Merlin and Arthur, and the Merlin story cycle may be completed without any Arthurian lore. In the works of Geoffrey of Monmouth, who began the popular restoration of Arthur in medieval literature, Merlin and Arthur hardly meet, though their relationship was soon to be developed by authors who elaborated upon lore set out by Geoffrey.

But in Geoffrey's *Vita Merlini* there is an important scene described, almost as an aside, in which Merlin and the bard Taliesin remind one another of the Fortunate Isle, ruled by the priestess or goddess Morgen. They carried the wounded Arthur to this magical Otherworld island for his cure by Morgen, who was skilled in therapeutic arts (see our Trump The Priestess). This curious scene, reflecting a Celtic tradition of kingship and the Otherworld, is the source for later developments of the relationship between Arthur and Merlin, and the theme of the wounded Arthur being carried to the Otherworld, Avallach or Avalon for restoration.

Merlin and Taliesin are steered to the Fortunate Isle by a mysterious ferryman Barinthus who is a mythical figure related to ancient sea gods and to the important role of psychopomp or Otherworld guide for souls of the dead or initiates. Thus, we have a significant grouping in the legend: *Merlin/Taliesin/Arthur/Barinthus/Morgen*. This grouping is reminiscent of similar relationships or structures that run through tarot in general, and may be used for meditation, farsight and insight, as shown in our Figure 24.

The basic *personae* may be interpreted as follows, with each one forming the basis for a position within a card layout.

1. *Arthur* (The Wounded King, who is to be restored): represents the personality, which is a wounded, distorted image of our true inner self

Figure 23: (opposite) THE COURT CARDS AND THE FOUR MODES

or spirit. Thus, this position reveals the inquirer's question, problem or difficulty. It will also suggest the true inner nature of a situation or sources of internal conflict or wounding.

2. *Taliesin* (The Bard of Knowledge, who teaches cosmology and traditional lore): represents intellectual and initiatory knowledge; reveals mental analytical aspects of the query, and may indicate the means towards solving any problems.
3. *Merlin* (The Prophet or Wild Man): represents intuitive emotional and poetic insights or inspiration; primal responses or magical transformations within a query situation. Indicates unusual or unexpected solutions to any problems.
4. *Barinthus* (The Otherworld Ferryman who enables the Wounded King to travel towards healing): the power of movement, resolution of situations, means whereby beneficial change may be achieved. May also indicate means of access to deep energies of change on a spiritual transformative level. Barinthus 'knows well the ways of sea and stars' (*Vita Merlini*), thus may work on an unconscious collective level (the sea) or on a transpersonal spiritual level (the stars). His route is across the Middle Pillar or Spindle of the Worlds, from the Earth to the stars.
5. *Morgen* (The Priestess or Power of Redemption and Healing): represents the outcome of a situation or query, the point or person or inner state upon which the entire matter depends for its answer, just as the Wounded King depends upon Morgen for his ultimate healing.

Each of these five positions may be given emphasis by the presence of Trumps which relate either positively or negatively to the legendary *personae* described above. Thus a Spindle or *Axis Mundi* Trump (Moon, Sun, Star) on the position of Barinthus will indicate a strong mediating motivating factor of change, ranging from the Lunar to Stellar Worlds

Figure 24: (opposite) THE FERRYMAN
(From the legend of King Arthur in the *Vita Merlini*.)

1. *King Arthur:* Wounded *persona* or lame Fisher King.
2. *Taliesin:* Bard of knowledge.
3. *Merlin:* Prophet of future potential.
4. *Barinthus:* Mysterious Ferryman of the soul.
5. *Morgen:* Feminine power of redemption, transformation, therapy.

1. Indicates the querent's true nature/question/problem.
2. Reveals an initiatory rational analysis and answer (or a person who embodies such qualities).
3. Reveals an intuitive prophetic answer (or a person who may embody such an answer).
4. Symbolizes the power of movement towards balance, resolution, inner truth.
5. Indicates the outcome in terms of transformation and inner rebirth.

accordingly. By consulting our master key of the Trumps upon the Tree of Life (Figure 2) the reader can establish such relationships; it is useful in the early stages of development in tarot work to write out lists of such correspondences and learn them by heart. A typical preliminary list might read as follows, though this is not definitive:

1. *Arthur:* typified by The Fool/The Emperor/more subtly by The Hanged Man.
2. *Taliesin:* typified by The Magician/The Chariot/more subtly by The Innocent (Hierophant).
3. *Merlin:* typified by The Guardian/The Hermit.
4. *Barinthus:* typified by the three Spindle Trumps/Temperance.
5. *Morgen:* typified by The Priestess/The Empress/Strength.

Thus the polar opposites are:

1. The Universe/Death *(Arthur)*.
2. The Priestess/The Lovers *(Taliesin)*.
3. The Empress/The Innocent (Hierophant) *(Merlin)*.
4. The Three Wheels or threshold Trumps of Fortune, Justice and Judgement *(Barinthus)*.
5. The Magician/The Guardian/The Blasted Tower *(Morgen)*.

All 22 Trumps are included in the above basic correspondences. There is no implication that the two sets listed are 'good' or 'bad', only that they have a polar relationship. Meditation upon the meaning of each Trump and its relationships with other Trumps will gradually open out an understanding of their meaning when they appear in the highlighted or significant positions listed above.

The Ferryman uses only five cards, but is one of the most powerful and informative layouts for the Merlin Tarot.

Appendix 1
MERLIN, DRUIDISM AND THE THREE WORLDS OF TAROT

An interesting relationship may be found between what we know of druidism, the twelfth-century *Vita Merlini* and the Three Worlds of tarot symbolism in general. This relationship is clarified in the context of the Merlin Tarot, but there is no suggestion here that we are attempting to restore any type of formal 'druidism'. The connections and symbolic values exist within a broad Western tradition of esoteric lore, regardless of specific forms, historical periods or reconstructions.

An indigestible mass of spurious nonsense has been written about the druids; unfounded pretentious claims from 'druid orders' derive entirely from nineteenth-century fabrication through clubs and societies or Masonic orders and occult lodges. None of these groupings may truly lay any claim to being druidic, separated as they are by at least a millennium from the last vestiges of practising druid religion.

More to the point is the sad fact that such self-styled druids hardly seem to have made any study of what is known about the original druids, and are often unaware of bardic and Celtic traditions which alone preserve the remnants of the druidic or ancestral culture. Revival bardic contests and themes in Wales or Cornwall are less open to criticism, as they are poetic and romantic reconstructions based upon literature, and make few grandiose claims to a relationship with the original druidic order; nevertheless, it must be stated that even they do not have such connections, either in historical or social terms. In favour of Welsh or Cornish or Breton modern bardism and druidism we might add, however, that at least the members are part of a Celtic culture, while so-called 'druids' in English lodges or Masonic style orders are not.

Despite the depressing situation outlined above, there is considerable evidence concerning druids, druidism, Celtic religion, and the later traditions of bards and poets. Such evidence ranges from classical literature to archaeology, and may also be found in medieval texts, folklore, Celtic cultural or social history, and the early literature, where preserved, of Celtic regions. Some of the evidence corresponds strikingly both to the Merlin texts and to tarot: a common tradition enlivens them all.

A detailed survey of the genuine evidence of druidic and bardic beliefs and practices cannot be included here, but a brief summary of the aspects that relate to tarot is worth while.

The Three Orders of Druidism

Three orders or degrees of druid were known, a triple pattern that was preserved in an attenuated form for many centuries after pagan druidism had ceased to exist as a formal religion. By approximately the first century AD the Romans had begun a serious campaign against the druids, and the druid religion was proscribed throughout the Empire. Many aspects of the religion were retained in modified form as late as the medieval period in Wales, however, and even later in Ireland and Scotland, where druidism was suppressed not by the Roman Empire, but by the spread of Celtic Christianity and later Roman Christianity.

The triple order of druidism is traditionally defined as follows:

1. DRUIDS or priests, judges, mediators of wisdom.
2. VATES or knowers, seers, prophets, inspirers of frenzy.
3. BARDS or singers of praise, reciters and preservers of poetic lore.

The original druids were a highly aristocratic caste within early Celtic culture, covering all of Celtic Europe regardless of regional or tribal differences. It was this political power that caused the Romans to destroy the druids, whom they believed originated in Britain. Welsh druids persisted until the famous attack made by Suetonius Paulinus in AD 61, when Roman troops destroyed the great sanctuary or college on the island of Anglesey off the north-west coast of Wales, but, as mentioned above, their traditions continued in a modified form, while the Romans did not reach into Ireland or Scotland, and we may reasonably assume that druidism persisted for several centuries in those lands. Certain sixth-century Celtic saints are described as having contests with druids and magicians for sacred locations and the support of the populace.

While druids, as an aristocratic priesthood and international judiciary, declined as a formal order, vates (or seers) and bards endured in Celtic culture. So deep rooted was the system that they endured and were accepted within early Christian society, and many aspects of bardism and seership survived as folklore into the nineteenth-century. Bards and poets were an important part of society in post-Roman Britain, especially in

Wales during the sixth to eighth centuries. It is to this bardic tradition that we should look for the Celtic and druidic lore in the works of Geoffrey of Monmouth, writing in the twelfth century and drawing from a diffuse oral tradition. In Ireland, complex bardic and poetic orders survived until the eighteenth century or later, through the activity of itinerant poets, scholars and harpists.

None of the above, however, constitutes proof for the secret survival of a formal druid order as has occasionally been suggested by persons claiming membership. A clear distinction is found world-wide between formal philosophies, religions, priesthoods and orders (such as the druids undoubtedly once were) and traditional practices and wisdom teachings or arts that derive from the collapse of an earlier culture. Oral traditions are, in any case, the foundations of formalized religion, and not merely the fragments or relics, even though they do incorporate such fragments with their protean body.

Druidism and the Merlin Tarot

How does the triple order of druids, vates and bards relate to Merlin and the tarot? Firstly, we can find the triple order in the adventures of Merlin himself, as told by the *Vita*. In the opening scenes he exhibits the typical symptoms and behaviour of the vates or prophet: he is frenzied and makes utterances or predictions. Towards the close of the *Vita*, we find that Merlin has undergone a cycle of transformations which bring him to a state of extreme wisdom, whereupon the chiefs and princes of Wales ask him to act as their judge. Thus two of the druidic orders are fulfilled directly by Merlin at the opening and closing of his life; significantly, we find that Merlin refuses to be a judge or druid for the princes, but chooses to retire into spiritual contemplation. So, while he undergoes the changes and orders of druidism, he also reaches beyond them for something else.

The order of bard is fulfilled in the *Vita* by Taliesin, who is called 'a bard newly arrived from learning in Brittany'. The name is famous in Welsh bardic poetry, and Taliesin is the formal instructor of Merlin into the attributes and correspondences of cosmology, geography and natural history. Thus bardic lore (that of preserving knowledge in poetic form) is a major part of Merlin's experience. The musical aspect of bardism is also represented in the *Vita*, for Merlin is cured of fits of madness by a bard or minstrel who plays upon the crwth, a type of bowed lyre known to be an early bardic instrument.

The motif of the teaching companion is found two to three centuries later in the *Triumphs* of Petrarch, which, like the *Vita* and the *Prophecies*, is a series of allegorical poems containing images similar to tarot Trumps. It seems likely that both Geoffrey of Monmouth in the twelfth century and Petrarch in the fourteenth were drawing upon a common tradition, which later became formalized as sets of images in tarot cards.

So each of the three degrees or orders of druidism is found in the life of Merlin, which also contains a major cosmology and psychology. It seems likely that we are encountering a literary reworking of a tradition of druidism, albeit confused and mingled with classical sources and refined into Latin by Geoffrey in his own inimitable and powerful style. The cosmological and psychological patterns, taught by the bard Taliesin, are based upon the Four Elements, the stars, Sun, Moon and life on Earth. In other words, this is the same system as found in tarot.

We may draw the following connection between the three degrees of druidism, which are ultimately three interconnected modes of con-sciousness or development of wisdom (from bard to vate to druid) and the Three Worlds of tarot:

DRUIDS	JUDGEMENT	STAR	Priests, judges, masters of wisdom.
VATES	JUSTICE	SUN	Seers, inspirers, prophets.
BARDS	FORTUNE	MOON	Preservers of lore, poetry, music.

These relationships may be restated in a modern manner as follows:
STAR: Transhuman or super-consciousness.
SUN: Illuminated or inspired consciousness.
MOON: Collective and generative/creative consciousness.

It must be stressed that these orders are *not* hierarchical, but harmonic. A *druid* priest or judge may also be a knower or *seer*, phrasing the inspiration in a poetic or *bardic* form. *The Prophecies of Merlin* is a striking example of this harmonic process rewritten from an oral tradition.

Conversely, the collective lore and poetry of bards, which remains in very simple form in folklore and song, preserves patterns of stellar or cosmological teaching. A famous example is the 'Dilly Song' or 'Keys of Heaven' found in oral traditions all over Western Europe, and with many world parallels. In this song, verses reach numerically from heaven to Earth, including religious, astrological and mystical symbols. It is a variant of that same teaching expounded by Taliesin in the twelfth-century *Vita Merlini*, yet it has been preserved and sung by ordinary people well into the twentieth century, people who have never heard of Latin texts or medieval cosmologies.

Various songs from oral tradition with both tenfold and twelvefold patterns of creation may be found in published collections of folk songs; a typical example would be the Cornish 'Dilly Song':

Come and I will sing you
What will you sing me?
I will sing you anew
What is your One-O?
One is One and all alone and ever more shall be so.

Come and I will sing you [etc.]
Two of them are lily white boys clothed all in green-O
Three of them are strangers, o'er the wide world they are rangers
Four it is the dilly hour when blooms the gilly flower-O
Five it is the dilly bird that's seldom seen but heard-O
Six is the ferryman in the boat that o'er the river floats-O
Seven are the seven stars in the sky, the shining stars be Seven-O
Eight it is the morning break when all the world's awake-O
Nine it is the pale moonshine, the shining moon be Nine-O
Ten forgives all kinds of sin, from Ten begin again-O.

This sequence is a simple variant of both the Tree of Life and the numerical/Elemental pattern of the tarot, especially of the Number cards or energies, as are many related songs. Songs of this sort declare simply how the universe was made – by a series of numbers. Thus, common folklore preserves the philosophies of Plato and Pythagoras, or perhaps the cosmology of the druids or of Western tradition. The varieties of form and changes of number are not important, but the principle of preservation is astonishing.

It would be inaccurate to suggest that the Merlin Tarot is a druidic tarot, or derived from the druidic equivalent of the tarot in the lost past. Picture images such as we use today would have been quite unknown to the ancient Celts, and possibly would have been regarded as corrupters of the memory and imagination, as the culture was based upon profound oral traditions kept in the memories of the three druidic orders.

The connection, however, is in the two main themes of tarot: the Great Story and the Creation of the Worlds. Julius Caesar wrote that the Celts and their druids spent much time discussing the patterns of the stars and creation, and we have the hard evidence of the Coligny calendar from the first century BC, by which period certain artefacts and written lore had been developed through contact with Rome. We may also consider the remarkable pre-druidic alignments of megalithic monuments that remind us that star-watching and pattern making are very ancient arts indeed in the West.

By the time of the writing of the *Vita*, Merlin takes over the Great Story, for he fuses many myths and legends and the theme of the first and last man within himself; furthermore, he is also the child of magical origins (as is Mabon, the Celtic Apollo) and develops ultimate wisdom through meditation upon the wonders of the universe. By traversing the Three Worlds and the Three Wheels, he passes through the degrees of consciousness and abilities associated with vates, bards and druids.

Appendix 2
ASTROLOGY IN THE
MERLIN TAROT

Tarot cannot be studied in any system or method of interpretation or development without encountering astrology. Even the most superficial use of tarot for temporal divination has many connections to the planets, Signs, elements and correspondences that are found within astrology. In the more convoluted systems of nineteenth-century cartomancy, and particularly in literary occultism, a great deal is made of astrology within tarot, although the correspondences vary considerably, often with 'authorities' within any one system or order arguing furiously over the placing of a Trump or Sign. This type of mental and literary juggling and disputation has been carried over into modern occultism, and expanded on in many publications that deal in depth with the relationships between modern astrology and materialist psychology.

While some of the published theories, particularly those of modern astrology, are comprehensive and efficient, there is no overview or final system of relationship between tarot, the Tree of Life and astrology. There are, however, a small number of significant theories which help us to understand the relationship between tarot and astrology and cosmology during the Renaissance, as there seems little doubt that tarot and related philosophical images were consciously and creatively related to the astrology and theosophy which flourished during the period. A number of expanded sets of images exist from that time which include detailed developments and extra cards relating to astrology and Elemental philosophy.

Such historical cards and theories, however, do not tell how or why tarot and astrology are related; furthermore, the Trump images evident in the twelfth-century Merlin texts, and the stellar symbolism related to them, are different in many ways from the developed astrology of the

Renaissance. How then does this earlier system employ astrology?

To grasp the primal connection between tarot and astrology, we need to dispose of theories of source, derivation, cause and effect. While historical and literary analysis demands the study of sources and derivations, such as Renaissance literature and images, or the Merlin texts, which prove the systematic use of tarot images at a much earlier date, such analysis does not truly improve our understanding of the origins of or the essential meaning in tarot. Both tarot and astrology derive from visions of cosmic affinity, of harmonic relationship; they are not deliberately contrived and assembled systems, built, as it were, brick by brick or unit by unit. Our failure to grasp the essential *holism* or poetry of such systems runs through most modern interpretations and representations; we concentrate upon details rather than the essential vision.

Tarot and astrology both reveal cycles and structures or paths of energy reflected through and within the psyche; both systems contain little-used methods of inner transformation through techniques of meditation, visualization and ritual pattern making. Yet they are hardly ever employed for such means. Detailed and scientific modern astrology leans towards 'accuracy' rather than spiritual vision, with much lip-service to materialist psychology, while modern tarot is generally far behind the development of astrology, and is almost exclusively concerned with trivial prediction or, in more recent years, with humorous or novel styles of imagery. At the height of its general popularity, tarot has never been more decadent; paradoxically, this current period of popularity has also led to new developments out of the ferment of trivialization.

Astrology refined and disciplined specific tarot packs during the Renaissance, just as it may do today, but it does not serve as an original for tarot in general. Conversely, we cannot claim that the earliest tarot images in literature, found within the *Vita Merlini* and *The Prophecies of Merlin*, played a formative part in the growth and development of astrology. Both systems are branches from the root of an ancient, loosely defined cosmology and magical psychology; we might define this older conceptual model as 'proto-astrology', or 'magical astronomy'.

The concept of magical astronomy is very important, as the primal symbols of this organic conceptual model are still active at the foundations of modern tarot, astrology and occultism. If we can grasp this model, we find that it reveals a dynamic world view that may transform our consciousness. Such transformational dynamics are related to catalysis through motion. In simpler terms, we could summarize the concept by saying that inner and outer journeys are attuned to one another. The nearest equivalent is the concept of pilgrimage or formal travel to a sacred site with dedicated purpose; but in the world view of magical astronomy, all movement, all journeys and all life fused together in a harmony that could be directly apprehended. It is this direct vision that is so different from later refined systems in which calculation and copious correspondences must be employed before any understanding may be risked. Paradoxically, however, we have ample proof that very detailed calculations and astronomical alignments were undertaken by ancient cultures in the siting of religious structures such as temples, stone circles or other works; but we need to grasp that these were based upon *observation*.

A direct and powerful observational astrology, linked to potent archetypical or magical images, does run through the Merlin texts. Both the *Vita* and *Prophecies* employ archetypical stellar figures such as Orion, the Pleiades, and more obscure but no less important *personae* such as Barinthus, the divine ferryman, or Ariadne, the creatrix. Such images are dealt with in detail in our analysis of each Trump within the earlier chapters. These images are not employed in modern astrology, nor are they generally found in tarot correlations, but in the Merlin texts they are included in coherent symbolic patterns that employ the planets, Signs, houses and elements. They refer us to magical astronomy, psychology and cosmology, not as theoretical and abstract structures, but as part of regular life.

Magical astronomy (proto-astrology) was not only concerned with great stellar cycles and divine archetypes (as we often grandly assume) but with the actual rotations of the Seasons, the weather, daily travels and activities such as essential farming, hunting, fishing, sailing, and all the fundamentals of collective and individual life. In modern Western culture we tend to hide such fundamentals, or be divorced from them to such an extent that it is hard to grasp concepts that would have been self-evident to our ancestors. In medieval and later astrology, it was quite common to observe celestial phenomena and draw up charts to predict mundane matters. This type of astrology is seldom practised today, and is the remnant of a coherent world view of magical astronomy in which all life danced together, with outer movement unified with awareness and spiritual insight.

This world view is shown in the *Vita Merlini*, when Merlin asks, 'Why are the four Seasons not identical, why do we have changes of weather?' This apparently childlike question gives rise to a profound holism of answers, ranging from adventures and experiences to direct cosmological vision and instruction. The culmination of the cycle of answers is instruction from the bard Taliesin, under the guidance of the goddess Minerva, which ranges from divine origination as Four Powers out of one source, through cosmology, metaphysics, planetary geography and biology, and Otherworld locations and beings.

The Seven Directions

The primal model, which may be seen as proto-astrology or magical astronomy, is based upon the concept of the Seven Directions. This may be applied directly by humans on Earth without complex mathematics or long lists of correspondences (though such developments are natural and valuable providing they do not replace intuition with arid or obsessive correlations). The Seven Directions form the basis of all modern systems of astrology, tarot, magical and esoteric symbolism, no matter how detailed complex and recondite such systems may have become in specific areas of development (or confusion).

The pattern is based upon the relative sphere, defined by East, South, West, North, Above, Below and Within. This relative sphere is used as a model in the Three Worlds (Moon, Sun and Star) and not merely in a geocentric sense: the Four Elements of Air, Fire, Water, Earth correspond to the Four Directions of Before, Right, Behind and Left (E/S/W/N as shown in Figure 5). When the relative Directions are defined within the Worlds, we find patterns of interaction are generated; these are the Spheres and other topological or mathematical models used in metaphysics. The Tree of Life is the classic example of this type of model, though there are other ways of demonstrating such relationships, such as the Platonic solids.

The Four Elements are harmonics of the Four Originative Powers, or four modes of consciousness in being prior to the manifestation of the Worlds. This is really a matter of intuitive vision rather than word-based philosophy; such concepts arise from meditation rather than through intellectual analysis, which is only a proper servant when it is applied after spiritual insight. We may apply our basic knowledge or pattern of Seven Directions and alignments of Moon, Sun and planets or stars, moving through the Four Elements, Quarters and Seasons – this is still the basis for modern astrology and magical arts, though the two are now widely separated. The analogy may be employed directly in terms of both physical journeys (in which we consider the Season, the planetary positions, the weather and other factors before setting out) and inner or metaphysical journeys, such as meditations or visualizations. Metaphysically, a meditation or transformation of consciousness is a journey from state to state or place to place. In primal magical arts, outer and inner journeys are fused as one. This is the basis of ritual working and still applies today.

It must be emphasized that we are not suggesting a complex magical system here, but something profoundly simple: the rotations of the superficially geocentric world are applied inwardly, through imagination, visualization and ritual movement such as dance or posture. These fundamental analogies are found world-wide, and they are not obscure or difficult in any way, no matter how complex certain schools of thought or practical disciplines and specializations may have become. Ultimately, we return to the Great Story, which is the journey and adventures inherent in the tarot, demonstrated by the *Vita Merlini* and other literary and oral variants of the endless theme.

The astrology found in the Merlin texts, particularly that of the *Prophecies*, is observational and poetic; it has the curious property of being practical and applicable by sailors, farmers or travellers within the cycle of the Seasons, yet at the same time subtle and magical or metaphysical. The rising of Orion, who appears in the *Prophecies* as a symbol of destruction, marked the beginning of the Seasons of dangerous weather for sailing; the movement of the Pleiades marked key turning-points of the year, and is used is the *Prophecies* to mark a key turning-point in the Great Year or cycle of the solar system relative to the universe. Neither of these major astrological events (which still occur, as the patterns are astronomical bodies in space, time and energy) play any part in modern astrology. We could add a number of other significant events/symbols which have disappeared from modern usage. Thus our primal astrology was paradoxically simpler and yet more complex than the modern art. Most important of all is the suggestion that these 'lost' elements of astrology are still valid and potent in meditation today. They work by harmonics, by rhythm, by analogy, as they have always worked, and these connectives are found within the Merlin Tarot.

Astrology in the Merlin Tarot, therefore, is not a matter of detailed mathematics or computerized correlation. It is a poetical and intuitive strand, like the thread of Ariadne, that links each and every image together through the fundamental relativity of the Elements, Worlds and Directions.

REFERENCES

1. Stewart, R. J., *The Prophetic Vision of Merlin* and *The Mystic Life of Merlin* (Penguin Arkana, London, 1986-7; in single volume, 1992). Also Stewart, R. J. (ed.), *The Book of Merlin* and *Merlin and Woman* (Blandford Press, Poole, 1987-8).
2. Raine, Kathleen, *Yeats The Initiate* (Allen and Unwin, London, 1986).
3. Stewart, R.J., *The Way of Merlin* (The Aquarian Press, London, 1991). Practical work within the Merlin tradition for modern men and women.
4. Dummett, Michael, *The Game of Tarot* (Duckworth, London, 1980); Moakley, Gertrude, 'The Tarot Trumps and Petrarch's "Trionfi" ' in *Bulletin of the New York Public Library*, vol.60, No.2, February 1956; Shephard, John, *Tarot Trumps* (The Aquarian Press, Wellingborough, 1985).
5. *The Mabinogion*, various translations; Matthews, C., *Mabon and the Mysteries of Britain* (Routledge and Kegan Paul, Arkana, London and Boston, 1987).
6. Stewart, R. J., *Celtic Gods, Celtic Goddesses* (Blandford Press, London, 1990; paperback, 1992). A survey of the divinities, myths and religions of the Celts, with colour illustrations by Miranda Gray and Courtney Davis.
7. H = *The History of the Kings of Britain* (c.1135); PVM = *The Prophetic Vision of Merlin* (*Prophecies*, c.1135); VM = *The Mystic Life of Merlin* (*Vita Merlini*, c.1150).
8. Stewart, R. J., *The Underworld Initiation* (The Aquarian Press, Wellingborough, 1985); also *Earth Light* and *Power Within the Land* (Element Books, Shaftesbury, 1992), two volumes exploring the Faery Realm and Underworld traditions, with emphasis upon practical work with these traditions for contemporary transformation. Kirk, Robert, *Walker Between Worlds* (Element Books, Shaftesbury, 1990), a new edition of *The Secret Commonwealth of Elves, Fauns and Fairies*, edited in modern English with commentary by R. J. Stewart.

9. Graves, Robert, *The White Goddess* (Faber, London, 1961).
10. Stewart, R. J., *The Waters of the Gap* (Bath City Council Publications, Bath, 1980; Ashgrove Press, 1990).
11. For detailed development of magical traditions represented by the Merlin Tarot, see Stewart, R. J., *Living Magical Arts* (Blandford Press, Poole, 1987), also *Advanced Magical Arts* (Element Books, Shaftesbury, 1988).
12. Stewart, R. J., *Where is Saint George?* (Moonraker Press, Bradford on Avon, 1976/80; Humanities Press, New Jersey, 1977; Blandford Press, London, 1989).
13. Stewart, R. J., *Music Power Harmony* (Blandford Press, London, 1990); *Music and the Elemental Psyche* (The Aquarian Press, Wellingborough, 1987): both books contain concepts and techniques involving music and changing consciousness. A cassette tape of Elemental Chants and visualizations from these books is available from Sulis Music, BCM 3721, London WC1N 3XX.

Further Reading
14. Stewart, R. J., *Magical Tales* (The Aquarian Press, Wellingborough, 1989). A collection of stories, many using patterns and images from the Merlin Tarot.

INDEX